Unmasking the African Dictator

UNMASKING THE AFRICAN DICTATOR

Essays on Postcolonial African Literature

Tennessee Studies in Literature,
Volume 46

Edited by Gĩchingiri Ndĩgĩrĩgĩ
With a Foreword by Ngũgĩ wa Thiong'o

THE UNIVERSITY
OF TENNESSEE PRESS
Knoxville

TENNESSEE STUDIES IN LITERATURE
Editorial Board:
Don Richard Cox, Allison Ensor, Marilyn Kallet,
Mary Papke, Janet Atwill, John Zomchick.

"Tennessee Studies in Literature," a distinguished series sponsored by the Department of English at The University of Tennessee, Knoxville, began publication in 1956. Beginning in 1984, with Volume 27, TSL evolved from a series of annual volumes of miscellaneous essays to a series of occasional volumes, each one dealing with a specific theme, period, or genre, for which the editor of that volume has invited contributions from leading scholars in the field.

Inquiries concerning this series should be addressed to the Editorial Board, Tennessee Studies in Literature, Department of English, The University of Tennessee, Knoxville, Tennessee 37996–0430. Those desiring to purchase additional copies of this issue or copies of back issues should address The University of Tennessee Press, 600 Henley Street, 110 Conference Center Building, Knoxville, Tennessee 37996–4108.

Copyright © 2014 by The University of Tennessee Press / Knoxville.
All Rights Reserved. Manufactured in the United States of America.
First Edition.

The paper in this book meets the requirements of American National Standards Institute / National Information Standards Organization specification Z39.48–1992 (Permanence of Paper). It contains 30 percent post-consumer waste and is certified by the Forest Stewardship Council.

Library of Congress Cataloging-in-Publication Data
Unmasking the African Dictator: Essays on Postcolonial African Literature / edited by Gichingiri Ndigirigi.
  pages cm. — (Tennessee Studies in Literature; Volume 46)
  Includes bibliographical references and index.
  ISBN 978-1-62190-055-9 (hardcover)
  1. African literature—History and criticism.
  2. African literature (English)—History and criticism.
  3. Postcolonialism in literature.
  4. Postcolonialism—Africa.
  5. Dictators in literature.
  I. Ndigirigi, Josphat Gichingiri, editor of compilation.

PL8010.U77 2014
809'.8896—dc23   2013047065

CONTENTS

FOREWORD
Ngũgĩ wa Thiong'o
vii

ACKNOWLEDGMENTS
ix

INTRODUCTION
Gĩchingiri Ndĩgĩrĩgĩ
xi

NURUDDIN FARAH'S
*VARIATIONS ON THE THEME
OF AN AFRICAN DICTATORSHIP*
Gĩchingiri Ndĩgĩrĩgĩ
1

COLONIALISM, THE MODERN AFRICAN DICTATOR
AND THE POSTCOLONIAL STATE
Nada Halloway
29

THE UNFAITHFUL CHRONICLER:
ON WRITING ABOUT THE DICTATOR
IN HENRI LOPÈS'S *LE PLEURER-RIRE*
(*THE LAUGHING CRY*)
Magalí Armillas-Tiseyra
47

TOXIC FATHERS:
HENRI LOPÈS'S *THE LAUGHING CRY*
AS EMBLEMATIC AFRICAN DICTATOR NOVEL
Gĩtahi Gĩtĩtĩ
65

THE LAST KING OF AFRICA
THE REPRESENTATION OF IDI AMIN
IN UGANDAN DICTATORSHIP NOVELS
Oliver Lovesey
85

JACOB'S LADDER AND *ANTHILLS OF THE SAVANNAH*:
NARRATIVIZING THE INTERNAL-EXTERNAL
DYNAMIC OF AFRICAN POLITICAL POWER
Joseph McLaren
111

THE DICTATOR AND HIS OBJECTS:
THE STATUS OF THE FETISH
IN THE AFRICAN DICTATOR NOVEL
Magalí Armillas-Tiseyra
125

FIMBO YA NYAYO,
WHEN THE KENYAN DICTATOR CALLED THE TUNES!
Maina Mũtonya
141

DIAGNOSING THE DICTATOR'S BODY POLITIC
IN *WIZARD OF THE CROW*
Robert L. Colson
167

PERFORMING RESISTANCE
IN NGŨGĨ'S *WIZARD OF THE CROW*
Gĩchingiri Ndĩgĩrĩgĩ
183

FRATERNAL OPPRESSION AND THE
"AESTHETICS OF VULGARITY" IN
ALAIN MABANCKOU'S *BROKEN GLASS*
Awa Sarr
207

"A NATION OF ONE'S OWN":
FICTIONAL INDICTMENT OF
CANNIBALISTIC AFRICAN STATES
Ng'ang'a Mũchiri
221

CONTRIBUTORS
233

INDEX
237

FOREWORD

Ngũgĩ wa Thiong'o

There was a time when African fiction in whatever languages was dominated by themes of anticolonial resistance. Despite their varying handling of the theme, the fiction captured the sense of optimism in the air: independence would usher a new era. But the dawn of independence was followed by dwindling hope. The colonial had turned into the neocolonial. In general African fiction was able to dramatize the end of an illusion. Fiction became the voice of democratic reason. But the new regime responded by shutting all avenues of democratic dissent. Military coups became the order of the day in country after country. Even civilian regimes became indistinguishable from the military, both mirror images of the undemocratic authoritarianism of the colonial era. An aspect of this authoritarianism was the rise of the one party states, which soon mutated into a one person rule that in turn mutated into full fledged dictatorship, which, in its practices, combined the tragic, the comic, and the absurd. This was once best described by Daniel Moi of Kenya when he publicly called on his ministers and politicians never to ask questions—theirs was to do exactly what he told them to do: put a comma or a full stop or an exclamation mark only when he told them to do so. Specifically, he called upon them to behave like a parrots. To the ears of the dictator in general, parrotry became poetry.

Slowly, fiction began to capture this combination of the tragic, the comic, and the absurd. African dictator fiction was born. The dictator novel had earlier emerged in Latin America. This is because Latin America, which experienced its anticolonial disengagement from Europe earlier than Africa, was also the first region to mutate into neocolonialism in relationship to North America. Neocolonialism was the fertile ground for the rise of the Grand Patriarch.

African literary criticism was slow in catching up with dictatorship fiction as a particular variant of that which depicted the authoritarian state. But with this collection of essays, Gĩchingiri Ndĩgĩrĩgĩ has rectified the situation. The collection brings together a variety of voices that illuminate the different aspects of dictator fiction in Africa and in the process enrich our experience and deepen our understanding of African literature, politics, and culture. The essays should prove useful to the literary specialist as well as the general reader of African literature, history, politics, and culture.

ACKNOWLEDGMENTS

A collection like this is the work of many hands. I would like to thank my colleague Michael Lofaro who first suggested the idea of this collection. The board of the Tennessee Studies in Literature has been very supportive of this project, and I especially want to thank Mary Papke, the board's current chair, for personally reading though the manuscript and catching those errors that easily slipped by me once the essays became too familiar, and for shepherding the manuscript through the internal and external reviews. I would also like to thank the two anonymous reviewers for their perceptive comments.

The collegial collaboration of all the contributors made it a joy editing this collection and I want to thank them all. I am especially indebted to Gītahi Gītītī and Oliver Lovesey for commiting early to the project and giving me the confidence to cast further afield for the other contributors. Their running commentary on the project has been really helpful. I also want to acknowledge the inspiration from Ngũgĩ wa Thiong'o, whose novel, *Wizard of the Crow,* forced me to start searching for a suitable lens to read the African dictator novel and became the germ for this project. I am especially grateful that Ngũgĩ agreed to write the foreword for this collection.

My work on this project has been supported by the Provost's Office and the English Department at the University of Tennessee. A teaching-free semester funded by the Office of the Provost in fall 2009 enabled me to do much of the research on the material for the introduction and my chapters on Nuruddin Farah's *Variations on the Theme of an African Dictatorship* and Ngũgĩ's *Wizard of the Crow*. A Hodges summer stipend from the English Department enabled me to write the two chapters in summer 2011. I am grateful to my colleagues Bill Hardwig and Chuck Maland for their insightful comments on the latter one.

INTRODUCTION

Gĩchingiri Ndĩgĩrĩgĩ

At the beginning of Chinua Achebe's *Arrow of God*, Ezeulu, the chief priest of Ulu, contemplates the limits of his ritual power within traditional Igbo society. Rejecting the thought that he was merely a watchman of the people's calendar, Ezeulu reflects: "If he should refuse to name the day [for the feast of the Pumpkin Leaves and for the New Yam feast] there would be no festival—no planting and no reaping. But could he refuse? No Chief Priest had ever refused" (293). Swearing that the woman who will bear the man who will say that he would not dare "has not been born yet," his mind flounders "on the brink of knowing" his limits (293). Shortly thereafter, Ezeulu leads the six villages of Umuaro in celebrating the Feast of the Pumpkin Leaves, a ritual cleansing of their sins before they can plant the year's crop. It is a rich spectacle that enables the community to temporarily transcend the tensions among some of the six villages and stage a show of unity for this one occasion. As the scapegoat who carries the community's sins and buries them in the ground, Ezeulu is central to the festival, the other purpose of which is the reenactment of the founding of Ulu, the god that was supposed to unite the six villages, and his triumph over the obstacles put in his way by the four days that made the traditional Igbo week (358–359). We later learn that central to the Chief Priest's office is the obligation to confront danger before it reached his people. Having decided at the amalgamation of the six villages that Ezeulu's ancestor would be the Chief Priest, the people went to him and said, "*You will carry this deity for us.*" Entranced by the people's song of support and the flute man who "turned his head," the ancestor accepted and went down on his knees: "[T]hey put the deity on his head. He rose up and was transformed into a spirit. His people kept up their song behind him and he stepped forward on his first and decisive journey, compelling the four days in the sky to give way to him" (473), thus ceding control over the Igbo calendar to him. Clearly, the Chief Priest only carried the deity for the people and his power was constructed, rather than intrinsic to his body.

It is ironic that the clarity that the Chief Priest's power emanated from the people occurs to Ezeulu at the point when he has confused his power as emanating from the god. Seeking to reward Ezeulu for telling the truth against his own people in the land case between Umuaro and Okperi, Captain Winterbottom, the Colonial Officer, summons Ezeulu to Okperi, the seat of the colonial government, where Ezeulu is offered the chance to become a Warrant Chief. Captain Winterbottom assumes that all Africans are drunk with power and that Ezeulu will jump at the opportunity. Refusing to subordinate his ritual authority to colonial authority, Ezeulu rejects the "great favor" (459) to the consternation of Mr. Clarke, Captain Winterbottom's deputy, who cannot believe that the "fetish priest" would have the "cheek" to make a fool of the British Administration in public (459). Despite his moral scruples that he could not "just clap an old man (yes a very old man) into jail without reasonable explanation" (462), Clarke is sufficiently blinded by the power he exercises in Winterbottom's absence to dismiss that language of rights as "very silly really" (462), and he locks Ezeulu up in the colonial jail for thirty two days. Having failed to get his people's backing in his attempt to resist the summons from Winterbottom, Ezeulu vows to punish his people upon his release. Using the specious excuse that the moon he sees in Okperi is different from the one in Umuaro, barely six miles away, Ezeulu seizes on the fact of his absence to argue that he did not see two new moons and that he cannot therefore declare the Feast of the New Yam because he still has to eat the remaining two yams that he would have eaten had he seen the two new moons during his absence. Because he had consciously resolved "to hit Umuaro at its most vulnerable point—the Feast of the New Yam" (486), he stubbornly refuses to eat the extra yams in one go when his peers try to persuade him to act in the interests of the people. In the end, his community deserts Ezeulu for the Christian church.

The figure of Ezeulu is an interesting window into the construction and performance of authority in traditional African spaces. The fantasy that he has absolute power that he could wield against his own people to settle a personal score is destabilized at the end of the novel when the community appeals to him to modify the code to save the community, essentially arguing that laws were made for man and not man for laws. The intervention of the colonial officer and the attempts to impose a figurehead on the people of Umuaro who would not be answerable to this very republican people speaks to the distortion of African modes of governmentality by colonialism around Africa. Throughout the conflict, the people exercise their sanction by progressively alienating Ezeulu and eventually deserting his god. By adapting to the new god, they win out in the end. But the demented Chief Priest who in the end still imagines that he is an arrow of his god, punishing the people in the name of a narrow traditionalism, reminds us of the mobilization of tradition by many an African despot. The adulation of the people that gets into the original Chief Priest's head, the deployment of spectacle in re-enacting the social body, the Chief Priest's control of time in the traditional society, and the assumption that his power is god-sent are all features that the modern dictators would appropriate to legitimize their monopoly of state power. As Michael Schatzberg has shown in his study of despotic regimes in Côte d'Ivoire, Zaire, Cameroon, and Kenya, the leaders' manipulation of spirituality—both the formal world religions of Christianity and Islam, and the occult—and the assumption that power was indivisible and had to be eaten whole by the power holders, went a long way in shoring up support for these regimes (*Political Legitimacy* 37). Emmanuel Yewah has argued that the modern dictators "have arrogated for themselves the power to define national character and have systematically subverted the process of recapturing collective memories by rewriting their personal stories in the guise of the collective history of the nation" (49). The twelve essays assembled in this collection uncover the ways that various fictional African rulers subvert popular sovereignty by appropriating divine powers and routinizing their majesty, producing Michel Foucault's effects of truth that naturalized their rule.

In Achebe's work, it is a short leap from the imposition of Warrant Chiefs in *Arrow of God* to the scramble by the smart, the lucky, and hardly ever the best who take over the colonial governor's mansion in *A Man of the People* and remind the people that dissenting voices outside the mansion would threaten the foundations of the new state (37). It is an even shorter leap from the subtle coercion and the politics of the belly that characterize *A Man of the People* to the forcible silencing of dissenting voices that begins *Anthills of the Savannah*. Tracing this evolution of the figure of the African despot in Achebe helps to map the trajectory of the distortion of traditional authority to the Machiavellian Chief Ngongos who so recently dotted the African political landscape. Taking his cue from Chief Ngongo, Sam in *Anthills* exercises power with all the pomp and pageantry, complete with a Christ-like mythology supplemented by his inaccessibility. Ironically, for someone who controlled the fictional Kangan so closely, Sam's overthrow and "disappearance" will be marked casually and compared to a woman in the village complaining that her goat is missing (197). Comfortingly, a wisecrack reckons that the people can "make another President"; it is not hard to do, in spite of the rulers' pretensions to the contrary (197).

Among others, Simon Gikandi, Achille Mbembe, and Michael Schatzberg have explored the place of state ceremonials and spectacle in dramatizing the majesty of the modern state. Gikandi has noted that in Ngũgĩ's writing of the 1980s, the performance of power in the postcolony had become its sole claim to legitimacy (35), a useful comment in reading most of the novels discussed in this collection. The analysis of the ways that the state deploys both spectacle and the more subtle disciplinary apparatus would also profit from an engagement with Achille Mbembe's insights on the despotic postcolonial African state's aesthetics of performance of power and ceremonial routinization.

Writing persuasively on the immutable truths that the postcolonial state circulates about itself, Mbembe posits that "festivities and celebrations [are] the vehicles for giving expression to the commandment and for staging its displays of magnificence and prodigality..." (107). Mbembe singles out "pomp and extravagance as classical ingredients in the production of power" (108). He explains that "the *commandment* must be extravagant ... [;] it must furnish proof of its prestige and glory by a sumptuous (yet burdensome) presentation of its symbols of status, displaying the heights of luxury in dress and lifestyle, turning prodigal acts of generosity into grand theater" (109). Through these grand gestures, the high command attempts to institutionalize the ruling elite's world of meanings as a "socio-historical world" (103) that entangles both the rulers and the ruled in a shared authoritarian episteme. Urging that there is a need to understand how the ruling elite comes to dominate the public space, Mbembe unmasks the specific settings in which the state offers spectacles for its "subjects" to watch" (104), paying attention to "those ceremonies that make up the state's liturgical calendar" (119). He shows how Paul Biya's regime in Cameroon "ultimately created its own rhythms of time, work, and leisure, and from them acquired a degree of predictability" (120). State celebrations and holidays would be held to mark Biya's important days; sports victories by the national team would be attributed to the leader's greatness; his departure for official trips abroad and his return would be marked with pomp and ceremony that disseminated Biya's image as a gifted visionary able to operate on the world stage.

Beyond the pomp and ceremony, Mbembe paints "the postcolony as a hollow pretense, a regime of unreality.... By making it possible to play and have fun outside the limits set by officialdom, the very fact that the regime is a sham allows ordinary people to simulate adherence to the innumerable official rituals that life in the postcolony requires" (108). Downplaying the narrow binarisms of domination/resistance, Mbembe places emphasis on the logic of "'conviviality,' on the dynamics of domesticity and familiarity, inscribing the dominant and the dominated within the same *episteme*" (110). As he argues, both rulers and ruled toy with each other: "[T]he relationship between the rulers and ruled in the postcolony is forged through a specific practice: simulacrum[.] ... This explains why dictators can sleep at night lulled by roars of adulation and support only to wake up to find [that they have been overthrown] ... that the applauding crowds of yesterday have become a cursing, abusive mob" (111). By seeming to obey their rulers, "the people turn the *commandement* into a sort of zombie" (111). But whereas Mbembe explicates an unconscious process, the toying with power ultimately leads to conscious resistance in some of the texts discussed in this collection, like Ngũgĩ's *Wizard*. Granted, grand narratives of liberation may now be unfashionable, but the people in *Wizard* eventually understand the hollowness of the pomp and ceremony that the Ruler uses to zombify them and they stage their own counternarrative.

Introduction

Mbembe's original reading of the postcolony attracted quite a reaction from Coronil (89–108), Mudimbe (61–62), and Tejumola (47–55), critics who, for the most part, contested Mbembe's pessimism and what they saw as citational colonialism. But Judith Butler defended Mbembe's reading of the postcolony for its recognition of "the ways in which power compels its subjects ritualistically to perform, within and through the mundane practices of civil society, a ratification of its own spectacular excess" (68). In a Foucauldian vein, she also praised Mbembe's recognition that sites of resistance are not always locatable outside power, which "is itself already multiply situated, diversified from the start, so that even the *commandment* is not a stable notion of sovereignty; on the contrary, this is a *commandment* that governs to the extent that it is perpetually and extravagantly ratified, and whose extravagance and theatricality is central to its operation" (68).

Mikael Karlström's more recent article (2003) rehashes some of the criticism leveled against Mbembe's original reading of the postcolony, and he seems to have missed Mbembe's retooled arguments in *On the Postcolony* (2001).[1] But the more he critiques Mbembe, the more he seems to be making the same point that Mbembe was making, a tendency apparently shared by quite a few of Mbembe's critics who have commented on "The Aesthetics of Vulgarity," the reworked chapter that originally appeared in *Public Culture*. A few examples from Karlström should suffice. He decries Mbembe's failure to see that the situations he described were changeable and contests the position that both the state and the people were involved in processes of mutual zombification. More troubling, Karlström seeks to flatten the relationship of zombification, wondering whether its episteme or aesthetics of power are intrinsic to it or contingent:

> By implying the former, Mbembe gives the impression of a pathological contradiction at the heart of African political subjectivity. Africans criticize and ridicule the excesses and grandiosity of their rulers, using lewd humor to deflate their pretensions. But the very same Africans also expect and even demand such grandiosity, seeming to positively relish rulers who indulge in excesses, amass illicit fortunes, and gorge themselves on scarce resources. Vacillating incoherently between these extremes, they systematically disempower both themselves and their political leaders. (61)

However, it would appear that the situation is not as clear cut or incoherent as Karlström presents it. As we see in Achebe's *A Man of the People*, the people of Chief Nanga's home region will keep electing him if he goes to the legislative and administrative capital of the modern state and brings "their" share to them, or if he gets his kith and kin into positions around the table where the state largesse is shared out. Unlike the village where a sense of propriety and accountability prevails and a villager dare not steal so much that the owner notices (87), the centralized state has no perceived "owner" (149). Conversely, the elected politician is only redistributing back to the people what paradoxically belongs to them. As long as Chief Nanga redistributes to "his people," they have no qualms about how corruptly the largesse is acquired. On the contrary, it is the supposedly uncorrupted Odili who proves unelectable because "his hands are empty"; he has nothing to give the people. The trouble is not to "eat" when other people are "eating" (149). It is a contradiction, yes, and Karlström paradoxically seems to recognize this when he presents the situation in Uganda:

> If it is true, as Mbembe claims, that a certain voracity and grandiosity are expected of power holders, it is equally the case that they are expected to submit to fattening and exaltation by their subjects. Discourses of "eating" and the size of political "bellies" are thus anchored in a moral economy of politics, in which the engorgement of politicians' bodies takes place within a social matrix of substantive reciprocities, and thus confirms the legitimacy of their authority. This relational matrix is experienced by many rural Baganda as more reliable and effective than the abstract mechanisms of distribution and legitimation of the modern "rational"-bureaucratic administrative system and the liberal democratic state, in so far as these have been operative in Uganda. (68–9)

Surprisingly, Karlström argues that contrary to the implications of Mbembe's account, "there is nothing intrinsically paradoxical or perverse about the eagerness of ordinary Africans to participate in the ceremonial exaltation of power and the fattening of rulers" (68–9). Contrarily, it is Karlström who seems to find the people's demand for such grandiosity, their fascination with rulers who indulge in excesses, amass illicit fortunes, and gorge themselves on scarce resources, and the resultant disempowerment of the people as incoherent vacillation.

Karlström argues that "the disabling paradoxes of postcolonial politics identified by Mbembe do not arise out of any inherent pathology of the African political imagination, but rather out of the postcolonial state's tendency to deploy local models and practices of the public sphere in ways that evacuate them of much of their legitimating content" (57–8). Adopting a Bakhtinian formulation, Karlström contests what he sees as an error in Mbembe's analysis, finding that "the ceremonialist state conducts an official 'monologue,' in which the people are spoken to, but cannot speak back" (60). Karlström observes that in traditional Baganda hospitality rituals, the local people were able to talk back to or at their elites, but paradoxically, he, like Mbembe, finds that the state deploys the formal features of traditional ceremonies while evacuating them of the reciprocity and legitimacy that characterized traditional society (69).

Karlström notes that even for the populist Yoweri Museveni regime of the 1990s, "the underlying performative pattern, which symbolically constitutes

Introduction

power as singular and transcendent" is deeply ingrained in both the ceremonial legacy of the postcolonial state and the subjectivity of political elites (70). Further, he says, "Depending upon the character of the regime, this ceremonial gulf between state and people may or may not be implicated in a broader pattern of state-society estrangement" and the state may engage in "forms of substantive reciprocity and popular accountability" (70). However, he comments that for insecure or despotic regimes "this performative paradigm can easily lead to an inflation of sovereign transcendence that evades the obligations and reciprocities upon which that transcendence is ideally predicated," of which Idi Amin's "malignant hypertrophy of transcendent singularity detached from all reciprocity and accountability" was a good example (70). Karlström remarks that Amin was "notoriously fond of public ceremonial, of occupying centre stage, and of receiving public adulation and obeisance" (70–1). By foregrounding the specificity of the structure of feeling that characterizes the Baganda experience, Karlström overcomes one of the shortcomings in Mbembe's analysis: the overemphasis on textuality and broad generalizations.

Whereas an underlying tone of horror at the breakdown of the circuits of reciprocity that should ideally tie the rulers and the ruled justifiably pervades Karlström's reading of the despotic postcolonial state, in *Dialectics of Power* Michael Schatzberg admirably demonstrates how the perversion became naturalized and attained its own logic in Mobutu Sese Seko's Zaire (1965–97). In *Political Legitimacy in Middle Africa*, Schatzberg extends the discussion to Côte d'Ivoire, Cameroon, and Kenya. Because Mobutu was obviously one of the prototypes of the dictators portrayed by Lopès in *The Laughing Cry*, Soyinka in *Opera Wanyosi*, and Ngũgĩ in *Wizard*, an understanding of the ceremonial gulf marking state-society estrangement in Zaire is appropriate. As Schatzberg says, "[L]egitimate governance in Zaire, and in much of Africa, is based on the tacit normative idea that government stands in the same relationship to its citizens that a father does to his children" (*Dialectics* 97), a position that reminds us of Moi's autocratic one-party state of the 1980s, in which the ruling party was officially constructed as "baba na mama" (father and mother) of the interpellated Kenyan children subjects. Schatzberg argues that when Mobutu "assumes the role of generous father-chief he speaks directly to a broad cultural and historical understanding of generosity, reciprocity, and obligation among kinsmen" (*Dialectics* 81). It is a short leap from the magnanimous father of the nation to the despot whose rule is naturalized, as Schatzberg shows with ample examples from around Africa that lead him to conclude that "[b]ecause the 'father's' authority is 'natural,' people may have greater tolerance for paternally-based authoritarian rule than we might expect" (*Dialectics* 90). Like the typical postcolonial Father-of-the-nation types, Mobutu cast himself as father of the Zairian family/nation with the expectation of deference from children/subordinates (*Dialectics* 72), and pervasive paternal and familial metaphors provided part of "the ideological cement of the *Mobutiste* state" (*Dialectics* 73). As Schatzberg reports, "[To] read the local press, one would never think a national budget existed" (*Dialectics* 79), because all routine matters and expenditures were disseminated as consequences of presidential magnanimity. The presidential "gifts" created "bonds of dependence between leader and follower and contributed to the leader's ability to maintain his power and control" (*Dialectics* 79). Applying Marshall D. Sahlins's analysis of generosity and reciprocal obligations in Polynesia, Schatzberg shows how the generosity of the chief ensured the loyalty of kinsmen: it is "a manifest imposition of debt, putting the recipient in a circumspect and responsive relation to the donor during all that period the gift is unrequited" (qtd. in Schatzberg 80). Schatzberg remarks that in Mobutu's Zaire, "[w]hen Mobutu assumes the role of 'generous father-chief' he speaks directly to a broad cultural and historical understanding of generosity, reciprocity, and obligation among kinsmen" (*Dialectics* 80). In his "Big Man" model of governance, the Big Man conspicuously takes care of the welfare of social inferiors; they equally conspicuously show their gratitude, respect, and deference (*Dialectics* 80). Using this logic, the state's resources were Mobutu's to give.

Among postcolonial Africa's despots, Mobutu was particularly noted for his dramatic displays of magnificence, generosity, firmness, and even ruthlessness. Through clever manipulation of state ceremonialism, he was able to remind the people of the invincible might of the state, represented in public functions by elaborate parades of a few units of the military that had some of the most up-to-date military hardware, financed out of the sale of Zaire's vast mineral resources. It was therefore a surprise to many when a seemingly rag-tag militia overran this military might within the span of six months in 1996/7. Schatzberg sums up the secrets behind Mobutu's longevity in power: Mobutu and his henchmen used "the state's coercive arms to terrorize and intimidate"—viewed from abroad, the state appeared "teetering and on the brink of dissolution," but seen from the perspective of ordinary Zairians, "its power [was] awesome and terrifying" (*Dialectics* 141). In addition, the state successfully manipulated ethnicity, regionalism, social class alliances, and the imagery of family. As Schatzberg concludes, the Zairian state—like most despotic African states—has not planted deep roots, and Mobutu and his clique deployed the metaphor of the nation as family and Mobutu as father "to build on the complex, culturally based moral matrix of legitimate governance" (*Dialectics* 141), using symbols and images "that help to maintain political quiescence" (*Dialectics* 141). Ethnicity, regionalism, and social class alliances were subordinated to the imagery of family. In *Political Legitimacy* Schatzberg shows that as father-chief, Mobutu manipulated the populace by reminding them of their familial dependence on him for their food, and he went further to combine

Christian, familial, and paternal imagery: "In the act of political resurrection, of course, God the Father is subtly confused with Mobutu, father of the national family. And because Mobutu is the father who resurrects Zaire from the chaos of the First Republic and all of its ills, Zairians owe him filial thanks and devotion" (51). They all recognize that power is indivisible and has to be eaten whole by the beneficent father figure who supposedly acts in the best interests of the national family (82). But, as Schatzberg concludes, the "father-chief could, and did, traffic with the forces of the occult and was able to bring these to bear, using fear as an implement of rule when necessary" (203). This model is particularly applicable to a reading of Daddy Bwakamabé, the dictator in *Laughing Cry*, and the Ruler in *Wizard*. The discussion of the African father-chief's investment in the occult is also helpful in reading the fetishes in Ahmadou Kourouma's *Waiting for the Vote of the Wild Beasts* and Sembene Ousmane's *The Last of the Empire*.

It is important to historicize both the African "Big Man" and his performance of power. In his cogent discussion of the emergence of centralized despotism in postcolonial Africa, Mahmood Mamdani recognizes that the African despot did not spring up fully-grown as a product of a postcolonial African political pathology: there was nothing particularly democratic about colonialism. Mamdani notes that in those societies that had not yet evolved into centralized states, the colonizers imposed chiefs "shorn of the rule-based restraint" (43). He shows that this restraint on precolonial authority "flowed from two separate though related tendencies: one from peers, the other from people." Without these, "the full-blown village-based despot" emerged (43). Further, he says, "[f]rom African tradition, colonial powers salvaged a widespread and time-honored practice, one of a decentralized exercise of power, but freed that power of restraint, of peers or people. Thus they laid the basis for a decentralized despotism" at the local level, serving a centralized and equally despotic state (48). In centralized states the traditional rulers were shunted aside to make way for colonial governors who had enormous powers without corresponding accountability to the governed. The colonial state thus created the foundation for the centralized despotism of the postcolonial era. Whereas Schatzberg shows that the paternalism of the African Big Man was a corruption of traditional African cultural modes, Mamdani posits that even the most liberal and sincerely motivated colonizer "displayed a deep-seated paternalism" in the formulation and implementation of colonial policy (85). As the good boys of the colonial administration, the new African rulers of the 1960s would carry this paternalism into the postcolonial phase. But as Mamdani remarks, "Although independence deracialized the state, it did not democratize it" (64).

Mamdani observes that "[d]irect rule was Europe's initial response to the problem of administering colonies. There would be a single legal order, defined by the 'civilized' laws of Europe. No 'native' institutions would be recognized. Although 'natives' would have to conform to European laws, only those 'civilized' would have access to European rights" (16). In a perceptive reading of the connections between colonialism and modernity, Biodun Jeyifo has taken issues with what he sees as Mamdani's characterization of the broken "promise of modernity" (612). However, like Mamdani, Jeyifo finds that under colonialism those promises were "negated by the very fact that it was such a profoundly illiberal, undemocratic regime of political governance which laid the foundations of despotism and even anti-modernity in postcolonial Africa" (612). Jeyifo's reading of the "civilizing process" in Europe that produced the modern subject complete with good "manners, conduct, personality" (608), defined "[the] ideal 'civilized' modern subjectivity . . . in opposition to instincts, dispositions and expressions which are considered wild, unsanitary, spontaneous and carnal" (609). He flags the separation of what is considered "'civilized', rational and modern from what is deemed savage, irrational, and unmodern," observing also that the process coincided with the formation of economic classes in Europe as the transition from late feudalism to early capitalism took place (609). The dichotomy provided the cultural sanctions for the separation of the lower social orders from the middle and upper classes: the civilizing process "in Europe did manage to consolidate a bourgeois subjectivity as the model of the properly 'modern' and 'civilized' subject" (609). It is this bourgeois subjectivity that paved the way "for all the economic and cultural projects of modernity" (611), and colonialism was core to those projects. But as Mamdani shows, the European civilizing mission ran into the challenge of controlling multitudes, thus forcing a shift in perspective and practice, "from a civilizing mission to a law-and-order administration" (109). As he argues,

> The hallmark of the modern state was civil law through which it governed citizens in civil society. The justification of power was in the language of rights, for citizen rights guaranteed by civil law were at the same time said to constitute a limit on civil power. The key claim was that this form of power was self-limiting. Against this description was the reality: the regime of rights was limited and partial. Citizen status was not conferred on all within the ambit of civil society. The primary exclusion was based on race. (109)

And thus, even though colonialism set out to "civilize" the "natives," it excluded those natives from citizenship in the colonial state, gave them few rights and exercised power that was not self-limiting. The authoritarian paternalism gave rise to the African "Big Man."

As Robert Price found in his study of postcolonial Ghana, British colonialism reinforced and increased the authoritarian expectations and leadership style already associated with authority roles. First, by "strengthening the hand of authority and significantly weakening, if not nullifying, the institutional mechanisms that provided the 'threat from below,'" even protecting chiefs from threats of destoolment as among the Akan. The second way was through "institutionalization of a new polity, the colonial regime, characterized by a sharp differentiation between the elite who ruled and everyone else. Those in authority were not held responsible or accountable to the public at large, and were thus left free to behave in an arbitrary and domineering manner to those they ruled" (184). He finds the roots of the Big-Man syndrome in that attitude: "Those in official position [usually Europeans] are, by virtue of that fact alone, to be considered masters treating all those without official position—that is, all Africans—with a mixture of authoritarian contempt and paternalist benevolence." After independence, the Africans occupying the European posts "behaved, and were expected to behave, in much the same manner as their predecessors" (184). Indeed, for the leaders of the postcolonial era, differences over issues became battles over personal status or esteem; hence, as Price argues, the Big-Man Small-Boy Syndrome hampered the institutionalization of the principle that public criticism of government policy is a legitimate activity (190). The big men came to have a monopoly of responsibility for public affairs and exacted deference to that responsibility from those without authority (190). They were also hypersensitive to criticism. The situation described by Schatzberg in relation to Zaire where "the state tries to occupy all available political space within the system" by delegitimizing other parties, co-opting or suppressing emerging opposition groups (141), and "ideological obfuscation" (142) became prevalent around Africa in the postcolonial era. In retrospect, it would appear that Europe's "civilizing mission" in Africa gave rise to fairly undemocratic colonial administrations whose paternalism and exercise of unlimited power became a model for postcolonial authoritarianism and paternalism, thus hampering the institutionalization of legitimate governance. The entrenchment of the African Big-Man supported by Western powers during the Cold War ensured that those artists and writers who dared to question Africa's "arrested decolonization" ended up in detention, if not in exile. But their writings gave birth to a large body of poetry, drama, and the African dictator novel, the predominant genre that fictionalizes these dictatorships.

While the Latin American dictator novel has been extensively studied, fictional and dramatic African representations of dictatorships in Africa have not been as comprehensively explored.[2] Mbembe's insightful analysis of the postcolony still painted African realities in overly broad strokes. The essays collected in this volume represent individual attempts to fill out some of the gaps in Mbembe's study. Twelve contributors undertake representative readings of the African dictator in the novel, drama, film, and music. It was not possible to put together a collection of essays that surveys all the dictator fictions written in the last half century. The list is long and includes Camara Laye's *A Dream of Africa* (1966), Yambo Ouologuem's *Bound to Violence* (1968, 1971), Ahmadou Kourouma's *The Suns of Independence* (1968), Sembene Ousmane's *The Last of the Empire* (1981, 1983), Naguib Mahfouz's *The Children of Gebelawi* (1981), Nuruddin Farah's trilogy—*Sweet and Sour Milk* (1979), *Sardines* (1981), *Close Sesame* (1981), Sony Labou Tansi's *The Antipeople* (1983, 1988), Nawal El-Saadawi's *The Fall of the Imam* (1987, 1989), Chinua Achebe's *Anthills of the Savannah* (1987), and Ngũgĩ wa Thiong'o's *Matigari* (1987). Representative of more recent dictator novels are Ahmadou Kourouma's *Monnew* (1990, 1994), *Waiting for the Wild Beast to Vote* (1998, 2004), *Allah is Not Obliged* (2002, 2007), Helon Habila's *Waiting for an Angel* (2002), Yvonne Vera's *The Stone Virgins* (2002), Ngũgĩ wa Thiong'o's *Wizard of the Crow* (2004, 2006), Emmanuel Dongala's *Johnny Mad Dog* (2005), Alain Mabanckou's *Broken Glass* (2010), and Sony Labou Tansi's *Life and a Half* (2011). From Uganda alone, Peter Nazareth's *The General is Up* (1984, 1991), Giles Foden's *The Last King of Scotland* (1998), Moses Isegawa's *Abyssinian Chronicles* (2001) and *Snakepit* (1999, 2004), and Goretti Kyomuhendo's *Waiting* (2007) are representative novels that portray Idi Amin's dictatorship. In addition, the dramas of Wole Soyinka—*Kongi's Harvest* (1967), *Opera Wonyosi* (1981), *and A Play of Giants* (1984)—treat the dictator theme. In the arena of film, Cheick Oumar Sissoko's *Guimba, the Tyrant* (1995) allegorizes African dictatorship through the ruse of a "classical" tale of a father-son struggle for power.

The papers gathered here cover postcolonial realities in Mali, Côte d'Ivoire, Senegal, the Congo, Nigeria, the Central African Republic, Somalia, Kenya, and Uganda. They constitute representative backdrops of recent dictator novels. Even though the papers could have been easily grouped into discrete Anglophone and Francophone sections, they are arranged here in a way that covers the dictator fictions from the earlier Farah in the 1980s to the translation of Sony Labou Tansi's *La Vie et Demie* (first published in 1979) as *Life and a Half* (2011). A cursory review of the list reveals the dearth of women writers in fictionalizing dictatorships. But as Susan Andrade has cogently observed, "Female writers, themselves excluded from the hierarchies of national politics" concentrate on domestic stories (21). While novels written by men "evolve out of their understanding of the economic and legal underpinnings of cultural acts, which bear directly on their representation of national phenomena," novels written by women "converge around the sphere of the familial as the orchestrating unit that looms over and plays out national dramas" (34). A novel like Chimamanda Ngozi Adichie's *Purple Hibiscus*, which portrays the interpenetrations of domestic and national tyranny, is the exception, rather than the rule. The fact that this collection of essays does not have

Introduction

a chapter devoted specifically to the interrogation of the ways women writers have fictionalized dictatorships is a gap that future scholarship should attempt to fill. As the product of a general call for papers centered around the figure of the dictator in African arts, this collection is a reflection of the scholarly interest that was expressed by the various contributors who survived the review process.

The first chapter surveys Nuruddin Farah's trilogy, *Variations on the Theme of an African Dictatorship*. While historicizing Siyad Barre's dictatorship, Gĩchingiri Ndĩgĩrĩgĩ argues that state power in Barre's Somalia was superstructural, operating on the basis of other traditional institutions—kinship, gender, and religion—which it corrupted. Showing that what Foucault calls elsewhere "the panoptic modality of power" (*Discipline* 201) functions in the fictional Somali society only on the basis of these other, already existing power relations, the chapter focuses specifically on the figure of the fictional president, the deified stand-in for General Siyad Barre whose ninety-nine praise names echo the praise names of Allah. Probing what Achille Mbembe calls "an intimate tyranny [that] links the rulers with the ruled" in the postcolony (128), the chapter shows that Barre was adept at producing regimes of truth that sought to disguise the effect of power as a negative force of repression.

Chapter Two analyzes Farah's *Sweet and Sour Milk*, *Close Sesame*, and Wole Soyinka's *Kongi's Harvest* and *Opera Wanyosi*. Nada Halloway argues that while the constitutions of many African nations at independence promised democratic rule, thirty-seven years after independence, those promises have, by and large, been replaced by autocratic rule. It was inevitable that such a development would occur as the bureaucratic institutions that the colonialists created in Africa could not and did not address the socio-cultural realities of Africans. The chapter shows that while Africans in general accepted European-style rule after independence, they still had ties to traditional forms of government, a dualism that characterizes the modern African nation. Halloway reads Nuruddin Farah's novels and Soyinka's plays as they examine the tools used by dictators to maintain power.

Chapter Three is a reading of Henri Lopès's novel, *Le Pleurer-rire* (*The Laughing Cry*, 1982), which is populated by multiple and competing narrators, and opens with a "serious warning" (*sérieux avertissement*) from the Inter-African Association of Francophone Censors, which insists the text is a fiction and the dictator, Daddy (*Tonton*), does not and cannot exist. Challenged by other characters who accuse him of fabricating the "fiction," the novel's principal narrator, Mam'he, the dictator's butler (*Maitre*), ends the novel with this assertion: "I have borrowed nothing from reality, nor yet invented anything." The novel presents an interesting portrait of the authoritarian practices of the African postcolonial (client) state. As Magalí Armillas-Tiseyra shows, the repeated ruptures of the narrative frame in the novel put into play two key issues of writing about dictators:

first, the concern with complicity (Mam'he, after all, works in the dictator's house) and, second, the question of authority. The latter is of particular importance because it is by claiming the position of authority that the writer can challenge the dictator. But Lopès does not allow such easy configurations. Magalí shows that the novel ruptures the monologic utterances of the state; however, it is not clear that an alternative can be rescued from the resulting chaos. Rather than attempting to claim the position of authority, Lopès takes on the question of authority itself similar to the canonical Latin American dictator novels of the 1970s, in particular Augusto Roa Bastos's *Yo el Supremo* (*I the Supreme*, 1974), which uses similar formal and narrative tactics to unfold its argument. Jumping off the reading of Lopès Magalí articulates a theory of practices of formal rupture as a new strategy in the dictator novel, a genre that has, in recent decades, become transnational. She concludes that the dictator novel is a space in which we can begin to think of a literary engagement with politics beyond the exigencies of particular political programs.

Chapter Four also examines Henri Lopès's *The Laughing Cry*, seeing it as one of the most representative African dictator novels. Gĩtahi Gĩtiti makes a detour into contemporary scholarship on postcoloniality to provide the necessary historical and critical/literary frameworks against which to read the ruinous effects of runaway dictatorships that bridged the twentieth and the twenty-first centuries in Africa. Reading Lopès's *The Laughing Cry: An African Cock and Bull Story* as a complex exploration of the Mobutu years that typified the postcolonial African dictator, Gĩtahi shows that the Bwakamabé, the dictator in the novel, is a composite of Idi Amin Dada, Jean Bedel Bokassa, Jomo Kenyatta, Marion Ngouabi, Hastings Kamuzu Banda, Félix Houphouët-Boigny, Ahmadou Ahidjo, Jaafar Numeiry, Paul Biya, Mobutu Sese Seko, and Eyadema. Deconstructing the Chief's "inherited" entitlement to the "systematic application of pain" ostensibly endorsed by a think-alike community, which crushes the dissenter "like a cockroach," Gĩtahi reveals the sleight of hand by virtue of which the Chief is *automatically* rendered variously as *always* "the wisest, the best orator, the man with the strongest fist" (74). Arguing that there is not a big leap from "the best orator" to the *only* orator, the one uniquely qualified to speak to, about, and for his country, the contributor shows how Bwakamabé takes recourse to a "logic" of allegedly African authenticity which sees the secret ballot as a distortion, a kind of *falsity* "dead against the education of our ancestors" (75). Reading the paternal imagery that Bwakamabé deploys to legitimize his rule, Gĩtahi celebrates the novel's denunciation of despots and its rallying call for solidarity among those who must act to bring about change.

Chapter Five, "The Last King of Africa: The Representation of Idi Amin in Ugandan Dictatorship Novels," explores one of the most grandiose of African

Introduction

dictators. Reading Peter Nazareth's *The General is Up* (1984, 1991), Giles Foden's *The Last King of Scotland* (1998), Moses Isegawa's *Snakepit* (1999, 2004), and Goretti Kyomuhendo's *Waiting* (2007) as representative Ugandan dictatorship novels, Oliver Lovesey shows how these texts written over three decades consider Idi Amin, his regime, and his legacy from very different perspectives, focusing on the historical figure or the devastation he caused, with the hope that he might be the last African dictator, the last self-styled King of Africa. The essay argues that the novels' accounts of the dictator's performances of false or invented traditionalism, distorted historiography, and bogus decolonization, as well as his media celebrity status, suggest that the spectacle of Amin has destabilized the integrity of Uganda and partly enabled a process of psychological re-colonization, given that his dictatorship was enabled by colonial tropes of subservient African chiefs. Lovesey argues that the texts indicate that perhaps Amin's most heinous legacy is the reinforcement of racist stereotypes about African dependence and helplessness, as well as a propensity to a distinctly "savage" brand of African fascism.

Chapter Six, "*Jacob's Ladder* and *Anthills of the Savannah*: Narrativizing the Internal-External Dynamic of African Political Power," analyzes John A. Williams's *Jacob's Ladder*, an African American perspective on despotic power in Africa, together with Chinua Achebe's *Anthills of the Savannah*. Joseph McLaren traces how both writers produced novels that present the crisis of national leadership in imagined West African states, where stability and governance practices determine the direction of the nation and its pursuit of political power. The contributor argues that for Williams, the cause of instability in West Africa in the mid-sixties can be linked directly to the West, while Achebe views political fractures in the eighties as stemming from internal contradictions. The reading explores these "internal-external" factors and illuminates the failures of leadership in the fictional African states.

In Chapter Seven, "The Dictator and his Objects: The Status of the Fetish in the African Dictator Novel," Magalí Armillas-Tiseyra reads Ahmadou Kourouma's *Waiting for the Vote of the Wild Beasts* (1998). The novel narrates the performance of a purificatory narrative for the dictator Koyaga, of the fictional Republic of the Gulf. Koyaga has been removed from power following the recent loss of his two fetishes: a meteorite and a Koran. As the narrator/performers state, the purpose of the *donsomana*—the purificatory narrative—is to help Koyaga find these fetishes and thereby return to power. At the end of the novel, however, it remains unclear whether Koyaga will return to power, and the narrative closes with a profoundly ambivalent proverb: "The night lasts a long time, but at last the day arrives." Magalí asks: what, then, does this novel tell us about authoritarian power? Alternately, what does it tell us about the place of writing (storytelling) in authoritarian politics? Taking its lead from the novel itself, the chapter begins with the fetish as a means for making sense of the narrative's apparent ambivalence. Attending to the multiple modalities of the fetish and fetishism in order to demonstrate the extent to which the dynamics of disavowal and substitution—fundamental to fetishism—are also fundamental to the novel's development of the theme of the link between narrative and power, Magalí shows how the novel parodies discourses of "African fetishism," revealing the meaning of a given object to be radically contingent. Precisely because it is articulated in a heterogeneous epistemological space, the fetish is also always ambivalent, signaling the coexistence of contradictory tendencies, both marking and negotiating the problem of difference. Magalí shows that within the space of the novel, disparate elements are brought into new, uneasy, and revealing relationships, with terms such as "democratic" being revealed to be as changeable as "meteorite" and "Koran." More broadly, the chapter also touches on invocations of African fetishism in other dictator novels—including Sembene's *Le Dernier de l'Empire*—in order to contextualize its claims about the role of the fetish in the dictator novel at large.

In Chapter Eight, "Fimbo ya Nyayo, When the Kenyan Dictator Called the Tunes," Maina Mũtonya analyzes the relationship between politics and music during Daniel arap Moi's dictatorship (1978–2002). Against the backdrop of the expression of the idiom of age and gerontocracy in Kenyan politics, the chapter explores how music became an important site where the dictatorial regime of arap Moi asserted its authority, while also probing the ambivalent space that music occupies in politics. Informed by the understanding of music as a "trenchant political site in Africa" (Allen 1), the chapter principally analyses the body of music that was produced as praise songs and propaganda tools during Moi's reign as well as the opposing voices from other artists who had to endure the eye of censorship during that time. Mũtonya also touches on the Kenyan "literature of the dungeon," a sub-genre that emerged in the 1990s that narrativizes the prison experiences of political prisoners in Moi's Kenya of the 1980s.

Chapter Nine, "Diagnosing the Dictator's Body Politic in *Wizard of the Crow*," is a reading of the body of the dictator in Ngũgĩ wa Thiong'o's *Wizard of the Crow*. As Robert Colson shows, the Ruler in the novel suffers from a curious malady: an illness, dubbed self-induced expansion or SIE, which causes his body to start "puffing up like a balloon, his whole body becoming more and more inflated, without losing the proportion of parts" (*Wizard* 469). The chapter argues that the representation of the Ruler's illness and, more particularly, the attempts to diagnose and treat his illness by both characters and narrators in the novel serve as potent modes of satirical critique of the excesses of his autocracy. Colson shows how the novel achieves this critique through its sustained attention to the body of the sovereign, revealing that when the Ruler begins to lose control of his body as a result of SIE, he also loses his hold on the body politic. This attention reveals

Introduction

the physical weakness of the Ruler's body and the underlying instability of his authority, which derives from a hidden history of complicity with the colonial and neocolonial powers that be. Colson brings into conversation the work of Giorgio Agamben on sovereignty and the sovereign body with Michel Foucault's work on the medical gaze and biopolitics in order to produce an account of how illness and diagnosis work, in the novel, as a narrative mode of political critique.

Chapter Ten, "Performing Resistance in Ngũgĩ's *Wizard of the Crow*," uses a performance lens to read Ngũgĩ's monumental novel. Showing that the state deploys ceremonialism as a means of staging its majesty, the analysis pays attention to the people's staging of their resistance by seizing on the inherently dialogic nature of performance. Reading the dramaturgy of the state ceremonials in *Wizard*, Gĩchingiri Ndĩgĩrĩgĩ presents the Ruler as a bungling scriptwriter, actor, and director. Foregrounding the constructedness of state spectacles that implies that the situation can be imagined otherwise, the chapter shows how the elites in the novel dramatize their prestige, planning events that are discursive affirmations of a particular pattern of domination. Partly informed by James C. Scott's article "Prestige as the Public Discourse of Domination," the chapter shows how hierarchical relations are routinized in the novel. Guided by the understanding in performance studies that an audience is actively involved in the construction of the meaning of a performance, the analysis shows how, as co-participants, the people appropriate and deform state ceremonies. Ndĩgĩrĩgĩ shows that the postcolony may be a dramatic stage and it may be filled with the disciplinary apparatus of state power as Mbembe says, but through Kamĩtĩ and Nyawĩra, the central characters in the novel, *Wizard* challenges Mbembe's assertion that subjection is the natural corollary of discipline.

Chapter Eleven looks at Alain Mabanckou novel, *Broken Glass*. Mabanckou is a member of the new generation of African writers born after independence. As Awa Sarr shows, in this postcolonial Africa, an indigenous minority exploits an indigenous majority. Drawing on Kwame Anthony Appiah's incisive reading of the novels of the second wave of African writing—the wave of disillusionment—the chapter shows that while the first generation of writers favored realism often associated with nationalism to denounce colonial occupation, the new generation is opting for surreal and burlesque modes of representation to portray postcolonial Africa stifled by its own people. This new generation of African writers did not experience the "colonial night," and, as a result, they blame the failures of the continent on Africans more than anybody else. Mabanckou is one of the most prolific writers of this new generation of Francophone writers. The chapter analyzes how Mabanckou mixes the grotesque, satire, and scatological writing in *Broken Glass* to represent the African postcolonial state marked by despotism and cynicism; and how he characterizes the disintegration of individuals that results from such maladministration. Borrowing the expression "aesthetic of vulgarity" from Achille Mbembe's *On the Postcolony*, the contributor elaborates on Mbembe's argument that the lower classes are not the only practitioners of the carnivalesque: vulgarity is the very principle by which the all-powerful postcolonial state machinery functions. Awa presents *Broken Glass* as a literary translation of Mbembe's theory.

In the last chapter of the collection titled "'A Nation of One's Own': Fictional Indictment of Cannibalistic African States," Ng'ang'a Mũchiri reads *Johnny Chien Méchant* by Emmanuel Dongala and *La Vie et Demie* by Sony Labou Tansi. Beginning with a discussion of the ubiquity of the nation-state as a political community and highlighting its life-endangering traits, the contributor explores the cannibalistic nature of African states, and the attendant sacrifice in human life. Arguing that, contrary to popular belief, state invocation of democratic ideals does not guarantee social justice, Ng'ang'a shows the interesting ways in which Dongala and Tansi disagree with the idealism contained in national constitutions that are typically considered foundational in setting the tone for civic engagement. Exploring the premier human rights documents on the African continent, The 1986 Banjul Charter—the African Charter on Human and People's Rights—and its supplement, The Women's Protocol of 2003, Ng'ang'a interrogates the idealism encompassed in the two documents, juxtaposing it with Dongala's cynicism of human rights discourse, as well as Tansi's ridicule of national constitutions. The analysis problematizes human rights praxis in post-war and/or authoritarian societies as a possible strategy for grassroots movements seeking to deploy and achieve democratic ideals while locating themselves within the universalist tendencies of human rights theory. Originally given as a paper at the 38th African Literature Association Conference in Dallas, Texas in April 2012, Ng'ang'a's paper was adjudged the best paper presented at the conference by a graduate student.

Finally, a note on the title of the collection, *Unmasking the African Dictator*.... There are at least two things that the African dictator of the last half century was good at: mastery of the rhetoric of obfuscation, and bluff. It has to be remembered that by and large, the dictators engaged in monologic utterances through state media, about which the chorus in the prologue of Soyinka's *Kongi's Harvest* complains that one could not bandy words with government rediffusion sets that talk and talk and never take a word of reply (*Collected Plays* 61). With beneficent paternalism, a Daddy Bwakamabé can argue that elections are a Western imposition, and in the same breath posit that every nation needs a good orator at the same time that he ensures that he is the only orator in the national space, with a good fist—no less. For him, civil peace is reducible to the security of his kin. Similarly, a ruler like the Ruler in *Wizard of the Crow* can state that there is no difference between him and the country, without any fear of contradiction (161, 513).

Introduction

In the chapters that follow, the rhetoric of obfuscation is flagged as the rhetoric of dictatorships that, to appropriate the words of Roberto González Echevarría writing on the Latin American dictator novel, masks the dictatorship of rhetoric (64-85). As Echevarría persuasively demonstrates, both power and rhetoric go together (1). As for the bluff, it might be helpful to remember the crowning of Bokassa, or Amin's self-investment as "The Last King of Scotland," among others who feature in the African dictator novel and drama. Some of the essays in this collection defetishize the body of the ruler and his fetishes that go together with his enlightened ritualism and supposedly confer divine authority that cannot be shared. They also show how this power is actually constructed, routinized and theatricalized in ways that draw attention to the bluff that the rulers stage, and the man-madeness of their spectacles of power which can be re-imagined otherwise. As Robert Colson observes presciently in chapter nine, "Much like the iconic scene in the film *The Wizard of Oz*, the dictator novel pulls back the curtain on the tyrant and exposes that behind the curtain and all the pyrotechnics and scary voices, there is just a man using a microphone and some machines" (Page 173) Most of the dictators fictionalized in the texts analyzed here have already fallen, but their pyrotechnics are laid bare in the chapters that follow.

For those who would argue that the literary text did not have any efficacy, one is reminded of the Elder in Achebe's *Anthills of the Savannah* who meditates on the relative power between the man of action and the storyteller. To him, the storyteller is supreme. Long after the men of action have fallen—and all the tin-pot despots took pride in themselves as men of action—the storyteller will have the final word. And to use an anecdote from that wizened Elder, the story of the leopard and the tortoise—asked why he was blowing up a dust storm instead of confronting leopard, the bully who was at that moment itching for a fight, the mismatched tortoise explained that "even after I am dead I would want anyone passing by this spot to say, yes, a fellow and his match struggled here" (*Anthills* 117). The writers may not have been able to overthrow dictatorships, but they have won the discursive war. The dictators met their match in the African writer who, like an anthill, survived to tell the story of last year's drought of human rights.

Notes

1. Admittedly, as one perceptive critic noted, *On the Postcolony* is "at heart a collection of essays rather than a book with an argument developed throughout" (Ellis, *African Affairs* 670). Unsurprisingly, it has also received some fairly mixed critical reviews. In two articles published months apart that seem to rehash the same argument, Jeremy Weate identifies what I also see as the weakness in Mbembe's theorization of power—"[T]he heavy privileging of *power over* (power as limitation and imposition), and scant attempts to theorise *power to* (power as capacity and agency)" (*Research in African Literatures* 32; *African Identities* 7). Weate also problematizes what

he sees as Mbembe's refusal to acknowledge resistance as "the name we must give to the force that modifies power" (*Research in African Literatures* 35; *African Identities* 9) in a way that refuses to recognize the situationality of power and the play with it. Having flagged Mbembe's alienation from the "continent's travails," Titi Adepitan denies him the office of African spokesperson on the basis that at core, Mbembe's desire is to entertain the West (*Canadian Literature* 155). In a much more nuanced critique of Mbembe's text, Ato Quayson recognizes the ways that "consent and coercion go hand-in-hand in the totalitarian African postcolony, but in such a manner as to appear quite unstable and difficult to identify completely or sorely with the politically dominant authorities" (*African Studies Review* 158). Still, Quayson notes the theoretical discontinuity in the book after chapter 3. While this collection was under review, two studies were published that mark a new extreme in the critique of Mbembe's reading of the postcolony. Dismissing Mbembe in an endnote, Robert Spencer still ends up reading power as a performance (147), a core argument in Mbembe. His reading of the continuities between colonial and the postcolonial despotisms (148–150) is also startlingly similar to Mbembe's. Neil Lazarus in his more substantive disagreement—which appears to inform Spencer—also dismisses Mbembe's work in an endnote (*The Postcolonial Unconscious* 232). The gaps and blindspots in these last two works need not detain us here.

2. Gītahi Gītiti's "Ferocious Comedies: Henri Lopès' *The Laughing Cry* and Ngugi wa Thiong'o's *Matigari* as 'Dictator' Novels," and Josaphat Kubayanda's "Unfinished Business: Dictatorial Literature of Post-Independence Latin America and Africa" are among some of the early studies that would be of interest.

Works Cited

Achebe, Chinua. *Anthills of the Savannah*. New York: Anchor, 1987. Print.

———. *Arrow of God* (*The African Trilogy*). New York: Alfred Knopf, 2010. Print.

———. *A Man of the People*. New York: Anchor, 1967. Print.

Adepitan, Titi. "Views of the Postcolony: Achille Mbembe *On the Postcolony*." *Canadian Literature* 178 (2003): 155. Print.

Andrade, Susan. *The Nation Writ Small: African Fictions and Feminisms, 1958–1988*. Durham: Duke UP, 2011. Print.

Butler, Judith. "Mbembe's Extravagant Power." *Public Culture* 5.1 (1992): 67–74. Print.

Coronil, Fernando. "Can Postcoloniality be Decolonized? Imperial Banality and Postcolonial Power." *Public Culture* 5.1 (1992): 89–108. Print.

Ellis, Stephen. "*On the Postcolony*, by Achille Mbembe." *African Affairs* 100.401 (2002): 670–671. Print.

Gikandi, Simon. *Ngũgĩ wa Thiong'o*. Cambridge: Cambridge UP, 2000. Print.

Gītiti, Gītahi. "Ferocious Comedies: Henri Lopès' *The Laughing Cry* and Ngũgĩ wa Thiong'o's *Matigari* as 'Dictator' Novels.'" *Ngũgĩ wa Thiong'o: Texts and Contexts*. Ed. Charles Cantalupo. Trenton, NJ: Africa World Press, 1995. Print.

González Echevarría, Roberto. *The Voice of the Masters: Writing and Authority in Modern Latin American Literature*. Austin: U of Texas P, 1985. Print.

Jeyifo, Biodun. "In the Wake of Colonialism and Modernity." African *Literature: An Anthology of Criticism and Theory*. Eds. Tejumola Olaniyan and Ato Quayson. Malden, MA: Blackwell, 2007. Print.

Karlström, Mikael. "On the Aesthetics and Dialogics of Power in the Postcolony." *Africa: Journal of the International African Institute* 73.1 (2003): 57–76. Print.

Introduction

Kubayanda, Josaphat. "Unfinished Business: Dictatorial Literature of Post-Independence Latin America and Africa." *Research in African Literatures* 28.4 (1997): 38–53. Print.

Lazarus, Neil. *The Postcolonial Unconscious*. Cambridge: Cambridge UP, 2011. Print.

Mamdani, Mahmood. *Citizen and Subject: Contemporary Africa and the Legacy of Late Colonialism*. Princeton, NJ: Princeton UP, 1996. Print.

Mbembe, Achille. *On the Postcolony*. Berkeley: U of California P, 2001. Print.

Mudimbe, V.Y. "Save the African Continent." *Public Culture* 5.1 (1992): 61–62. Print.

Olaniyan, Tejumola. "Narrativizing Postcoloniality: Responsibilities." *Public Culture* 5.1 (1992): 47–55. Print.

Price, Robert. "Politics and Culture in Contemporary Ghana: The Big-Man Small-Boy Syndrome." *Journal of African Studies* 1.2 (1974): 173–204. Print.

Quayson, Ato. "Breaches in the Commonplace." *African Studies Review* 44.2 (2001): 151–165. Print.

Sahlins, Marshall D. "Poor Man, Rich Man, Big-Man, Chief: Political Types in Melanesia and Polynesia." *Comparative Studies in Society and History* 5 (1963): 285–303. Print.

Schatzberg, Michael G. *The Dialectics of Oppression in Zaire*. Bloomington: Indiana UP, 1988. Print.

———. *Political Legitimacy in Middle Africa: Father, Family, Food*. Bloomington: Indiana UP, 2001.

Scott, James C. "Prestige as the Public Discourse of Domination." *Cultural Critique* 12 (1989): 145–166. Print.

Soyinka, Wole. *Collected Plays* 2. London: Oxford UP, 1974. Print.

Spencer, Robert. "Ngũgĩ wa Thiong'o and the African Dictator Novel" *Journal of Commonwealth Literature* 47.2 (2012): 145–158. Print.

Weate, Jeremy. "Achille Mbembe and the Postcolony: Going Beyond the Text." *Research in African Literatures* 34.4 (2003): 27–41. Print.

———. "Postcolonial Theory on the Brink: A Critique of Achille Mbembe's *On the Postcolony*." *African Identities* 1.1 (2003): 1–18. Print.

Yewah, Emmanuel. "The Nation as a Contested Construct." *Research in African Literatures* 32.3 (2001): 45–56. Print.

Nuruddin Farah's *Variations on the Theme of an African Dictatorship*

GĨCHINGIRI NDĨGĨRĨGĨ

In "Why I Write," Farah characterizes Siyad Barre as an omnipresent maestro performer. Written after the publication of his entire trilogy, *Sweet and Sour Milk* (hereafter *SSM*), *Sardines* (*S*), and *Close Sesame* (*CS*), the article paints a picture of Barre that is not fully realized in the trilogy. The reader who encounters the article before reading the novels would expect some grand theater staged by Barre in a veritable society of the spectacle. However, a close reading of the novels reveals that what Farah has presented us is really the carceral state. The ruler functions as a master puppeteer who manipulates the administrative, coercive and ideological arms of state power from behind the scenes. In fact, he hardly appears in person. And thus, as in Bentham's panopticon, the ruler's power is everywhere at once but it is largely unverifiable (Foucault, *Discipline* 201). The family functions as an agent of state surveillance and power, a situation Farah paratextually signals through the Wilhelm Reich epigraph preceding Part Two of *Sweet and Sour Milk*: "In the figure of the father the authoritarian state has its representative in every family, so that the family becomes its most important instrument of power" (103). A variation of the epigraph is verbalized by two different characters in *Sardines* (67) and *Close Sesame* (114). The enmeshing of authoritarianism at the domestic and state level is therefore significant in the three novels and merits the kind of sustained analysis undertaken in this chapter.

My reading of the protean fictional dictator in Farah's *Sweet and Sour Milk*, *Sardines*, and *Closed Sesame* is informed by Foucault's arguments in *Power/Knowledge* that "the relations of power, and hence the analysis that must be made of them, necessarily extend beyond the limits of the state [. . .] because the state, for all the omnipotence of its apparatuses, is far from being able to occupy the whole field of actual power relations" (Rabinow 64). Following Foucault, I analyze the Somali state as superstructural in relation to the power networks that invest the body, sexuality, the family, kinship, gender, and knowledge with the "metapower" structured around prohibitions in the society. Foucault's "panoptic modality of power" (*Discipline* 201) functions in the fictional Somali society only on the basis of other, already existing power relations in ways that illuminate the figure of the fictional president, the deified stand-in for General Siyad Barre, whose ninety-nine praise names echo the praise names of Allah. Probing what Achille Mbembe calls "an intimate tyranny [that] links the rulers with the ruled" in the postcolony, that conditions the ruled to internalize "authoritarian epistemology to the point where they reproduce it themselves in all the minor circumstances of daily life—social networks . . . [,] styles of dress . . . [,] rhetorical devices, and the whole political economy of the body" (128), enables an exploration of how the state ensures that family and clan heads act as surrogate enforcers for the General. Running their families with unquestionable authority, they become extensions of the repressive apparatus of state power, delegitimizing dissent as an affront to the father figure(s)—or the aged mother in *Sardines*—by children who do not know any better. In turn, the General dismisses dissent against the state either as tribal jealousy or a reflection of the failure of parental authority. In both cases, the duty of reining in dissent is devolved to clan heads and father figures: it ceases to be a civil matter involving the rights of citizens. In order to maintain a place in the General's patronage networks, each family has to discipline the members within its ranks. Inevitably, generational tensions erupt, pitting the older generation—who almost invariably side with the perverted traditional authoritarianism deployed by the General—against the younger generation that is a product of modern education and desires change. The more progressive women in the novels act as agents of change of the patriarchal order, while the more conservative ones are complicit in their own oppression, having internalized the domination of both the patriarchy and the state.

Extending Michael G. Schatzberg's discussion of the deployment of the paternal imagery in Mobutu's Zaire (26) to read the positions of fathers and clan heads as non-elective offices whose decisions were not open to question by children (or competition), I study the reproduction of the authoritarian epistemology of the state at the family level. Locating the men's power within the fluid "Big-Man Small-Boy Syndrome" that Robert Price discusses in a Ghana-specific context illuminates how, in the Somali situation, the "Big Men" of social weight, worth, and responsibility become "Small Boys" to the General's "Big Man," their interactions governed by the "conspicuous power-authority versus conspicuous obedience and sycophancy" that Price found in the Ghana study (176). By controlling access to state patronage resources that were largely distributed through kinship networks, Barre was able to act the "Big Man" and reduce clan heads and family heads to sycophantic "Small Boy(s)," reproducing the situation that Marshall D. Sahlins discusses cogently: "Because kinship is a social relation of *reciprocity*, or of *mutual* aid[,] hence generosity is a manifest imposition of debt, putting the recipient in a circumspect and responsive relation to the donor during all that period the gift is unrequited" (qtd. in Shatzberg 80). Constructed as a large family—in real life Barre ruled Somalia through five related clan heads—the Somalis in the three novels are trapped within patronage networks based on kinship and reciprocity. But Farah shows that these traditional ties inevitably fracture when more cosmopolitan dissidents interrogate the Somali imaginary. These agents destabilize the paternalism and sexism of the postcolonial Somali state and articulate the need to move beyond familial/kinship-based structures of Big-Man/Small-[Wo]Man and reciprocal gifts that re-energize the paternal hold to the language of rights to citizenship, free expression, and free choice unfettered by patriarchal discourse. Deconstructing the co-optation and ideological obfuscation deployed by the state, the leaders of the fictional Somali resistance "multiplied their identities," to borrow Mbembe's reading of the postcolony (102–4), so that the same bodies that danced and dressed in party uniforms to better spread the pseudo-revolutionary ideas of "The Great General" were at the same time playing with his power. Mbembe posits that the postcolony is defined by a "convivial tension" between rulers who set rules that they modify at will and the ruled who pretend to be following the rules while subverting them: both operate in a simulacral world (128–129). This chapter explores this simulacral world in the Somali context.

Without proper historical context, it is possible to misread the dictatorial regime in the trilogy as a reflection of a pathological Somali condition. Mbembe and Mahmood Mamdani both historicize postcolonial despotisms in relevant ways. Mbembe suggests that the privatization of public prerogatives and the socialization of arbitrariness became the cement of postcolonial African authoritarian figures but they were inherited almost intact from the colonial order (32). Elaborating on the same, Mamdani traces the emergence of decentralized and centralized despotism in different African colonial environments, depending on whether they endured direct or indirect colonial rule. Under indirect rule that relied on a hierarchy of local state apparatus comprising chiefs and headmen who would have held elective office that was subject to peer sanction in the traditional society, that power to elect and to sanction office holders was removed from the local community and vested in the centralized colonial state.

The administrative chief thus "emerged as the full-blown village-based despot" (43) whose power was "freed ... of restraint, of peers or people ... [thus laying] the basis for a decentralized despotism" (48). In the already centralized states, the rulers were made answerable to colonial authority. At independence, Mamdani notes, conservative states reproduced the decentralized despotism that was the form of the colonial state in Africa while the radical regimes sought to refine it: "The outcome, however, was not to dismantle despotism through democratic reform; rather it was to reorganize decentralized power so as to unify the 'nation' through a reform that tended to centralization. The antidote to a decentralized despotism turned out to be a centralized despotism" (25). He says of the despotic nature of emergent power: "[T]he more it centralized coercive authority in the name of development or revolution, the more it enforced and deepened the gulf between town and country" (26). In the trilogy, that gulf is bridged by the big men of the country realizing that they have to act like small boys to the General so as to access the largesse that reinforces their status as big men in the country/ clan/family.

Elements of both the conservative and radical postcolonial state are in evidence in Farah's fictional Somalia. State power is seemingly diffused to the "people" through their non-elective heads of clans and families. It is a hierarchical system that reproduces the gender and generational exclusions and the uneven distribution of the benefits of colonial modernity. The centralized, despotic postcolonial state reinforces the non-elective power holders at the clan level and uses them to keep family members in check, as we see in the case of Keynaan in *Sweet and Sour Milk*, the clan members in *Sardines*, and Sheikh Ibrahim in *Close Sesame*. Even though all three texts are dominated by the same authoritarian General at the national level, the figures of domination in the micro-social domestic and regional spaces are an authoritarian father figure in *SSM* and a mother figure in *S*, while the authoritarian figure in *CS* is contrasted with an almost gender-blind figure of moderation. As such, it is productive to discuss the novels individually.

SSM establishes a foundation for reading the trilogy. The delimitation of Somalia as a carceral state; the interpenetration of ageism, kinship, and gender with state power; and the state's production of "regimes of truth" to naturalize the General's hold on power and the people's zombification are aspects that run through the trilogy. As Margarita observes in *SSM*, the post-independence rulers like Somalia's Barre were career soldiers in the colonial army. Halfway through the novel, Margarita states that acting on behalf of the civilized world, all colonial powers in Africa "administered the colonies barbarously, savagely, [and] never considered it expedient to allow the sub-human subjects under their administration the same democratic rights as they themselves had, both in their own countries and in their privileged positions as rulers, viceroys or governors" (134).

Further, she says, the postcolonial Africa was "a textbook reproduction of European values and western thinking.... There was no equal distribution of responsibility" (134). Prodded by Loyaan to comment whether "African dictatorships are but a re-creation of the same methods... these career-soldiers learned from their colonial masters during the toughest struggles" (135), Margarita replies in the affirmative. To achieve his ends, the General resorts to a combination of despotism, surveillance, and discipline.

Whereas the rise of the modern state nurtured institutions that settled differences in society without recourse to violence, Foucault remarked upon the centrality of prison in the regulation of society, seeing it as a reproduction of the mechanisms found in the social body (Rabinow 217). He has argued that the rise of the modern state in the 16th and 17th centuries was defined by the establishment of a professional army, the police, and administrative bureaucracy (Rabinow 63). He traces the emergence of discipline that was characterized by surveillance and normalization—the psychiatric hospital rehabilitating the "abnormal" for reintegration in society—and later, the emergence of punishment, correction, and education (63). Connecting the panoptic modality of power to the rise of the bourgeoisie as the politically dominant class in the 18th century, Foucault shows how the class masked its dominance in the establishment of an explicit, coded, and formally egalitarian juridical framework made possible by the organization of a parliamentary, representative regime. But the ostensibly egalitarian system of rights was

> supported by these tiny, everyday, physical mechanisms, by all those systems of micropower that are essentially non-egalitarian and asymmetrical which we call the disciplines. And although, in a formal way, the representative regime makes it possible, directly or indirectly ... for the will of all to form the fundamental authority of sovereignty, the disciplines provide, at the base, a guarantee of the submission of forces and bodies. (*Discipline* 222)

The African despot inherited a centralized state devoid of the sanction of peers or people, or limits on civil power. He consolidated the state's monopoly of violence and its instruments of discipline without allowing the will of all to form the fundamental authority of sovereignty. In the trilogy, the entirety of Somalia is imagined as a large prison, and the people are subjected to permanent observation and archiving. The surveillance and regulation in the fictional Somali state is described in Soyaan's letter to Loyaan three years prior:

> The city is broken into thirteen cells, of which all but one is of manageable size. The security deems it necessary to break this sandy city into these, have each house numbered, the residents counted—and everybody screwed! The General has the master-key to all cells, whether numbered or unnumbered. He is the Grand

Warder, remember. Every civil servant and his family must register with the Centre nearest him. Thrice weekly, civil servants should report themselves to the Centres at which they are registered. Thrice weekly in the mornings, civil servants must attend a program of orientation organized by the Revolutionary Council for all Ministries. If any person is found missing on two counts out of six, he or she loses his or her job. (95)

Attendance at the Orientation Centres rises at the expense of mosque attendance, and the General becomes the substitute god: "People immediately, when their number exceeded five, found it expedient to sing the General's praises." It was illegal "to have an assembly of more than five persons unless they were at an Orientation Centre or unless they were there to chant the chorus of the General's ninety-nine good names" (95). Significantly, the people only find it "expedient" to worship the General to escape censure, and on top of the ninety-nine "good names," the General has some bad ones, and even the beggars choke on his praise names at the end of the novel (255).

Tracing the development of carceral institutions from the landmark opening of Metray Prison in January 1840, Foucault remarked upon the construction of a space where the "criminal cannot hide" (Rabinow 235), an image that is appropriate to a reading of the carceral state that is Farah's fictional Somalia. But whereas Metray Prison was subjecting criminals to surveillance, Farah constructs the entire state as a prison. Foucault observed the mobilization of the staff whose task was "to produce bodies that were both docile and capable," ensuring the orderliness of the inmates, physical exercises, military exercises, the routines of rising in the morning, going to bed at night, the walks to the accompaniment of bugle and whistle: "[T]hey checked cleanliness, supervised bathing. Training was accompanied by permanent observation; a body of knowledge was being constantly built up from the everyday behavior of the inmates; it was organized as an instrument of perpetual assessment . . ." (235).

The surveillance in the trilogy is pervasive. As in the carceral state, the body in the fictional Somali state is regulated in infinite ways in life and death. One of the key mysteries in *SSM* is what kills Soyaan, who becomes indisposed after a visit to Beydan, his stepmother, during which, together with the Minister who was also present, he is given a meal, according to Beydan's account (166). Even though suspicion falls on the Minister as the person who probably had the food poisoned, the polygamous family is encouraged to suspect Beydan, thus conveniently letting the Minister off the hook. As long as the family fights horizontally, they remain unable to confront the enemy above them. Keynaan is the tyrant in the domestic space who delegitimizes all dissent within his family on the basis of age, kinship, religion, and gender.

At the beginning of the novel, Keynaan is introduced as "a terror of a husband" (2) and associated with tyranny on at least three occasions in the novel (33, 142, 143). He specifically refers to himself as "The Grand Patriarch" (102), thereby equating himself to the General, who is variously referred to as "Grand Patriarch" (55), "father of the nation" (110, 120), "Grand Jailer" (153), and "Grand Warden" (95). But unlike the General, Keynaan's power in the family is not absolute: he acts Big Man/Small Boy situationally. We are told that when Loyaan and Soyaan were younger, "[w]henever some superior officer humiliated him, he came and was aggressive to the twins and his wife. He would flog them, he would beat them—big, and powerful that he was, the Grand Patriarch whose authority drenched his powerless victims with the blood of his lashes" (92). When Soyaan dies of the suspicious food poisoning, rather than pursue the clues that point to the state's role in the death, Keynaan sees it as an opportunity to advance his own interests in the state (102). He asserts paternal prerogative "to give life and death as I find fit[.] . . . The law of this land invests in men of my age the power" (102). This declaration comes immediately before the Wilhelm epigraph that foregrounds the authoritarian father figure as an extension of the state, and its most important instrument of power (103). Keynaan decides "to breathe life into [Soyaan's] name . . . [,] make him honourable . . . [,] give him life again" by getting a school or a street named after him, thus ensuring "the spiritual revival of his name" (101). This intervention is premised on his status as a father. He appears to have saved Soyaan's life once when part of the security apparatus reported to him that they were about to arrest his son. Keynaan reports that he went to the General and appealed to him: "I vowed to the General that I would speak to Soyaan" to tone down his anti-government activism (101). And thus, in the centralized despotic state, the General devolved authoritarian father figures to discipline their children on behalf of the state. To advance his parental prerogative, Keynaan mobilizes Qumman in shaming Loyaan into silence about the inconsistencies in the state's story.

Keynaan's disdain for the younger generation's resistance to the General is illustrative of the persistence of an anachronistic age-set mentality in the running of the modern centralized state. The younger generation is assumed to be working for the interests of the countries in which they received their academic training, be they Western or Russia, and lacking a common ideology and principles (99). But whereas the younger generation integrates ideas borrowed from the West in its quest for the civil liberties that should define the modern state, the state itself borrows its political ideology from Russia and its religious values from a perverted Islam. But it still claims to be legitimate. Reflecting the clever divide-and-rule policies that guide the state, the General gives the impression that he still cares for the legitimacy that his peers confer to him in the running of the state: his peers supposedly have a stake in the welfare of his reign and he treats them as equals, and thus the need to discipline the errant members within their ranks who show dissent because they do not know any better, whether as a result of parental failure or brainwashing from the West. Reflecting on the survival of kinship groups in the more unstable Somali society of the 1990s, Anna Simons makes some interesting observations that would help to put the individuation of the younger generation that Keynaan and the General seem to resent in context. Simons notes that by "embodying a history of mutual obligation genealogy can easily act as a ready-made safety-net and moral order(er)" (277), and since traditional social relations have never been fully dissolved, "vital social welfare services historically have had to be provided for by the extended family (extending into the lineage and clan)" (278). Cleavage from the family "could only be accomplished so long as kin did not have to count[;] . . . the more kin-as-safety-net could be (successfully) circumvented the more easily attachments between individuals and individuals and institutions at all levels could be reconfigured" (278). Exposed to other societies where individual freedoms and rights are respected, the younger generation seeks to break the anachronistic hold of the kinship group and strive for a more accountable state. Used to exercising unquestionable authority within the kinship group and the state, Keynaan and the General stifle all dissent, which, to their thinking, cannot conceivably be homegrown. What we see consistently in the trilogy is that the General cares little for the legitimacy of his peers or people.

The state is marked by a heightened distaste for individual autonomy: people belong to groups, and when one of them errs, the whole group bears the punishment. When the mysterious Mulki is suspected of typing a seditious manuscript, her whole family is punished, as three hundred members of Mulki's tribe are imprisoned (112). When youths near Margarita's home deface the billboard with the General's face, three hundred of them are hauled off to jail. Social identity is yoked to the individual, constraining the individual. But whereas the older generation is comfortable with this yoking, the younger generation resists it.

Keynaan's sons, Soyaan and Loyaan, oppose the regime and choose friendship and loyalty to the nationalist ideal over kinship, leading to fights between the father and the sons. Significantly, this opposition and generational tension does not die with Soyaan. Loyaan appears to take over where Soyaan left off, a situation that seems to be validated by his invitation to take Soyaan's place in the secret group of ten dissidents. But thinking of the groups coming to pay "tribal condolences" after Soyaan's death, Loyaan voices a defining thought: "I am nobody's tribe, neither was Soyaan" (32). Unlike the less educated, the Western educated do not privilege the seemingly primordial ethnic identity constructions of their parents. Their cosmopolitan national identity is premised on rational choice. But even this neat distinction between identity construction and identity choice is being challenged in African Studies. Robert Bates, for one, describes ethnic groups as "coalitions which have been formed as part of rational efforts to secure benefits created by the forces of modernization" (qtd. in Posner 3). As Daniel Posner shows, identity construction operates over the long term and "involves a mix of subconscious social learning and conscious investments by individuals in particular group memberships" (7). Identity choice is a short-term process "that is immediately sensitive to alterations in the rules of the political game and is viewed here as an outcome of strategic choice" (7). The consensus seems to be that ethnic identities are situational and strategic (9). Against this background, it would appear that even Keynaan makes rational calculations to secure benefits created by the modernization of the Somali state. By aligning himself with the General, and being quiet when his son dies in suspicious circumstances, Keynaan is assured of gratuity payments from the state, and a street is named in Soyaan's honor. Within the value system operative in the novel, he becomes a man of social worth.

If Somalia is a prison (210) and the General is the "Grand Jailer" (53) or the "Grand Warden" (95), and "Grand Patriarch" (55) and "father of the nation" (110, 120), that prison is reproduced in the homesteads presided over by the likes of Keynaan and in the various cells into which the city is divided. The fathers control the members within the family with a mix of paternalism and sexism—children obey their parents without question, and women have no voice; the clan heads control the various kinship groups; the older members are given the illusion that by virtue of their age, they share state authority with the General; but he controls all. Religious and gender prohibitions reinforce the functioning of the kinship and age groups, and women's silence is expected as a matter of tradition and religious observance. As "father of the nation," the General wields unquestionable authority that is not subject to competition by tradition, and he comes to be equated with Allah in the popular imagination, which honors him with ninety-nine praise names. Age, kinship, gender, and religious prohibitions are thus mobilized to reinforce state power. Individual and collective bodies are marked, policed, and made to serve the interests of the state while one is alive. But even in death, the body can either be obliterated if it will bring disrepute to the General, or it can be made to stand for something that glorifies the General. The ten sheikhs who oppose the General's appropriation of Islam are executed and buried in unmarked graves, reflecting the General's need to control the nation's narrative. If the graves were marked, the General would feel exposed and insecure since people would garland them with flowers and call them the tombs of martyrs, thereby converting the graves into an alternative fetish to compete with the General for symbolism (44). When Soyaan dies, his body is appropriated by the state to advance its own narrative. The reconstruction and dissemination of the words Soyaan speaks on his deathbed is a classic example of information control of public memory. It raises the question: what counts as truth/knowledge, and what power does that confer on the person who wields it?

Soyaan succumbs with Loyaan's name on his lips (17). But different stories are manufactured with the result that "new life [is] planted by the tellers" (28). Without state textualization of Soyaan's death, the certificate of death reduces him to a mere name on a piece of paper and a reference number (78). But the state then decides to appropriate Soyaan as a hero of the revolution, in ways that invert his anti-government activism when he was alive and delegitimize any further questions regarding the circumstances of his death. The mutability of bodies in advancing the state's narrative is foregrounded in the farcical substitution of Soyaan's picture with Loyaan's in the state-controlled paper, captioned: "Loyaan, Martyr of the Revolution, is dead but has left behind him a living legend of revolutionary vitality and loyalty to the highest of ideals. His last words were: *Labour is honour.* May he be remembered thus!" (80). The correction only draws attention to the fabrication of the original.

The textualization of Soyaan's last words is a battle of discursive control. In the first version of the appropriation of Soyaan's dying words, the Minister states that "they" were given "a different version. We prefer that" (46). The version morphs into the capitalized "LABOUR IS HONOUR" (47), but after being retold several times, its final rendition by the Minister deifies the General: "LABOUR IS HONOUR AND THERE IS NO GENERAL BUT OUR GENERAL" (222). As a convenient truism reported by the father—whom the reader knows was not present at Soyaan's death—the Minister wonders why they should believe Loyaan instead of his father. Keynaan's age validates the truth value in his statement, which becomes all the more unquestionable in its yoking of the pseudo-revolutionary slogan and its echo of Allah as the true God. A Foucauldian lens helps to unmask the vested interests motivating the Minister to the Presidency's adoption of this version.

Foucault presented "truth" as "a system of ordered procedures for the production, regulation, distribution, circulation, and operation of statements" (Rabinow 74). As he argued, "'Truth' is linked in a circular relation with systems of power which produce and sustain it, and to effects of power which it induces and which extends it" (74). The truth of the statement of Soyaan's death and validation of the General and his pseudo-revolution is thus tied in circular relation with the system of power which produces it and which it extends. It becomes part of the state's discourses, which, following Foucault, produce "effects of truth" which in themselves are neither true nor false (Rabinow 60). It is part of the massive fabrication of history, of which the "revolutionary billboards cashing in on the General's fabrications of the nation's realities" (41) are a part. As Medina says,

> He constructs showy pieces of timorous architecture, he gives to us monuments of false hope. He creates for the nation heroes of his own choosing[,] ... the roadsides are decorated with neon signs illuminating the sky of the city with the brilliance of his quotes of wisdom. Some of these sell to the masses ... [,] ideas which one is expected to buy uncritically—these being the General's wise sayings. (78)

Reflecting on his ambitions in writing *Discipline and Punish*, Foucault elucidates the focus on "a veritable technological take-off in the productivity of power" in the 17th and 18th centuries onward. The monarchies developed state apparatuses in this period of a "new 'economy' of power[,] ... procedures which allowed the effects of power to circulate in a manner at once continuous, uninterrupted, adapted, and 'individualized' throughout the entire social body" (Rabinow 61). Foucault presented these new techniques as both much more efficient and much less wasteful, less open to resistance than the techniques previously used—that were based "on forced tolerances (from recognized privileges to endemic criminality) and costly ostentation (spectacular and discontinuous interventions of power, the most violent form of which was 'the exemplary,' because exceptional, punishment)" (Rabinow 61)—in ways that are appropriate to a reading of the economy of power in the fictional Somalia depicted in Farah's trilogy. Elaborating on diffusion of power in the postcolonial state, Mbembe has argued convincingly about its reproduction as an episteme. As he says, power is not only repressive; otherwise nobody would obey it:

> What makes power hold good, what makes it accepted, is simply the fact that it doesn't only weigh on us as a force that says no, but that it traverses and produces things, it induces pleasure, forms knowledge, produces discourse. It needs to be considered as a productive network which runs through the whole social body, much more than as a negative instance whose function is repression. (61)

The Foucauldian echoes are evident in Mbembe's reading of power. Having looked at the power networks structured around the body, family, kinship, and gender that have the quality of prohibitions, discussion turns to the ways power traverses and produces things, forms of knowledge and discourse that naturalize the less overt domination.

The narrator in *SSM* remarks several times upon the retouching of the General's picture in the local daily to make the General appear younger and handsomer. Half the paper is devoted to his speeches and wise sayings. The portrait of the General is also retouched because, as Loyaan recognizes, image is everything (145). The General is hardly seen in public in the novel, but he is paradoxically omnipresent—on radio, on TV, newspapers, billboards, and on the arch commemorating the Revolutionary Victory in Afgoi (155). In addition, his thoughts are contained in a booklet that has been translated into four languages. All this is part of the ideological obfuscation that the sheikhs punctured, arguing that state tyranny was not legitimized by Islam (145). The sheikhs' opposition to the new economy of power forces the General to revert to the more spectacular and exemplary mode of punishment when he orders their execution and erases traces of their graves.

Information control is also critical to "[t]he politics of mystification [which] rendered rumours credible" (216). People are kept in their separate compartments of ignorance about what has happened to other people and things; no information is released "until a rumour had been published, and nothing was made official until the General's informants had reported back the mood, the feeling of the general public" (216). If the action was unpopular, unconfirmed reports would circulate "that so many persons of that tribe, or that class of people, or that pressure group had been imprisoned. The papers didn't carry the news, the radio either" (216). And thus, the state is able to control the flow of information through the regular broadcast and print channels, as well as official rumour.

In *SSM*, state surveillance is pervasive. Soyaan thinks of his father as "an informer," an "ear-servant of the National Security Service since he was semi-literate" (10). This "ear service" is in every homestead (151), planting fear and suspicion. The surveillance is concretized in the image of Dionysius's ear that basically listens in on every conversation. The people live in fear of being next after the knock on their neighbor's door at dawn; they fear standing up for principles, and the instinct for self preservation is captured in this dictum: "Raise your children, but not your voice nor your head. To survive you must be a clown[;] ... let's together humour the General" (37). The people clap and clown consciously to humor the General. That way, they can be left alone. As Mbembe has argued, it is productive to think of the state and its people as being entangled in a "convivial tension" where each side humors the other, and there are no clear-cut differences between oppression and resistance (104).

Connected to the surveillance is the ideological control, represented by the Orientation Centre that conditions the people into blind obedience. Like the city that is broken into cells, the social body is tightly regulated, its every movement entered into the state archive. On a trip out of the city, Loyaan observes of the Mogadiscio checkpoint, "In a ledger, every vehicle entering the city was registered, number of passengers, names, reason for vehicle's leaving or re-entering" (148). But attesting to the improvisatory nature of these rules, the ledger routine in Mogadiscio is waived when Loyaan travels later with Ahmed-Wellie because the traffic warden recognizes him (171), though he has to register on the return trip (177). Individual bodies are tightly regulated, studied, and recorded in numerous state archives/registers. Those who deviate from the norm set by the state are confined to mental institutions or prison, while the more ordinary folk have to submit to weekly ideological renewal at the Orientation Centre. It becomes the locus for mapping people's coordinates. In his search for Margarita's house in Mogadiscio, Loyaan finds no huge monumental placards bearing the General's portrait, yet the directions he gets are mapped in reference to the Orientation Centre (121). It is through these subtle gestures that power becomes a network operative through the whole social body, producing "a regime of truth" and what passes for knowledge.

Having looked at the ways power is diffused in the fictional Somali society in *SSM*, attention now turns to *Sardines*. A lot of the power networks portrayed in the first novel are also operative in the second novel in the trilogy. Discussion of this novel foregrounds the difference in the operation of this power when the person at its apex at the family level is female, and the negotiations women are forced to do with the authoritarian General at the top.

Sardines, Like *SSM*, presents authoritarianism at the level of the family as a reproduction of state tyranny. The action of the novel traces the conflict between two headstrong women: Idil, the mother-in-law to the novel's heroine, Medina. A socially conservative woman who accepts the inferior status accorded women in Somali tradition and in Islam, Idil seeks to enforce a patriarchal order in her son's house, but the son—Samater—is comfortable sharing domestic duties with the maid. Eventually, Medina leaves her house to Samater and his domineering mother, hoping to find a room of her own in a direct echo of Virginia's Woolf's feminist text (3, 4, and 6).

Whereas the connections between family and state authoritarianism were suggested paratextually in *SSM*, they are made more integral to the universe of discourse in *Sardines* with the fictionalization of Wilhelm's epigraph. As even Sagal, a minor character who sees revolution as a fad, remarks to Medina, it is an accepted fact that "in an authoritarian state, the head of the family (matriarch or patriarch) plays a necessary and strong role; he or she represents the authority of the state" (67). Sagal's recognition that matriarchs can also reproduce the authoritarianism of the state is particularly useful in a reading of Idil. We are told that even when Samater was twenty-one, Idil "pummeled [him] every time he answered back," thus turning his childhood into "a long unslept nightmare" (16). But suffering from separation anxiety and without recognizing her own emasculating influence on her son, Idil tries to shore up his masculinity when she surmises that Medina seems to call the shots in their marriage: she does not cook or do the dishes, she owns the house, and the car and the bank account are in her name. Samater therefore appears like a weakling to the tradition-bound Idil (17). Medina herself has these ghosts of authoritarianism. Her grandfather is described as "monstrous" and conservative: he specifically wanted to keep Medina from acquiring an education, but her more liberal-minded father had refused and exposed her to a fairly cosmopolitan education that included college in Italy. Still, she "opposed the present dictatorship because it reminded her of her unhappy childhood" and the General reminded her of her grandfather who was an unchallengeable patriarch (17). Medina herself is introduced as being "strong-minded as she was unbending in her decisions[,] . . . as confident as a patriarch in the rightness of all her decisions" (6). These decisions might appear suffocating sometimes, especially where her daughter, Ubax, is concerned. We are shown a thin line between the nurturing mother and the smothering one who has difficulty letting her daughter grow into her own person. Whereas, according to Idil, Samater was "as weak in the head as he was in the knees . . . because he had not grown up with a strong father to emulate or imitate" (6), Ubax runs the risk of growing up feeling overwhelmed by Medina's all-knowing presence.

Medina's mother, Fatima bint Thabit—who is of Arabic extraction—recognizes her imprisonment in a room that is not her own, but she wishes the same for her daughter: "The tradition of my people encages me in a four-walled prison and makes me the exclusive property of a man" (144). As a conservative, she cannot contemplate a woman who is not attached to a man or her mother's hearth—and therefore indirectly to a man. She tells Medina: "If you are not with Samater, a wife to a caring husband, then come back here and be the grown child of your mother" (145). Medina reads echoes of the General in Fatima's authoritarian power, her inclined head, her body, and her insistence on inequality between parents and children (148).

Samater is progressive, but his mother sees this as weakness. He is dependent on Medina, but because of this, Idil finds Samater unmanly, while she thinks that Medina is irresponsible, untraditional, and un-Islamic (70–71, 74). She criticizes Medina for not molding Ubax into a traditional girl and threatens to get Ubax circumcised (71). She seeks to control expenditure in the household, cut down on toys and even Medina and Samater's books that, to her, cost too much. While she only vows that she will burn the books (71), she bans liquor in Medina's house as long as she is around as un-Islamic (81). In Idil's gendered spaces, the kitchen is woman's territory where men have no business. She is therefore shocked to learn that Samater cooks meals for Medina and Ubax and functions as his family's "official dishwasher" in the maid's absence (74). Apart from Medina, the mature women have internalized their domination and seek to convert those around them into pliable subjects of the state.

Politics is constructed as a male space, and resistance is also male. Medina is merely sacked for editing the General's speech, but some of those men who hear her story are jailed. Before we learn the full extent of her actions, we are invited to marvel at Medina's guts—editing the General's speech in a country where the control of text and reception is the state's monopoly. Given a fuller explanation of her action, Samater thinks that only a mad person would dare to seemingly tamper with a text emanating from the Solomonic lips of the General (89). We are told that his speeches were always carried in full, to the exclusion of other news. Medina is only interrogated and then banned from writing, but the other journalists—all men—are jailed for subversion. This discrimination reinforces the perception that there is no opposition, or it is only misguided opposition, or it is only by men. As we see throughout the trilogy, the General's state apparatus is able to disaggregate Somalis in terms of age, gender, clan, class and religion. Medina concludes that she is not imprisoned because the General thinks "that women are not worth taking seriously" (48). But there is little evidence that the General is "dueling" with her besides her sacking and getting her banned from publishing. Somalia is an oral culture anyway, and that is why the General has Dulman imprisoned because she is modernizing the oral culture by taping her anti-government songs and distributing them abroad where much of the dissent comes from. As an indication of the frivolity of the elites' opposition to the state, those who are able to address the largely illiterate popular masses constitute the biggest threat to the regime. Even the ill-informed Idil recognizes the inconsistencies in the opposition: the Samaters and Medinas are leaderless and lacking an ideology to articulate what would replace what they are rejecting (83).

As in *SSM*, the individual is flattened into a clan identity. The clan structure runs parallel to the state. The General fills most of the state offices with his clansmen. Those who are not his clansmen are made to answer to figureheads within their own clans. The clan dictates to the individual, as we see in Samater's appointment as Minister for Constructions, in the state's resolution of Amina's compensation for politically tinged rape, and in Dulman's silencing which is negotiated with her clan. In turn, the clan is punished for the transgressions of the individual. When youths are arrested for subversive activities, they are released only after the parents are bonded, and the "tribal chieftains" promise that the children would not take part in uprisings against the regime or write on walls in future (206). At the beginning of the novel, Samater is offered a cabinet position specifically because he is considered clean and "free-thinking." He can therefore bring some legitimacy to the corrupt and undemocratic government. Faced with the choice of standing by his principles that motivate his opposition to the regime, and thus risking the ire of a society that will not forgive, or sacrificing those principles to obey the authority of her aged mother (24), Samater decides to take the position. Nasser, Medina's brother, ponders the report on his choice: "Had Samater refused to accept the nomination, fifteen or twenty of his clansmen would have gone to prison. Or so the story goes. The General gave him an ultimatum: Samater's clansmen were told: 'Convince him to take the ministerial position, or else I will destroy you one and all'" (44). As Samater himself remembers it, he had been left with little option. Summoned from his home by state security, he had been driven from the house in the same car that the Security used to take prisoners away (182). The action suggestively sends two messages: he could end up in prison if he refuses the position, but taking the cabinet position is also akin to imprisonment. Then a flood of relatives had come begging him to take the position or they would all be ruined. Piling on pressure, the General had imprisoned thirty of his tribesmen, forcing the clan elders to come and plead with him to take up the position so as to save them (182).

Samater temporarily liberates himself from both Medina and Idil. While Medina leaves of her own volition to escape the tyrannical and patriarchal Idil, and to ostensibly free herself from contact with extensions of the regime on which she is writing a critical book, Samater kicks Idil out of Medina's house after she sets herself up as a domestic tyrant who micromanages his every move. She insists that he should marry a more submissive wife, the maid that she makes available. To his credit, Samater resolutely rejects the girl. But the threats Idil makes against him remind us of the interpenetration of authoritarian power. She threatens both clan sanction, and an appeal to the General to discipline him by sacking him now. And thus, if he took the cabinet position to safeguard the interests of his mother and her clan, they would have him lose the position when he refuses to conform to the clan. But it is arguable whether it is the clan or Idil herself who makes rational calculations about the benefits of a son in government, on the one hand, and the need to contain disobedience to her authoritarian, familial, age-based power on the other. Medina's own liberation is incomplete—she abandons her own house to the tyrannical/patriarchal Idil and escapes to her liberal brother's house. She does not appear to have the stomach to fight the domestic tyrant in her space, or to eject Samater, the other extension of the state in her domestic space. Paradoxically, it is Samater who will seek to liberate himself from her benign control: he gets a room at the hotel to complete the quest for freedom that is motific in the novel. Six months pass between Medina's departure and his own self-liberation.

Sitting in his hotel room as he contemplates resigning and fully regaining his freedom, Samater's gaze encounters the framed portrait of the General that "stared down at him from several angles, a portrait made handsomer and younger by the photographer " (182). And thus, if he thought he was escaping tyranny in the domestic space, he walks right into the gaze of Orwellian Big Brother: his move to the hotel is monitored, two state agents take up the rooms next to his, and the nervous receptionist hands him a message from the General to "*Come and see me when you can*" (185). It is a thinly veiled threat that he cannot run very far, and he recalls his mother's threat as he was evicting her—tradition will win in the end. That tradition is bound up with the clan heads who lambaste his decision to eject his mother and intervene with the General to now sack him (185). But whereas the traditionalists think that they are exercising power as independent agents, by whatever action—getting Samater to take the position or appealing to have him sacked—the traditionalists reinforce the General's power and dramatize their own powerlessness.

Medina's brother, Nasser, thinks that Medina's confrontation with Idil is a direct challenge to tradition, to the General's generation (104). Both sides appeal to a vacuous tradition to legitimize their positions. Idil becomes a symbol of the age-based oppression, as the face of the General in the domestic space (258). But whereas Medina assumes that she is fighting for all women, Farah presents a multiple-centered category of woman. The traditional Idil and Fatima align themselves with the patriarchy, and Xaddia (Samater's sister) blames Medina for her politics that are destroying Xaddia's family (259). Medina thinks that by "demolishing 'families' like Idil's and regimes like the General's" that she is fighting for the survival of all women (259). But we are shown that women have diverse interests, as we see in the cases of Xaddia herself, Asli (Medina's replacement maid), Amina, and Dulman.

Xaddia sees Medina's activism as a charade and wonders why Medina will "never concede or accept defeat" so as to save her family (259). Xaddia's concern with family has more to do with social standing: the cabinet position that her brother has lost, and the honor that her mother has lost as a result (259). She cannot understand why they have to be the ones to make a sacrifice. Likewise, Asli, the new maid brought in by Idil wonders why the maid she replaces, who was of inferior status, should have been allowed to voice opinions, exercise freedoms, and experience equality in Medina's house (84).

If nationalism is inherently gendered as male and depends on a masculine symbolic content that constructs the nation as female and the patria rushing to its defense (Parker 6), Amina's body becomes the site for staging a perverted totalizing Somali nationalism. Males are constructed as guardians, and it is a requirement that the members of cabinet be physically and mentally fit to keep enemies at bay and lead in the praise-singing (75). We do not see much in the way of men rushing to the defense of the motherland, or Amina, who is raped by three men in punishment for her father's loyalty to the General. Even though men from the rapists' clan were alerted about the rape, they refused to help Amina because of the persecution of their people by the General with Amina's father's complicity—he is a major in the armed forces and a government minister. The rapists were throwing a challenge to the General but wrote it over the body of Amina (126). While her father reads the rape as political, the General insists that the case must be isolated, "treated as though it were devoid of any political significance ... whatsoever" (127). The father follows the orders "for the good of the Revolution," which raises questions about how fragile the revolution must be. But it is illustrative how the General is able to reconstruct Amina's traumatic story to erase its political significance: to acknowledge such would be to acknowledge that there is resistance to his rule. Like Keynaan in *SSM*, the father's embrace of the General's solution shows how gender and kinship are appropriated to prop up the state. The father states, "We'll give you a ticket to go anywhere you like and we'll pay for your university anywhere in the world" to give people time to forget about the rape. Pressed on the "we," the father responds, "The General and I. I haven't spoken to your mother. I've spoken to the General and his instructions are clear: no publicity, no scandal" (127). Thus, the victim's feelings are immaterial. The women from the rapists' clan recognize the interpenetrations of gender, class, and power, remarking that "[t]he pain is ours, the fat and wealth and power is the men's" (126). They ironically empathize with the marginalized woman whose body is used as a stage for battles between men over power. The father sees his silence and acquiescence as a means of advancing himself in the state apparatus.

Even though Amina insists on a public trial, the state facilitates the rapists' escape to minimize the scandal. Following a cabinet reshuffle, Amina's father is appointed to an ambassadorial position abroad, and Amina is eventually persuaded to move into her empty parents' house and paid monetary compensation to hush up. And thus, material considerations trump the gender agenda and the larger struggle for civil liberties. In this sense, Amina's story has some similarities with Dulman's.

Dulman's collaboration with the state and her eventual fall from favor reflects the General's ability to manipulate gender codes to advance his own power. Feeling inadequate and unfulfilled in a society that values women only as mothers, Dulman's search for a cure for her barrenness, what she sees as the "dark curse on her femininity," leads to her mounting debts that make her easy prey for the General's overtures. As she tells Nasser, she will sing the devil's lyrics if he will pay for her gynecology treatments that could help her conceive (165). As an oral artist who records her songs on audiotape, Dulman is a more potent threat to the General's hold on the largely oral Somali society. Because of her standing as a reputable oral performance artist, the tapes achieve wide circulation both in Somalia and abroad. Prior to the conscription by the General's handlers, Dulman was a folk play performer, and her rise to fame threatened the General, who believed that there could only be one star in the sky. Dulman was banished from the theater to cut her down to size (173). The General used artists like Dulman when he was consolidating his position because some of the artists were bigger stars. But once he entrenched himself, the General created his own troupe of sycophants. Eventually, Dulman was accused of planning an anti-revolutionary play and offered the choice of playing with the General's troupe or joining the General's enemies, "the anti-revolutionary reactionaries" from a rival clan (174). Before making the offer to Dulman, the General had already cleared with her clan the payback for her: she could go anywhere in the world for gynecological care and the government would foot the bills (174). Just like Amina's being offered the world at the state's expense, the General manipulates Dulman's kinship ties, her body and its medical needs, and her art to advance his own interests. If Amina's body is the site of rape staged as a contest over power by men, the medical experiments on Dulman's body extend the patriarchal reach of state power. Unconsciously, she helps to reproduce the phallocratic system by seeing her body as a site of reproduction. Unable to reproduce biological bodies that would in due course be part of the carceral state, Dulman's body and voice are appropriated to reproduce the discourses of the General and the state. According to the undercover agent who shows Nasser to Dulman's house, she is celebrated as the "Lady of the Revolution" for singing an adulatory song for the General that equates him to "the guarantor of God" and as a man whose "machine is made to order/to fulfill a need, the nation's and God's" (162). The suggestiveness of his apparent sexual prowess creates the image of the hypermasculine father of the nation, a dominant trope in African novels of dictatorship. But this hypermasculinity is called into question via references to the General's diseased body. It would be productive to probe "the anxious virility" of the phallocratic regime (Mbembe 110) a little further by reading the sexual politics in Samater's escapade with Ata.

Even though Ata is reportedly free with her sexual favors, Samater imagines that he would recover the manhood that has apparently been smothered by Medina if he raped Ata. Even as he contemplates his perverted masculine assertion, Samater still yearns for validation of this conquering masculinity by his mother (191). But if it is true, as it is rumored, that Ata had also been sleeping with the General and one of his vice-presidents—a kinsman—the questioning that Samater undergoes relating to Ata's real identity and her motivations in coming to Somalia would appear moot: given their control of the state apparatus, the General and his kinsman should know who Ata is. It seems likely that Samater is tortured for partaking of the same female body as his higher-ups. In a country where the body is constantly under surveillance, their conversation was monitored, and their compromising posture was captured by a photographer working for the state (202). Ata's playful admission that "[p]ower loves pussy," that she has slept with the General and that he is not much of a man—she says that Samater is more muscular, stronger, and more of a man—and that one of the two vice-presidents that she sleeps with "would come if you massaged his feet" (201), paints a picture of homosocial bonding attained through the sharing of her body. But in a society where the General is overly concerned with image and fancies himself a Casanova—he has two wives and reportedly keeps several mistresses—the dissemination of the image of the General's imperfect sexual body probably explains why the General deals so ruthlessly with Ata—she is deported soon thereafter—and Samater. The state security seeks to destroy Samater's credibility by planting the story of his fling with Ata and spreading it through Sandra, her nemesis, and also informing Nasser, Medina's brother (225). And thus, one woman is used to bring down another, while the hope in informing Nasser would be that the in-laws would discipline their transgressing son-in-law. But these machinations do not erase the image of the General's imperfect body that is already lodged in the people's imagination that consistently remarks that he is sick.

The General engages in elaborate image management in the novel. He is presented as an institution that controls public memory, with important events dated in reference to his actions (246). But he is defetishized just as consistently. Besides being recast as the greedy tortoise in Medina's rewriting of the story of "Tortoise and the Birds" from Achebe's *Things Fall Apart* (5), the General becomes the butt of children's jokes and is given "deprecatory anatomical nicknames" (13). In addition, speculation is rife that the General is afflicted with syphilis (246). We are told that the weirdest things happen every time the General is rumored to be ill—multitudes are locked up and later released as an indication of presidential magnanimity (251). But the panic that arises when the General is rumored to be seriously sick speaks to the paradox of the authoritarian African ruler being the glue that holds together a weak state. Even Sandra, the patronizing Italian journalist who is used by the state to cleanse its image abroad, recoils at the thought of his demise. She presciently remarks that "[t]he vacuums dictators leave are generally unfillable" (226). Looking at the situation in Somalia now would lead an observer to the same grudging concession: Barre did not nurture state structures that could survive him.

At the end of the novel, Medina sees herself as the sole survivor of a traumatic journey (261). Her activism is confined to writing to Amnesty International regarding the human rights situation in Somalia. While she refuses to see herself as a guest in her own country and instead constructs herself as an active participant in its history, she does not have much to show for her actions. The final image in the novel groups Ubax, Samater, and Medina as the recuperating nuclear family (263). But the family in *Sardines* is also presented as a site of repression. In her own nuclear family, Medina herself is a figure of repression just like Idil was in hers. Ubax feels suffocated by her mother's well-meaning attention, and Samater objects to Ubax's brain washing by Medina's equally dictatorial attentions (16).

Nuruddin Farah's *Variations on the Theme of an African Dictatorship*

Close Sesame is also dominated by images of confinement and reprises the same sites of power. However, the emphasis is much more on the figure of moderation represented in Deeriye, the main character. The novel is also much more focused on despotism as a reflection of the incomplete modernization of the state. Discussion in this section will therefore focus on these two areas.

At the beginning of the novel, Deeriye thinks of himself as a tethered beast—only walking as far as the rope will allow (7). While his daughter Zeinab meant well by having him sell his house and move into hers because he is too old to live alone, the alteration of his lifestyle and gentle restrictions imposed on him remind him of his limited freedom. His caring daughter's expectation that he will follow her regime of regular exercises and walks makes Deeriye want to move to the relative freedom of his son Mursal's house. However, he fears moving there because of Yassin, the yard/village bully/dictator, who harasses everyone, including animals on the street (68). The heroic Deeriye cringes on seeing Yassin (25). He has seen him in his dreams where Yassin struck him with a stone on the forehead, like he eventually does in real life (87). And thus, Deeriye is faced with two choices in the novel: submit to the benign regulations in Zeinab's house, or live under the perpetual terror of Yassin in Mursal's house. Yassin's reign of terror at the micro level mirrors that of the General at the national level. Deeriye's dependence on the favors that the family can provide—transport, water, and whatever modicum of security—reflects the hasty modernization of Mogadiscio, a city that has aged before it has teethed, as Deeriye comes to think (99). Such vital services would ideally be provided by the state.

The novel raises pertinent questions about the consolidation of the benefits of modernity. If the development of the modern state is marked by the settlement of differences without recourse to violence, by an arbiter who is recognized by all as representing the common will, what is the relationship between public justice and vengeance? Is justice a private matter or a public concern (*CS* 4)? If the administration of justice was transferred to the modern state, where is one to turn when it is the state that perpetrates the injustice? As Mursal wonders, is violence a legitimate option in overthrowing authoritarianism at the state level? At issue is the question of tradition (private justice) and state (public) justice. *Close Sesame* shows that the transfer of justice to the state was not accompanied by corresponding civil liberties.

For Mursal, traditional justice is private justice. The kith and kin of the aggrieved person, in order that the family or clan not be dishonored, uses the *lex talionis* system—a life for a life, an eye for an eye (10). Embedded in public justice is the sense of an all-encompassing justice, with the state as the arbiter of consensus. But as Deeriye recognizes, there is reason to doubt whether "the weak structures of the nation-state [can] bear the weight of the constitutional responsibilities ... of a clannishly ruled state" (189). He concludes that "the Somali doesn't [sic] believe in the logic of the state working justly for all, regardless of clan" (209), thus recognizing the incomplete integration into the centralized state of a people who were ruled by a plethora of decentralized institutions. Because the people's primary allegiance is to their own clan, individuals take it upon themselves to avenge their kin. In turn, the state apparatus is mobilized to protect the General's kin and insulate them from any association with dissent.

Given the foregoing, Deeriye dreads what his pre-teen grandson, Samawade, would do if he learnt that Yassin struck Deeriye. He can foresee a situation where kin defends kin, a reflection of the failure of the state to convince citizens that it is a just arbiter. When he learns of Yassin's attack on Deeriye, Samawade does indeed vow to avenge, and Deeriye has to talk him out of it. As in tradition, Yassin's family makes the formal visit to ask Deeriye for forgiveness—which he gives—but Deeriye rejects the compensation for blood spilt (86). But while it turns out that Yassin had already been punished by his family (83), doubts are raised about Yassin's character and motivations. He is described as "a good actor" merely performing the gestures of penitence (86), which indicates that he is not completely sorry for his actions. As a character whose excess, brutality, and play-acting are analogous with the General's, he becomes the device that Farah uses to question the General's theatrics and his sense of responsibility for the blood he sheds in the fictional state.

Related to the question of justice is the question of loyalty: is one's primary loyalty to the kin or the larger ideal of the nation? The nebulous resistance group navigates questions of loyalty to kin or loyalty to the resistance group whose core revolves around Mahad, Mursal, and Muktaar. For Mukhtaar, the question arises whether his loyalty to Mursal and the rebel group is greater than the ties of kinship/blood that tie him to his opportunist family (77). When Mahad stages the ill-fated attempt on the General's life and the group is rounded up, the state manipulates these kinship ties with the result that Mursal is released immediately to give the impression that Mahad's action was an isolated clan affair. Deeriye's own relatives are ordered by the General to stay out or heads will roll (181). It becomes clear that Mukhtaar would never betray a friend in order to safeguard the interests of the clan. But the members of the group are led to question each other's loyalty throughout the trilogy. Deeriye recognizes the tension between loyalty to state and kin bonds (133) in a way that recalls the earlier argument about ethnic identification as a rational choice. Deeriye's question—"why can't father and son disagree ideologically but live together in harmony?" (144)—speaks to the search for a moderate path between tradition and modernity. By the end of the novel, Mukhtaar's attempt to navigate the tension between clan identity and nation fails when Sheikh Ibrahim, his loyalist father, ends up killing Mukhtaar.

This is a culmination of the constant fights between the two over Mukhtaar's support for the nascent resistance. Deeriye, on the other hand, is the accommodating patriarch who is not threatened by the aspirations of his son, and there is an easy camaraderie between Mursal and Deeriye. He even integrates the feminine side of Naddifa, his departed wife.

During Mahad's incarceration, he is subjected to a lot of pressure to implicate only his own clansmen so as to advance the state's reductionist argument that resistance to the General is limited to particular clans (112). Due to Mukhtaar's relationship with the General—he is a cousin—his involvement in sourcing information for Mahad is hushed up and arrests are not made outside Mahad's clan (112). To advance the notion that dissent reflects a failure of parental responsibility, Mukhtaar's father is expected to "discipline" Mukhtaar (113), but he does so on behalf of the state. Like Keynaan in *SSM*, Mukhtaar's father is as heavily invested in the rewards he can reap from the state for playing along. The reported fight between Mukhtaar and the sheikh is detailed by Yakub, an uncle, who reports that Mukhtaar was fighting to defend the right to dissenting opinion and friendship with Mahad (121). In the end, when Sheikh Ibrahim clobbers Mukhtaar to death, the narrator reflects, "A father can beat his son to madness," and the state allows the parent "the prerogative . . . to do with life and property of an offspring" whatever he likes (131–2). And thus, Mukhtaar's fight with his father is delegitimized by tradition while his killing is sanctioned by both tradition and the modern state. This raises the tangled question for Mursal: acting for the state, the Sheikh kills Mukhtaar (134), the son for whom he would otherwise accept compensatory blood. What then is the dividing line between traditional/private justice and the public? (143). In a self-serving gesture, the state presents the façade of being the guardian of public justice, but it uses traditional agents and means to cut down its enemies. The clan actors make rational calculations about the patronage goods they can extract from the modern state. In their various ways, Mukhtaar, Mursal, and Mahad attain autonomy from "family first." (77, 132).

The controversy surrounding Mukhtaar's death and its dissemination in the government controlled press shows how tradition, religion, and knowledge are intertwined in the novel. The press attributes Mukhtaar's death to suicide and constructs the father as a do-gooder guardian of tradition and Islam, who was trying to prevent it. But because Mukhtaar committed suicide, according to state texts, he was therefore impure in Islam and not fit for full burial rights. The alleged shame of his action denies him the right to public burial and fetishization (154–5), a situation that is compounded by the postmortem on his body that willfully desecrates it in the eyes of fellow Muslims. As a marker of the state's complicity, the post-mortem naturally concludes that Mukhtaar committed suicide, and the examination is supervised by Dr. Ahmed-Wellie, who is more obviously an arm of the state's biopower in *Close Sesame*. The body of Muktaar thus becomes a text on which the state writes nationalist narratives in the same way that it appropriated Soyaan's in *SSM*, and Amina and Dulman's in *Sardines*.

More than the other two novels in the trilogy, *CS* also explores the role of class in enabling power to function at the superstructural level. The older men around Deeriye remark upon their inability to hold opinions, unlike Deeriye who is wealthy. According to them, he can afford to stick to principles because he has a wealthy son and daughter (107). The other men avoid "dealing" with ideas and national principles and confronting the despot because the latter gives handouts (107). The requirement to sacrifice their sons to the policies of a father-of-the-nation type is a minor inconvenience for the less wealthy (113). This is the kind of corruption Deeriye finds unconscionable.

While the workings of the clan—like the state's—have been fairly opaque in the other two novels, in *CS* we see a parody of parliamentary procedure in the clan meeting discussing the General's ultimatums both to Rooble's clan and Deeriye's. Because the General undermines the idea that identity is a matter of rational choice rather than the merely social and heritable, he puts pressure on Rooble's clan to excommunicate him for supporting his nephew's radicalism. It is the classic policy of isolation and rule perfected by British colonialism. But in a society structured around prohibitions, obeying one decree leads the clan to flout another. The tribal leaders are misled that the General wanted them to have a gathering of the clan to discuss the actions of Mahad, a clan member, and state a clan position. The elders are then arrested for holding a meeting of more than five people outside church or state function, and Rooble is among those arrested (126). Their release depends on the General's magnanimity, thus trapping Rooble's clan in reciprocal obligation.

Deeriye's clan is also expected to discipline him for his failure to discipline his son, Mursal. Threatened with detention if they do not excommunicate Deeriye, the clan meets, but it engages in some fairly sophisticated legalism. They argue correctly that Deeriye is not a clan leader, hence he does not represent the clan. The clan therefore cannot be held responsible for his individual views, and the General can seek him out if he thinks Deeriye should modify them, or bring a case against him in a court of justice (189). But they add the rider that if Deeriye is sought out unjustly, then the clan "will stand behind him as we would stand behind any other Somali in the same position, whether or not he or she is a member of our clan" (189–190). This penchant for looking beyond the sectional interests of the clan seems to define Deeriye's clan, and we are reminded several times of its sacrifice during colonialism.[1] In the same way that Deeriye's nationalist lens enabled him to see all Somalis as one clan/people with Italians as the common enemy during the colonial test (39), Deeriye clearly recognizes that the General is using the same divisive tactics that the Italians used. Thinking about the clan deliberations, Deeriye wonders whether the weak structures of the nation-state could "bear the weight of the constitutional responsibility clearly outlined therein" (189). Musing that "[t]he General uses the authority of the nation-state, of which he is now head in view of his military take-over, and lays this belabouredly on the structures of a clannishly ruled state," Deeriye now recognizes the place of *lex talionis* in resolving conflict (189). In a society marked by elements of both the radical and conservative state à la Mamdani, the state pays lip service to the language of rights and justice, but it leaves its people with little option other than to avenge injustice. It is this recognition that ultimately drives Deeriye to his attempt on the General's life once he learns that his son, Mursal, has been killed by the regime. Deeriye is also driven by the need to do something heroic to prove his continued relevance (222). As an indication of his own generational blind spot, Deeriye had been tempted to tell Mursal to leave "politics to us" (223), the men of his generation, so that Mursal could take care of his wife and child. Deeriye thus appears to have been trapped in the same ageism that powers the General.

Much more than the other texts in the trilogy, *Close Sesame* portrays the interpenetration of state power and existing power relations. Historicizing the disconnect between the state and the people, the narrator observes that Africans fought colonialism only to be ruled by nincompoops (101). The first threats to democratic institutions came from colonial governments imposing untraditional dictatorship on the Africans, appointing stipended chiefs as opposed to clan-recognized chieftaincies (183). The end result is that, as Deeriye comes to recognize, "[i]n the figure of the chieftain, the authoritarian state has its representative in every clan or tribe so the elders of the clan become its most important instrument of power" (114). According to Deeriye, tribal chieftaincy was an invention of the Egyptian viceroys who had been the absentee landlords of Somalia in the eighteenth century. But whereas the chieftains in the past had been chosen for their oratory and leadership, they are now chosen for their spinelessness (114). He traces a direct line of appointments running from Italian to British colonizers and on to the General in the post-independence era: men (never women) who are awarded political power and a stipend and made responsible to the state authority, "these days chosen for their lack of gut and leadership" (114). They enable the centralized modern state to reach deep into the recesses of traditional society and manipulate its institutions. Traditional patriarchy, sexism, ageism, and kinship bonds defined power relations in traditional society that are manipulated by the General to advance his own dictatorial agenda. Control of oral channels of communication and modern print and broadcast media enables the state to produce "effects of truth" that legitimize domination.

With both Mursal and Deeriye dead, the future in *Close Sesame* belongs to Samawade and Zeinab, two characters previously marginalized on the basis of age and gender. Samawade accepts his father's disappearance as the price to pay for liberation, and prepares to play his part like Mursal had to as a young boy when his father was detained (213). Even though women are not invited to the clan meeting that deliberates on what to do about Deeriye, the last words belong to Zeinab as she begins the search for Deeriye and Mursal's bodies so that she can inter them in a shared tomb where they can continue their dialogue. It is left to her to ensure that their death is not anonymous, that their heroism is recognized (260). It is a small gesture that speaks to the ways courageous, progressive women step into the vacuum created by the death of the men. Even though *Close Sesame* was supposed to be the novel that provides the key to reading the entire trilogy, Farah does not appear any more sure of the future direction the imagined society will take. But just before his death, Deeriye recognizes that only God has the prerogative to be sure of anything, but since Deeriye is human, he therefore doubts (253). At the end of the novel, only the General is allowed the arrogance of certainty in his power. History has not borne him out.

Tracing the survival of the kinship group as a safety net and a moral order(er) in modern Somalia, Anna Simons argues that "the Somali state never proved itself credible as the guarantor of a secure future to any of its citizens," and the extensive kin networks persisted specifically because nationalism had proven hollow as a social glue (277). A secure state would actually have enabled the kind of individuation that Soyaan, Loyaan, Medina, Samater, Mursal, Mahad, Mukhtaar, and even Deeriye himself, crave, where kin did not count. But in the trilogy, the state not only fails to safeguard the rights of the people, it also deploys kinship networks as weapons for smothering dissent. The state is marked by a heightened distaste for individual autonomy: people belong to groups, and when one of them errs, the whole group bears the punishment. By flattening people into their clan identities, the state is able to take advantage of the built-in ageism, sexism, and authoritarianism of the clan. Equating the General with Allah confers his actions with unquestionable religious authority. As Simons observes, had the state proved "(largely) solvent[,] (largely) stable, and (largely) responsible over generations" it would have come to be viewed as the credible guarantor of security by large enough numbers of its citizens (278), and nationalism would have become the social glue that held the nation together. However, as we see throughout the trilogy, the General's state apparatus is able to disaggregate Somalis in terms of age, gender, clan, class, region, and religion, enabling the General's power to be simultaneously nowhere and everywhere at the same time.

Notes

1. Deeriye's clan gave safe harbor to the dissident from a neighboring clan who bucked the Italian dethronement of traditional chieftains. The clan was ordered to give up the man or their wells would be poisoned, but the clan still refused in order to uphold a traditional notion of honor that protected fugitives. Deeriye's clan ends up paying the higher price than the man's clan (35).

Works Cited

Farah, Nuruddin. *Close Sesame*. Saint Paul, MN: Graywolf, 1983. Print.

———. *Sardines*. Saint Paul, MN: Graywolf, 1981. Print.

———. *Sweet and Sour Milk*. Saint Paul, MN: Graywolf, 1979. Print.

———. "Why I Write." *Third World Quarterly* 10.4 (1988): 1591-1599. Print.

Foucault, Michel. *Discipline and Punish*. New York: Vintage, 1979. Print.

Mamdani, Mahmood. *Citizen and Subject: Contemporary Africa and the Legacy of Late Colonialism*. Princeton: Princeton UP, 1996. Print.

Mbembe, Achille. *On the Postcolony*. Berkeley: U of California P, 2001. Print.

Parker, Andrew, et al. *Nationalisms & Sexualities*. New York: Routledge, 1992. Print.

Posner, Daniel. *Institutions and Ethnic Politics in Africa*. Cambridge: Cambridge UP, 2005. Print.

Price, Robert. "Politics and Culture in Contemporary Ghana: The Big-man Small-Boy Syndrome." *Journal of African Studies* 1.2 (1974): 173-204. Print.

Rabinow, Paul, ed. *The Foucault Reader*. New York: Pantheon, 1984. Print.

Sahlins, Marshall D. "Poor Man, Rich Man, Big-Man, Chief: Political Types in Melanesia and Polynesia." *Comparative Studies in Society and History* 5 (1963): 285-303. Print.

Schatzberg, Michael G. *The Dialectics of Oppression in Zaire*. Bloomington: Indiana UP, 1988. Print.

Simons, Anna. "Democratisation and Ethnic Conflict: The Kin Connection." *Nations and Nationalism* 3.2 (1997): 273-289. Print.

Colonialism, the Modern African Dictator, and the Postcolonial State

NADA HALLOWAY

> The actual and present condition
> of Africa is one of deep trouble,
> a deeper trouble than the worst condition
> imposed during the colonial years (9).
>
> —Basil Davidson, 1992

Decolonization was a landmark event in Africa. It promised to usher in an age of democracy with nationalist leaders like Kwame Nkrumah, who, on the eve of independence, promised to "create [an] African personality" (www.bbc.co.uk). Yet, independence did not usher in the age of "emancipation" and "total liberation" (www.bbc.co.uk)[1] that Nkrumah had pledged. In many countries, post-independence political power became vested in "dictatorships where rulers governed [their] countries without constitutional or legal restraints" (Corfield 301). This need for absolute power led to the creation of totalitarian regimes that subverted all constitutions whether written or unwritten. While written constitutions are meant to deter absolute power, these documents would not necessarily stop a dictator from assuming power. But, as Yomi Dorotoye has observed, the unwritten nature of precolonial African constitutions were, theoretically, supposed to stop the rise of dictators and dictatorship in Africa because "political order originate[d] from and is sustained by religion (especially creation myths and kinship)" (Dorotoye 299). Yet, much of post-independence African society has seen its fair share of violent coups and the imposition of totalitarian regimes led by highly educated and charismatic leaders "who had great intentions, inspired by the opportunities of their leadership, but who were often side-tracked or felt obliged to remain in power for as long as they could to see through their 'vision'" (Corfield 302). While the post-independence rulers like Kwame Nkrumah, Hastings Banda, Milton Obote, and Francisco Macias Nguema were all civilian leaders who stayed to "see through their 'vision,'" they were replaced with military commanders such as Gnassingbe Eyadema of Togo, Idi Amin of Uganda, Jean-Bedel Bokassa of the Central African Republic, and Siyad Barre of Somalia. These men had all served in the colonial armies and had learned their tactics and forms of intimidation and repression from their colonial leaders.

The rise of dictators and dictatorship then in Africa can be attributed to colonialism and the colonial powers who ruled the different countries. Colonialism, as Yomi Durotoye has observed, is "dictatorship par excellence . . . [that] essentially overthrew the existing African constitutions and in time rendered the surviving traditional rulers unaccountable to their people" (300). Colonialism overthrew existing governments by annexing territories and peoples through violence. As Richard Gott has observed, "[T]he creation of . . . [the] Empire caused large portions of the global map to be tinted a rich vermilion. Although not meant that way, the colour turned out to be peculiarly appropriate, for . . . [the] Empire was established and maintained for more than two centuries, through bloodshed, violence, brutality, conquest and war" (1). It is not an accident that the end of colonialism saw the rise of military and civilian dictators in Africa. "Eighty-six successful military coups were recorded on the continent between 1956 and 2002. . . . The most notorious of the military dictators were Idi Amin of Uganda, Jean Bedel Bokassa of Central African Republic, Mobutu Sese Seko of Zaire . . . and [of the civilian dictators], Francisco Macias Nguema of Equatorial Guinea" (Dorotoye 300). This cycle of violence that pervaded the lives of Africans under colonial regimes did not bode well for a postcolonial society as many of the bureaucratic structures that had been implemented during colonialism were not dismantled after independence. The promise that nationalist leaders like Banda made at the beginning of his presidency was never fully realized. For example, once Banda became president of Malawi, he "set about getting rid of his most loyal followers, employing the same security laws he had campaigned against so vigorously. He once said they should be 'food for crocodiles.' . . . Turning his back on former allies in the struggle for independence, Dr Banda gave diplomatic support to South Africa's white rulers, who built him a palace and a new capital in return. In Malawi his attitude to Africans was colonial. He saw them as poor, benighted people who needed his guidance and a British education" (www.economist.com). This contempt for his people translated into one of the most repressive regimes in Africa, and after his defeat in 1994, his successor, President Muluzi, brought criminal charges against Banda for crimes committed against humanity. While Banda's presidency could not be considered an absolute failure, he nevertheless routinely violated his people's civil rights by arresting them without charge and jailing them without trial. This format followed the pattern set by the British.

The abuses of power and authority by some post-independence African rulers are examined in the works of Nuruddin Farah and Wole Soyinka. Both writers explore how nations that had such promise at the dawn of independence would become the playground for dictators. The problem, as Frantz Fanon observed, is that "the national middle class [that inherited] power at the end of the colonial regime is an underdeveloped middle class . . . [and] to them, nationalization quite simply means the transfer of power into native hands of those unfair advantages of which are the legacy of the colonial period" (149–152). The real tragedy of Fanon's observation can be seen in the social and economic conditions of post-independence Africa. Africans have exchanged one oppressor for another, and in this post era, in some parts of Africa like Nigeria, Uganda, Somalia, and the Central African Republic, the oppressors are their own leaders. As Davidson observes in *The Black Man's Burden*, "[H]arsh governments or dictatorships rule over people who distrust them to the point of hatred. All too often one dismal tyranny gives way to a worse one. Despair rots civil society, the state becomes an enemy, bandits flourish" (9). This critique of rulers like Siyad Barre, Kwame Nkrumah, Idi Amin, and Jean-Bedel Bokassa is evident early on in Soyinka's plays *Opera Wonyosi*, *A Play of Giants*, *Kongi's Harvest*, as well as in the poem "Future Plans," and in Nuruddin Farah's *Sweet and Sour Milk* and the final chapter to the trilogy, *Close Sesame*.

Sweet and Sour Milk begins with oppressive and violent silence. Soyaan, a Somali government official, is in bed, violently ill with a stomach ailment. We later find out that he has been secretly plotting against the government. Soyaan does not survive his illness, but before his death, we are introduced to two members of his family: his twin brother, Loyaan, and his father, Keynaan. Father and son, in this text, inhabit opposite spheres. Loyaan constantly comes up against his father, who is an apologist for the Barre regime, as he searches for the reason behind his brother's death. Loyaan faces a dual struggle with the governmental forces and with his parents. Soyaan's displeasure with his father is centered on Keynaan's decision to marry a girl young enough to be his granddaughter, and so, we are told, "of late, the two had been on very bad terms" (9). So when Keynann enters Soyaan's sick room, their conversation is stilted and eventually dies down. But Soyaan cannot stand the silence: "Silence. He couldn't take it, Soyaan couldn't. His itching nerve, Soyaan's inner impatience hazarded a move: he switched on the radio. He turned the radio unnecessarily loud. Keynaan, to be heard, spoke at the top of his voice. When his throat pained him, Keynaan turned the volume down" (9). Soyaan's attempt to drown out his father's voice can be read as a moment of rebellion. The father, on the other hand, responds by shouting and eventually turning down the radio. This moment is fraught with tension—both father and son represent two divergent paths—the son as rebel and the father as the representative of a repressive regime. The father's shouts are an attempt to silence his son, and he succeeds when he turns down the radio. However, Soyaan refuses to be silenced even in the face of his father's displeasure. His question is: "'[I]s this Africa or Stalin's Russia? As soon as I feel better, I promise you. . . . ' He hiccupped . . . 'As soon as I feel better, I hic, will hic . . .'" (10). The hiccups do not end after his father leaves but continue when his brother visits. In the subsequent conversation with his brother, Soyaan describes their father as "a powerless *hic* patriarch, the grandest of them *hic* all. We are on the worst of *hic* terms" (15). In describing the father as "a powerless patriarch, the grandest of them all," Farah highlights patriarchy as equivalent to "political authoritarianism and police-state terrorism, demonstrating how he combines the roles of family head and ex-policeman-cum-informer to the regime and by conniving at the death and defamation of. . . . Soyaan, stamps out subversion, simultaneously, at both state and familial levels (Wright xxii). Farah, through Keynaan's role, explores the idea of rule whereby political authority comes from the individual ruler and extends through a system of cronyism in the form of the "father figure." Thus Keynaan functions in a dual role: both as the literal father and as the representative of the national "father figure." Soyaan is on the worst of terms with both fathers as both are responsible for silencing him. He admonishes Loyaan to "tell the *hic* masses in the simplest of terms what is happening. Demystify *hic* politics. Empty those heads filled with tons of rhetoric. Uncover whether hiding *hic* behind pregnant letters such as KGB, CIA, or other *hic* wicked alphabet of mysteries *hic*" (15). The fragmented nature of his speech parallels the gradual silencing not just of the intellectuals but of the opposition as well. His reference to the KGB and the CIA highlights the secretive nature of a regime that would force family members and friends to acts of betrayal. The hiccups are a direct result of the poison that has been administered by the State, and the interruptions that occur during Soyaan's speech are quite violent and render him inarticulate. This violence is captured in the death scene: "[F]irst, the warmth went out of Soyaan's hand. Then the brightness out of his eyes. Everything assumed an artificial quietness, for an unbroken fraction of a second. And Soyaan hiccupped his last" (16). The quietness of his death is indicative of the manner in which the government and its security forces deal with the opposition. The silencing of the dissenting voices is done in the darkness and in absolute silence. And in this manner, Soyaan's death is very much representative of the torture of the oppressed.

According to the United States Development Programme, "the 21-year regime of Siyad Barre had one of the worst human rights records in Africa" (42). The Africa Watch Committee wrote in a report that "both the urban population and nomads living in the countryside [were] subjected to summary killings, arbitrary arrest, detention in squalid conditions, torture, rape, crippling constraints on freedom of movement and expression and a pattern of psychological intimidation" (9). According to Amnesty International, Barre's National Security Service's method of torture included executions and "beatings while tied in a contorted position, electric shocks, rape of woman prisoners, simulated executions and death threats" (127). All of these methods were clearly designed to silence a population that was increasingly becoming restive under an oppressive regime. This silence becomes even more insidious in *Sweet and Sour Milk* before and after Soyaan's death. The newspaper, the official machinery of the state, canonizes Soyaan as a national hero and a fervent supporter of the General. Soyaan the rebel is replaced by Soyaan the standard bearer of the regime: "He died, and his last words were praiseful of the General's policies: 'Labour is honour and there is no general but our general'" (98). Here, we see two things occurring simultaneously, the attack on Soyaan's supporters and the re-writing of history. The dominant trope in this scene is "truth." What is the truth? In *Sweet and Sour Milk*, truth is an abstract concept. This is clear in the book when the announcement of Soyaan's death is filled with propaganda meant to elevate the General. Moreover, it is a concept that is reducible to each individual's perceptions. Farah explores this concept of truth in his essay "Why I Write." As he observes, truth is ever changeable:

> The "truth" that matters, indeed! What if I argue that truth must be "spoken" whether in the privacy of one's chambers or in the presence of others? What if I argue that it must be given a body, a physical existence, that truth must be clothed in the bodied concepts of words, of motions—so that *others* may share it, challenge it or accept it? My writings have been summarily described in Somali government jargon as "a selection of 'untruths,'" because I have not been to Somalia for years but have written books which challenge the propaganda which the official media give as "the truth." My books, say the anti-Siyadists, give a true picture of the state of affairs. To both camps it is not truth that matters but to whom it is given.... I can only tell them how I perceive things.... During this period, whenever anyone asked me why I wrote the kind of books I did, I answered that I wrote to put down on paper, for posterity's sake, the true history of a nation. (1598–1599)

This nature of truth is examined in the different positions that Soyaan and his father embrace. According to Soyaan, his father is an accomplice to the torture of the Somali people, and to Keynaan, his son is the equivalent of a rabble-rouser. Thus, Keynaan participates in the silencing of his son and, by proxy, is an accomplice to a murderous regime. As Keynaan makes clear to Loyaan, "I am the father. It is my prerogative to give life and death as I find fit. . . . And remember one thing Loyaan: If I decide this minute to cut you in two, I can. The law of this land invests in my age the power. I am the Grand Patriarch" (95). Keynaan's thought process is a microcosm of the larger problem—it is this type of thinking that leads to tyranny and oppression. In connecting patriarchy and governmental oppression, Farah argues that Africans are themselves ultimately responsible for their predicament as they choose to accept the status quo rather than fight for their freedoms.

The complicity of the Somali people in their continued oppression is fully explored in the last book of the trilogy, *Close Sesame*. In this book, Deeriye, the protagonist, straddles the past and the present—in this case, colonial and postcolonial history. Deeriye's story in both periods is eerily similar. As a young man under the colonial regime, he is imprisoned by the Italians because of his refusal to betray a neighbor who, in self-defense, killed an Italian soldier. For his loyalty to his people, he is imprisoned by the colonial government and separated from his family. The third imprisonment is the most significant as Deeriye is imprisoned by the postcolonial government for subversive activities. His imprisonment makes him a very public figure, but as we are told, his life "was a life developed, like a negative in the darkroom of isolation" (*CS* 31). While Deeriye is in prison, his wife is responsible for the care of their children, Zeinab and Mursal. Mursal's early memories of his father are of him in prison. As such, he comes to associate the government with imprisonment and injustice. But Mursal also represents the new "breed" of intellectuals who would agitate for more freedoms. As a member of this new breed of opposition leaders, Mursal is the founding member of Soyaan's opposition group, but this group is betrayed by a member, Ahmed-Wellie, who is loyal to the General. Because of this betrayal, Mursal and Deeriye are persecuted by the state (Ntalindwa 188).

The difference, however, in this book is the link between postcolonial tyranny and colonial tyranny. This link is explored in the stories that Deeriye tells his children and grandchildren. In the stories, we learn that the colonial forces overcame the indigenous forces because of Somali collaborators. Thus, Somalia was handed over to the Italians by her own people. "The betrayal made it possible for the colonialists" to impose their culture and their laws on a people that had once relied on their kings for guidance. This invocation of the past is a recognition of the Dervish, the revolutionary movement that Sayyid Muhammad Abd Allah al-Hasan put together to repulse the British, Italian, and Ethiopian forces (Ntalindwa 188). If Al-Hasan is the leader of the people, the General, who takes over after independence, is not a representative of his people as he uses coercion and fear to control his people. That Al-Hasan plays a dual role—that of religious and political leader—is no accident. He is the ideal because of his religious philosophy—a philosophy that is embraced by Deeriye but not by Keynaan, in the sense that Keynaan's version of this religious philosophy is at once brutal and oppressive (Dasenbrock 748). As fathers, they both represent the state and are the conduits of power. While Keynaan's oppressive nature leads him to torture his family, Deeriye is concerned for his family. When his son is murdered, Deeriye moves from the passive figure to an activist, and even though he fails in his endeavor, his attempt to kill the General is very much symbolic of the few people who would fight to regain their freedoms from repressive regimes. As he observes, "[W]e Africans did not struggle against the white colonialists only to be colonized yet again by black nincompoops" (84). This is one of the sharpest criticisms in the novels.

This criticism of the postcolonial nations and the rulers that came into power at the dawn of independence is furthered in several of Soyinka's plays and poems. *Opera Wonyosi*, a combination of John Gay's *The Beggar's Opera* and Brecht's *The Three Penny Opera*, and *A Play of Giants* are not as subtle, but the criticism is still the same. The leaders are thieves and criminals, and nothing is done to topple them. In *A Play of Giants*, the characters are easily discernible: Benefacio Gunema is Macias Nguema of Equitorial Guinea; Emperor Kasco is Jean Baptiste Bokassa; Field Marshal Kamini is Idi Amin; and General Barra Tuboum is Mobuto Sese Seko. Along with the critique of these leaders, Soyinka does not spare the international community as he sees them as responsible for the atrocities that these men committed. In the introduction to the play, Soyinka writes that "the tone, the varied disguises of their 'ignorance' left me with the confirmation of a long held suspicion that power calls to power, that the brutality of power evokes a conspiratorial craving for the phenomenon of 'success' which cuts across all human occupation" (vi). In other words, the monsters were accepted by the international community because of the power they exercised, and in *A Play of Giants*, the Sculptor is a representation of members of that community that allowed men like Amin and Bokassa to participate in a global agenda at the same time as they were murdering their people. The masks that the Sculptor creates are a symbolic representation of the cloak of respectability that the international community granted these men.

The central character of the play is Kamini/Amin and the monster that he was. Amin was a sycophant in the British army, and because of his loyalty to his superiors, he was rapidly promoted through the ranks. It is worth noting that Amin was virtually illiterate, and his promotion was simply based on the assumption of his loyalty, which he demonstrated during the Mau Mau insurgency in Kenya. Sent by the British to aid in suppression of the rebellion, Amin participated in the killing of innocent civilians from the Turkana tribe—an act that he was never prosecuted for thanks to the efforts of Sir Walter Coutts, who argued that the prosecution of Amin would endanger Ugandan independence (Horvitz and Catherwood 15–17). From the moment Amin came to power, he went on a systematic rampage, targeting ethnic tribes such as the Acholi and Langi. It is estimated that between 1971–1979, 300,000 people were killed in Uganda. While *A Play of Giants* does not deal with all this violence, it nevertheless deals with Amin's ignorance of economics and international politics when he attempts to borrow two hundred million dollars from the World Bank. Told by the chairman that the World Bank will only fund specific projects rather than hand over that amount of money, Amin is at a loss for words, and his ultimate response is to torture the chairman of the Bugaran Bank. As with Farah who uses the interruptions that Soyaan's hiccups offer to symbolize the silencing of the rebellious voice, Soyinka highlights Amin's ignorance and brutality through his mangled use of grammatical structure:

> KAMINI: What I care about Conditions? Agree to any conditions just get the loan.
> CHAIRMAN: It is not quite as easy as all that Your Excellency. They want to mortgage Bugara body and soul. . . .
> KAMINI: I say what I care about body and soul? If they can loan Bugara the two hundred million dollars, I give them body and soul. (5)

Here, we see Soyinka playing with the knowledge of Amin's illiteracy, and the irony is clear—if the man cannot understand simple economics, how can he be the president of a nation? Each character revels in the display of power. Toboum's (Mobutu's) personal army terrorizes the people in an attempt to "eliminate all foreign influences from our people," and his army, according to him, "are the elite, they bathe in the same ambience of power, terribly invincible" (18–19). Gunema's contempt for his people is evident in his declaration that "some people are born to power. Others are cattle. They need ring in their nose for us to lead" (11). It is Kasco (Bokassa), however, who is the most terrifying in his articulation of the meaning of power: "[P]ower comes only with the death of politics. That is why I choose to become emperor. I place myself beyond politics. At the moment of my coronation, I signal to the world that I transcend the intrigues and mundaneness of politics. Now I inhabit only the pure realm of power" (21). Bokassa came to power in 1965 with the support of the French, and recently, he was again in the news, but this time it was because he was being pardoned. According to a report in *The Guardian*, Francois Bozize, CAR's president, pardoned Bokassa in December of 2010. The president, in his speech, said that Bokassa "had given a great deal for humanity" and that "this rehabilitation of rights eases penal condemnations, particularly fines and legal costs" and stops any future liabilities that result from them. Bozize added that Bokassa was "a son of the nation recognized by all as a great builder [and] he built the country but we have destroyed what he built" (www.guardian.co.uk). How can Bozize claim that Bokassa built the nation when his coronation depleted the CAR's GDP? This movement to pardon Bokassa is a very interesting moment in the history of the CAR. It is almost as if the people have selective memory, and in the rehabilitation of Bokassa, we see a type of nostalgia for the past that is quite frightening and can be self-serving.

Soyinka explores this self-serving nature of politics in his poem "Future Plans." The poem is in form of an agenda for a meeting:

> The meeting is called
> To odium: Forgers, framers
> Fabricators Inter-
> national. Chairman,
> A Dark horse, a circus nag turned blinkered sprinter
> Mach Three
> We rate him—one for the Knife
> Two for 'iavelli, Three—
> Breaking speed
> Of the truth barrier by a swooping detention decree
>
> Projects in view:
> Mao Tse Tung in league
> With Chiang Kai. Nkrumah
> Makes a secret
> Pact with Verwood, sworn by Hastings Banda.
> Proven: Arafat
> In flagrante cum
> Golda Meir. Castro drunk
> With Richard Nixon
> Contraceptives stacked beneath the papal bunk . . .
>   . . . and more to come (778)

If Bokassa, Amin, and the others are "maggots" in *A Play of Giants*, in this poem, they are now forgers, framers, and fabricators, and their partners from around the world enable them in perpetuating the most egregious forms of oppression. Politics, in this poem, is based on deals rather than on personal beliefs. Nkrumah and Verwoerd were two diametrically opposed leaders whose ideologies could not be more different. This difference can be seen in a speech that Verwoerd gave in December 16, 1958, at Blood River in which he urged white South Africans to defend their notions of their superiority in the face of international criticism.[2] A year earlier, Nkrumah had led the Ghanaian people to independence. But, in having Nkrumah make "a secret pact with Verwood,"

Soyinka suggests that for politicians to succeed, they must participate in a game that would call their integrity into question.

This question of personal integrity would shadow Nkrumah[3] during and after his rule. While Nkrumah wanted to see all of Africa achieve political independence, his vision did not include independent countries. He wanted to become the sole president of Africa, and while he is responsible for creating the OAU, it became increasingly clear, a year after Ghana's independence, that Nkrumah was not the visionary that he claimed to be. In 1958, suspecting dissatisfaction within his government, Nkrumah proposed legislation that authorized him to detain anyone suspected of opposing his programs or ideas. Nkrumah's failure and the disappointment it generated on a continent that was looking for a leader is the subject of another of Soyinka's plays, *Kongi's Harvest*.

The tension in *Kongi's Harvest* is between Oba Danlola, who represents tradition, the past, and therefore, the people, and president Kongi, who is the present and presumably the future. This clash of cultures centers on Kongi's efforts to strip from Oba Danlola the right to eat the first yam, a rite that is symbolically important to a ruler whose hold on power is sanctioned through the use of terror (July, 480). If Kongi succeeds in eating the first yam, he would then replace the old culture with the new and modern one that he envisions. However, much of the reform that Kongi espouses is proven false, and his administration is exposed as corrupt. The corruption and tyrannical nature of Kongi's regime is exposed in the climax of the harvest festival when, rather than the ceremonial first yam, Kongi is presented with a platter containing the head of a fugitive killed by the police. At the end of the play, the past is effectively silenced, but Kongi is also exposed as a fraud.

The clash between the Oba and Kongi is immediately apparent in the opening sections of the play. The roll of drums that "accompanies a national anthem" (61) is at odds with the words of the anthem that the Oba and his retinue sing:

> Ism to ism for ism is ism
> Of isms and ism on absolute-ism
> To demonstrate the tree of life
> Is sprung from broken peat
> And we the rotted bark, spurned
> When the tree swells its pot
> The mucus that is snorted out
> When Kongi's new race blows
> And more, oh there's a harvest of words
> In a penny newspaper....
>   Who but a lunatic

> Will bandy words with boxes
> With government rediffusion sets
> Which talk and talk and never
> Take a lone word in reply. . . .
> For I do not bandy words
> No I do not bandy words
> With a government loudspeaker. (61–62)

Kongi has succeeded in marginalizing the Oba and his retinue. The past is seen as "rotted" and therefore something to be discarded, but it is clear that the "harvest of words" is mere propaganda aimed at silencing tradition and the people. This propaganda is necessary because without it, the people will see through the lies. The "ism[s]" that start the section are similar to the hiccups that Soyaan experiences in talking to his father. Neither Soyaan nor the Oba is granted the right to speak. Kongi does not allow the Oba and his people to be heard because of the fear that they might incite a protest. As such, he does not allow them to speak, and the loudspeaker assures him that the Oba would not be heard above the din of the speaker. The repression of the past is seen in the fact that Kongi has imprisoned the Oba and his followers and they, as leaders themselves, are forced to deal with Kongi's representative, the superintendent of the prison, thus highlighting their marginalization. The superintendent's agitation is symbolic of the divide that exists in Kongi's regime. While Kongi's henchmen are given the power to silence the Oba, they are nevertheless wary of the power that the Oba still possesses.

This fear of Oba Danlola and the spiritual power that he holds over the people is captured in the section entitled "First Part." Kongi and the secretary are discussing Kongi's image and his participation in the new harvest. Their wish to legitimize Kongi's regime is seen in the secretary's statement:

> . . . All we want is some way of persuading King Danlola to bring the New Yam to Kongi with his own hands. I have organized the rest—the agricultural show to select the prize-winning yam, the feat, the bazaar, the music, the dance. Only one thing missing—Oba Danlola. And gentlemen, that problem is yours. Kongi desires that the king perform all his customary spiritual functions, only this time, that he perform them to him, our Leader. Kongi must preside as the Spirit of Harvest. . . . (77)

In having Oba Danlola perform the customary rituals to him, Kongi would then attain the mantle of the divine. This symbolic gesture would affirm to the people the rightness and divine nature of Kongi's regime. Kongi's divinity is affirmed when he declares himself as "the SPIRIT of the Harvest" (91). Along with his secretary, he would go further to create history and present a Christ-like image to his people:

SECRETARY: Of course my Leader. And a benevolent Spirit of Harvest. This year shall be known as the year of Kongi's Harvest. Everything shall date from it.
KONGI: Who thought that up?
SECRETARY: It is among the surprise gifts we have planned for our beloved Leader. I shouldn't have let it slip out . . .
KONGI: You mean, things like 200 K.H.
SECRETARY: A.H. my Leader. After Harvest. In a thousand years, one thousand A.H. And last year shall be referred to as I B.H. There will only be one Harvest worth remembering.
KONGI: No, K.H. is less ambiguous. The year of Kongi's Harvest. Then for the purpose of back-dating, B.K.H. Before Kongi's Harvest.

In this scene, the revision of history and the creation of Kongi parallels Nkrumah's taking on the name of "Osagyefo"—the redeemer. In choosing this name, Nkrumah came to personify everything that was heroic. He positioned himself as the spiritual leader of his people who would be victorious against all odds. In addition, he would appropriate all the "traditional symbols of constitutional legitimacy for himself—the wearing of the 'royal' *kente* cloth, the fabrication and use of a 'royal' stool and linguist's staff containing a mélange of traditional symbols" (Le Vine 661). Nkrumah's arrogance at the appropriation of these symbols was met with resistance by the chiefs whom he had disparaged on his rise to power (Le Vine 661). In one of the telling moments in his autobiography, Nkrumah narrates the story of a man who had interrupted his rest and asked for help with his pregnant wife who was several weeks overdue. Nkrumah wrote that "'they had come all that way to see me because they know that I was the only person who could help her. . . . ' 'Don't worry,' I told her, placing my hand gently on her body. 'Your child will be born shortly and you will have no trouble. Have faith'" (qtd. in Rahman 156). The woman, it so happens, had a healthy baby boy the next day. Nkrumah presented himself as a Christ-like figure on this occasion. This deliberate re-imagining of his image and his life can be seen in his revision of Whitman's poem "Whoever You are, Holding Me Now in Hand." Nkrumah would change lines eight and nine of the poem to reflect his "divine nature." Where Whitman had written "You would have to give up all else—I alone would expect to be your God, sole and exclusive," Nkrumah wrote, "You would have to give up all else—I alone would expect to be your *Sole and exclusive standard*" (emphasis added). The final version, which he published in his autobiography, presented him as the hero ready for battle.[4] Incredibly, Nkrumah would assign the revised poem to Whitman.

The impetus for re-writing history and the manner in which he imagined himself for his people can be seen in his position on how European history had portrayed Africans. In his view, the movement towards decolonization could not be completed if Africans still held to the European presentation of Africans. In 1964, Nkrumah declared that

> In the new African renaissance, we place great emphasis on the presentation of history. Our history needs to be written as the history of our society, not as the story of European adventures. African society must be treated as enjoying its own integrity; its history must be a mirror of that society, and the European contact must find its place in this history only as an African experience, even if as a crucial one.... European contact needs to be assessed and judged from the point of view of the principles animating African society, and from the point of view of the harmony and progress of this society. (qtd. in Rahman 11)

From this position we can gather that history became the tool for the revolutionary in his fight for power. In consistently speaking to this idea of history as the determinant of a future, Nkrumah was able to rally his people to support his bid for independence. But the personality that had seen history as crucial to the self-definition of a continent and a people was also the personality who could not tolerate opposition of any kind. As *Time* magazine reported in 1959, the Prime Minister of Ghana was not satisfied when his Conventions People's Party

> won 71 out of 104 parliamentary seats.... [As retaliation for the seats lost, the Prime Minister] deported some critics, [and] jailed others. At least nine M.P.s belonging to the opposition defected to the C.P.P. when Nkrumah made it clear that, unless they did so, no government money would be spent in their constituencies. In persuading ordinary villages to see the light, Nkrumah's government got good service out of the Builder's Brigade—ostensibly a kind of Civilian Conservation Corps, but actually an army of young toughs in yellow shirts, green trousers and red caps. (www.time.com)

This coercion of opponents was preceded by the Preventive Detention Act of 1958, and by 1964, Nkrumah had stripped the judiciary of its powers, suppressed the opposition by detaining political opponents, and finally, in 1964, forced the inauguration of a one party state in Ghana.

The two different aspects of Nkrumah's rule, the reformer and the dictator, are best described by Ali Mazrui, who observes that "by some strange twist of destiny Kwame Nkrumah of Ghana was both the hero who carried the torch of Pan-Africanism and the villain who started the whole legacy of the one-party-state in Africa. To that extent, Kwame Nkrumah started the whole tradition of Black authoritarianism in the postcolonial era. He was the villain of the piece" (3–4; also qtd. in Biney 140). Mazrui would further argue that Nkrumah became a "Leninist Czar"(4; also qtd. in Biney 140) who combined two very disparate political traditions: the adoption of the title of "osagyefo" and his embrace of Leninist ideology set him on the path towards authoritarianism. Furthermore,

Nkrumah believed, according to Mazrui, that a one-party state was the only option to combat political tribalism. This view is supported, in a manner, by Zolberg, who argues that Nkrumah's embrace of authoritarianism stemmed from his belief that politics should not be influenced by ethnic affiliations, religion, and tribalism as these artifacts of culture and society could become corrosive in an emerging nation. Thus, he instituted a one-party system to move Ghana into the modern era (54; also qtd. in Biney 141). The two different views presented by Mazrui and Zolberg give us the negative and positive aspects of Nkrumah's rule.

In *Kongi's Harvest*, Soyinka focuses on the negative aspects of Nkrumah's rule. When the Builder's Brigade proclaim: "And Kongi is our Saviour/Redeemer, prince of power/For Isms and for Kongi/We're proud to live or die!" (116), the dictator here is presented as a poseur, one who surrounds himself with thieves and liars and is himself a coward, a bully, and an insecure ruler who defines his leadership through slogans and the nonsense that he calls positive scientificism, which is a reference to Nkrumah's personal philosophy of *Consciencism*. While the Oba's power comes through the rites/rights of succession, Kongi's power comes through fear, but he recognizes that this power can be short lived. However, before the final curtain, Soyinka summarily dismisses Kongi and his cohorts:

> Imprecations then, curses on all inventors of agonies, on all Messiahs of pain and false burdens[.] ... On all who fashion chains, on farmers of terror, on builders of walls, on all who guard against the night but breed darkness by day, on all whose feet are heavy and yet stand upon the world[.] ... On all who see not with the eyes of the dead, but with the eyes of death. (99)

In the final moments of the play, the secretary and Danlola are both running for their lives, and the final sound is that of an "iron grating [that] descends and hits the ground with a loud, final clang" (138), which represents the sounds of the prison bars consigning Kongi's enemies to a darkness from which they would never return.

Nkrumah, perhaps, could have gotten away with the Preventive Detention order[5] that he signed, or, perhaps, his people could have forgiven him for turning Ghana into a one-party state. But what was clear was that Nkrumah was losing and had lost touch with the people. The symbolism of Nkrumah's residing in and ruling from Christianborg Castle proved disquieting for the people. It was, after all, built by slave traders who had decimated the continent and had been utilized by British governors. For the British, it was a useful location as it distanced them from their subjects. For the Ghanaians, however, it symbolized power, dominance, and contempt. It was also a symbol of oppression—one that Nkrumah had fought to end. So it was a shock when their revolutionary leader occupied a castle with such a negative history. Furthermore, rather than change the bureaucratic structures that had existed with the British, he continued with the same administrative policies that the British had installed to protect their interests. It has been argued by several critics that he had no choice—he had to maintain the institutions that the British had implemented because he was surrounded by members of his cabinet who were all trained in the West. Perhaps that is so, but it could also be argued that since he was attuned to meanings and symbols, he should have known, had he paid more attention to the needs of his people, that taking up residence in the castle would not be viewed favorably; just as the British had elevated themselves to absolute power from Christianborg Castle, so, too, Nkrumah, from the castle, conceived of himself as the ultimate ruler—President of the United States of Africa. It is this ego that Soyinka satirizes in *Kongi's Harvest*. This not to say that Soyinka did not respect Nkrumah. His attitude to Nkrumah's legacy is rather more complex than the one-dimensional tone with which he presents Kongi. Soyinka, according to Oyin Ogunba, respected Nkrumah for his push for African unity, for his support of Pan-Africanism, and for creating the OAU, but he detested the Nkrumah who created the PDA and myriad laws to maintain power. In the end, while Nkrumah may have been an inspiration for Kongi, Soyinka argued that the play "should not be taken to mean that [it] is referring to some Yoruba dictator, of which there is none by the way at the moment, although I know at least half-a-dozen would-be-dictators in Nigeria, but . . . it is meant to apply to the whole situation, the whole trend towards dictatorship on all sorts of spurious excuses in the newly independent states in Africa" (Duerden & Pieterse 178–80). Soyinka's remarks are meant to highlight the universality of his play; that his audience see, in the character of Kongi, some relevance to their cultural and political circumstance.

The questions raised in these works are complex as they reflect the nature of the political and social problems that exist in much of Africa. Soyinka and Farah are both exploring their societies in an attempt to understand the problems that are inherent within African societies. The manner in which they examine the social context and problems suggests that African society itself has tragic flaws as it is too much tied to tradition and the past. While fiction does not necessarily function as the blueprint for social action, Farah suggests that the overall theme of his novels is "truth versus untruth" and his role was that of a social historian who "wrote to put down on paper, for posterity's sake, the true history of a nation" (1599). The integration of the individual struggle in the face of larger social and political oppression is something of a call to arms. In the end what both Farah and Soyinka show is the manner in which some postcolonial African leaders, in their attempts to hold on to power and authority, embraced colonial power in all its ruthless glory. Both authors question the legitimacy of a rule that is maintained by repressing popular opposition and dissent. Furthermore, we are reminded that the Barres, Amins, etc., could not have succeeded without the support of some of their own people and of members of the international community who were invested in maintaining and supporting the dictators.

Notes

1. On Thursday September 14, 2000 BBC world service, on its bbc.co.uk website ran a restropective on Kwame Nkrumah and his vision of and for Africa. The retrospective came on the heels of a December 1999 vote, by BBC's African listeners that named Nkrumah "Man of the Millennium." The programme and excerpts of Nkrumah's speeches can be found on the British Broadcasting website.
2. See Worger, Clark, and Alpers for Verwoerd's speech. As they observed, his racist speech was delivered on the anniversary of the Battle of Blood River when an armed force of Voortrekkers avenged the death of their leader by killing thousands of Zulus.
3. Much of the information about the life and leadership of Kwame Nkrumah used in this chapter was derived from the following texts: Basil Davidson's *Black Star*, Ahmad A. Rahman, *The Regime Change of Kwame Nkrumah*, and Howell and Rajasooria, *Ghana and Nkrumah*. Davidson and Rahman are very sympathetic to Nkrumah and the problems he faced post-independence.
4. This is Nkrumah's version:

    Whoever, you are, holding me now in hand,
    Without one thing, all will be useless,
    I give you fair warning, before you attempt me further,
    I am not what you supposed, but far different.
    Who is he that would become my follower?
    Who would sign himself a candidate for my affections?
    The way is suspicious—the result is uncertain, perhaps destructive:
    You would have to give up all else—I alone would expect
    to be your sole and exclusive standard,
    Your novitiate would even then be long and exhausting,
    The whole past theory of your life, and all conformity to the lives
    around you, would have to be abandon'd;
    For it is not what I have put into it that I have written this book
    Nor is it by reading it you will acquire it,
    Nor do those know me best who admire me, and vauntingly praise me,
    For all is useless without that which you may guess at many times and not hit—
        that which I hinted at;
    Therefore release me, and depart on your way.

    Nkrumah omitted lines 13–39 and 42–47 of Whitman's poem. See Rahman for a more detailed discussion of the differences between Whitman's poem and Nkrumah's revision.
5. The Preventive Detention order was colonial invention. As Basil Davidson observes in *Black Star* the order had been utilized by colonial governments to quell "unrest," and it was signed into law by Jawaharlal Nehru and was used by Colonial Secretary Lennox Boyd in Kenya (169). It is interesting to note that Davidson does not fault Nkrumah for using this tactic to put down the protest and challenge to his government that arose in 1958, and perhaps he would not have been criticized for the order if, in 1963, it did not increase his power to arrest people to "keep them from 'acting in a manner prejudicial to Ghana's defense, her relations with other countries or her security.' He assumed the right to restrict individuals' movement and to detain persons evading arrest for up to 10 years instead of the previous limit of 5 years" (103). See also Thomas and Rajasooria.

Colonialism, the Modern African Dictator, and the Postcolonial State

Works Cited

Biney, Ama. "The Legacy of Kwame Nkrumah in Retrospect." *The Journal of Pan African Studies* 2.3 (2008): 129–159. Print.

Coleman, James. *Nigeria: Background to Nationalism*. Los Angeles: U of California P, 1958. Print.

Corfield, Justin J. "Modern Dictator." *The Oxford Encyclopedia of African Thought*. Eds. F. Abiola Irele & Biodun Jeyifo. Vol. 1. New York: Oxford UP, 2010. Print.

Dasenbrock, Reed Way. "Nuruddin Farah: A Tale of Two Trilogies." *World Literature Today* 72.4 (1998): 747–752. Print.

Davidson, Basil. *The Black Man's Burden: Africa and the Curse of the Nation State*. New York: Times Books, 1992. Print.

———. *Black Star: A View of the Life and Times of Kwame Nkrumah*. New York: Praeger Publishers, 1973. Print.

Davis, Thomas J. & Nwiwu, Azubike Kalu. "Education, Ethnicity and National Integration in The History of Nigeria: Continuing Problems of Africa's Colonial Legacy." *Journal of Negro History* 86.1 (2001): 1–11. Print.

Duerden, Dennis & Pieterse, Cosmo. *African Writers Talking*. New York: Africana, 1972. Print.

Durotoye, Yomi. "Dictatorship." *The Oxford Encyclopedia of African Thought*. Eds. F. Abiola Irele & Biodun Jeyifo. Vol. 1. New York: Oxford UP, 2010. Print.

Fanon, Frantz. *The Wretched of the Earth*. Trans. Constance Farrington. New York: Grove Press, 1963. Print.

Farah, Nuruddin. *Close Sesame*. London: Allison & Busby, 1983. Print.

———. *Sweet and Sour Milk*. St. Paul, Minnesota: Gray Wolf, 1992. Print.

———."Why I Write." *Third World Quarterly* 10.4 (1988): 1591–1599. Print.

Gott, Richard. *Britain's Empire: Resistance, Repression and Revolt*. London & New York: Verso, 2011. Print.

Horvitz, Leslie Alan, & Catherwood, Christopher. *Encyclopedia of War Crimes and Genocide*. New York: Facts on File, 2006. Print.

Howell, Thomas A. & Rajasooria, Jefferey P., eds. *Ghana & Nkrumah*. New York: Facts on File, 1972. Print.

July, Robert W. "The Artist's Credo: the Political Philosophy of Wole Soyinka. *The Journal of Modern African Studies*, 19, 3 (1981), 477-498. Print.

Mazrui, Ali. *Nkrumah's Legacy and Africa's Triple Heritage Between Globalization and Counter Terrorism*. Accra: Ghana UP, 2004. Print.

———. *Soldiers and Kinsmen in Uganda: The Making of a Military Ethnocracy*. Beverly Hills and London: Sage Publications, 1975. Print.

Ntalindwa, Raymond. "Linkages of history in the narrative of Close Sesame. Journal of African Cultural Studies. Vol. 12, No. 2, December 1999, 187-202. Print.

"Obituary: Hastings Banda." *The Economist* 27 November 1997. Proquest. Web. Accessed 08/02/2013.

Rahman, Ahmad A. *The Regime Change of Kwame Nkrumah: Epic Heroism in Africa and the Diaspora*. New York: Palgrave, MacMillan, 2007. Print.

Said, Edward, *Selected Subaltern Studies*. Eds. Guha & Spivak. Oxford: Oxford UP, 1988. Print.

Smith, David. "Posthumous Pardon for former Dictator Bokassa". *The Guardian* 40, 4 December 2010: ProQuest. Web

Soyinka, Wole. *Collected Plays 2*. London: Oxford UP, 1974. Print.

———. "Future Plans." *Literature: Reading, Reacting, Writing*. Eds. Laurie G. Kirszner & Stephen R. Mandell. 5th ed. Canada: Thomson/Wadsworth, 2004: 778–779. Print.

———. *Opera Wonyosi*. London: Rex Collins, 1981. Print.

———. *A Play of Giants*. London: Methuen, 1984. Print.

"The Way of a P.M." *Time* 74:16 (1959): 44. Print.

Vine, Le Victor T. "African Patrimonial Regimes in Comparative Perspective." *The Journal of Modern African Studies* 18.4 (1980): 657–673. Print.

Weber, Max. *Economy and Society: An Outline of Interpretive Sociology*. Berkeley: U of California P, 1978. Print.

Worger, William, Nancy Clark, & Edward Alpers. *Africa and the West: A Documentary History*. Vol. 2. New York: Oxford UP, 2001. Print.

Wright, Derek, ed. Introduction. *Emerging Perspectives on Nuruddin Farah*. Trenton, NJ: African World Press, 2002: xv-xxv. Print.

Zolberg, A. R. *Creating Political Order: The Party States of West Africa*. Chicago: U of Chicago P, 1985. Print.

The Unfaithful Chronicler:
On Writing about the Dictator
in Henri Lopès's *Le Pleurer-rire*

MAGALÍ ARMILLAS-TISEYRA

Early on in Henri Lopès's *Le Pleurer-rire* (*The Laughing Cry*, 1982) the narrator, who is unnamed, declares to the reader: "To begin with, I haven't understood a thing about our politics since independence. A swamp of crocodiles—no one who ventures there manages to stay honest" (17).[1] The statement comes as yet another coup unfolds in the narrator's country, which is also unnamed. On first reading, this insistence on political ignorance, or even apathy, serves to position our narrator as one of the large mass of people whose lives are determined by the tug-of-war of post-independence politics, although they themselves have no ideological investment in those politics. However, the critique posited in the second sentence of the quote above belies the assertion made in the first: despite his disavowal of a particular ideological commitment ("I haven't understood a thing about our politics"), our narrator proves to have a keen eye for the vicissitudes of politics and power in his recently independent country. Soon, the narrator, a *maître d'hôtel*, becomes the new ruler's butler, and the narrative of *The Laughing Cry* is presented as the report of his time in the dictator's service.

As a novel about an African dictator, Lopès's *The Laughing Cry* shares many of the observations and narrative tropes of other African dictator novels.[2] Lopès's perspective on the figure of the African dictator and on authoritarianism in post-independence Africa is similarly negative; however, the novel is equally critical of those working in opposition to the dictator. This chapter will argue that, as we see in Lopès's *The Laughing Cry*, to write about the dictator is also to write about the writer's place in the political sphere. Lopès's novel, in turn, thematizes the difficulty of writing about the dictator by making visible the multiple perspectives and (political) interests at play: the narrator, as soon becomes clear, is not entirely reliable. In order to contextualize my argument about the dictator novel and the question of political commitment, I will begin with some reflections by Ngũgĩ wa Thiong'o on politically committed writing and writing about authoritarian rulers. From here, I will proceed to a reading of *The Laughing Cry* that puts the novel into dialogue with Lopès's comments on politics and literature in interviews and essays. Finally, I will show that Lopès imagines the political import of literature not as an immediate question of reference to a particular political program that the text supports, but rather as a long-term project of change whose effects remain uncertain in the present. The figure of the African dictator, therefore, is the locus around which a discourse about the making of political subjects begins to cohere.

Ngũgĩ's decision to write fiction in Gĩkũyũ stands as one of the more powerful—and notorious—statements of political commitment on the part of an African writer. The language debate, as the kernel of the definitional challenge posed by the category "African literature," rages on. I will not directly engage this debate, but gesture to it as another place in and around which conversations about the social and political role of the writer take place. For Ngũgĩ, it is the responsibility of the African writer to communicate with the people in a language that is comprehensible to them. "Language" here is both literal and figurative: the form and content must also be accessible, as Ngũgĩ makes clear in the essay, "The Language of African Fiction."[3] Here, Ngũgĩ recounts the challenges encountered in the process of writing his first Gĩkũyũ-language novel, *Caitaani Mũtharaba-inĩ* (*Devil on the Cross*, 1980). The committed writer must not simply choose content that is familiar to his reader but also point readers to their surrounding political reality. This poses particular difficulties:

> How do you shock your readers by pointing out that these [the dictator; politicians] are mass murderers, looters, robbers, thieves, when they, the perpetrators of these anti-people crimes, are not even attempting to hide the fact? When in some cases they are actually and proudly celebrating their massacre of children, and the theft and robbery of the nation? How do you satirize their utterances and claims when their own words beat all fictional exaggerations? (80)

As Achille Mbembe illuminates so well in his theorization of the "aesthetics of vulgarity" in *On the Postcolony*, a defining characteristic of the post-independence African dictator is his embracing and foregrounding of vulgarity as a defining characteristic of his rule. This undermines the potential for critique. In the face of extreme and unmediated violence, wild bombast, shameless exploitation, what is left for the writer to say? Within a larger framework, this question can be pushed further: What does it mean to be a committed writer in post-independence Africa? The arc of Ngũgĩ's career offers one response. Lopès and *The Laughing Cry*, I will argue, offer another.

The narrative of *The Laughing Cry* is largely retrospective, as the dictator's butler records his experiences only after going into exile. However, the novel ends with an interruption that puts the story as a whole into question: a letter from the butler's mistress, Soukali. Having read the manuscript, she accuses her lover, who she reveals is actually a doctor in a provincial town, of having spun a tall tale from the details of their quotidian lives. In a sense, Soukali's disclosure is redundant—after all, the French original opens with the standard designation *roman* (novel) on the title page—but it comes as a shock to the reader, unsettling the narrator's authority.

Soukali's intervention draws, in turn, a rebuttal from the narrator. Declaring that he has only included Soukali's "insidious and malicious" letter in the spirit of democracy, the narrator adds:

> In fact, I have borrowed nothing from reality, nor yet invented anything. Here I end the telling of a rosary of dreams and nightmares that have followed one another with the cadence of a chronicle [*à la cadence d'un feuilleton*] and from which I cannot be free [*débrasé*] until the last word is written. (258–59)

Playing with the distinction between history (reality) and fiction is a common feature of narratives about dictators. In the most immediate terms, this has to do with the dangers of writing about a present oppressive political reality. Sony Labou Tansi's opening warning in *La Vie et demie* (*Life and a Half*) is exemplary: he designates his text a fable.[4] But Lopès pushes the traffic between fiction and reality further, issuing a logical contradiction—"I have borrowed nothing from reality, nor yet invented anything"—about the novel's origins. If the text is based on nothing (neither, nor), "reality" is made relative. The narrative is then compared to both dreams and nightmares and, finally, to a *feuilleton*; it unfolds with the "cadence of a *feuilleton*." Gerald Moore's translation renders this as "chronicle." The associations of this term with historiography make it a potent choice, as it privileges the perception of the text as a continuous record of events as they occur in time. But the exposition in *The Laughing Cry* is anything but linear and, indeed, resists many of the ordering imperatives of historiography. The French term *feuilleton* points us down another interpretative path.

In the most literal sense, *feuilleton* refers to a serial or serialized narrative; it is currently used to refer to soap operas. The emphasis of the word is not so much on facticity or referentiality—as in Labou Tansi's use of the term "fable"—as on temporality and repetition. The term *feuilleton* suggests that the work of writing about dictators extends across time and space: it has multiple and potentially infinite iterations. Iteration is also a thematic and structural concern within *The Laughing Cry*: the novel is concerned with the problem of authoritarianism as a *recurring* phenomenon—the return of the same story over and over that is the same cycle in which the narrator is caught.[5]

Accordingly, the plot of *The Laughing Cry*, properly speaking, does not end: the dictator, having survived a coup, remains in power. It is the narrator who goes into exile, not for his politics but rather to escape punishment for his affair with the dictator's wife. Composed of a series of frames and riddled with interruptions, ellipses, and abrupt breaks between segments, the novel does not allow its reader many certainties. The lack of resolution in the story points to the fact that there is another story—an argument—in the text to which we must attend. It is in the context of this conception of political authoritarianism and the place of the writer that Lopès's novel takes up the question of literary commitment and considers what it might mean to be a committed writer. Rather than simply presenting the African dictator as a deplorable figure, Lopès's novel thematizes the challenges of writing about the dictator by making visible the multiple perspectives and (political) interests at play.

The narrator of *The Laughing Cry*, the dictator's butler, is only referred to by his professional title, *Maître d'hôtel*. The dictator dubs him Maître (Master) because the full title is too long. This winking inversion of roles—the butler as the dictator's master—is of a part with the novel's humorous tone, and it serves to characterize the dictator's own lack of sensibility for the playful potential of language: he is a clumsy and unsophisticated reader and, the narrator tells us repeatedly, a poor speaker of French. The dictator, Hannibal-Ideloy Bwakamabé Na Sakkadé, is a military man who, at the beginning of the story, removes the sitting president, PoléPolé. He is known as "Tonton," a diminutive for uncle that suggestively echoes the term used for the former French colonizers in the country: *les Oncles* ("the Uncles").[6] This is one of the novel's most explicit statements about the neocolonial entanglements on which post-independence authoritarian regimes in Africa depend for their survival. Tonton is a "little Uncle," continuing a relation of domination, violence, and denial of individual rights between the people and the state. Moore playfully renders the dictator's epithet as "Daddy," which loses the connection to the colonizers but emphasizes the ways in which Tonton, in his political discourse as well as his actions, presents himself as the father of a national "family."

While the country in which the story takes place is pointedly not named, the dictator is given a fictional ethnicity, "Djabotama," as well as that of the ethnic group against which he organizes his people, Djassikini, the ethnic group of the former dictator.[7] The politics that take shape around these markers, in their intersection with French, are part of the representation of the figure of the African dictator and gesture to many possible models. Despite the coy refusal to properly name its referents, the narrative of *The Laughing Cry* is filled with references to mainstream global culture of the 1970s and 1980s.[8] The literary figure "Tonton" stands for a multitude of African dictators, both historical and textual. Tonton's politics, in turn, are a curious and shifting mix of reformism and traditionalism; his mode of rule is fundamentally charismatic with his personality filling the void of ideological consistency. Political flexibility is the trademark of the client politician dedicated to fulfilling the requests of external interests, and it allows for trenchant critique; Tonton, for example, at one point pursues a policy of "Cultural Resurrection" (*Résurrection culturelle*) and later accepts aid in exchange for support from the apartheid government of South Africa.

Maître, an outsider to political power with an insider's perspective, presents a privileged view of the dynamics of the dictatorship, as he points out to the reader. This privileged perspective is the foundation on which his authority as narrator in the novel is based. But this authority is consistently challenged. Soukali's closing letter in *The Laughing Cry* is just one of many interruptions of the narrator's story. The novel is populated with multiple and potentially competing voices, from the censorial "warning" that opens the novel to the "editor" who attempts to make adjustments to the butler's account.

The Laughing Cry opens with a disclaimer ("Be Warned") addressed to the reader by the "Inter-African Association of Francophone Censors." The censor's primary criticism of the novel is that it fails to provide the reader ("the people") either with entertainment (*littérature d'évasion*) or with a positive image of Africa; the censor calls for a literature "exalting our positive moral values and our ancestral cosmology."[9] Censorial discourse demands commitment from the writer, in this case, service to the propagandistic imperatives of the authoritarian state. The role of the writer here is to provide a celebratory or aspirational image of Africa; the writer is part of the forward movement of the continent. The introduction of the imperative to produce a "useful" literature in the voice of the state operative here codes, from the beginning of the novel, exhortations to commitment as necessarily suspect. The "warning" that opens the novel conditions the reader to be suspicious of such demands, which will be made by other characters over the course of the novel.

The text in *The Laughing Cry* is divided into segments, the different purposes of which are typographically marked: the primary narrative appears in roman type, it is inter-cut with italicized passages of interior monologue whose speaker is often unidentified and occasionally shifts, as well as by editorial interjections that are offset from the margins and in smaller type. It is in the interactions between these segments that *The Laughing Cry* illuminates and explores the competing interests at work in writing about the figure of the dictator. Opposition here is not a guarantee, and, more importantly, the novel demonstrates the way in which the insistence on a text that opposes and critiques the dictator is itself an authoritarian imperative. The committed writer is not, therefore, *a priori* a positive figure and always risks falling into the trap of propaganda, regardless of the cause.

Maître addresses his memoirs to an ex-functionary of Tonton's government, the former Cabinet Secretary [*directeur de cabinet*].[10] It is the Directeur who makes the editorial interjections in the Maître's narrative, and the conversation that emerges is about the nature and purpose of properly politically committed (and intended) writing. The Directeur, as editor, objects to Maître's interpolation of what he deems to be extraneous and distracting material, particularly about Maître's sexual activities, which are described in exhaustive and at times comic detail. The Directeur, on the other hand, hopes that Maître's account of his time with the dictator will be a document to use in the campaign against Tonton. For his part, Maître is defiantly a-political, repeatedly reminding his reader—the Directeur as well as the audience—that he wants no part in politics: the phrase "politics and I," followed by an ellipses, is a common refrain in Maître's writing. This political ambivalence allows the text to represent more fully the attitudes of interested groups: Maître is able to take an ironic distance from Tonton's announcements, particularly his paranoid declarations about "-isms" or "ists," as well as from the imperatives that the Directeur sets for his memoir as a piece of committed writing. But for all his resistance to politics, Maître is inevitably caught up in the political tide.

The first break in Maître's narrative comes relatively early on. Following a chapter break, he announces to the reader: "Feeling some lack of confidence in myself, I have consulted a compatriot, the former Cabinet Secretary [Directeur] to Daddy [Tonton]" (33). The text that follows is an inserted letter from the Directeur, distinguished by its smaller type. The letter is initially invoked as a means to shore up the narrator's authority; the Directeur begins by confirming the precision of Maître's depiction of one of Tonton's ceremonies. In this instance, the Directeur's congratulations have a mutually benefiting effect: in confirming Maître's account, the Directeur establishes his own authority to do so. However, he quickly turns to making editorial interjections and objections to the details of Maître's account. In response to Maître's criticism of some young intellectuals, the Directeur warns, "Consider that in scoffing too much at us in the name of some undigested truth [*vérité irresponsable*] you may be playing the enemy's game. If you want to be of service to the country, make haste to offer us a positive hero [*héro positif*] in your story" (34). Much like the censor, the Directeur worries about the implications that negative representations of certain characters will have for his political plans. Once again, the responsibility of the committed writer is to provide a positive image (the positive hero) to which the reader can aspire or which may inspire the reader to action.

The Directeur's concerns about content are repeated on the level of form; he continues:

> As for the rest, I hesitate to pronounce an opinion. Whilst reading your work, I was constantly asking myself how to classify it. Sometimes you aspire to the precision of a historian or a sociologist; sometimes you resemble more the *griots* [*ces griots*] in whom some see only dream-peddlers and entertainers, and others a key to decoding the life of the village. (34)

Classification is a central problem for the committed work of literature: the unclassifiable work is also the work that cannot be properly marshaled in support of any argument as its extra-generic excess, an uncontrollable surplus, will always be open to other interpretations. At the same time, as becomes clear over the course of the disagreements between Maître and the Directeur, a work that is too easily classified risks becoming mere propaganda and therefore suspect. In this passage, the Directeur marks the instability of the narrator's discourse as much as he outlines the requirements for the properly committed work of literature. In negative terms, the committed work of literature as defined by the Directeur must be focused, generically stable, anticipate its possible interpretations (the Directeur is particularly concerned with how he is represented in the text), and, above all, offer a positive (prescriptive) model to be followed by the reader. Maître is largely unaffected by the Directeur's concerns and simply responds, "I'll continue, all the same" (34).

In subsequent comments, the Directeur becomes increasingly and particularly concerned with Maître's focus on his sexual activities; he writes, "I ask myself whether one has any right [*si l'on a le droit*] thus to confuse [*mêler*] politics and porn [*politique et porno*], without risking that one will spoil the other?" (95). Although the Directeur has admitted that the material is riveting—he begins, "I've read your last installment in one go" (94)—it is also cause for trepidation. Rather than declaring the material inappropriate outright, he wonders whether the (committed) writer has the *right* to mix genres. The language of rights necessarily opens toward the question of who has the authority to grant such rights to the writer. In the Directeur's estimation, Maître would have no right because his writing (will) must be subsumed to a larger purpose. The term "porno" here stands for pleasure or distraction; the concern is that the one (pleasure) will spoil the other (politics). And yet the text has held the Directeur's attention. Pleasure here—and, indeed, the sexual register in general—stands in for the comic and, in particular, the critical popular humor that Lopès celebrates in the novel, but the two are not necessarily equivalent. Rather, sex and the Directeur's reaction to sexual passages are used to point to underlying problems in his conception of politically purposeful writing.

It is in these comments that the Directeur provides the fullest articulation of committed writing in *The Laughing Cry*:

> When you first broached to me your idea of writing these satirical and critical memoirs of a slice in the life of a dictator during the last part of our century, I encouraged you, and even offered my collaboration. It's a question for me, I repeat, of contributing to the struggle against that tyrant Bwakamabé. Now, by the way the manuscript is developing, as for instance in this last installment, I fear that in yielding too much to intimate memories, you are mixing up genres and losing sight of the objective [*l'objectif fondamental*] of all committed writing [*écrit engagé*]. And the African book coming from these times, and having any respect for itself, cannot choose but be committed [*ne peut être qu'engagée*]. . . . (95)

The basis of the Directeur's thinking on commitment is expressed in the closing claim—contemporary African literature cannot but be committed—a foundational assumption for the Directeur's (standing in for the "native intellectual's") worldview. In order to be literature, it must somehow be connected to a larger political project; otherwise, it is simply entertainment or, recalling the censor, a source of confusion. The link to politics shores up the Directeur's personal motivations for participating in Maître's memoirs as editor: he hopes to contribute to the fight against the dictator. But Maître's story quickly slips from the Directeur's control. Importantly, the objective of committed writing remains grammatically unclear and effectively unsaid: "the fundamental objective" [*l'objectif fondamental*] is unqualified here and elsewhere in the novel, suggesting that the Directeur's goal of "critique" remains amorphous and undefined. Recalling the questions Ngũgĩ posed at the beginning of this chapter, Lopès here satirizes official censorial discourse, as much as the Directeur's discourse on political commitment, not through exaggeration but rather by the use of juxtaposition. In placing these two discourses together, he shows how the demand for commitment too often recalls the call to propaganda on the part of the state; both are rooted in the authoritarian imperative to control meaning-making.

In *The Laughing Cry*, the differences between Maître (the writer) and the Directeur (his editor) become the space in which the novel articulates the problematic nature of the ideal of politically committed writing. Drawing a thread between the demands made by the censor and the demands made by the Directeur on the text, the novel demonstrates the ways in which any writing that aims to be committed always risks being overly determined by external interests. Within the narrative, the journalist Aziz Sonika, the editor of the state newspaper *Le Croix du Sud*, stands as an example of the writer whose work is entirely determined by such external interests: he is the archetypal propagandist, writing first for Polépolé and then quickly shifting his allegiance to Tonton. Maître makes frequent reference to Sonika's writing as the mouthpiece of the state. Sonika draws his authority from the fact that he is in the service of power. In their glancing similarity, Maître reserves a degree of admiration for Sonika: "I've got to admit that the man is an artist endowed with a certain talent [*certaine valeur*]. No one knew better than he how to distract attention [. . .] " (61). Even in the most flagrant collusion, there is a measure of value, indeed, of art, in the manipulation of language. But Sonika is also a figure of derision—Maître refers to his "boot-licking style"—whose writing is not taken seriously (27).

In contrast to Sonika, there is the figure of Matapalé in *The Laughing Cry*, a celebrated writer arrested by Tonton's government whose disappearance becomes a major issue in the international press. Maître is unimpressed by the coverage, commenting that the unknowns jailed by Tonton are no less important: "The European papers knew of no one but Matapalé, whom they presented moreover as a writer of genius. There, they were certainly exaggerating" (43). This is followed by Maître's carefully articulated negative evaluation of Matapalé's work. Matapalé—the author of books with titles such as *Les Légendes du Lac Eworowo* (*The Legends of Lake Eworowo*) and *Les Chants du Baobab* (*Songs of the Baobab*)—stands for the kind of "native" writer lauded by the colonizers.[11] He may represent the "local" for the Europeans, but both Maître and *The Laughing Cry* more generally privilege more popular sources. The contrasting force to the individual genius such as Matapalé or the pliability of Sonika's political allegiances is the popular consciousness embodied by what Maître calls Radio Grapevine [*radio-trottoir*]—the shared knowledge and rumors carried by the people who inhabit the working-class area of the city, Moundié.

In working through the question of committed writing in *The Laughing Cry*, it is necessary to distinguish between the kinds of "committed" texts that the censor or Directeur require and the model of commitment that a writer like Ngũgĩ articulates. We should recall that both the censor and Directeur desire clarity, which is not the same as producing a text that is accessible to the broader public with which Ngũgĩ hopes to engage. A case in point: in "The Language of African Fiction," Ngũgĩ describes his turn to oral and vernacular narrative forms for inspiration and guidance in the writing of *Devil on the Cross*. Ngũgĩ's privileging of what he conceives of as a popular critical consciousness—embodied in the vernacular tradition—has echoes in Lopès's own thinking on the question of commitment. However, we should look more closely at how Lopès himself outlines the problem. If *The Laughing Cry* stages the multiple interests that weigh on a narrative that aims to talk about politics, what is the conception of literary commitment that his novel articulates?

In a 1982 interview with Denis de Saivre, Lopès directly addressed the relationship between the fictional world of *The Laughing Cry* and possible historical referents:

> [I]f by chance it happens that an historian, many years after I am gone, becomes interested in this work [*The Laughing Cry*], he may be able to establish a comparison between real key persons and this one that I call "Tonton." But he would soon find that I have been an unfaithful chronicler [*un chroniqueur infidèle*], that I have pushed the traits of this one here, that I have moderated those of that one there, that I have attributed the characteristics of one single man to many, in brief, that I have transformed reality. (De Saivre 121)[12]

Lopès's is "unfaithful" because his work is not in fact a history—this is where *feuilleton* rather than "chronicle" (*chronique*) becomes a useful concept in our analysis. Lopès draws a clear line between the work of historical accounting in the chronicle and the play of the novelist who creates "types" (*personnages typiques*), which recall for the reader the world in which they live. The "unfaithful chronicler" is the author of the *feuilleton*. The novel, Lopès continues, is not a report; it is a narrative. Commitment here is to a mode of representation—the play with types, critical humor—rather than to generic or topical unison or an overarching political teleology.

In an essay written a few years after the publication of *The Laughing Cry*, "My Novels, My Characters, and Myself" (1993), Lopès addresses the inspiration for his work. The essay, which begins with a comment on the frequency with which Lopès himself is compared to or confused with his narrators, is a reflection on the writer's role in society that draws on Lopès's own connection to politics.[13] Writing, in this essay, is not merely a matter of storytelling but also of invention; once again, Lopès's "chronicler" is unfaithful. According to Lopès, African literature in the post-independence period has been closely linked to politics; Lopès characterizes this as a "confusion" of the political struggle with artistic creation. "Confusion" here is also conflation, with one term ("aesthetics") being taken as co-terminal with the other ("politics"). This takes place in the postcolonial moment of national consolidation. Literature becomes—following Frantz Fanon, Ngũgĩ, and a whole generation of thinkers—a key part of consolidating and validating national culture. In this framework, such validation is in a feedback loop with the consolidation of the state, both within national borders and on the global stage.[14] But this fundamentally limits the writer because it determines the content and shape of his work rather than allowing him the space for invention.

The writer, in Lopès's estimation, needs to be slightly outside of this circuit of cultural and national foundation; fundamentally "unfaithful" and inventive, he is in fact an occasional agent of productive disorder. Lopès here provides his own definition of the function of the writer in society: "As African writers, we have the duty to help the Africas [sic] of the *Le Pleurer-rire* period make the transition between the paranoia of the 1960s and the critical humor that begets democracies" (85). In *The Laughing Cry*, the model of literary commitment desired by the Directeur is that of the "faithful chronicler" invested in furthering particular political goals. Maître, in his a-political attitude, is outside of the terms of this model of commitment; put another way, in his writerly politics as much as in his sexual practice, our narrator is fundamentally unfaithful. For Lopès, the committed writer is one dedicated not so much to a particular cause or politics—this would be the kind of *a priori* external determination of the text attributed to the censor and the Directeur in *The Laughing Cry*—as to literary invention as an end in itself. The text should refer to its surrounding reality, as in the use of "types" (*personnages typiques*), but not be determined by that reality. This, in turn, engenders in the reader a particular kind of critical humor and attitude toward authority and authoritarian acts more generally. As a model, Lopès's conception here is fundamentally oriented toward the future.

Within *The Laughing Cry*, Maître's shift from resisting the Directeur's editorial remarks to rejecting his intervention marks a key turning point. Instead of including another letter from the Directeur, Maître takes it upon himself to interrupt the narrative:

> I will spare my readers the long pages of rhetoric in which my young compatriot ex-Cabinet Secretary [*mon jeune compatriote ancien directeur de cabinet*], in the name of revolutionary modesty, takes issue with exotico-pornographic writing. Some will certainly miss these pieces of eloquence, in which the pen of a gifted polemicist demolishes with implacable dialectic the depraved tendencies of a decadent bourgeoisie, which insists on contaminating a virginal Africa by the systematic export of its dissolute values. But I couldn't publish them without adding my own reflection upon these edifying lessons in morality. To his venerable and learned ethic and to my own banalities and platitudes, each in turn ridiculous in their conviction of revealing new truths, I have preferred the forgotten voice of the good Diderot. (209)

In the inserted quote from *Jacques le fataliste et son Maître* (*Jacques the Fatalist and his Master*) which follows this introduction, the narrator upbraids notions of propriety in regards to sex and, in particular, to writing about sexual matters; it is clearly pointed at the Directeur.

Diderot's novel is an important intertext for *The Laughing Cry*: particularly in its articulation of the relationship between servant and master, it serves as a palimpsest for Lopès's novel. In this scene, the choice of passage marks a clear distinction between the Maître and the Directeur and constitutes the break between them. The turn to Diderot marks the end of Maître's dependence on the Directeur to buttress his authority, and the act of substitution itself points to the authorizing function that the Directeur served all along. Here Maître himself assumes the editorial function, pushing the Directeur out of the narrative. But this turn also marks the moment in which Maître is pushed into exile in the story, bringing about a fundamental narrative shift: the text begins to lose its segmented structure as the italicized reminiscences become increasingly melancholy and the order of the structure begins to unravel.

While the discussion to this point has depended on the distinctions drawn by the separations between sections, as *The Laughing Cry* progresses, the apparent order instituted by the segmentation of the text comes apart. If initially the novel set up a series of opposing pairs, the most central of which is Maître (writer) and the Directeur (editor), by the point at which Diderot is invoked, these symmetries no longer hold. The breaks and interruptions between sections are no longer absolute, and voices, themes, and issues begin to overflow their boundaries. From this later perspective, it is clear that the initial segmentation of the narration in Lopès's novel expresses the wish for an order that cannot be maintained; but this is only perhaps the case from an editor's perspective. Our narrator, as has been made clear, is fundamentally unfaithful. Our author, too, has identified himself as an unfaithful chronicler. It is in the break with the Directeur/editor and the rupture of the order which had previously disciplined the narrative that *The Laughing Cry* leaps toward critical humor and, most importantly, toward invention.

At the beginning of this chapter, Soukali's interruption at the close of *The Laughing Cry* was presented as an act that radically undermined the status of the narrative in the novel by exposing it as a fiction. It functioned as a way, to recall Ngũgĩ's comments on writing about authoritarian rulers, to shock and unsettle the reader. But the break that Soukali's letter represents also has rich potential for our interpretation of Lopès's perspective on the question of what it means to be a committed writer. In the context of this argument, Soukali's letter becomes the key moment in the novel precisely because it celebrates literature not just as storytelling but also as *invention*. What seems to be a rebuttal to the narrative in fact proves to be the antidote to the censorial warning that opens *The Laughing Cry*. Soukali's description of what the narrator has done echoes Lopès's comments on the "types" (*personnages typiques*) above:

> Despite a few transpositions, your friends will have no difficulty in recognizing every one of the actors under their masks [*sous leurs grimaces*]. Daddy [Tonton] is obviously the celebrated prefect of a certain province, which was inhabited for three years by a young heart specialist, then fresh from university in Europe, to whom I now entrust the care of my health. I easily recognize him, even if he defends himself

by taking the precaution (while remaining grossly obvious) of shuffling the cards, borrowing a trait here and there from one of his relatives, not the *maître d'hôtel* at the *Relais Aériens*, but bouncer at a fashionable nightclub. (257)

Soukali reveals to the reader that what we thought was testimony is in fact fiction. The types described are recognizable, but much has been changed: the small stories of provincial drama are recast as the grand narrative of the *roman du dictateur* (dictator novel). Soukali confirms for the reader that the narrator of *The Laughing Cry* has in fact transformed reality, just as Lopès has done in writing the novel. The reality transformed within the world of *The Laughing Cry* and in Lopès's writing of the novel are very different, but the fundamental dynamic of invention and transformation through writing begins the same way. In this sense, Soukali reveals to the reader the extent to which the novel stages its production for the reader.

Soukali then goes on to give an evaluation of the narrative as an aesthetic object; she points out the parts she thinks are excessive and admits that she does not think it is particularly strong as a work of art. Nevertheless, and perhaps despite the identifiability of its source material, she treats the narrative as art:

> But the magic and teaching power of art [*puissance pédagogique*], isn't it less to resemble reality than to lend to reality the colors of the painter's heart? If that is your aim, your bleeding vision [*rêve débridé*] is certainly more acceptable than the prissy and edifying images demanded by the young compatriot Cabinet Secretary. (258)

"To lend to reality the colors of the painter's heart" is the transformative function of art. In the voice of Soukali, Lopès offers the most cogent definition of another model of literary commitment, beyond those demanded by the Directeur or by the Censor. In this model, the author's commitment emerges in the nature of the aesthetic object itself ("the colors of the painter's heart") rather than in the political purposes to which it can be put. The "magic"—or, more programmatically, the instructive potential—of art lies in its difference from reality, that is, in its excess. If the narrative in *The Laughing Cry* represents the resistance of the writer to a variety of political imperatives, Soukali's letter effectively frees Maître's story, allowing it to be the author's invention. The capacity for invention, in turn, represents the writer's greatest potential for resistance to the monologic utterances of the state.

Although *The Laughing Cry* stages the work of writing about the dictator, it is anchored by its representation of real political dynamics—both in the dictator's government as well as between those who might possibly form an opposition. The literary text isolates and illuminates these dynamics for the reader; it does not propose a solution but rather gives the reader the means with which to recognize these dynamics as they operate in the real world. This is the primary intent of Lopès's novel: to provide a critical lens—what Lopès in the essay "My Novels, My Characters, Myself" calls, "the critical humor that begets democracies" (85)—through which to view the dictator. It is also what Lopès conceives of as the social and political role of the writer. Writing that is too ascetic in its commitment to externally determined political goals ceases to be writing of interest; it risks, as always, being reduced to the propaganda to which it so often responds. "Commitment" here is not programmatic so much as revelatory, and its politics is experiential.

There remains, in our discussion of Lopès's conception of commitment, the question of time. While the model of commitment put forward by the Directeur in *The Laughing Cry* is rooted in the political present, Lopès's conception of the potential of literature is fundamentally oriented toward the future. In the interview with De Saivre, he states, "The political project of this book is not to bring down [*faire tomber*] this or that regime. This is not what interests me and I don't think that a novel can do that [. . .]" (83). Instead, the potential of literature lies in the ways in which it can transform the reader's perspective, with the potential for change being displaced toward the future.[15] Lopès's "long term" perspective on literary commitment complicates the incorporation of the writer into any political program—such as the Directeur tries to do in the novel—by pointing to the incommensurability between the teleology of political programs in relation to real social change.

A final consideration: in 2006, Lopès took over the editorship of the journal *African Geopolitics*. In the editor's note that opens his first issue, he writes:

> Africa has undoubtedly had her fair share of visionaries (Nkrumah, Sekou Touré, Lumumba, Ben Bella, Frantz Fanon, even Chiekh Anta Diop) but perhaps their dreams were too much inspired by intuition, too closely linked to ancient principles and based on a gamble. In their day, such inspiration had the power to stir and sway the crowds. But the orator's day has passed. The crowds they used to harangue and which chanted simple beliefs at their behest have matured, aged, and are no longer willing to accept flights of lyricism as common currency. Today's African man and woman in the street want to form their judgment on the basis of actual evidence. (7–8)

The day of the orator as the authoritative speaker—and of oration as the rhetorical or argumentative mode of the authoritarian ruler—has passed. In his place is a mass of critical subjects no longer amenable to being swayed by visionary discourse. This is a hefty declaration and no doubt more of a hopeful expression than measurable fact. But, three decades after *The Laughing Cry*, we can read in this declaration the desire to assert that the vision of literary commitment articulated therein has indeed borne fruit. We can read in Lopès the fervent wish for the perceived or desired political relevance of literature to be substantiated in real social change, specifically, to break out of the cycle of repetition—*la cadence d'un feuilleton*—and, finally, to achieve the potential of freedom. Here we have, then, a realization of the democratic potential represented in the critical humor through which Lopès hoped to instruct his reader.

However, the novel *The Laughing Cry* and the editor's note to *African Geopolitics* are two disjointed statements that cannot be read on the same discursive plane. As Soukali makes clear at the close of *The Laughing Cry*, the novel (the aesthetic object) colors reality with another brush. While in the 1982 interview with Denise de Saivre (quoted above) Lopès presents literature as representing a popular reality (*realité populaire*) different from the official story, thereby opening up its readers to new modes of thinking, in this same interview he raises the possibility of the *chroniqueur infidèle*, which, Soukali's intervention shows us, is not limited to the writer's relation to official accounts but, rather, to the writer's relation to reality as a whole. This infidelity to, or in, the moment has the effect of opening up possible futures. What is important, therefore, is not what the text represents—its historical referents, its facticity—but *how* and with what effects. Commitment, such as it is conceived by Lopès, lies not in the political argument in which the writer immediately hopes to intervene but in the futures that the text aims to make possible.

Notes

1. English quotations are from Gerald Moore's translation, *The Laughing Cry: An African Cock and Bull Story* (1987). The subtitle of the translation serves a similar function to the *roman* on the title page of the French edition; however, "cock and bull" here carries further implications, designating the novel as a whole as a "tall tale."
2. Specifically, I have in mind Sony Lab'ou Tansi's *La Vie et demie* (1979), Ousmane Sembène's *Le Dernier de l'Empire* (1981), Henri Lopès's *Le Pleurer-rire* (1982), Chinua Achebe's *Anthills of the Savannah* (1987), and Aminata Sow Fall's *L'Ex-père de la nation* (1987), all of which are roughly contemporary to *The Laughing Cry*; as well as Ahmadou Kourouma's *En Attendant le vote des bêtes sauvages* (1998) and Ngũgĩ wa Thiong'o's *Wizard of the Crow* (2004–2007).
3. "The Language of African Fiction" appears in the seminal collection *Decolonizing the Mind: The Politics of Language in African Literature* (1986). The first essay in the collection, "The Language of African Literature," outlines Ngũgĩ's philosophical position while subsequent essays explore its implications; "The Language of African Literature" and the "Language of African Fiction" should be read as a complementary pair.
4. "*Life and a Half* becomes this *fable* that sees tomorrow through today's eyes" (3).
5. This is emphasized at the conclusion of the narrative, prior to Soukali's letter, as Maître observes: "It is a story told only in scrupulously closed venues, or on certain evenings of a wake where those gathered in mourning are quite homogenous. It's like those songs of which no one knows the composer, but which everyone learns without a false note, from generation to generation, from century to century. Soundiata Keïta, Almamy Touré, Chaka, Bouéta Bongo, Mabiala Maganga, Roland at Roncevalles, the Emir Abd-el-Kader . . . and others, many others" (256).

6. Tonton's full title is "President of the Republic, Head of State, President of the Patriotic Council of National Resurrection, President of the Council of Ministers, President of the Supreme Council of the Magistrature, Minister of many departments, intellectual author of the policy of national cultural resurrection" (191).
7. For further information on the connotations of these fictional names, see T. Zezeze Kalonji's "Eléments pour une analyse plurielle du *Pleurer-Rire* de Henri Lopès."
8. The narrator references everything from the Brazilian football player Pelé to Abba's "Fernando." References are also made to Latin American revolutionary politics and Ché Guevarra in particular; toward the end of the story, the narrator reports the rumor that a certain "Tché" or "Chez" has infiltrated the politics of the country and is organizing the opposition to Tonton.
9. These pages are unnumbered in Moore's translation.
10. *Directeur de Cabinet* is generally translated as "Chief of Staff;" although Moore chooses the term "Cabinet Secretary." I maintain the French *directeur* for consistency with the use of "Maître."
11. Maître declares: "They [Matapalé's works] offer nothing of the marvelous or the fantastic, no real fire, and what magic there is, is displayed with great clumsiness. The *Grand Prix* of the French Union which we won proves nothing, if not that in those days other blacks wrote no better and that the Uncles stood astounded, as at a marvel, before even twenty pages written by a negro" (43).
12. Translation mine, with thanks to Katharina Piechocki for help with revisions.
13. Lopès has had a long and distinguished career in politics, holding several ministerial posts under a series of presidents and was Prime Minister from 1972 to 1975. His involvement with politics has drawn criticism; most notably, from David N'Zitoukoulou in a critical review of *Le Pleurer-rire*. In the 1980s, Lopès's relationship with politics and politicians began to shift; in 1981, Lopès left his post in government and went to work for UNESCO; later, he served as the Congolese ambassador to France. For a more complete biography of Lopès, refer to Apollinaire Singou-Basseha's "Chronologie de la vie et de l' ouvre de Henri Lopès" in *Henri Lopès: Une écriture d'enracinement et d'universalité*.
14. Lopès writes: "[M]any of our authors have become accustomed to confusing the political struggle with artistic creation. Thus, they set out to defend and to illustrate our cultural identities, but they foundered on a sort of nationalism which, when we encounter it in other people, seems anti-humanistic. In actual fact, true literary creators are never chauvinists or lackeys" (84).
15. Lopès states, "The greatest [*le plus grand*] political effect [*action politique*] that a writer can hope to have on his reader is, let's say, that he [*the reader*] is if not transformed at the end of the work, at least that he does not have the same [self-assurance] [or certainty] [as he did before] when he finds himself in the face of certain situations" (83).

Works Cited

Bobika, André-Patient and Antoine Yila. *Henri Lopès: Une écriture d'enracinement et d'univeralité*. Paris: L'Harmattan, 2002. Print.

De Saivre, Denyse. "Entretien avec Henri Lopès." *Recherche, pédagogie et culture* 59/60 (1982): 118–20. Print.

Kalonji, T. Zezeze. "Eléments pour un analyse plurielle du *Pleurer-rire* de Henri Lopès." *Peuple Noirs Peuples Africains* 37 (1984): 30–34. Web. 5 June 2011.

Labou Tansi, Sony. *Life and a Half*. Trans. Alison Dundy. Bloomington: Indiana UP, 2011. Print.

———. *Le Vie et demie*. Paris: Editions du Seuil, 1979. Print.

Lopès, Henri. Editor's note. *African Geopolitics* 23 (2006): 7–11. Print.

———. *The Laughing Cry: An African Cock and Bull Story*. Trans. Gerald Moore. London: Readers International, 1987. Print.

———. "My Novels, My Characters, and Myself." *Research in African Literatures* 24.1 (1993): 81–86. Print.

———. *Le Pleurer-rire*. 1982. 2nd Ed. Paris : Présence Africaine, 2003. Print.

Mbembe, J.A. *On the Postcolony*. Berkeley: U of California P, 2001. Print.

Ngũgĩ wa Thiong'o. "The Language of African Fiction." *Decolonizing the Mind: The Politics of Language in African Literature*. London: Heinemann, 1986. 63–86. Print.

N'Zitoukoulou, David. "*Le Pleurer-rire* de Henri Lopès." *Peuples Noirs Peuples Africains* 35 (1983): 103–119. Web. 1 June 2011.

Toxic Fathers:
Henri Lopès's *The Laughing Cry* as Emblematic African Dictator Novel

GĨTAHI GĨTĨTĨ

> Its entrance gives onto a vast esplanade, in the middle of which rises a statue of Bwakamabé, all in ivory and rising to a height of many feet. . . . Whenever it rains, I never tire of watching the slow dripping of rivulets over the polished surface, and I allow myself some doubtful thoughts about History and Immortality.
>
> —Narrator, *The Laughing Cry*

> Why not recognize a certain sincerity in the dictatorships that today oppress the majority of our countries? Freedom of enterprise means, in times of crisis, the deprivation of freedom for the people. Latin American scientists emigrate, laboratories and universities have no funds, industrial "know-how" is always foreign and exorbitantly expensive; but why not recognize a certain creativity in the development of a technology of terror? Latin America is making inspired universal contributions to the development of methods of torture, techniques for assassinating people and ideas, for the cultivation of silence, the extension of impotence, and the sowing of fear.
>
> —Eduardo Galeano, *Days and Nights of Love and War* (1983)

The Uruguayan-born writer and political activist's comment about Latin American dictators may very well have been written about Africa, so compelling is its truth. A considerable portion of postcolonial African literature—the novel, drama, poetry, short fiction—has been preoccupied with the ubiquitous phenomenon of the military or civilian strongman, who has been the bane of African economies, politics, and culture. What began in the early 1960s as the theme of "disillusionment" has extended into the twenty-first century; the novel arguably carries the bulk of the burden. As Gĩtahi Gĩtĩtĩ has argued, while the dictator novel is a familiar enough literary object in the African context, what it lacks in comparison to, say, its Latin American counterpart is sufficient critical attention as an arena in which contending ideologies as well as the discourse of authority engage in a dramatic display of claims and counterclaims all geared toward the acquisition of a form of hegemony (212). As is to be expected, the essay and autobiography/memoir succeed more in the elaboration of the dictator spectacle than other formats.

This chapter will closely examine Henri Lopès's *The Laughing Cry* (1987), one of the most representative African dictator novels, through a detour into contemporary scholarship on postcoloniality to provide the necessary historical and critical/literary frameworks against which to read perhaps the most enduring topic bridging the twentieth and the twenty-first centuries in Africa—the ruinous effects of runaway dictatorship. So numerous are/have been African dictators, and so devastating their rule, that no region of the continent has been spared. As Alemayehu Mariam has written,

> The inconvenient truth about Africa today is that dictatorship presents a more perilous threat to the survival of Africans than climate change. The devastation African dictators have wreaked upon the social fabric and ecosystem of African societies is incalculable. Over the past several decades, bloodthirsty dictators . . . have been responsible for untold deaths on the continent. Millions of Africans have starved to death because of the criminal negligence, depraved indifference and gross incompetence of African dictators, not climate change. (1)

In his seminal *On the Postcolony*, Cameroonian critic Achille Mbembe incisively examines what he calls the notion of the postcolony, which, he writes, "identifies specifically a given historical trajectory—that of societies recently emerging from the experience of colonization and the violence which the colonial relationship involves" (102). The postcolony, adds Mbembe,

> is characterized by a distinctive style of political improvisation, by a tendency to excess and lack of proportion, as well as by [the] distinctive ways identities are multiplied, transformed, and put into circulation. But the postcolony is also made up of a series of corporate institutions and a political machinery that, once

in place, constitute a distinctive regime of violence. In this sense, the postcolony is a particularly revealing, and rather dramatic, stage on which are played out the wider problems of subjection and its corollary, discipline. (102–103)

While Mbembe's focus is his native Cameroon, the insights in *On the Postcolony* apply widely and pertinently to the rest of Africa, and especially to so-called sub-Saharan Africa. Mbembe uses the term *commandement* to designate both the political machinery and the regime of violence mentioned above. Accordingly,

> In the postcolony, the *commandement* seeks to institutionalize itself, to achieve legitimation and hegemony (*recherché hégémonique*) in the form of a *fetish*. The signs, vocabulary, and narratives that the *commandement* produces are meant not merely to be symbols; they are officially invested with a surplus of meanings that are not negotiable and that one is officially forbidden to depart from or challenge. To ensure that no such challenge takes place, the champions of state power invent entire constellations of ideas; they adopt a distinct set of cultural repertoires and powerfully evocative concepts; but they also resort, if necessary, to the systematic application of pain. (103)

Within the context of Africa, the Democratic Republic of the Congo, once called Zaire, has its dubious claim to fame largely through the iconic Mobutu Sese Seko and his 32-year-long dictatorship. Congolese novelist Henri Lopès's *The Laughing Cry: An African Cock and Bull Story* (1987), first published in French as *Le Pleure-Rire* in 1982, typifies the postcolonial African dictator through a complex exploration of the Mobutu years. Lopès's compatriot, Sony Labou Tansi, published his *La Vie et Demie* in 1979; its English translation, *Life and a Half*, was published in 2011. An interesting relation exists between these two texts, to say nothing of the two authors' other works in the form of the novel, poetry, drama, short fiction, and the essay. Labou Tansi dedicates *Life and a Half*, which he adroitly characterizes as "this *fable* that sees tomorrow through today's eyes," partly "[t]o Henri Lopès too because when all is said and done I have written nothing but his book." Labou Tansi apprehends the world in which Lopès's "cock and bull story" plays itself out as "a place of fear in this vast world that's going to hell" (3). Concerning the beleaguered world of *Life and a Half*, Achille Mbembe truculently observes that it is "a place and a time of half-death—or, if one prefers, half-life. It is a place where life and death are so entangled that it is no longer possible to distinguish them, or to say what is on the side of the shadow or its obverse" (197). Quoting Mbembe, Dominic Thomas discerns that "the power of the sovereign, encapsulated in *Life and a Half* in the emblematic figure of the Providential Guide, is expressed in terms of the tenuous relationship between life and death," whereby the ultimate expression of sovereignty resides, to a large degree, in the power and the capacity to dictate who may live and who must die. Hence, to kill or to allow to live constitutes the limits of sovereignty, its fundamental attributes (11–12).

Lopès's "sovereign" is Marshal Hannibal-Ideloy Bwakamabé Na Sakkadé who, upon seizing power in a coup d'état, promises his country that "[t]here'll be political stability. No opposition. I, Bwakamabé Na Sakkadé, son of Ngakoro, son of Fouléma, son of Kiréwa, will never become an ex-President, like that coward Polépolé" (21). This self-appointed Recreating Father of the Nation and President of the National Council of Resurrection must be addressed as "Daddy [who came down to us from on high]," thus cementing his claim both as symbolic father of the nation and one elected by divine will. The democratic-minded former president, Polépolé, had been deposed and forced into exile because he was perceived to have been an advocate of "the corrupt and individualistic morals of western countries" (74). Bwakamabé had appeared, with courage, "to save the nation when it was on the brink of the abyss into which Polépolé threatened to plunge it" (74). Bwakamabé's defense of autocracy is premised on a supposedly African tradition of the right of the *chef* to accede to power without opposition or discussion:

> Ever since Africa was Africa, the chief of the village, in our culture, had never been elected. To thirst nowadays for innovation in this domain was to be as uncustomary as asking a man to do the cooking or carry a calabash on his head. Notions of European pederasts! No. The chief, that was always the wisest, the best orator, the man with the strongest fist. He imposed himself through the occult will of the dead, and everybody recognised him. Whoever dared question his authority was immediately called to public account and punished by the community, which crushed him like a cockroach. The vote was a hypocrisy of the white mentality. (74)

During the investiture ceremony, Bwakamabé is placed before an altar and presented with a drum and a lion's tail, "both symbols of strength and all-powerful authority" (30). He is ceremonially invited to "receive the power of the ancestors," which, the narrator editorializes, is to be understood to mean the power of the chieftains of the Djabotama. *Litassa*, the Djabotama word for power, "[i]s at once the power to command, the intelligence to dominate others and the strength of a bull, or more, of a supernatural being. These are powers in which the Uncles don't want to believe, and which place us beyond the reach of our enemies. Whoever has received *litassa* can communicate directly with the ancestors . . ." (30). Significantly, the Chief also receives a *tounka*, a chain with many pendants to be worn on his back,

> as a woman bears her child. For a chief has nothing in common with the kings in the Uncles' history books. He is, before everything else, a father who must occupy himself with his subjects as with his own sons. The President could no more

separate himself from his chain than from his lion's tail. They also proffered him a bag, which symbolized the power to raise and receive tribute. (31)

The lion's tail, which must never leave his grasp, is a symbol of formidable power and authority that will in time become an artifact with which the *chef* can bless his subjects, or alternatively, act as an instrument of punishment. Henceforth, Bwakamabé will assume extravagant titles, such as "Supreme Strategist, Creator of the New Regime of Popular Liberties," but will be unable to exercise his full power without the "Great-Historic-Courageous-and-Intrepid Armed Forces" (151).

Bwakamabé, a composite of Idi Amin Dada, Jean Bedel Bokassa, Jomo Kenyatta, Marion Ngouabi, Hastings Kamuzu Banda, Félix Houphouët-Boigny, Ahmadou Ahidjo, Jaafar Numeiry, Paul Biya, Mobutu Sese Seko, and Eyadema, to name but a few of the vicious dictators, invokes the Chief's "inherited" entitlement to the "systematic application of pain" ostensibly endorsed by a think-alike community, which crushes the dissenter "like a cockroach." It is hard to miss the sleight of hand by virtue of which the Chief is *automatically* rendered variously as *always* "the wisest, the best orator, the man with the strongest fist." There is not a big leap from "the best orator" to the *only* orator, the one uniquely qualified to speak to, about, and for his country. As Bwakamabé furiously remarks after Captain Yabaka has given an interview to "some European daily" in which the latter "had attacked American imperialism" and expressed the opinion that "the dictatorships of puppet regimes [were] condemned by history" (221): "Who does he think he is, this fellow, to go giving interviews? Only one person can speak in the name of the Nation, in any well-organised country: the Chief" (222). As a military man steeped in a culture of obedience and ready compliance, the Chief construes all acts of dialogue as leading inexorably to chaos, hence his literal and symbolic banning of opposition. Interestingly, during an interview that Bwakamabé grants to a renowned American author, the Chief dryly remarks that there were still enough military men like him left in the world "to save a humanity in full decomposition, threatening every day to throw itself, all withered, into the maw of some totalitarian dictator! Happily, the military saviours were watching it! Perhaps everything would go better when the day came that Africa was governed exclusively by military men. That day couldn't be far off, anyway. One had only to see the wind of history. Civilian regimes were living under sentence of death" (234). Bwakamabé imagines a fraternity of dictators across the continent and an ideology that both tolerates and invests in dictatorship as its *esprit de corps*. This proliferation of dictators, many of whom provide moral support and/or sanctuary to their sitting or ousted fellow presidents—as in Soyinka's *Opera Wonyosi*—is a theme shared with the Latin American dictator novel, as in Gabriel García Márquez's *The Autumn of the Patriarch*.

Speaking through his narrator, Lopès underscores the sheer scope of African despotism through an act of defamiliarization:

> Ah yes! the Country, the Country—but which Country? Somewhere on this continent, for sure. Choose for yourself, after a hundred calculations, or just follow your hunch, take a point on the equator, and steer either northward or southward, keeping your nose with the wind, and at a slightly oblique angle. Your craft then, after surviving air-pockets and overcoming tornadoes, will arrive, after a certain time, at a point from which you can just discern the capital of our country. (34–35)

The ineptitude and greed of successive African regimes has failed to create successful African infrastructural and capital modalities. With regard to travel, the result is that, "to save time, it's a hundred times better to go to Paris, London, Lisbon or Madrid, from which . . . one can arrive at one's destination in a flight of a few hours" (35). The cost to the country of the roundabout way is nothing to Africanists and wealthy businessmen of all nationalities, and the route is made complex to suit the dictator's paranoid sense of security (for himself and his cohorts), but as the narrator sarcastically remarks, why would the ordinary people of the Country have any "reason for voyaging at random from a state where the people live perpetually in Nirvana" (35)? The reverse is true: those subjects who somehow manage to evade arbitrary arrest and torture/death languish in a state of internal exile; those who manage to elude the dictator's hunting men, like Polépolé, the compatriot Cabinet Secretary, and eventually the *maître*, live forever in external exile. True to Mbembe's observation regarding the ultimate expression of the sovereign, the ruling patriarch reserves the absolute power to dictate not only who may live and who must die but also the right to pursue exiled "dissidents" wherever they may reside. Thus, the power of life and death is exercised both within and without the country, with no small assistance from the dictator's agents and allies abroad.

In the chapter of *On the Postcolony* titled "Of Commandement," Mbembe observes succinctly that

> dealing with human behavior and how it is regulated in a state framework and with state instruments means not simply to look at what constitutes the strength and reason of the state, but also to ask questions about the actual forms of power, its manifestations, and the various techniques that it uses to enhance its value, distribute the product of labor, and either ensure abundance or manage poverty and scarcity. And since, in Africa both before and after colonization, state power enhanced its value by establishing specific relations of subjection, something must be said about the distribution of wealth and tribute, and the more general problem of the constitution of the colonial subject. (24)

Importantly, Mbembe goes on to argue that "postcolonial African regimes have not invented what they know of government from scratch. Their knowledge is the product of several cultures, heritages, and traditions of which the features have become entangled over time, to the point where something has emerged that has the look of 'custom' without being reducible to it, and partakes of 'modernity' without being wholly included in it" (24–25). As we have seen above, Bwakamabé's exercise of power is premised on the notion of hereditary power, which is then ritualized both as divinely sanctioned and unaccommodating of dissent. Lopès's novel opens with an official note from the Secretary-General and Assistant Secretary-General in Charge of Written Works of the "Inter-African Association of Francophone Censors" explaining why it has been decided not to ban the book, even though it is considered "an offence to good taste." The powers that be have decided that, instead of censoring books, "[f]rom now on, we shall allow publication and sale of all works. In exchange, every book, every film, every record, every cassette that ought to be struck by our interdiction for the safeguard of our morals, will be preceded by an introduction: written, visual or oral; prepared or delivered by Us." Interestingly, Lopès's novel was, in matter of fact, banned by Mobutu's operatives for several months after its publication. The author of "Be Warned" opines that "Daddy [Bwakamabé] does not exist, cannot exist, in these days and on this continent. He is the fruit of a macabre imagination that is close to frenzy: a comic strip character." The official stance, issued in regal tones (the use of "Us") is to deny that dictators like Bwakamabé can and do exist in Africa, and to threaten dire consequences for those who may dare to suggest that Bwakamabé's regime is anything but benign. Furthermore, the government censor is of the opinion that the novelist is "a white man who has had the chance to spend some time in Africa. An African worthy of the name would never dare to write such trash. A true son of Africa would never describe his milieu and epoch with such detachment. We are dealing with an unscrupulous forger, whose work is stitched together with threads . . . WHITE ones, for sure" (np). Thus, written or audiovisual materials will still be banned; only the method will have changed. Conscientious African writers and thinkers are blackmailed into silence or mediocrity by the prospect of being viewed as "playthings of a vast plot orchestrated by obscure forces that seek to spread subversion to every corner of our dear continent and introduce foreign, destructive ideologies" (np). The equation of dissent with treason is rather obvious, as is the equation of the local/internal with goodness and the foreign/external with danger or negativity. The value of an idea or thought is associated not with its potential to do good, but with whether it is "ours" or "theirs." The designation of a "true son of Africa," or "an African worthy of the name," is the preserve of the "sovereign." Effective citizenship has more to do with the sovereignty's notion of the subject's loyalty than with the rights inherent in birthright. And if, as Mbembe writes, "[t]o exercise sovereignty is to exercise control over mortality and to define life as the deployment and manifestation of power" (12), the exercise of free will, conscience, and fundamental human rights can and does expose those subjected to sovereignty to injury or death, or both. The Censor's warning is but an extension of the voice of the dictator, which never tires of issuing decrees and proclamations, all of which have a tremendous terror component. The unspoken injunction not to express dissident opinions or thoughts is daily issued through State Radio. Bwakamabé's accession to power, for instance, is proclaimed over the national airwaves while "the radio thrust its speech into every hearth of a town suddenly turned to stone" (3). The thrust of the despot's ordinances is as terror inducing as the military and police weapons endlessly leveled against the populace.

The effective silencing of the general population is a recurrent theme in *The Laughing Cry*. The narrator's tone emphasizes the ponderous weight and harshness of this silence, in counterpoint to the ubiquitous tones of military music. State Radio and "*The Southern Cross*, the one and only weekly newspaper of the Republic" (12), dominate the public space and opinion. The unchanging nature of everyday life is exemplified by a typical reference: "All day the radio had kept its *battery* of military music, interrupting it at regular intervals, without any additional comment, to *rebroadcast that morning's communiqué, delivered in the tones of a pedantic schoolmaster. Twiddling the knobs, I managed to pick up everything, except what was happening now and what I wished to know*" (10; my emphasis). A population without any reasonable recourse to the one-sided verbal and psychological assault of the dictator is here couched as a population constantly battered by a hardened schoolmaster accustomed to giving dictation unto others. The Chief has arrogated to himself the privilege of virtually closing off alternative modes of information and thinking, choosing instead to deliver repetitions of the same message in the same *master* voice. Alternative interpretations of the internal status quo may be heard on Radio France-International, through the voice of the departed Polépolé, for instance, but only at the risk of capture and punishment because, since the Chief's accession, "[his] eyes watched the whole country, under the sun's rays, under those of lightbulbs and kerosene lamps, as well as in the dark. Whenever we passed a public building, they gazed down on us. Whenever we entered shops or offices, we met their stare[.] ... Whenever we picked up a newspaper, there they were. Whenever we flicked through a book, they jumped out of the pages" (26). The ever-watching and everywhere eyes of the Chief underscore the surveillance exercised by his regime, but of greater note is the ritualized and mandated imprinting of the image of the *chef* on both private and public spaces. It is in the newspaper headlines and in all published books. His image (and putative presence) transgresses the boundary between the public and the private, going so far as to invade the intensely personal and private sphere: "Whenever my mother undressed, she took care to cover his photo with her scarf, a photo that she always kept near her bed beside her crucifix and her *gri-gri*" (26). The juxtaposition of the narrator's mother's crucifix and *gri-gri*—as objects that empower and protect their user from harm—is in itself revealing and troubling. His spies and informants, we are told, operate both in the open and in the dark.

In his *The Dialectics of Oppression in Zaire*, Michael Schatzberg writes extensively on "The State as Ear," "The State as Bandit," etc. In the former, Schatzberg notes, "We should view surveillance in Zaire both in [Anthony] Giddens's sense, as a means of gathering and storing information necessary to exert control and supervision, as a means of constant reassurance to a psychologically insecure politico-commercial bourgeoisie" (31). Schatzberg relevantly quotes a source in which, for Mobutu, vigilance means

> keen attention, sustained surveillance, exercised on all elements susceptible of making an attempt, from near or far, from the interior or exterior, on the life or survival of the State, its basic institutions, or its organs. Vigilance must lead the masses to unmask the enemies of the fatherland in their physiognomical changes and, in all their forms, to seek them out in their lair [*repère*], to master them and to smother their calling to destruction, anarchy, and trouble. (31–32)

Moreover, Bwakamabé takes recourse to a "logic" of allegedly African authenticity, which sees the secret ballot as a distortion, a kind of *falsity* "dead against the education of our ancestors" (75). After all, "the country was one big family: *I, I am the father. And you, you are my children. All the citizens are my children . . .*" (75, author's emphasis). Schatzberg observes that

> legitimate governance in Zaire, and in much of Africa, is based on the tacit normative idea that government stands in the same relationship to its citizens as a father does to his children. There is a substratum of belief which views paternal authority as legitimate as long as the implicit understanding of rights and duties contained in the moral matrix of legitimate governance is not violated. When African political leaders behave as responsible fathers; when they care for, nurture, and provide security; when they do not seek eternal power and they respect the normal rotation of generations; legitimacy, and thus stability, are maintained. But when they violate the implied cultural norms and unarticulated promises of political "fatherhood," legitimacy erodes, tensions mount, and instability, repression, or both, ensue. (97)

Whatever the merits of this postulation may be, tropes of infantilization and the authentic/inauthentic are at work here. Citizens are posited as immature children incapable of understanding or meaningfully participating in their own governance. The father as head of the family invokes the symbology of the division of the body into zones of descending importance: the placement of the father ("Daddy" Bwakamabé) as the (thinking) head of the (national) family implies not only the authority (and authoring capacity) of the patriarch but also the supposed irrationality of those subordinated to/by the father. As Schatzberg writes concerning Mobutu's Congo,

> The incessant refrain that there can be but one chief, one father, as well as the tendency toward the centralization of power it rationalizes, legitimizes, and reinforces, is replicated at each lower level of the state hierarchy. Every little father-chief wants to act as a small-scale model of the president, as one who ostensibly encouraged subordinates to make decisions and demonstrate initiative, but who by subtle gesture and attitude actually discourages it. (95)

The conflation of gender and social class categories serves in the impeachment of the unlettered and women. Bwakamabé's all-purpose *maître*, who narrates most of the story, observes acidly that "[f]or him [Bwakamabé] a minister must instantly obey the Head of State, like a woman and children their husband or father" (49). As a hypermasculine and idolized entity, Bwakamabé has perfected strategies for the feminization of his ministers, none of whom is female, as well as the general male population. So widespread is misogyny that even the *maître*, himself no more powerful than his own wife, comments, apropos of a married woman and her husband, that "she's just a space in which to leave his signature" (8). Moreover, he adds, "[m]arriage is an institution for the benefit of the family, the clan, the tribe" (8). As for the civilian population, except for short-lived, strategic moments, Bwakamabé has little use for "the illiterate and irresponsible populace," which he considers as chaotic and as an impediment in the acquisition and maintenance of despotic power. Thus, according to him,

> To abandon the choice of guides for the community to a chaotic mass, was to renounce that innate sense of responsibility that resides in the breasts of all those who feel themselves to be chiefs. He knew he had been chosen by the Eternal Will, and that it would be a sacrilege to put that in the balance with a population armed with votes. There could be from thence forward ... no question of ceding power to a rabble bemused by Satan. (75)

Consequently, this "chaotic," "irresponsible," "impressionable" ("bemused by Satan") "rabble" must be kept under surveillance at all times: "He was ready to fight, to die and to kill to keep in his pious hands the power conferred on him by God. Yes, African societies, by tradition and historical necessity, needed to be controlled and well directed" (74–75). Schatzberg reports that in Mobutu's Zaire, "[t]here is still another way that leaders abuse the imagery of father and family.

Henri Lopès's *The Laughing Cry* as Emblematic African Dictator Novel

Since flexible symbols permit political leaders to portray those who rebel as wayward children, political repression against them becomes parental discipline" (95). Little wonder, then, that at a meeting with members of his government to discuss new approaches to governance, "[s]omeone immediately replied by extolling the virtues of the one-party system. It was the only realistic solution to the country. Democracy must be pursued, of course, but not by aping the whites. Authorizing several political parties would only encourage a realignment in antagonistic tribal blocs, and encourage fratricidal conflict" (73). Multiparty democracy had never worked in Africa, argued this speaker, because "Africa was not Europe" (73). More shocking than this self-negating thinking is the rhetoric of the need for a strongman: "The next speaker stressed that the fight against underdevelopment imposed the need for a strong regime: 'Don't be afraid of words, we must have a dictatorship: a dictatorship expressed in the interests of the people.' And he cited, by way of examples, pell-mell, Nasser, the countries of the Far East, Stalin, Hitler and Mussolini" (73). The speaker here enunciates the official attitude that the pursuit *and* maintenance of power for its own sake—at all costs—takes precedence over the interests of the people in whose name the dictator overthrew his predecessor. Early in the novel, the narrating *maître* timidly reports that "we, the common people, understood nothing of . . . the war of the Great" (16). Repeatedly throughout the novel Bwakamabé asserts that (the game of) power is no joke, and routinely complains about "the solitude of those who govern" (232), setting himself up as the exemplar of the statesman and visionary in opposition to "[our] intellectuals here [who] only want to play politics" (162).

Mbembe argues that the commandement defines itself as a cosmology, or, more simply, as a fetish. Quoting M. Coquet, Mbembe defines a fetish as, "among other things, an object that aspires to be made sacred; it demands power and seeks to maintain a close, intimate relationship with those who carry it" (111). At the ceremony marking Bwakamabé's investiture, reports the narrator, "one of the traditional priests announced that all disquiet should be chased from our hearts: that the Nation was saved, because the sun of the shadows, which that night diffused its pale yellow light, had transmitted to us the message of the ancestors: they had chosen Bwakamabé Na Sakkadé to lead all the Djabotama and impose their will upon all the other tribes of the new country, as defined by the Uncles" (30). A number of things are significant about this passage. First, a *traditional* priest announces the new *chef* as a messianic figure come to save the Nation. Secondly, Bwakamabé comes to bring light to a new country allegedly threatened by the darkness of oppositional politics advocated by Polépolé. Significantly, as Schatzberg has observed, one of Mobutu's most used honorifics was Mobutu Moyi ("Mobutu the light, the sun"). As "supreme chief of the Bangala and father of the large Zairian family, [Mobutu] has absolutely no intention of letting other sources of light and competence compete for popular allegiance" (95). Thirdly, though Bwakamabé is ritually invested with ancestral authority to become leader of all the people of the country, he will go on to identify with, and promote, solely the interests of his ethnic group, the Djabotama. Elsewhere in the text, Bwakamabé insists, "I must be surrounded by my own people and no one else" (20). Since the hated Polépolé was a Djassikini, the Djassikini become the pariahs of the country by virtue of association to the exiled Polépolé. Indeed, all national misadventures will be blamed on the Djassikini, including their alleged support of communism (which is never mentioned by its overt name). Fourthly, the interests of the Djabotama will be imposed upon the rest of the country, a country whose political and economic interests are overseen by the French. Indeed, Bwakamabé has no greater role model than Papa de Gaulle, nor a political ally more loyal than "France, our mother country" (180). After all, Bwakamabé's de facto minister of security is an "Uncle," Monsieur Gourdain, more powerful than any member of the president's cabinet. A former soldier who fought for France in all the major colonial wars and was rewarded for it, Bwakamabé continues to consider himself a French citizen. The high point of his visit to France, at his own insistence and high cost to the country's treasury, is marked by a speech made by his hosts, "a eulogy for a country whose history was common with that of France and whose President was a tried and true friend of the French people, tied to them by many bonds, beginning with that incomparable common instrument of thought: language" (216). It is important to note that Bwakamabé's most enduring trait is his capacity for dictation. The narrator reports that in primary school "[Bwakamabé] had learned more quickly than his fellows and had distinguished himself in the eyes of the monitors by his exceptional qualities," and though he was not admitted to the great French colleges, "he would never make a single spelling mistake in his dictations" (12). Accordingly, as Recreating Father of the Nation, he is routinely depicted speaking a kind of "received" French: "Daddy was reading aloud, following the words with his finger and articulating each syllable with the care of a master giving dictation, bringing out as clearly as possible the difference between the é, the è and the *ai*, on the one hand; the *o* and the *au* on the other; and, finally, between the *i* and the *u*" (95). This fastidiousness with things learned by rote is not lost on his hosts:

> By the approving nods of the French authorities, one noted their satisfaction in tasting the correctness of his accent. They had something to be proud of in the education they had given. Colonialism, contrary to fashionable notions, had other things than crimes on its conscience. The Chief expressed himself *as custom demanded in all the speeches delivered in such circumstances, not omitting to celebrate the secular bonds, the communality of the linguistic instrument, the eternal glory of*

Henri Lopès's *The Laughing Cry* as Emblematic African Dictator Novel

> France, land of liberty and the rights of man, which she had so generously exported to the African continent, hitherto sunk in barbarism. (216–217; my emphasis)

Bwakamabé emerges as one who has, in all his years of service to the French, including during his presidency, learned his lessons passively and gratefully, and who prizes obedience and submission. When his subjects show signs of "laziness," resistance, or possible insurrection, he readily responds that the remedy is "[n]othing for it but the methods of Indochina and North Africa" (168). It is instructive that, during the torture of Captain Yabaka before his ultimate killing for allegedly challenging Bwakamabé's supremacy, one of the soldiers involved muses that what they were doing in the post-independence era was "exactly as they had been taught during the colonial epoch . . . as blacks yesterday thrashed their fellow blacks. Yesterday, they took their orders from the white man. But today, . . . ?" (246).

Mbembe's thesis in his essay "Necropolitics," that "the ultimate expression of sovereignty resides, to a large degree, in the power and the capacity to dictate who may live and who must die" (11–12), applies as much to the excesses of rampant despotism as depicted in Lopès's novel. Bwakamabé appropriates power under the guise of saving his nation "from the abyss" of a liberal politics and praxis. Henceforth he will be bitterly opposed to "intellectuals," however wrong-headed their understanding of sovereignty. At the beginning of the novel, the university-educated young men rightly argue that "de Gaulle was a paternalist," and that "France was not our friend. We were merely her neo-colony" (5) and must, therefore, "cut the umbilical cord" (3). This stands in sharp contrast to the dependency-conscious politics of Bwakamabé and his cronies who cannot tolerate the idea of striving for complete independence. At one moment in the novel, one of the Chief's sisters, Za Héléne, reports that her house has been burglarized; that, therefore, the bandits who did it are creating a serious security situation in the country. The people, she claims, are disappointed:

> And the whites, above all the Uncles, they say if it goes on like this, they want to go home, *wo!* They think highly of the countries of coffee, cocoa and oil. Paradises upon the continent, free of bandits, and most important of all, with guaranteed security of capital. *But now,* if they really go, what will become of the country? *But now,* if they stop investing, where will you draw your power from? This must stop. You must punish. Make examples. (97)

At an extraordinary meeting of the Council of Ministers that same night, draconian measures are announced concerning the stealing of things big and small: "Any person (citizen of the country or foreigner) who stole a bull, or just a piece of wool, or anything inferior, equivalent, intermediary or superior; furniture, building or ringing piece of metal, would have an ear cut off; in case of a second offence, the second ear would go; in case of a third, amputation of the right hand

and in case of a fourth, public execution in the main square" (97). The fictional account here is clearly an allusion to Jaafar Numeiry's Sudan after his imposition of *sharia* law. What is involved here is clearly an act of devaluation of the life of the alleged offender in an exercise that privileges private property, especially where that private property is the desired object of (white) foreigners.

Soon after the reported burglary at the Chief's sister's home, Bwakamabé is depicted musing about the relationship between instituting ruthless discipline and protecting national wealth—and one's reputation as a resolute and respected leader. His point of reference is "Jeddah, the emirs, the oases, the harems, the oil, the royalties, the dollars, the dollars, the dollars . . ." (95). He concludes that the reason for the temporary relapse is

> Discipline. Discipline. Civic spirit. We have lost that. People don't work any more. They steal. The black man has reverted to his blackness. We must reintroduce the lash[.] . . . [In the French army] we were well trained[.] . . . Could do sensational things, that I could never have attempted in an army commanded by blacks. In any case, there weren't any in those days. Learnt discipline. A soldier is nothing if he doesn't know how to obey. All men must learn how to obey. If not, no question of being able to lead. And it was precisely in the French Army that I learned how to obey. (95–96; italics in text)

Immediately after the Council of Ministers has passed the new laws against so-called indiscipline,

> the whole capital, civilian, military and diplomatic, was summoned . . . for a [light and sound] spectacle in the marketplace. Daddy wanted to kill two birds with one stone: 'Punish with maximum suffering' all the robbers and the 'Gang of Twenty,' with their accomplices—all in one go. The officials, as if in rank, were ranged along the stands, fascinated by the circle of white light. An orchestra opened with the popular *beguine*, 'May Daddy Bwakamabé live for centuries and centuries.' (98)

In the silence imposed by his infamous *juju* over the audience, Bwakamabé reiterates his theme that "we were in Africa and that in the real Africa of our ancestors, the chief of the village was the sole master. In Africa, opposition was unknown. There was applause, and it was difficult to decide whether it came from the *labouring masses*, the national officials or the diplomatic corps" (98; emphasis in text). He berates the accused gang of "Moscow's apprentices," declaring that "if these puppets didn't like the country, they had only 'to go and make themselves heard among the snows of the Red gulags'" (98). What follows in this spectacle of blood and death, summoned ostensibly to demonstrate the Chief's management of order and discipline, is so horrific that the narrator confesses himself unable to adequately tell all about it: "Let no one look here for an account of this bloody circus stunt. How could one describe the scene of violence which followed, and grew ever more atrocious, with the devilish rhythm of an animated cartoon?" (100). The narrator's rueful meditation above raises the important question of the inadequacy of language to apprehend accurately or comprehensively the atrocities perpetrated by postcolonial dictatorships. Elsewhere in the novel, the narrator comments on the shortcomings of prose, or even his own narrative capacity, to encompass the daily, the routine, happenings at the palace and wherever else his duties take him: "To recreate the meetings of the Council of Ministers a book cannot serve my purpose. A film would offer greater possibilities" (71).

Stylistically and discursively, Lopès's novel succeeds in explicating how a product of the colonial school, faced in his own country with the challenges of modernization and social uplift occurring in a rapidly changing continent, opts to reproduce both the discourse and the practices of colonization. Achille Mbembe writes,

> [T]hroughout the nineteenth and first half of the twentieth centuries, governing in a colony meant first and foremost having *commandement* over the native. "Civilization" initially made its presence felt in its brutal form, war, through the act of conquest—that is, the right to kill and make force prevail. Exercising command thus meant to compel people to perform "obligations." It also meant, as in an army, to proceed by orders and demands. *Commandement* itself was simultaneously a tone, an accoutrement, and an attitude. Power was reduced to the right to demand, to force, to ban, to compel, to authorize, to punish, to reward, to be obeyed. (32)

The rise of the dictator in Lopès's novel follows a trajectory informed by the values of the "command and be obeyed" discourse of the colonizing enterprise, and the role played by the police and military in the promotion of "progress" in a zone considered "dark," "backward," "chaotic." And none is more qualified to effect the "civilizing" project than the fetishes steeped in the lore of power-taking. As Mbembe eloquently posits,

> In the postcolony, fetishistic power is invested not only in the person of the autocrat but also in the persons of the *commandement* and of its agents—the party, policemen, soldiers, administrators and officials, middlemen, and dealers. It turns the postcolonial autocrat into an object that feeds on applause, flattery, lies. By exercising raw power, the fetish, as embodied in the autocrat and the agents of autocracy, takes on an autonomous existence . . . In this situation, one should not underestimate the violence that can be set in motion to protect the vocabulary used to denote or speak of the *commandement*, and to safeguard the official fictions that underwrite the apparatus of domination, since these are essential to keeping the people under the *commandement*'s spell. . . . (111)

Regarding the "light and sound" spectacle above, the narrator states, Bwakamabé "assured [members of the diplomatic corps] that such things had never been seen, but that, thanks to God, and above all thanks to Himself, inspired by God, this slide into decadence was going to stop[.] . . . He described what was done in the Persian Gulf. They didn't joke there. They cut off the hands of the robbers. Gba!" (99). Importantly, no thought is entertained about the objective economic and social conditions that produce so-called criminals, or why only those who allegedly rob the Chief's sister are worthy of being made an example of. That the accused robbers are publicly savaged alongside political dissidents is telling: even the appearance of political dissidence is regarded as egregious a crime as, say, robbery with violence. Not to be missed is Bwakamabé's emulation of the Persian Gulf states as a model for how to govern, that is, in Mbembe's words again, to "exercise control over mortality and to define life as the deployment and manifestation of power" (12). Nor can it elude our notice that Daddy's carefully orchestrated spectacle is a distillation of raw power, an occasion to send a serious warning to all and sundry that any deviation from his mandates will meet the same end as those publicly and officially, and to this extent *legally*, murdered, since the Chief *is* the law. This last point is emphasized by Schatzberg:

> Interactions between the political sector and the judiciary are complicated further because since February 1972 the spoken words of the Zairian head of state have had the force of law. After each of Mobutu's public speeches, the minister of justice prepares relevant extracts for promulgation as laws of the land. Now a major source of Zairian law, legislation through Mobutu's spur-of-the-moment remarks creates special difficulties for Zairian justice because presidential asides rarely provide concrete guidance for magistrates who have to prosecute or render judgment. (108)

In the novel, under Bwakamabé's regime, people are drilled to accept the status quo as natural, therefore eternal. The system is identified with the fatherland; an enemy of the regime is by extension a traitor or a foreign agent.

One more example of the dictator's megalomania and capacity for violence will suffice. The event is the International Book Day, organized by the writers' society in the gymnasium named for the dictator, exhibiting literary works by all the "acceptable" writers of the country, but not including a recently released writer whose works were still banned. Bwakamabé opens the exhibit and is hailed as "the new black Augustus, great friend of literature and the arts, protector of all creative spirits" (101). The writers' society had neglected to include the Marshal's publication in the exhibit, so an impromptu Council of Ministers is called to explain why. In the oppressive silence of the meeting chamber, "[m]embers of the presidential entourage kept bringing more copies of the same book, laying them like bricks on Daddy's table" (102). The failure to exhibit Daddy's one book results in another cabinet reshuffle, with the portfolio of the Minister of Culture being taken on by the Marshal himself. Daddy's fury—"He hammered the table with his fist. And he talked, abused, talked, abused, showed his fist, insulted, talked" (102)—may proceed from a sense of being slighted, but it is patently misplaced, given how much verbiage his regime produces in the form of "patriotic" speeches, edicts, proclamations, radio and newspaper addresses, communiqués, bannings, exhortations, etc. Yet, for all that, the paranoia demonstrated during this incident underlies the ever-present sense of insecurity. While there is State Radio—"Our guards are still there, the radio blaring out military music. Played by whom?" (117)—and *The Southern Cross* with its maladroit Aziz Sonika of the "pen steeped in hyena's bile, and his own oaths full of spittle" (13), there is radio grapevine (*radio trottoire* or "pavement radio") of Kinshasa fame, one of the very few weapons that the oppressed must use to counteract the heavy-handed rhetoric of the *commandement*.

The Laughing Cry is a polyphonic novel whose multiple voices encompass those of the *commandement* and its functionaries, the sometimes ambivalent voices of the "common masses," as well as excerpts from local and foreign newspapers, political slogans and chants, popular songs, proverbs, and folktales. The complex tale of a chronic dictatorship could not be told otherwise. The narration of *The Laughing Cry* alternates between that of the palace *chef*-cum-procurer and that of the exiled "young compatriot ex-Cabinet Secretary." The latter often chides the former for his lack of political consciousness. In the first exchange of communication between the two, the narrator admits to a lack of understanding of all that is going on, which prompts him to write to the ex-Cabinet Secretary. The latter excoriates the *maître* for writing so negatively about the intellectuals and those who, in general, were critical of the newly acceded Chief. The ex-Cabinet Secretary advises his correspondent to "[c]onsider that in scoffing too much at us in the name of some undigested truth you may be playing the enemy's game. If you want to be of service to the country, make haste to offer us a positive hero in your story" (34).

As to the narrative form, the "young compatriot" ventures, "Whilst reading your work, I was constantly asking myself how to classify it. Sometimes you aspire to the precision of a historian or a sociologist; sometimes you resemble more the *griots* in whom we see only dream-peddlars and entertainers, and others a key to decoding the life of the village" (34). In other words, the "young compatriot" urges a broader perspective, and a more critical consciousness. Elsewhere, in tones reminiscent of the writing of the African American slave narrative, the "young compatriot" urges caution against revealing information that could harm those still vulnerable to Bwakamabé's power. He counsels that in the struggle against such a formidable force, it is necessary to keep anonymous the names of those organizing against the dictator. The *maître* is warned against revealing his amorous escapades with the dictator's wife and the Custom Inspector's: "I ask myself whether one has any right to confuse politics and porn, without risking that the one will spoil the other?" (95). In a clever twist which "flips" the narrator and the author, Lopès uses the ex-Cabinet Secretary's correspondence to broach the dual subject of the why and how of writing—the use of appropriate form and the taking of a political stance. From exile, the ex-Cabinet Secretary reminds his correspondent,

> When you first broached to me your idea of writing these satirical and critical memoirs of a slice in the life of a dictator during the last part of our century, I encouraged you, and even offered my collaboration. *It is a question, for me, I repeat, of contributing to the struggle against the tyrant Bwakamabé.* Now, by the way the manuscript is developing, as for instance in this latest installment, I fear that in yielding too much to intimate memories, *you are mixing up genres and losing sight of the objective of all committed writing. And the African book coming from these times, and having any respect for itself, cannot choose but to be committed.* . . . (95; my emphasis)

Faced with increased opposition at home, including armed resistance, and a withdrawal of support by his European allies, Bwakamabé faces crisis after crisis. At the height of it all, the narrator records his astonishment at reading the news of the arrest of seven members of a group called the Telema Seven: "*An opposition declaring itself at home? An armed opposition, working as commandos?* As life went on, I had finally convinced myself that the heroes would never more emerge from legends and epics where earlier epochs had definitively enclosed them. I looked attentively at each of the names. *All of the tribes were represented, including the Djabotama. And among them, a woman!*" (224; my emphasis). The narrator will soon flee into exile, finally having understood that the politics he has so far studiously avoided has already snagged him in its coils: "But nowadays, in our country, politics no longer waits for you to come to it. A wild beast that bursts blindly into the village, in all the rage of despair[.] . . . Who, in these circumstances, can still find his philosophy in peacefully mending his nets?" (242). Stylistically, his now more astute observations of conditions in the country he recently fled become part of the overall fabric of the novel. Two such observations—"Yabaka was only a mango fallen in the first rains. Since then, other storms have struck even the soundest of our plants" (250); and "A man can root out a mango tree, or even a plantation of mangoes, but never the whole species" (256)—derived from orature, speak to Lopès's unapologetic mining of African literary resources demonstrated in the writing of this novel, as in his other works. Secondly, tribute is paid to the unyielding Yabaka (his sister would later join in the now full-fledged struggle against the dictator) and all those who, over the decades, heed the call to fight injustice. Lopès's provocative novel metaphorically offers testimony of a season of dishonor in a continental context. Its act of denunciation of those who stop their nations from becoming what they can become is accompanied by a rallying call for solidarity among those who must act to bring about change.

Works Cited

Gĩtĩtĩ, Gĩtahi. "Ferocious Comedies: Henri Lopès' *The Laughing Cry* and Ngũgĩ wa Thiong'o's *Matigari* as 'Dictator Novels.'" *Ngũgĩ wa Thiong'o: Texts and Contexts*. Ed. Charles Cantalupo. Trenton, NJ: Africa World Press, 1995: 211-226. Print.

Labou Tansi, Sony. *Life and a Half*. Trans. Alison Dundy. Bloomington: Indiana UP, 2011. Print.

Lopès, Henri. *The Laughing Cry: An African Cock and Bull Story*. New York: Readers International, 1987. Print.

Mariam, Alemayehu. "The Toxic Ecology of African Dictatorships." *Pambazuka News* Dec. 2009: 1. Print.

Mbembe, Achille. "Necropolitics." *Public Culture* 15.1 (2003): 11–12. Trans. Libby Meintjes. Durham: Duke UP, 2003. Print.

———. *On the Postcolony*. Berkeley: U of California P, 2001. Print.

Schatzberg, Michael. *The Dialectics of Oppression in Zaire*. Bloomington and Indianapolis: Indiana UP, 1988. Print.

Thomas, Dominic. "Sony Labou Tansi—The Conscience of Africa and the Voice of the People." Introduction. *Life and a Half*. By Sony Labou Tansi. Trans. Alison Dundy. Bloomington: Indiana UP, 2011: ix-xii. Print.

The Last King of Africa: The Representation of Idi Amin in Ugandan Dictatorship Novels

OLIVER LOVESEY

Idi Amin Dada (1925–2003), self-proclaimed President of Uganda (1971–79) after a military coup against Milton Obote, may be the prototype of the brutal African dictator. He was a masterful media manipulator who ruled through the power of both a bewitching charisma and spectacles of unimaginable terror. A man of questionable sanity, though supremely capable of manipulating such a reputation to his benefit, Amin claimed to be the last "uncrowned" King of Scotland, though in his surreal flamboyance he was rivaled by Jean-Bédel Bokassa, who had himself crowned as the emperor of the Central African Republic in a ceremony modeled on that of Napoleon.[1] Amin was a homicidal, kleptocratic megalomaniac who drained the national treasury, gutted his country's infrastructure, murdered nearly half a million Ugandans, threatened war with three of his neighbours, and directly or indirectly inaugurated genocidal actions that have contributed to the ongoing destabilization of much of central Africa. He may be seen as the precursor of the murderous and possibly insane Joseph Kony, whose Lord's Resistance Army continues to operate with its child soldiers in northern Uganda and elsewhere today. Though Kony was indicted in 2005 by the international criminal court on charges of crimes against humanity and war crimes, he remains at large.[2]

As the Arab Spring or Jasmine Revolution that has witnessed the demise of dictators and dictatorships throughout North Africa enters the fall and winter of its hope and challenge, it is difficult to appreciate the absolutism enjoyed by dictators such as Idi Amin just over three decades ago. He fashioned himself as a pro-colonial stalwart and also as an anticolonial provocateur at will, playing the game of global, Cold War power politics for personal gain. Amin had been a member of a British colonial regiment, the King's African Rifles, and he had taken part in anti-Mau Mau (Kenya Land and Freedom Army) military actions in Kenya, as one of what Giles Foden calls the "colonial bloodhounds" (129).[3] He was widely admired for his athletic prowess in swimming, boxing, and rugby, but feared for his clandestine involvement in the affairs of Sudan and the Congo as well as illegal activities. Facing arrest for atrocities and smuggling, Amin staged a coup, stating that he would hold elections and free political prisoners. A week later the semi-literate Amin declared himself president and rapidly established Uganda as a military state and began a series of moves against all intellectuals as well as a virtual policy of ethnic cleansing.[4] Amin had styled himself a Field Marshal in the postcolonial Ugandan army, and in the mid-1970s he was the Chair of the Organization of African Unity. He had appeared to be the model of the pro-colonial postcolonial ruler until his outrages made him a liability to the former colonial overlords and he sought the fraternity of other dictators in Libya and East Germany.

Amin's police state would quickly become what Henry Kyemba, the health minister, would describe as "a state of blood."[5] In 1972, he expropriated property from Asians and Europeans in Uganda, and in August of that year expelled nearly 100,000 "people of East Indian origin, extraction, or ancestry" (Nazareth 111), many Ugandan-born, leading to economic collapse. The 1976 Israeli hostage crisis at Entebbe airport and the Israeli military's daring rescue in Operation Entebbe intensified the growing international condemnation of the Amin regime, and the following year he claimed to be the Conqueror of the British Empire. His increasingly erratic behaviour in this period sparked widespread rumours that he was mentally ill and that he engaged in cannibalism.

Amin's self-mythologizing and catachrestic modes of expression gained much Western media attention, though he was represented as a comic buffoon and, in racist fashion, as a typical African dictator rather than an opportunistic fascist. Recent texts such as *Dictators' Homes: Lifestyles of the World's Most Colourful Despots* (2006)[6] and *Sex Lives of the Great Dictators* (1996) and even comedy recordings such as *The Collected Broadcasts of Idi Amin* (1975) by British comedian John Bird overlook the suffering of victims and gloat on the cartoonish outlandishness of dictators like Amin, as if their "lifestyles" are merely variations on those of other wealthy, powerful celebrities. Amin's time in the spotlight quickly came to an end following his grandiose claims to territory in other African countries, when he launched an invasion of Tanzania. His defeat at the hands of President Julius Nyerere—the war was fashioned in personal, pugilistic terms by Amin—signaled the demise of Amin's power. He lived in exile in Libya and then Saudi Arabia until his death in 2003, though there was a failed attempt to re-establish him as president during an abortive invasion in 1989, and during his final illness there was a bid to allow his return to die in Uganda.

Such an almost cartoonish monster, a self-styled, jovial African Mohammad Ali and a terrifying African Adolf Hitler, poses a particular challenge for novelistic representation, as his reality appears to be the stuff of magical realism with a shadow of the macabre, the grotesque, the gothic, and the apocalyptic.[7] As Ngũgĩ wa Thiong'o wrote nearly two decades ago of the difficulty of finding a narrative mode to represent the outrages of neocolonial Kenya:

> A writer inhabits two places at the same time: the land of facts and that of fiction. But in a neo-colonial situation fiction seems to be more real than the absurdity of the factual world of a dictator. The world of a dictator has an element of pure fantasy. He will kill, jail, and drive hundreds into exile and imagine that he is actually loved for it. (*Moving* 157)

Peter Nazareth's *The General Is Up* (1984, 1991),[8] Giles Foden's *The Last King of Scotland* (1998), Moses Isegawa's *Snakepit* (1999, 2004),[9] and Goretti Kyomuhendo's *Waiting* (2007) are representative Ugandan dictatorship novels that employ variations of a realist mode of representation, unlike Ngũgĩ's own recent *Wizard of the Crow* (2007), though Foden's and Isegawa's novels engage with the melodramatic and sensational modes of popular adventure fiction. Written over three decades, they consider Idi Amin, his regime, and his legacy from very different perspectives, focusing on the historical figure or the devastation he caused, with the hope that he might be the last African dictator, the last self-styled King of Africa.[10] These novels consider the effects of Amin himself, his cult, and his reign of terror in different communities: the Asian-Ugandan, European expatriate, Ugandan professional middle class, and rural peasantry. They all consider the vexed question of who was responsible for Amin. The novels that tackle representation in close proximity to Amin or Amin surrogates (*The Last King of Scotland* and *Snakepit*) focus on the psychic battlefield within Amin himself or the poisonous symbiotic relationship that develops between him and some of those close to him. Paradoxically, the greater the distance from the person of Amin in the novels' focalization in temporal and geographic terms, the more powerful is the evocation of the pervasive destruction of his dictatorship on bodies and minds, locally, nationally, and internationally. Given the sobering legacy of Amin's oppression in Uganda and the rest of Africa, all of the novels encounter a perhaps inevitable difficulty with narrative closure. This chapter argues that the novels' accounts of the dictator's performances of false or invented traditionalism, distorted historiography, and bogus decolonization, as well as his media celebrity status, suggest that the spectacle of Amin has destabilized the integrity of Uganda and partly enabled a process of psychological re-colonization, given that his dictatorship was fostered by colonial tropes of subservient African chiefs. The texts indicate that perhaps Amin's most heinous legacy is the reinforcement of racist stereotypes about African dependence and helplessness, as well as a propensity for a distinctly "savage" brand of African fascism. Another enduring legacy of Amin's reign that these texts represent is the suppression of Ugandan literature within the nation's schools, a problem that is only recently being addressed.[11]

The General Is Up concludes with a coda or delayed epigraph from Ali Shalash: "History is sometimes changed by idiots" (145). While internationally-famous, Ugandan-born novelist Peter Nazareth's novel, first published in 1984, does not name Amin as its central, idiotic general, there are many parallels from his colonial past, seizure of power when the rightful president was out of the country, obsession with the British monarchy, and belief in a divine right to govern that point to Amin. Nazareth's first novel, *In a Brown Mantle* of 1972, had anticipated the coup and the later Asian expulsion. *The General Is Up* opens with the General's paranoid reasoning for expelling "diasporic and descended Asians" in Uganda,[12] but then its perspective broadens to show the effects of this policy on members of the country's civil service, obsessed with their own careers, their clubs, their community, and their sexual conquests. It resembles a novel by Graham Greene, cited later in the novel (137), about an outpost of empire into which a gothic monster has wandered whose viciousness they initially underestimate. Their office politics are juxtaposed with the delusional motivations and power politics of the ruler who appears to recognize the advantage of operating in an atmosphere of suspicion, paranoia, and perpetual uncertainty. He is the "new conqueror" before whose "iron throne" the bureaucrats "quiver" as in Christopher Okigbo's elegy from which Nazareth takes the novel's title (Okigbo 69). As Nazareth's character Ronald D'Mello—*The General Is Up*'s author, as the novel's metafictional epilogue indicates—recognizes, "[T]he rulers had succeeded in entering the minds of the conquered" (17), a process of a type of psychological re-colonization witnessed around the world when political crises make

> the American Jew [. . .] anglicise his name and reshape his nose[, . . .] the American black [desire] to leave his family and pass for white[, . . .] the Goan to insist that he is not an Indian[, . . .] the Indian to insist he is a college graduate and not a *dukawalla*. [. . .] They were the ultimate victims. (43)

The narrative gradually constricts to the day of expulsion, and in the process characters note the similarities in the strategies of control used by the colonial and neocolonial authorities in the country. Central to these strategies is the creation of division within and between cultural, ethnic, national, and other communities and the promotion of the spectre of particularly ethnic animosity that plays on the Western stereotype about African "tribalism" as the central cause of all African problems.

The novel strongly implies that England created Idi Amin, a postcolonial Frankenstein or Frankensteinian monster. In a bid to maintain its power over the country, the colonial power enabled the General, trained in its military, to stage a coup against his socialist predecessor, failing to anticipate that the puppet would quickly discover his muscles and become a major embarrassment and liability. Neocolonial exploitation "was a game that had to be played with finesse and skill! Instead, he was bull-headed" (56). The General operates through expulsion and murder on a grand scale, but he learned to manipulate from the imperial power whose forces have been "able to deceive half the world and rake in its wealth to build up that tiny little lump of shit growing out of the Atlantic" (34), as David D'Costa thinks. The expulsion of Asians is also treated as another example of conventional imperial practices: "Wherever they went, they brought in a buffer, scapegoat middle-class, usually from another part of the empire. So when Independence came, the people would be made in a thousand ways to blame these foreign scapegoats as the real cause of continued problems facing the people" (55). The expulsion itself was inspired by the British resistance to accepting its East Asian colonial subjects as citizens, the General's perverse Anglophilia, and, much later, the General's claim that his inspiration was divine. The role of all postcolonial survivors from all parts of the former commonwealth, laments D'Costa, is to be "the pallbearers for the dying British Empire" (63) and to continue to carry the freight of its legacy, though the novel indicates that divisions do arise between different communities, such as when D'Costa questions George Kapas, a Damibian, about his own commitment to the socialist policies of the previous regime. He suggests that George was devoted to merely "cocktail socialism" (93), a postcolonial version of radical chic, implying his responsibility for the General's takeover. D'Costa's departure is interpreted by George as the selfish act of a "not-yet-decolonized mind" (94).

The General is perceived in different ways by the novel's different diasporic communities, and he reinvents himself to suit his different audiences. As if to respond to some of the people's desire for a return to traditional values, for example, he bans miniskirts, and as if to satisfy the people's expectations of prophetic history, he claims to be a seer predicted in the Bible. He is by turns a Moslem, who makes alliances with General Effendi (probably Colonel Gadaffi of Libya), a supporter of his displaced predecessor, Milton Obote, a promoter of democracy, an opponent of dictatorship, as well as an apologist for the

British monarchy, apartheid South Africa, and Adolf Hitler. He is described in the novel variously as "the Devil Himself," "The Grim Reaper," "a real monster," or "an honorary White Man, a leper in the ranks of the non-white people" (39, 43, 109, 44). He is either a savvy manipulator or a psychopathic idiot savant who consistently wants to "remind the people how he had saved them from dictatorship" (52). He does speak truth occasionally by accident. Intending to declare that he had taken power to "restore democracy and suppress corruption," for example, he says instead that his plan was to "destroy democracy and impress corruption" (38). Later he proclaims, "I am the government and the government is me [....] I am the chosen one, the prophet, the representative of God!" (127).

The state of perpetual instability Amin inaugurates is illustrated by the bureaucratic limbo into which D'Costa and his family enter as their status as citizens shifts amid changing colonial and postcolonial realities. He is adrift in a Kafkaesque nightmare with elements of tragicomic farce in which at one stage he must renounce allegiance to the Queen of England as a colonial citizen and then swear allegiance to the queen as the head of state of a newly independent former colony. He must then attempt to verify his claim to be a citizen of Damibia as a member of the Asian diaspora. Nazareth extends the depiction of D'Costa's dilemma to involve the dehumanizing, ethical compromises powerless people are sometimes forced to make in impossible situations.

Nazareth's novel contains a type of self-conscious apologia for itself as an African dictatorship novel. Over and above its metafictional epilogue, there appears to be a recognition in the narrative's interrogation of postcolonial verities that the dictatorship novel is itself a generic stereotype about perceptions of Africa. The novel is both a conventionally "exotic novel about Africa" and "a work of fantasy or a draft horror film-script" as it is regarded by at least one of its naive readers, a fallible narratee (144). Its General is merely one of the ubiquitous "dictators of the banana republics" (141); he blandly claims that his coup was a "Liberation from dictatorship" (101). The murder of the General near the end of the novel displays performative justice that does not exist in the historical record. Despite a number of assassination attempts and the perpetual hope that international outrage—especially post-holocaust—would "not stand for it" (74), Amin departed only after he had almost destroyed Uganda, and the cost of his ousting—as Giles Foden and Goretti Kyomuhendo indicate in their first-person dictatorship novels about Amin—undermined the economy of Tanzania and the geopolitical stability of eastern Africa.

Unlike *The General Is Up*, which represents an Amin-like dictator from the perspective of the General's state apparatuses, *The Last King of Scotland* (1998) by English author Giles Foden, who spent many of his formative years in different parts of Africa, enables access to Amin via a foreign interloper. Foden's novel is set shortly after the expulsion that ends Nazareth's novel. Foden's focus is the psychological and moral effect of dictatorship on the dictator's erstwhile supporters and sycophants, and it appears to echo the Western media's fascination with the psychic conundrum of the Amin complex. As in a gesture more popularly performed in films such as *The Year of Living Dangerously* (1982) and *Missing* (1982)—and Foden's novel was the basis of a much celebrated, highly successful film from 2006[13]—the intrepid Westerner ventures by accident or design or via the dictates of career into an international disaster zone and an ethical quagmire. It is a formula presumably designed to enable the Western implied reader's easy access to alien worlds. *The Last King of Scotland* dramatically supplies more direct access to Amin than *The General Is Up* and far more immediate exposure to the physical danger of anyone in his presence. However, after the initial shock of the retrospective account of an encounter with Amin, there is a lengthy delay anticipating the dreaded first meeting. The protagonist of Foden's novel then quickly becomes a kind of shadow self, double, or doppelganger of the dictator in his role as personal physician—on arrival in Uganda he feverishly dreams of himself as both devil and Christ, as one guilty of horrendous crimes, and also, quoting *Hamlet*, as "the king of infinite space" (25)—and he must save his sanity in a terrifying situation though he uses his personal danger to justify his moral inertia. He is the type of the teflon expatriate, denying responsibility for protecting a Kenyan official tormented by Amin's soldiers in the matatu; or the Asians mistreated prior to expulsion; or Kay Amin, who dies after a botched abortion; or those, including his friend, about to be murdered in Amin's secret torture chambers; or the Israeli hostages at Entebbe airport.

The Last King of Scotland is a kind of latter-day *Heart of Darkness*, with a sometimes charming monster at its center. Conrad's "blank spaces" on the map of Africa that mesmerize Marlow (a continent that for Conrad collects all the anxieties about otherness and allows a space for the existential soul-searching and hand-wringing of one displaced European sailor and subsequent waves of modernist interpreters) (Conrad 66) are here represented by Uganda in the grip of Amin. Foden's narrator, Nicholas Garrigan, was "mad for maps" as a boy (19), and on his arrival in Uganda on the day of Amin's coup, he recalls the Fanonian image of the outline of the continent as "a gun in a holster" (33). This Scottish doctor at the center of Foden's discursively-diverse popular novel—a well-researched,[14] highly descriptive, action-packed historical thriller, with extracts from tourist tracts, historical documents, and medical texts, and intertextual connections with Conrad—has been co-opted by Amin, relocated into somewhat luxurious surroundings in the capital, and given a generous salary and a Toyota van expropriated from an expelled Asian. Like Conrad's Marlow, who is complicit in keeping Kurtz's last words hidden from his fiancée and by extension in covering up the enterprise of greed and murder that operates in King Leopold's private colony in the Congo under cover of a grand humanitarian mission, Garrigan narrates retrospectively from a position of guilt, self-justifying frustration, or convenient moral ambiguity. Foden suggests, however, that everyone was responsible for Amin, from Amin's cronies in the civil service and expats on the make to foreign powers and international media, but particularly the former colonial overlords. Just as "[a]ll Europe contributed to the making of Kurtz" (Conrad 116), so the world made Amin. The narrator conjures his memories of Amin as if he were talking to or even interrogating himself about his own responsibility, solipsistically trapped in a state of post-traumatic stress. Moreover, like Marlow in his anticipations of Kurtz, Garrigan's memory of Amin is a voice on "dictatorphone" tapes and finally on the telephone (20).

Idi Amin is represented here, as in *The General Is Up*, partly through his own extravagant, flamboyant, comically outrageous, threatening words, his fondness for hyperbole, and "his gangster sophistry" (324) that gained so much attention in Western media accounts and traded on stereotypes of the African big man. At the Ambassadors' Dinner, he is introduced with a string of titles and accolades, including "Lord of All the Beasts of the Earth and Fishes of the Sea and Conqueror of the British Empire in Africa in General and Uganda in Particular" (9). He styles himself a soldier, not a politician, the head of the national family, "the hero of Africa" (200), Africa's "saviour" (183), "the greatest politician in the world" (200), and even the "sexual lion" who contains "all the world's fathers" (226, 152). Before the end of the first chapter, Amin boasts that he has eaten human meat, as if he has gained power from violating every taboo. The dinner unfolds after his acknowledgement of cannibalism—he will later claim he learned the practice when he was a Mau Mau prisoner (298)—and the assembled local and foreign dignitaries fall with gusto on the roast kudu. In the aftermath of the shock of Amin's declaration and his canny catering to stereotypes about Africa and Africans, the collective gorging mimics Amin's actions as if there is a collective appetite for and a sharing of responsibility for moral myopia and even for eating Uganda itself. The chapter ends with a reference to crocodiles,[15] one of Amin's favourite methods of disappearing his enemies, and later Garrigan will witness Amin extracting organs from murdered military officials.

Amin's perverse fascination works on the protagonist, and it assumes a quasi-erotic power. It is "a quality of naked, visceral attraction that commanded the attention, mustering assent, overcoming resistance—fostering the loss of oneself, or so it felt, in the very modulations of his voice" (92). However, as with the young Scottish doctor's assertions that he can control wild animals like leopards, Amin's "elemental force" is associated with the animalistic, and Garrigan deludes himself that he can manage Amin, and he similarly does not question the racist stereotypes underlying his fascination. He can't shake his "deadly, addictive curiosity" regarding Amin, but despite increasing evidence of Amin's erratic violence, he continues to believe he can control his obsession (246). He has been amused and partly flattered by one particular delusion of Amin's: "Many of the Scottish people already consider me last King of the Scots. I am the first man to ask the British government to end their oppression of Scotland. If the Scots want me to be their King, I will" (111). Garrigan responds to Amin's physical breadth, his mythic force, his fondness for Scotland, and his somewhat old-fashioned, formal charm as well as his proverbial sayings. He experiences a quasi-erotic affection for Amin. He feels "[a]s if [he] were his subject" (115), or Amin's twin, and "[t]he strange idea came into [his] head that [his] body and Idi's were connected. Like the King's umbilical cord" (190).

Foden's Amin has been able to play the postcolonial card with considerable deftness, however. He calls for "African solutions to African problems" (160), and he refuses to be the puppet of the British or of any superpower. He plans to nationalize foreign businesses. Moreover, he speaks for the African diasporic community in his condemnation of slavery in the Americas, and he supports liberation movements and the rights of nations like Scotland and Ireland to independence. While clearly recognizing the fatuity of Amin's claims, Foden's protagonist is mesmerized by Amin's "wicked brilliance" (315), his "Jekyll-and-Hyde character" (316), and his always-impressive physicality even as his health declines. At the end of the novel, to a degree resembling Conrad's Marlow, but more like Francis Ford Coppola's Vietnam-war version of *Heart of Darkness* in his film *Apocalypse Now* (1979), where the Marlow character merges with the jungle as Colonel Kurtz does on first introduction, Garrigan recognizes, "I have become him," after admitting that he could contemplate murdering Amin (244). He knows that Amin is the state, the body politic, and Garrigan treats his body, afflicted, like the dictator of Ngũgĩ's *Wizard of the Crow*, with a mysterious illness.[16] Garrigan rejects syphilis as a diagnosis, settling instead for "a type of impulsive grandiose delusion that I now see might have been common to dictators" (185). Dictatorship is a viral pathogen infecting an individual but devastating a nation.

Isegawa's *Snakepit* focuses, like Nazareth's *The General Is Up*, on the Ugandan civil service, but in the period after the expulsion of Asian Ugandans and the departure of intellectuals when opportunities develop for the unscrupulous to gain fabulous wealth as "flag independence was giving way to economic independence" (6).[17] The central character, Bat Katanga, returns to his homeland after completing his degree at Cambridge to seek his fortune in the Ministry of Power and Communications. He works in close proximity to the powerful General Samson Bazooka Ondogar, who approximates Amin, and like him affects an aura of eccentricity "to impress or intimidate" (7). Bat, however, is the still—even empty—center of a novel concerned with the widespread effects of dictatorship within Uganda. It is, in Thackerayean mode, a novel without a hero, but it does have multiple centers of consciousness. The novel portrays the fatal moral compromises some are prepared to make to gain great wealth before a frenzied departure. It shows the demoralization of those swept up in or willfully entering the "snakepit" of greed, exploitation, incompetence, arbitrary brutality, terror, and chaos around Amin. Amin's regime is presented as a "national catastrophe" that engulfs everyone in widening circles around Bat and the General—their families, associates, rivals, and enemies—whose power and peril depend on Amin as the dictatorship's chaos accelerates (91). The overdetermined novel is in many ways a fast-paced, sometimes off-balance, morality play, but also, in its author's words, "an adventure story, set in the seventies . . . but with generals and intellectuals" (qtd. in Vazquez 149). The novel's dramatic confrontations between the powerful that have disastrous results for the powerless are motivated by petty jealousies. This dangerous game, ruled by the law of the gun and deftly described in scenes of graphic violence—scenes often illustrating the jarring shifts in levels of diction in the novel—is set against the great beauty of Uganda, the fabled "pearl of Africa" (196), with plentiful, restrained descriptions of water- and mountain-scapes, lush vegetation, shifting light, dramatic sunsets, and weather events.

Just as the reader can become entrapped in the novel's relentlessly hectic pace and its orgies of violence, so too the novel's characters seem to lose their ethical balance in Amin's Uganda. Isegawa's narrative strategies reinforce the notion that there can be no neutral spectatorship: all those who become voyeurs of the dictatorship are transformed. Isegawa's novel portrays the main effect of Amin's dictatorship as a collective moral debasement in which everyone is caught up, though those close to Amin have been long-schooled in the amoral use of spectacles of terror to reinforce their own and others' perception of their power. There are brief, apocryphal references to Amin's banning of miniskirts, indulging in cocaine, and collecting human heads in his fridge, but the novel mainly details the sweeping effects of individuals suspending moral judgment until sufficient wealth will allow their rapid exit from the fallen paradise, and their entrance into tropical paradises elsewhere. Bat, for example, participates in increasingly reckless manoeuvres to secure his portion of spoils resulting from the systematic rape of the country's infrastructure. His girlfriend, the mother of his daughter, Victoria, becomes a spy for the regime after she witnesses her parents brutalized and experiences the General's murderous exploitation. Thrust into the role of terrified, brutalized victim, she becomes an amoral assassin who preys upon Bat's new girlfriend, Babit, when she can no longer exploit others. Perhaps the most extreme and illustrative examples of moral debasement lie in the riots of violence and vulgarity enacted by those closest to Amin as exercises of their untouchable status. The General has a special house for "hosting orgies":

> In the middle of the night, with every guest drunk or stoned, with nothing to aim at except the trees, the whole group would go outside and start shooting at the stars. There were often Russian roulette competitions, beer-drinking contests and duels fought out in bulletproof vests. The General loved holding beer in his cheeks and spraying his guests, especially his dates or pick-ups. At other times, they all pissed in the bathtub all night long, rolled the dice at the end of the party, and the loser would be made to strip and bathe in the piss. (98)

These activities display the General's power and also ease his perpetual anxiety while reinforcing his perception of invulnerability. His power is usurped by the arrival of Robert Ashes—Isegawa's fictionalized version of the controversial historical figure Robert Astles—whom Amin promotes according to the prophecy of his alchemist. The General aims at various ways of eliminating Ashes, but he cannot anticipate the ruthlessness of Amin's new anti-corruption leader. When he is double-crossed by British businessman Alan Witherthrush of Cooper Motors, and particularly insulted at the attempt because in "Amin's Uganda [...] [p]eople died for a pancake, a kilo of sugar, for nothing" (120), Ashes abducts Kate Witherthrush and then her husband. Before burning them alive, he calls for

> the Pounder. The giant man came feeling with his free hand the weight of a metre-long pestle, smooth as an egg. The woman was held down and the man started to work on her feet. Two blows and they were gone. She fainted, frothed, and oozed all over the place. The exercise lasted barely four seconds; it was so fast that Bossman [Witherthrush] could hardly believe it had occurred. [...] In another four seconds the woman's arms were gone. Bossman soiled himself and let out a long tortured wail that would have chilled the blood of less hardened mortals. Ashes barely took notice. (121)

This extended scene of torture illustrates that Ashes's personal pride—not his greed—nurtures his extreme violence; he competes with others to perpetrate yet more macabre acts.

The nation's demoralization also belongs to a collective delusion in which the ever-present madness of the nation compels a type of magical thinking. In particular, virtually all of the characters suffer from fantasies of their own invulnerability and invincibility despite the omnipresent spectacles of arbitrary horror around them and their own private fantasies of violent death. It is as if their witness to unimaginable horror will shield them from its worst expression. Bat naively believes that he can survive due to his bureaucratic expertise and efficiency as well as his willingness to use clandestine surveillance to rule over subordinates. Even after a lengthy detention in the bureaucracy of makeshift prisons, he still believes that if he were released, he wouldn't leave the country. When he is suddenly, arbitrarily released—functioning as a pawn in the struggles between Ashes and the General—after witnessing and then participating in indiscriminate murder, he travels to England but returns to satisfy some type of vaguely defined revenge and thus helps finance his brother's dissident group. The General also thinks that he is guaranteed impunity because he helped install Amin; later he considers that his personal record of survival despite many near-disasters and his own involvement in murder "just cemented his belief in his own invincibility" (189). Victoria feels the General's "might" will protect her from any threat (218), though he is as much her tormentor as protector. Even Kate and Alan Witherthrush cannot imagine their fate, partly due to their extensive experience of previous governments' rising and falling, and having "witnessed lynchings, shoot-outs, beatings, burials, flamboyant weddings[, . . .] pleasure and pain see-sawing on an invisible, ever-changing pivot"; thus, they "at times [. . .] felt invincible, like gods walking among the uniformed scum and the people yearning for salvation from tyranny" (116–17). Alan Witherthrush has "been too confident of the protection of the local British Embassy [. . .] contacts in the British government in London; friendly generals in the Uganda army; his connections in the murky world of business; his reputation as a tough guy who not only faced down dictators but made lesser men cringe and do his will," and even the fantasy that Ashes's fear of Amin would restrain Ashes's murderous cruelty (121–22). Moreover, it is this couple's competitive challenge to his power, his private army, his reputation for unspeakable violence, and, particularly, "his feeling of infallibility" that infuriates Ashes and drives him to eliminate the couple and thus squander millions of dollars in bribes. Petty jealousy and paranoid anxiety—rather than grand political motives or even greed—generate the most extreme violence.

A perverse false traditionalism also motivates some of the excesses of the General and Bat's brother-in-law, though it also supplies a justification for deep-seated inferiority. Before marrying Bat's sister, Mafuta was the husband of a former princess of the royal line, and he willingly accepted her verbal and sexual abuse to maintain his proximity to the traditional Buganda monarchy. Only after meeting Bat's sister does he recognize that psychological inferiority compelled him to endure the parasitic relationship with the princess. As a man who resents southerners as much as intellectuals, the deeply insecure General associates his arbitrary acts of violence with the actions of the royal house of the Kabaka or King of Buganda: "I am a prince[. . . .] I can do whatever I want, I can assure you. If I want somebody's eye, I pluck it. If I want somebody's arm, I harvest it, ha-ha-ha. It is what the princes of old used to do" (98). The General's family lives in a district housing the tombs of the old monarchy, and he feels the royal connection when he drives in an entourage of luxury cars to his mansion or sits on his throne for audiences with supplicants to whom he dispenses largess or contempt. Though he appreciates the triumph of the will that power affords, he regrets the prevalent atmosphere of disdain. He envies

> the old kings [...] the loyalty of their subjects. However grotesquely they misused their power, however many people they killed, people still loved and obeyed them, ready to give their lives for them. He remembered the lines of mourners filing past the coffin, orderly tear-sodden kilometres peopled by men and women who would have braved the hottest sun or the heaviest rain just to have the chance to peek at their king for the last time. (99–100)

He is never able to overcome his feelings of inferiority and illegitimacy, due to his peasant origins and lack of education.

Snakepit interrogates the bogus radical politics that motivated the dictatorship's early supporters. For some of Amin's military leaders in Isegawa's novel, the dictatorship represents a legitimate postcolonial revolution with important traces of the traditional monarchy. Even those officers in the army who dislike the "reptile" Amin maintain that the possession of arbitrary power by a new elite "is what we fought for" (98). The last King of Buganda "had been in exile when Marshal Amin, King of Africa, created the new line of kings and princes now in power" (99). In this new atmosphere, no one wants to be "[a]nother sad-eyed case left behind by the revolution" (104), a member of the hopeless, exploited masses. The General wants to be "king of the lake" (105), and even Bat, who admires Amin's ejection of "foreigners" (132), feels regal as he presides over the collapse of the nation's infrastructure and assists with the sale of its resources to foreign powers. Bat justifies his success as a consequence of the democratization of feudalism:

> He himself felt like royalty of sorts. Kingship had become democratized by money and power. Soldiers and the elite were the new royalty, with new rituals and hierarchies. Mimicking the princes of old by stabbing, poisoning, and burning each other in a quest for a little more power and money and prestige. (80)

Bat is surprised, nevertheless, when the Saudi businessman from whom he accepts bribes expresses a desire to appropriate all of East Africa, a re-colonization justified in his mind by the Arab roots of towns on the Swahili coast and by his inability to compete with the princes in his Saudi homeland (71). In another example of the perverse melding of self-interest and postcolonial assertions, Bat's brother Tayari rationalizes his own drunkenness as "an act of resistance" if only to display the linguistic debasement of dictatorship (77). Amin himself acknowledges the neocolonial mimicry of Africa's post-independence dictators, as he comes to fear the fate of Emperors Selassie and Bokassa. More cynically,

Bat, thinking of Amin, appears to recognize historical doom at work in postcolonial Uganda:

> It was the biblical land where riches got eaten by locusts. The present did not last, the future got rancid before you touched it, blighted by the looming past: the stultification of slavery, the humiliation of colonialism, the debilitation of neo-colonialism, the raging war between capitalism and communism. The colonials, the Asians, the royals, the dictators, had all tasted the bitter truth. Amin and his cohorts knew it; they had their luggage ready. (74)

Snakepit has a certain ideological unwieldiness.[18] It appears to focus on the nature of evil and its roots in human fallibility, self-delusion, and pride, as well as on purely psychological drives to explain the tolerance for dictatorship and Amin's longevity. Even the anti-Amin dissidents are motivated by adrenaline and a desire for adventure, rather than a concern for social justice. Bat is released from detention through the action of a British MP, and he immediately resumes his work for the regime. Bat's brother, who becomes an expert bomb-maker for the Ugandan dissident group, was first allied with Amin's private army until a power struggle left him and the rest of his group imprisoned for a week without food. His motivation is only partly personal and fraternal revenge, and he projects a post-Amin future for himself as a spy for the new regime. Other than a few initial instances when he discusses "the personality problems of different dictators" with his astrologer (65) or converses with Ashes (242–46), Amin himself appears in the novel only at a distance. Amin is "a spectre floating on rumour" in the narrative as he is for rural villagers (131), and as a result he is, paradoxically, a more plausible presence, filtered through those around him who often seek to fashion themselves after him. Amin is a shadowy double who nevertheless requires the support of others to keep his bearings in the chaos and unreality of his own regime:

> like many tyrants, he was lonely amidst a crowd of worshippers, sycophants, wives. He needed a confidant, somebody on his level, a mirror to make the enchanted nebulous world he inhabited real, a thorn to prick him with the occasional pang of inadequacy he needed to spur him on. (112)

Ashes fills this role, as directed or foretold by Amin's chief astrologer, Dr. Ali, who also advises Bokassa and Mobutu. Ashes appears to be an amoral, affectless monster. His encounter with the stoicism of Mau Mau detainees only taught him to assess the possibility of breaking individuals through torture. Ashes

> kept thinking about Mau Mau women caught with guns under their robes. Two decades later, he could still see them, their immobile faces giving away nothing even after rigorous torture, dying with their secrets and ruining a perfect day, a week or month's campaign. (118)

For Ashes here as for Amin in Foden's novel, the colonial action against Mau Mau in Kenya supplied important knowledge for the project of dictatorship in Uganda.

Though not explicitly Christian, *Snakepit* contains a myriad of somewhat arbitrary Christian references, though they usually appear to indicate the "fallen" nature of life without principle, a mythological grid drained of meaning. These references may also of course indicate *Snakepit*'s author's personal knowledge and his awareness of his country's immersion in Christine doctrine and dogma. Tayari's dissident group refers to a possible Tanzanian invasion force as the "Lamb," but such biblical references usually denote roles rather than political codes. Babit's murderers offer to deliver her head on a plate to Victoria, "a bonus as well as a warning; a bonus for its Biblical dimension: Herod's daughter receiving the head of John the Baptist; a warning to keep her quiet if things went wrong" (218). Victoria earlier has thought of herself as Mary Magdalene, as does Babit when she feels compelled to rub—though not wash—the feet of Bat's British "saviour" Damon Villeneuve (173). Upon release from detention, Bat feels like Lazarus and the prodigal son; shortly afterwards, he sees his sister lying on a bed "like a sweet cross to carry and get crucified on before entering the paradise of motherhood" (168). In the aftermath of his release, he perceives Babit as "an open chalice," but this image prompts his "greed" to say, "Let us fuck all afternoon" (166), his psychomachia-like passion play rapidly becoming carnal. After Babit's murder and his witnessing of the horrific crime scene, he rejects an eschatology in which there is "resurrection of bodies"; instead, she becomes "a trinity" of the remembered woman, the desecrated corpse, and "the ethereal Babit, the one he wanted to see again" (224).

The reference to resurrection here offers one suggestion of what appears to be the novel's handling of the theme of suffering's purification or, rather, the annihilation of meaning amid apocalyptic conflagration. Bat's motives shift rather abruptly after his six months in detention and his own enforced participation in the murder of other detainees with a hammer, and then the brutal death of Babit. He wonders about the origins of the omnipresent violence and resolves not to seek revenge for Babit's murder: "I don't want anybody's death on my conscience" (215). After the fiasco of the trial, however, when Victoria is not murdered by outraged dissidents, Bat believes that Tayari was "not beyond salvation" (239). Far more dramatically, the General experiences an about-face when he confronts the ruin of the countryside. He has gone on tour to escape the impasse of his confrontation with Ashes in which he has felt "like some dog's dick trapped inside a bitch's pussy" (148). The further he moves from the city, the more he realizes that "government was a very thin concept [. . . .] He stopped several times to buy things, taking the trouble to enter the small dusty shops [. . . .] The goods he wanted were almost always unavailable [. . . .] There was no cooking oil, no paraffin, no food, nothing" (151). He recognizes the near collapse of state institutions like schools and hospitals, and that "the gun had risen to become [...] an integral part of the culture" in portions of the country that were now virtually state-less zones where violence, smuggling, and different regional associations ruled (153). He sees that empty government promises are just another nearly worthless currency. However, it is the explosion that nearly kills his wife, an event the General blames incorrectly on Ashes, that makes him confront his own mortality and recognize the catastrophe of Amin's rule. He becomes "obsessed with eternal life and Judgment Day," but he has passed beyond redemption (236). He knows he should have supported a coup against Amin, though he finally violates his own perverse code of military honour when he respects a private pact made with another officer by cutting off his own toe. He knows finally that he is "already erased from memory" even before his suicide (256).

Walter Benjamin writes in *The Origins of German Tragic Drama* that "[t]he enduring fascination of the downfall of the tyrant is rooted in the conflict between the impotence and depravity of his person, on the one hand, and, on the other, the extent to which the age was convinced of the sacrosanct power of his role" (72). At the end of *Snakepit*, amid the detritus left by a retreating dictatorship, Bat, representative of his age, acquires his old job under the new regime and feels strangely victorious. He has just returned from America and witnessed Amin's entry into pop culture as a buffoon, displaying the primarily bemused disinterest with which the West viewed the tyrant. The novel's comic—even banal—closure seems artificial and superimposed, the overall sense of national tragedy and unspoken complicity is so overwhelming.[19] In this setting, unlike in England, as Bat realizes, tragedy is not "erased and carted away into library files where it lost bite, later coming off the page like a shadow, bland in its weightlessness, almost a figment of the chronicler's imagination" (172). However, despite its assertion of history's living presence in Uganda, the novel's conclusion appears to render recent historical horrors as being easily, effortlessly shrugged off. This may be an inevitable and fully comprehensible psychological response to trauma, both historically and notionally, in reading or representing trauma. Benjamin, for example, wrote of the impossibility of obtaining "an easy moral satisfaction [...] from the tyrant's end. For if the tyrant falls, not simply in his own name, as an individual, but as a ruler and in the name of mankind and history, then his fall has the quality of a judgment, in which the subject too is implicated" (72). This novel's final image of Bat as "victor" with his final dreaming thoughts given to his memory of Babit and his lust for a friend's wife ignores any responsibility for complicity and perhaps inadvertently sets the tone for the next, differently tragic stage of Ugandan history.

Goretti Kyomuhendo's spare novel *Waiting, A Novel of Uganda at War* makes no attempt to portray Amin at close hand, or to mythologize him, or to consider the colonial or other causes of his dictatorship, or to assess the outlandish representation of Amin in Western media. Instead, the novel's oral history—dialogue predominates in its evocation of somewhat fractured traditional lifeways—describes the aftermath of Amin, his legacy of instability, violence, deprivation, and chaos in Uganda and surrounding African countries shortly after his departure and the impact of this legacy on the next generation of Ugandans.[20] It is history from below, from the perspective of the powerless and, particularly, of women.[21] Kyomuhendo's female characters are the first and the last to suffer in the senseless catastrophe perpetuated by a single man. They appear to be virtually stateless, receiving no direct benefits as Ugandan citizens but only enduring the economic and military fallout of power struggles in Kampala that make their already difficult lives increasingly wretched. Like Isegawa and Foden, Kyomuhendo refers to the rumours of Amin's fridge full of human heads as well as to visits to the dictator's private quarters. Foden's Garrigan, however, encounters Amin there and facilitates his departure, but Kyomuhendo's novel merely mentions that some soldiers have removed pornographic magazines from Amin's already looted private rooms. Kyomuhendo's focus is not the aura of the dictator but the extensive collateral damage of the breakdown of the state effected on Uganda's peasantry.

The novel begins at the historical moment when Isegawa's novel ends with an extended family's immediate dread of the arrival of undisciplined soldiers, either from Amin's retreating army or those of the liberating Tanzanian armies. Terror is normalized, as the family and particularly its female members attempt to survive amid the day-to-day grind of trying to locate and prepare food for a large extended family, to search for natural remedies in the face of hospital and clinic closures, to secure their few possessions from marauding armies and termites, and to decide if and when to run from their temporary shelter on a banana plantation. The narrator's mother is in the last stages of a difficult pregnancy in this impossible situation, and just when Amin's drunken soldiers arrive looking for "women, food, and money" (37), she is in labour. What might be a sign of promise in post-Amin Uganda is yet another disaster. The soldiers murder the old woman, Kaaka, who is assisting at the delivery in the absence of a midwife, after she furiously shouts at them the reckless words of the powerless:

> Go, you beasts! I have to attend to a woman giving birth to a baby who will be more useful than you. How can you beat a woman old enough to be your great-grandmother? Do you think you can scare me? Me, who used to beat my husband until he urinated in his trousers? (38)

Though they don't understand her language, they fire two bullets. Her funeral is shared with the narrator, Alinda's mother, whom Kaaka attempted to save, but there is a third spectre at the gravesite: the remains of an undelivered foetus that has left Kaaka infertile over many decades, an infertility that caused her husband to end their marriage. Behind the spectre of post-dictatorship chaos lies the unequal balance of power between men and women and the weight of gendered prejudice.

The combination of the everyday and the extraordinary in Kyomuhendo's account of gender relations in post-Amin Uganda recalls the artistic assurance in the lengthy first section of Chinua Achebe's *Things Fall Apart* or Buchi Emechetta's ironically-titled *The Joys of Motherhood*, though the focus here is on the sufferings of women that have only worsened through the disaster of Amin's rule and the new helplessness of some men faced with their powerlessness before the armed soldiers and the new, mindless, testosterone-driven bravado of other men. Even in a modern war zone, however, there is time for the telling of folk tales and the origins of names, orature indicating the survival of cultural practices as forms of resistance, particularly in female communities. Nyinabarongo, for example, has been driven away by her husband's family and forced to leave behind her son after being coerced into the marriage:

> The problem started with the birth of her first child, a boy, who had presented his legs first during a difficult childbirth. That is why he was given a twin name and various rituals were performed. When she bore her second child, a daughter, she was also given a twin name because the child's two upper teeth grew before the lower ones. That's how Nyinabarongo got her name, meaning "mother of twins," even though her children are not really twins. (8)

We learn later that Kaaka, the woman murdered after her tirade against Amin's marauding soldiers who had an even more troubled reproductive history, had defied colonial authorities in the past when they tried to force all girls to wear manufactured dresses they couldn't afford instead of cheaper, durable calico wraps. She repeats the folk tale of the white dove with a revolutionary message that galvanized women's resistance, and the young girls recite the tale in her memory.

Faraway political tragedies, however, do impinge upon the already difficult lives of these rural women. The narrator's friend Jungu, for example, is the offspring of an exploitative, violent relationship between a poor widow and a wealthy Asian manager of a cotton mill who refuses to pay her deceased husband's wages. Jungu's ashamed mother had attempted to murder her child, but neighbours and the police rescued the baby and forced her mother to nurse it. Traditional anxieties about the suicidal tendencies of the offspring of "mixed" parentage provide Alinda with an explanation for Jungu's tragic flight after her lover in the departing Tanzanian forces, not realizing he had stayed behind to be with her. Alinda's uncle Kembo loses his job as a night watchman at a sawmill "when

Idi Amin chased the Indians away from Uganda" (57), but he is coerced into becoming a Muslim through the offer of an expropriated Indian shop. His wife won't convert, and family tensions escalate until his business collapses, his newly married wives leave him, and he returns to the village with his long-suffering first wife, who also then deserts him. The woman from Zaire who is regarded as a witch by the men has gained her knowledge of herbs as an indirect result of high-level political manoeuvres: "When Patrice Lumumba was killed by the Americans in 1961, there was a lot of fighting in Zaire" (55). Though only fifteen years old and without having any schooling, she begins to assist her aunt in nursing at a hospital without medicines in Stanleyville, and she learns the uses of different plants.

Birth and rebirth in a post-dictatorship war zone—in the aftermath of the departure of a brutal tyrant, his undisciplined troops looting and murdering indiscriminately—delimit the hope remaining at the end of *Waiting*. It is, moreover, a somewhat mechanical, superimposed hope given the coming decade of post-Amin chaos. A new non-traditional family composed of pregnant women and babies, new marital partnerships, and Pan-African members from Zaire and Tanzania provides the main promise of stability and survival.[22] There is more food and the prospect of employment in the city for the family patriarch, but hope for the future rests primarily on education and a shared commitment to return to school.[23] Moreover, this future unfolds in a denuded landscape stripped bare by the liberating armies, crops and livestock replaced by landmines that blow off the leg of an old man.[24] His fate symbolizes his delayed punishment for murdering his wife, chopping up the body, and delivering the grisly remains in a sack to her parents. Amin released the man from prison for becoming a Moslem, and he is now cared for by the physically and psychologically wounded survivors. Significantly, there is virtually no reference to Amin, "that monster" (87), in the ending, as if the survivors lack the strength even to contemplate what they have survived or its cause. There is, however, time to consider the end of other dictatorships nearby: "The Lendu woman asked them [the Tanzanian soldiers] to go and liberate Zaire too, after they were finished with Uganda, and kill or chase away that dictator, Mobutu" (78). There is no appetite or energy for retribution or even for justice for Amin in the face of the daily hardships amid the wreckage left by dictatorship. While members of the family have dispersed and the wars continue just beyond the border, they no longer wait to see "[w]ould we survive this war?" but they concentrate with the enforced pragmatism of the very poor and without pause for heroic hyperbole or lamentation on how they will build the future in the face of the national economic collapse and regional instability enabled by Amin (60).

The muted hopefulness and fatigue at the end of *Waiting* demonstrate in particular the weight of the catastrophe wrought by Idi Amin. These four novels all represent the sweeping damage effected by Amin's dictatorship locally, nationally, regionally, and internationally, and the difficulty of representing him and the monumental scale of the disaster he caused in something approaching the dictatorship novel genre. The legacy of Amin is witnessed in the traumatized, exiled diasporic Ugandan community, the reinforcement of negative Western stereotypes about Africa and Africans, and in the rural poverty and instability in Uganda and within regional conflicts.

Notes

1. Samuel Decalo, in a study of the pathology of dictators, refers to Bokassa, Amin, and Equatorial Guinea's Francisco Macias Nguema as the "dictatorial triumvirate" (ix). Teodoro Nguema Obiang Mangue, the son of the present dictator of Equatorial Guinea, appears to stand in waiting to become the next "King of Equatorial Guinea" (Silverstein 3). Teodoro's father, Theodoro Obiang Nguema Mbasogo, is celebrated on state radio for being in "permanent contact with the Almighty"; the dictator empowers himself "to kill without anyone calling him to account and without going to hell" (qtd. in Birrell 26). The country's possession of oil wealth appears to allow its dictatorship freedom from international scrutiny.
2. In October 2011, US President Barak Obama sent a letter to Congress outlining a plan to dispatch one hundred troops to Uganda who would work in an advisory capacity to destroy the Lord's Resistance Army and capture or kill Kony.
3. Foden recounts Amin's describing to the OAU his method of murdering Mau Mau suspects by strangulation (128). Amin's actions against the Mau Mau as the proxy of the colonial powers may have been Amin's major training in the deployment of the psychology and violence of terror (Robins and Post 257–58).
4. Amin was not a "one-man genocide," as Natalie Haynes describes Achilles (40), but rather a modern-day Caligula (Rush 1).
5. See Henry Kyemba's *A State of Blood*, one of a number of survivor accounts by high-level officials near the Amin regime. Kyemba recalls Amin's fondness for meeting for a drink or dinner with unsuspecting individuals he was about to have murdered. *Guardian* journalist John Fairhall, arrested in Uganda in 1972 on suspicion of being a foreign soldier, recalled particularly brutal methods of murder in Amin's makeshift jails: "the normal method of execution was by 'tapping' a man's skull with a 20 lb. hammer," in some cases with lines of detainees being forced to murder the next person in line in succession (Fairhall 209).

    Uganda also became a paranoid state under Amin, as what Robert Robins and Jerrold Post diagnose as the dictator's personal "paranoid psychopathology" was reflected in the nation (262, 256–65).
6. This was the title given to the American edition of the book, presumably to capitalize on the popular TV show "Lifestyles of the Rich and Famous." In the introduction, Canadian novelist and artist Douglas Coupland, in an anecdotal reflection, comments that the book's analysis of dictator style in home decorating—which is certainly not dictator chic—shows that the dictators are guilty of crimes against humanity and also good taste. The examination deflates the dictator's supersized egos, but its focus on a kind of grotesque camp tends to underplay the enormity of these individuals' exploitation.
7. As Dominic Thomas writes of Congolese dramatist Sony Labou Tansi's phantasmagoric 1979 novel of dictatorship *La Vie et demie*, translated and republished as *Life and a Half* in 2011, "There

Representation of Idi Amin in Ugandan Dictatorship Novels

is evidence of a new and original variation of the dictatorship novel, where humor, sexuality, violence, and corporeal activities inform simultaneously the world of the living and the world of the dead" (xi).

8. The first edition of the novel was published by the Writers Workshop, Calcutta, in 1984, and the "new edition" in 1991, as the "Acknowledgements" in that edition indicate. This chapter's discussion is based on the 1991 edition of Nazareth's novel.

9. *Snakepit* was first published as *Slangenkuil* by Uitgave De Bezige Bij, Amsterdam, the Netherlands, in 1999. The novel was published by Knopf in hardcover in 2004, and in paperback by Vintage International, a division of Random House, in 2005.

10. Isegawa's narrator says that *Snakepit*'s General Bazooka, acknowledging that he lacks the power of Amin, "realized that a prince was no king: he still had to take crap from his king, especially if he was a self-declared king of Africa. As a prince, he could piss on the heads of peasants, but he could not get his way all the time" (149).

11. Isegawa, in an interview with Jacqui Jones, presents the devaluation of books and reading in the Amin years, when people were focused on obtaining the bare necessities of life, as his reason for leaving Uganda (90); once outside Africa, he says in another interview, "you become African for the first time, in a sense" (Vazquez 144). One sign of the more positive attitude towards books and reading in Uganda at the present is that *Waiting* itself was drafted while Kyomuhendo was studying for an MA in Creative Writing at the University of KwaZulu-Natal in 2004–05 (Daymond 113). She also knew Peter Nazareth when she studied at the University of Iowa's International Writing Program in 1997. Kyomuhendo has been involved in FEMRITE, the Ugandan Women's Writers Association, one of whose goals is the development of Ugandan literature by women.

12. The phrase is John Scheckter's in a useful discussion of transformational or hybrid diasporic Goan identities in Nazareth's work (83–84).

13. The film is a pared-down and slightly distorted version of the novel with a much greater emphasis on Garrigan himself (played with great authority and a certain James Bond-like rakishness by Scottish actor James McAvoy) as "our man in Uganda" and a de-emphasis on Amin (played by American actor Forest Whitaker in a much-commended, Academy Award-winning performance). Garrigan's somewhat caddish romantic and sexual interests receive greater attention in the movie, and it is Garrigan, not an African official, who has an affair with Amin's wife Kay. In addition, Garrigan is himself the victim of vicious torture. Amin is generally the more jovial, buffoonish monster of Western stereotype.

14. Foden was concerned that his research might overwhelm his novelistic intentions, though he was simultaneously aware of the self-created fictional quality of Amin himself and of the questionable uses to which a mesmerizing account of the dictator might be put. He interviewed many people associated with Amin's regime, including the notorious enabler Robert Astles, and he even attempted to interview Amin himself in Saudi Arabia. See "Bold Type: Interview with Giles Foden" at <http://www.randomhouse.com/boldtype/1298/foden/interview.html>.

15. Isegawa's celebrated *Abyssinian Chronicles* (2001) audaciously begins with crocodiles, in a narrative gesture evoking a very different event concerning the narrator's father at the beginning of Laurence Sterne's *Tristram Shandy*.

16. There is speculation that Amin's peculiar cluster of symptoms and behaviors indicated the presence of syphilis, perhaps none clearer than his typically bombastic injunctions to students about promiscuity (Carlton 207), or schizophrenia or hypomania (Kiwanuka 709). The root of Amin's pathology may lie in childhood trauma, though Eric Carlton points to the theory of contingency in leadership (4) and the various tensions playing in 1970s Uganda as more significant: fascism's atavistic quest for a pre-modern ideology, the desire for modernism with a traditional face,

the legacy of Baganda despotism, and Obote's over-reliance on Amin's strong arm to maintain a one-party state. Carlton significantly underplays the effect of the colonial legacy (202–13). That Amin was both the product of the colonial creation of Uganda as well as the main cause of the nation's problems informs the collection of essays in Holger Bernt Hansen and Michael Twaddle's *Uganda Now* that begins with the assertion that in 1988 Uganda exemplified "Third World disaster" (1).

17. Isegawa's *Abyssinian Chronicles*, the author's first-published novel, a Rushdie-like family saga, national narrative, and bildungsroman, refers to the "post-Independence political elite" as a group who had gained a great deal but at a terrible cost in the manner of "hardened thieves" (121). While the novel only makes incidental references to Amin, it does point to Ugandan young people's admiration for the despot's pugilistic bravado that in its early stages fostered pride and self-assurance. He is a larger-than-life, quasi-Biblical figure who can even offer "spiritual help" (135). Isegawa credits Mahmood Mamdani's portrayal of Amin as intelligent in his *From Citizen to Refugee* (1973) for influencing his account of the dictator (Vazquez 134). In that work, Mamdani refers to Amin's Uganda as a "bottomless pit" (37), but he acknowledges Amin as an astute, tactical populist, a "masterful performer" with "the decisiveness of a tiger" (59, 60). Mamdani's later *Imperialism and Fascism in Uganda* (1983) importantly indicates popular resistance to Amin. After a brief period of popular support due to Amin's catering to different interest groups within Uganda using strategies ranging from "nationalistic chauvinism and demagogy, to petty reforms and privileges for a section of the oppressed" (55), popular resistance took hold (57, 105–06).

18. However, as Ian Kershaw explains in *The "Hitler Myth,"* the dictator and the public were locked in a system that superseded narrow ideological identification in favour of shared popular values represented by a figure of charismatic authority at its center. In Uganda, as Isegawa shows, the urban public and particularly the intelligentsia in the civil service did not so much consent to Amin's authority as relinquish their power to consent and turned instead to the distractions of career and the growing need to concentrate on survival as the economy collapsed. However inept and chaotic he was as a leader, Amin ostensibly stood for certain common values and for the enterprise of postmodernity and postcoloniality, almost as if the people had forfeited their critical, political will until the state virtually collapsed.

19. Norman Rush addresses the disjunction between the horrific subject of Isegawa's novel and its detachment. He locates the disconnection in the novel's "often breezy, rococo prose" and its unwillingness to provide "a closer approach to Amin, to the nature of his power" (5, 6). However, he also points to moments of implausibility, such as when Bat, having experienced the horrors of detention in Amin's jails, returns first from England, and then after witnessing the effects of the brutal butchery of his wife, from America to Amin's Uganda. Andrew H. Armstrong, in an essay on Isegawa's first two novels, argues that all novels attempting to narrate a traumatic history inevitably confront a crisis of representation in terms of both language and genre (127–43).

20. Kyomuhendo has said that "as a writer, I write best about something I know" and particularly about the experiences of women who were "the traditional storytellers" ("Goretti Kyomuhendo" 124). She further clarifies the circumstances that inspired the novel as well as her aims:

> I wanted to write a story that would reflect the lives of ordinary people during the Idi Amin era. These are people who were far removed from the centre of politics, the politics of things like trade embargoes, exile or even the killings. Amin was not interested in killing ordinary people—he was interested in eliminating people he perceived as enemies—politicians, lawyers, academics, judges, etc. People who were bound to oppose him and threaten his power. I wanted to focus on these people: the night watchman, the herbalist, the Post Office clerk, farmer, tailor, housewife etc. How did Idi Amin's reign of terror affect them? Did their

lives change after he was overthrown? Could it change? What did the new regime mean for them? Most of the literature produced about Idi Amin focuses on the macro politics and I felt that the ordinary people were being written out of this particular literature, of this history. Secondly, I also wanted to show the role, importance, resilience of women during times of war. (Goretti Kyomuhendo, Director of the African Writers Trust, personal communication, January 2013).

21. Kyomuhendo's focus on rural women and particularly a young woman whose independent life has yet to begin distinguishes her novel from Isegawa's *Abyssinian Chronicles*, a novel that is as much a bildungsroman as a narrative unfolding in the shadow of dictatorship.

22. Daymond maintains that the new, extended family's "transnational linguistic exchanges" are "the novel's greatest sign of hope for the future" (125). Emilia Ilieva and Lennox Odiemo-Munara consider the linguistic paradox in the novel's "mosaic community" (188): while highlighting the need for a common, rural language such as Swahili to facilitate communication between diverse linguistic communities, the novel makes clear that Swahili is associated with the divisive, draconian policies of Amin and the oppression of his soldiers (198–99).

23. The great Ugandan poet Okot p'Bitek, however, would call for an African cultural revolution in education in the face of political oppression, as he responds when asked about an earlier declaration of bitter despair: "The most striking characteristic of all African governments is that they are all without exception dictatorships which practice such ruthless discrimination as to make apartheid look tame" (100). See, too, Bernth Lindfors's "Okot's Last Blast: An Attempt at Curricular Reform in Uganda after Idi Amin" (101–09).

24. The old man is bothered by the traumatic sensation of having pains in his leg after it is amputated by the slandered but wise and compassionate Lendu woman from Zaire, and this image may embody the notion of "writing as phantom limb" in Kyomuhendo's fiction in Andrew H. Armstrong's provocative interpretation, though he doesn't consider *Waiting*: "The narrators perform the task of creating a phantom limb that enables a 'bearing of witness' to the traumas of their protagonists" (260).

Works Cited

Armstrong, Andrew H. "Narrative and the Re-co[r]ding of Cultural Memory in Moses Isegawa's *Abyssinian Chronicles* and *Snakepit*." *Journal of African Cultural Studies* 21.2 (2009): 127–43. Print.

———. "Reporting from the Edge of Reality: Writing as Phantom Limb in Goretti Kyomuhendo's Fiction." *Journal of International Women's Studies* 10.4 (2009): 259–75. Print.

Benjamin, Walter. *The Origin of German Tragic Drama*. Trans. John Osborne. Introduction by George Steiner. London: Verso, 1990. Print.

Bird, John. *The Collected Broadcasts of Idi Amin*. London: Transatlantic, 1975. Print.

Birrell, Ian. "Public Face of a Dictatorship." *The Guardian Weekly* 11–17 Nov. 2011: 25–27. Print.

Carlton, Eric. *Faces of Despotism*. Aldershot, Hants: Scholar P, 1995. Print.

Cawthorne, Nigel. *Sex Lives of the Great Dictators*. London: Prion, 1996. Print.

Conrad, Joseph. *Heart of Darkness*. Ed. D. C. R. A. Goonetilleke. Peterborough, Ontario: Broadview, 1995. Print.

Coupland, Douglas. "Tree Forts and Love Shacks." Introduction. *Dictator's Homes*. By Peter York. London: Atlantic Books, 2005. vii–viii. Print.

Daymond, M. J. Afterword. *Waiting, A Novel of Uganda at War*. Goretti Kyomuhendo. New York: The Feminist Press, 2007. 113–34. Print.

Decalo, Samuel. *Psychoses of Power: African Personal Dictatorships.* Boulder: Westview, 1989. Print.

Fairhall, John. "Prisoner of Idi Amin: Four Days in Makindye." *The Guardian Century.* Ed. Giles Foden. London: The Guardian, 1999. 208-09. Print.

Foden, Giles. *The Last King of Scotland.* London: Faber and Faber, 1998. Print.

Hansen, Holger Bernt and Michael Twaddle, eds. *Uganda Now: Between Decay & Development.* London: James Currey, 1988. Print.

Haynes, Natalie. "Human, not hero." Rev. of *The Song of Achilles*, by Madeline Miller. *Guardian Weekly* 21 Oct. 2011: 40. Print.

Ilieva, Emilia and Lennox Odiemo-Munara. "Negotiating Dislocated Identities in the Space of Post-Colonial Chaos: Goretti Kyomuhendo's *Waiting*." *Negotiating Afropolitanism: Essays on Borders and Spaces in Contemporary African Literature and Folklore.* Amsterdam: Rodopi, 2011. 183-204. Print.

Isegawa, Moses. *Abyssinian Chronicles* [1998]. New York: Vintage, 2001. Print.

———. *Snakepit* [1999]. New York: Vintage, 2005. Print.

Jones, Jacqui. "Traversing the Abyss: Moses Isegawa: An Interview and Commentary." *English in Africa* 27.2 (2000): 85-102. Print.

Kershaw, Ian. *The "Hitler Myth": Image and Reality in the Third Reich.* Oxford: Oxford UP, 1987. Print.

Kiwanuka, Semakula. *Amin and the Tragedy of Uganda.* London: Weltforum Verlag, 1979. Print.

Kyemba, Henry. *A State of Blood: The Inside Story of Idi Amin.* New York: Ace Books, 1977. Print.

Kyomuhendo, Goretti. Interview by Stephen Gray. *Research in African Literatures* 32.1 (Spring 2001): 123-25. Print.

———. *Waiting, A Novel of Uganda at War.* New York: The Feminist Press, 2007. Print.

The Last King of Scotland. Dir. Kevin Macdonald. Based on the novel by Giles Foden. Fox Searchlight Pictures, DNA Films Ltd. and FilmFour, 2006. DVD.

Lindfors, Bernth. "Okot's Last Blast: An Attempt at Curricular Reform in Uganda after Idi Amin." *Long Drums and Canons: Teaching and Researching African Literatures.* Trenton, NJ: Africa World P, 1995. 101-09. Print.

Mamdani, Mahmood. *From Citizen to Refugee: Uganda Asians Come To Britain.* London: Frances Pinter, 1973. Print.

———. *Imperialism and Fascism in Uganda.* Nairobi: Heinemann Educational Books, 1983. Print.

Nazareth, Peter. *The General Is Up.* Toronto: TSAR Publications, 1991. Print.

Ngũgĩ wa Thiong'o. *Moving the Centre: The Struggle for Cultural Freedoms.* London: James Currey, 1993. Print.

———. *Wizard of the Crow.* Trans. Ngũgĩ wa Thiong'o. New York: Anchor Books, 2007. Print.

Okigbo, Christopher. *Labyrinths with Paths of Thunder.* New York: Africana Publishing, 1971. Print.

Okot p'Bitek. *Africa's Cultural Revolution.* Nairobi: Macmillan, 1973. Print.

Robins, Robert S. and Jerrold M. Post. *Political Paranoia: The Psychopolitics of Hatred.* New Haven: Yale UP, 1997. Print.

Rush, Norman. "The Last Word on Evil." Rev. of *Snakepit*, by Moses Isegawa. *The New York Review of Books* 7 Oct. 2004: 1-9. Web. Accessed 9/21/2011

Scheckter, John. "Peter Nazareth and the Ugandan Expulsion: Pain, Distance, Narration." *Research in African Literatures* 27.2 (1996): 83-93. Print.

Silverstein, Ken. "Teodorin's World." *Foreign Policy* Mar.-Apr. 2011: 1-3. Web. Accessed 9/21/2011

Thomas, Dominic. "Sony Labou Tansi—The Conscience of Africa and the Voice of the People." Introduction. *Life and a Half* by Sony Labou Tansi. Bloomington: Indiana UP, 2011. Print.

Vazquez, Michael C. "Hearts in Exile: A Conversation with Moses Isegawa and Mahmood Mamdani." *Transition* 10.2 (2001): 126–50. Web. Accessed 9/21/2011.

York, Peter. *Dictators' Homes*. London: Atlantic Books, 2005. Print.

York, Peter and Douglas Coupland. *Dictators' Homes: Lifestyles of the World's Most Colorful Despots*. San Francisco: Chronicle Books, 2006. Print.

Jacob's Ladder and *Anthills of the Savannah*: Narrativizing the Internal-External Dynamic in African Political Power

JOSEPH MCLAREN

The internal-external theory of African political causation has been advanced by a number of academics from differing disciplines, especially as it relates to international foreign policy, political economy, and globalization. It is well known that "[t]he leadership of many African nations hardened into autocracy and dictatorship" during the 70s as a result of the deterioration of "political and economic matters" (Collier and Gunning 3). However, in explorations of the failings of African states as a result of the rise of dictatorial or military regimes, there is the danger of placing Western democracies as the superlative system because "the very sharpness of the clash between democracy and dictatorship exposes us to the danger of simplifying both and of thinking of them as two absolutes" (Lerner 4). In other words, it should be recognized that in traditional structures "African society is profoundly democratic," despite the reality of certain dictatorial regimes in the modern era (Brown 4).

Numerous African novelists, such as Chinua Achebe, Wole Soyinka, Ayi Kwei Armah, and Ngũgĩ wa Thiong'o, have used the internalist approach to explain the pitfalls of political leadership in their respective nations. Soyinka's *Kongi's Harvest* (1967), Armah's *The Beautyful Ones Are Not Yet Born* (1968), and Ngũgĩ's many novels, culminating in *Wizard of the Crow* (2006), have each developed fictional formats for a neocolonial critique. Ngũgĩ has also consistently developed the external perspective, maintaining the complicity of global power in the support of despotic African leadership. In the academic arena, one of the most severe critics of African autocracy has been George B. N. Ayittey. Ayittey's *Africa Betrayed* (1992), *Africa in Chaos* (1998), *Africa Unchained: The Blueprint for Africa's Future* (2005), and *Defeating Dictators: Fighting Tyranny in Africa and Around the World* (2011) all reiterate a similar internalist argument.

> Internalists are those who believe Africa's woes are due more to internal than external factors. This school of thought maintains that while it is true that colonialism and Western imperialism did not leave Africa in good shape, Africa's condition has been made immeasurably worse by *internal* factors: misguided leadership, systemic corruption, capital flight, economic mismanagement, senseless civil wars, political tyranny, flagrant violations of human rights, and military vandalism. (*Africa in Chaos* 44)

In other words, as Cameron G. Thies describes it, "the interplay between domestic and international factors is crucial to understanding state building over time and space" (Thies 716).

The argument for external causes of Africa's state crises, especially during the independence era, was put forth cogently by Kwame Nkrumah in *Neo-Colonialism: The Last Stage of Imperialism* (1965), where he defined "neo-colonialism" as "modern attempts to perpetuate colonialism while at the same time talking about 'freedom'" (Nkrumah 239). Nkrumah, who considered the U.S. as the "[f]oremost among the neo-colonialists," also argued that "[i]n order to halt foreign interference in the affairs of developing countries it is necessary to study, understand, expose and actively combat neo-colonialism in whatever guise" (Nkrumah 239). Most importantly, "the government of Kwame Nkrumah was confronted with a rather complex international system with repercussions for both internal politics and Ghana's external relations" (Gebe 161).

Although for some like Ayittey the externalist perspective, associated with the Left, is considered dated, it has been given support by those who recognize the U.S. role in "destabilization." John Stockwell's *In Search of Enemies: A CIA Story* (1978) and *The Praetorian Guard: The U.S. Role in the New World Order* (1991), or William Blum's *Killing Hope: U.S. Military and CIA Intervention Since World War II* (2004), are works that delve into U.S. interventions in clandestine global activities.

John A. Williams's novel *Jacob's Ladder* (1987), although published well after the independence era, develops the externalist theory and Nkrumah's Pan-Africanist conception through a retrospective narrative. The novel concerns the predicament of an African American military attaché during the 1960s who is reluctantly involved in U.S. destabilizing efforts in the fictional country of Pandemi. In contrast, Achebe's *Anthills of the Savannah* (1988), a "fable" that shows "that even the most devastating political and emotional turmoil gives way to renewal," is set in the 1980s in the imagined state of Kangan (Ohaeto 252–53). When placed together, both novels show how the internal-external theory, in whole or in part, can be actualized in fictional form and to what extent the "solution" to leadership excesses can be solved by a return to African traditional attitudes towards governance, increasing vigilance of the intellectual class, and an unhampered media.

JACOB'S LADDER AND EXTERNAL INTERVENTION

Williams, the prolific African American writer, author of *The Man Who Cried I Am* (1967), based on the life of Richard Wright, *!Click Song* (1982), and *Clifford's Blues* (1999), among others, covered Africa as a journalist and authored as well *Africa: Her History, Lands and People* (1962). *Jacob's Ladder*, a rare novel by an African American set in Africa, is named after its main character, Jacob Henry, and also evokes the Biblical allusion to Jacob, suggesting reunion and spiritual ascendancy. Supposedly written by an "angry black writer," it was thought by one reviewer that in the work, "Africans are drawn with more clarity than the Americans" (Jaffe 5). The novel portrays especially two African leaders, Chuma Fasseke of Pandemi and Taiwo Shaguri of Temian, a neighboring state. (Shaguri's name mirrors that of Nigeria's Shehu Shagari, president from 1979–1983.) Pandemi is meant as a version of Liberia; Temian a parallel to Nigeria; and Ulcuma, a third West African country, described as having little resources, a pawn of the U.S. in undermining Pandemi. However, Williams also implies that his fictionalized leader, Fasseke, might be a version of Nkrumah, especially in his pursuit of technological power and his Pan-African ideas. Like Nkrumah, whom "[t]he United States wanted...out," Fasseke is also the target of destabilizing interventions (Blum 198).

The Africa developed in *Jacob's Ladder* reflects the internal and external pressures generated by the geopolitical dynamics of the Cold War era, in which U.S.-Soviet rivalries were played out in Africa in attempts to align newly independent African nations. As Kenneth Waltz observes ironically in *Theory of International Politics* and in relation to the "bipolar" system, "[S]ince World War II the United States has responded expensively in distant places to wayward events that could hardly affect anyone's fate outside of the region" (Waltz 172). Another perspective on U.S. foreign policy was expressed by Cyrus Vance, Secretary of State during the Carter administration, who saw it as "'grounded in the conviction that we best serve our interest there by supporting the efforts of developing nations to advance their economic well-being and preserve their political independence'" (Kirkpatrick 41).

In creating Pandemi, Williams reconstructs a history that resembles that of Liberia in several ways. The establishment of Pandemi results from the migration of free and formerly enslaved African Americans to West Africa in the early nineteenth century. In Liberia's past, early indigenous leaders were rivals of the returnees, who were repatriated as part of a design by the American Colonization Society as an alternative to emancipation, thus creating a group later known as Americo-Liberians, who established the Republic of Liberia in 1847. In his *Memoir* of 1961, C. L. Simpson, former Ambassador to Washington from Liberia, described the experiences of the early settlers from whom he was descended. "But having set foot upon the soil of Africa, these people changed almost overnight from docile drudges into dignified, defiant and fearless fighters, able to stand their ground against experienced warriors brought up for generations in the atmosphere of military prowess" (45). In Pandemi, Chuma Fasseke, the new president, has replaced the former government of the Franklins, a family descended from the stock of returning nineteenth-century African Americans. (Although in Liberia William Tubman was president during the time when the novel is set, the military coup that deposes Fasseke resembles the actions of Samuel Doe, who deposed William Tolbert in a 1980 coup. Williams's novel was published a year after Samuel Doe became president of Liberia, which had no president from 1980–1986.) Most importantly, the return of former populations of African descent is not idealized or romanticized by Williams, who shows the discrepancies in social hierarchies: "The generations had witnessed their American attitudes of caste and class, their making the English language into the official language. They had been the new tribespeople with their American names and silk hats, striped pants and swallow-tailed dress-of-state" (26). Also, Pandemi is a major exporter of rubber, like Liberia, whose rubber resources had been used to equip the U.S. military in World War II. The harvesting of rubber deeply affected Pandemian society, for it created a class of workers or slaves, as described by Williams, whose livelihood and housing patterns were determined by U.S. interests in rubber. Fasseke's family owed its prominence to their planting of rubber to be sold to U.S. industries. Like certain African leaders of the 1960s, such as Azikiwe of Nigeria and Nkrumah of Ghana, Fasseke, whose lineage stems from a "long line of ironsmiths," studied in the U.S. and is aware of the historical connections between African Americans and indigenous Africans (*Jacob's Ladder* 17).

In addition to the larger national and external challenges of Pandemi, there is also the personal struggle of Jacob Henry (Jake), who, as an African American agent of the U.S. military, must face the contradictions of his identification with Africa and Pandemi, having been born there, and his loyalty to the U.S. To achieve a presentation of these complicated elements, Williams models the novel on devices of espionage fiction in which there is a strong element of suspense

Narrativizing the Internal-External Dynamic of African Political Power

and impending confrontation. The novel's plot centers on attempts by the U.S. through the CIA to destroy Pandemi's newly constructed fast breeder nuclear reactor. Although one critic thought the novel "hits a roadblock at every turn" (Packer 26), this element can be explained by Williams's goal to combine a novel of political ideas with one of suspense and action.

Jake's perceptions are joined with memories of the Atlantic slave trade, a significant opening to a novel that questions the destabilizing activities of the CIA in consort with U.S. embassy officials. For African Americans returning to the continent, the first sighting of the coastline can be a symbolic moment, a connection to diaspora consciousness and heritage: "From here, he thought, right from here, they left in their hundreds of thousands" (*Jacob's Ladder* 4). Jake also functions as an ironic perspective on the return to the Motherland theme: "What brought Jacob physically, spiritually, emotionally and psychologically home was embracing African culture" (Glocke 213). As one reviewer expressed it, the "novel explores in quite intriguing and provocative ways the ramifications of power—both political and personal" (Kalb 130).

Jake, who is also aware of the dynamics of global power and Africa's place at the table of players, admires Fasseke, who "had flown in the face of power, and against the entire history of what that power had always done to people," for his decision to achieve power through the building of a nuclear reactor, similar perhaps in concept to Nkrumah's interest in modern electrical power generation and the Akosombo Hydroelectric Project (*Jacob's Ladder* 81). It is relevant that Nkrumah supported the idea that the "Atomic Energy Commission" was part of "The Invisible Government," comprised of such agencies as the CIA, the National Security Council, and the FBI (Nkrumah 240).

The Pandemi of Fasseke, who gained control in 1960, is considered an improvement over the previous government of the Franklins, which had created internal ethnic battles in order to preserve its own power. Fasseke's progress is measured in the life expectancy rates of the people, which were extended three years as a result of the health programs supported by the WHO (World Health Organization). In this regard, Fasseke is presented as a Nkrumah-like Pan-Africanist leader who realizes that "[t]he struggle went on even as the bushbeaters of foreign companies slipped across the continent like vipers, stalking oil, uranium, cobalt, ferrochrome, bauxite, gold, iron, copper, diamonds" (*Jacob's Ladder* 11).

In the novel, the coup that topples Fasseke, a parallel to Nkrumah's ousting, is engineered by the CIA and described indirectly: "SOURCES SAY CIA AIDED IN COUP THAT DEPOSED PANDEMI'S FASSEKE" (242–43). This implies externalist intervention and perhaps the extreme end product of "destabilization," defined by former CIA agent John Stockwell as "put[ting] pressure on the targeted government by ripping apart the social and economic fabric of the country . . . but what they mean is making the people suffer as much as you can until the country plunges into chaos" (61). In Nkrumah's case, the 1966 coup was brought on by a combination of factors, both internal and external:

> When he [Nkrumah] attempted to lessen his country's dependence on the West by strengthening economic and military ties to the Soviet Union, China and East Germany, he effectively sealed his fate. . . . Those Ghanaians who carried out the coup suffered from no doubts that a move against Nkrumah would be supported by the Western powers. (Blum 198)

Williams also complicates the novel by including Nmadi Ouro, Fasseke's close friend and a writer-poet, who represents the artist-critic-intellectual; his poetic sensibility often runs counter to political expediency. The role of the intellectual has been addressed as well by Ayittey, who argues that "Africa's best hope lies with its intellectuals" although there are also those thinkers who "grab every opportunity they get to serve the dictates of barbarous military regimes" (*Africa Unchained* 427–428). For Williams, characters such as Fasseke, a somewhat flawed leader because he does not encourage democratic elections, and Ouro, the progressive intellectual, were the hope of the newly independent African states. Moreover, the Pan-Africanist ideas of Fasseke, "'to help our people and all of Africa,'" (*Jacob's Ladder*), reflect the argument of Nkrumah, who saw the counter to neocolonialism as "act[ing] on a Pan-African basis, through a Union Government" (Nkrumah 259). These were the ideals of Pan-Africanism and African nationalism, in general, which would themselves be challenged by succeeding generations in their criticism of African leaders of the past.

ANTHILLS OF THE SAVANNAH AND THE INTERNAL DILEMMA

Achebe's *Anthills of the Savannah*, published the same year as *Jacob's Ladder* and short-listed for the Booker Prize, is less concerned with U.S. interventions and more with internal neocolonial issues in the imagined state of Kangan in the 1980s, some twenty years beyond the independence era explored in *Jacob's Ladder*. *Anthills of the Savannah* shows how literature can go beyond fictional representation and serve a social end, as Achebe articulated in his essay "What Has Literature Got to Do with It?": "But we must not see the role of literature only in terms of providing latent support for things as they are, for it does also offer the kinetic energy necessary for social transition and change" (167).

Anthills of the Savannah was a long time in the making, having been published more than twenty years after *A Man of the People* (1966). In 1982, about five years before *Anthills of the Savannah's* publication, Achebe "had not found an adequate story to carry the themes he had in mind" (Ohaeto 223). The turning point in Achebe's progress on the novel occurred in 1985 near the publication of his *The Trouble with Nigeria*, which might have "'helped to ease the passage of the new story'" (Ohaeto 242). The novel, which was published when General Babangida was the military head of state in Nigeria, is implicitly a commentary on his rule and those of other Nigerian military figures. Nigeria experienced some four military coups and five military leaders after 1966: Generals Gowon, Murtala, Obasanjo, Buhari, and Babangida.

Achebe is especially concerned with the kind of power wielded by military leaders, of whom Wole Soyinka expressed scathing criticism in *The Open Sore of a Continent: A Personal Narrative of the Nigerian Crisis* (1996). For Soyinka, "[a]ll that is served by the chest-thumping rhetoric is the right of the military to do anything, adopt and execute any policy no matter where it leads" (33).

The publication of *Anthills of the Savannah* elicited critical reviews from two prominent writers from Africa, Somali novelist Nuruddin Farah and South African novelist Nadine Gordimer. Farah, who has also written novels about national leaders, especially in Somalia, such as the trilogy, *Variations on the Theme of an African Dictatorship* (1980–1983), which includes *Sweet and Sour Milk* (1979), *Sardines* (1981), and *Close Sesame* (1983), praised *Anthills of the Savannah* and underscored Achebe's achievement: "Achebe is, in my opinion, Africa's best novelist and craftsman, and one of the world's greatest, living or dead" (Farah 1828). However, regarding the plot, Farah thought, "Now and again, there is a stylistic stutter. Often the points in the novel are made in a roundabout way or else in a cryptic manner," but, ultimately, the work was a "rich treasure of transferred meanings" (Farah 1828). Nadine Gordimer's review was somewhat controversial in that she introduced the question of her own authority and a defense of her position as a reviewer: "I need no special knowledge of a writer's people, country or continent." Despite these opening comments, Gordimer recognized the complexity and challenge of Achebe's task: "This drama is no triangle on which a single clang is sounded. It reverberates through and gains resonance from linkage with other, richly complicated formations" (Gordimer 1). Another reviewer thought that Achebe "indulges in editorializing which strains credibility" and that he had created a "simple morality tale" (Pryce-Jones 1106).

Achebe has described his overall novelistic conception as "re-creations of the history of Africa in fictional terms" (Gordimer 1), and *Anthills of the Savannah* shows the additional interest in politics, governance, the role of the intellectual, the media, and traditional systems. As in *Jacob's Ladder*, the novel portrays a head of state, Sam, or "His Excellency," but also emphasizes the role of the intellectuals and the media. Chris Oriko, the Commissioner for Information, and Ikem Osodi, editor of the *National Gazette*, a state-run newspaper, serve this function, the latter used to show that "[a] free and independent media" is an integral part of governmental reform (Ayittey, *Defeating* 245).

Achebe uses the writer-intellectual in a more extensive manner than does Williams, whose development of Nmadi Ouro is a minor thread of his work. Also, Chris and Ikem are paired with women characters, Beatrice and Elewa. Of the female characters, Beatrice has special prominence as a narrative voice, and, as Farah noted, is given "a lioness's share in the telling of the story itself" (1831). The novel also develops intrastate rivalry, particularly the contestations brought forward by a delegation from the northern province of Abazon, their appeals for services, and their reluctance to agree with His Excellency's "presidency for life" quest.

Kangan in *Anthills of the Savannah* is a military state, and the portrayals of His Excellency and the machinery of government are handled with a sharp satiric style. Achebe achieves the kind of mockery also found in Ngũgĩ's *Wizard of the Crow*, which is based more on a magical realism style, but also mocks the "Ruler" of a mythical African state, the Republic of Aburĩria. In *Anthills of the Savannah*, "it is the ludicrous aspects of his [His Excellency's] regime that receive the most attention" (Gross 18). The edge of humor and mockery is apparent in the opening section narrated from the perspective of Chris, whom His Excellency acknowledges as the one who "owns all the words in this country—newspapers, radio and television stations" (*Anthills* 6). Through the interventions of the various cabinet members, such as the Commissioner for Justice and Attorney General, the Commissioner for Education, and the Chief Secretary, Achebe satirizes parliamentary imitations. Certain cabinet ministers display exaggerated obeisance to His Excellency, and Chris's observations about the source of their attitudes raises questions about the intellectual class: "I am not thinking so much about him as about my colleagues, eleven intelligent, educated men who let this happen to them, who actually went out of their way to invite it, and who even at this hour have seen and learnt nothing, the cream of our society and the hope of the black race" (2). Chris occupies a "silly observation post" from which he makes "farcical entries in the crazy log-book of this our ship of state" (*Anthills* 2). (A mocking presentation of cabinet ministers is also projected with greater exaggeration in *Wizard of the Crow*.) Professor Okong, an academic who is the Commissioner for Home Affairs, and His Excellency are both attired in ways that suggest a mockery of their positions. Rather than wearing military garb, His Excellency wears a white *danshiki* embroidered in gold, implying a cultural nationalist leaning. Professor Okong, on the other hand, wears khaki safari suits with epaulettes, a kind of quasi-military garb or a colonial administrator's attire, a style preferred by the "crew from the Universities." In this way, the novel raises questions about the relationship between intellectual elites, university professors, and military rule; at one point Chris observes, "It is amazing how the intellectual envies the man of action" (4). Closely associated with a liberated media, "intellectual freedom" is also associated with state "reform," which is most effective when it is "[i]nternally initiated" rather than "dictated from the outside by, for example, the World Bank" (Ayittey, *Defeating* 196).

Similar to a pattern used by Williams, Achebe also describes the method through which the head of state came to power. His Excellency, who had no preparation for political leadership, attended a private military college in England, which did not train officers to "take over Her Majesty's throne" (*Anthills* 11). This is a replication of the actual circumstances of certain African military leaders, such as Nigeria's General Murtala Muhammed, who attended Sandhurst Military Academy in England. In the novel, military school training had a counterproductive result for Sam, detachment from the matters of state, a state in which the former leaders of the civilian government are described as ending up "unloved and unmourned on the rubbish heap" (*Anthills* 11). In its place, the military government is unprepared for leading a state, unlike the government of Fasseke from *Jacob's Ladder*, which emerges as potentially progressive because its leader is aware of international power politics and Pan-Africanism.

Achebe's mockery of government workings echoes the prominent internalist arguments about the inefficiency of military leaders in operating governmental structures. The manner in which His Excellency relies on recommendations and advice in the forming of his cabinet, a group brought together in an uncertain manner, exemplifies this ineffectiveness. Chris's role in advising and helping to select the cabinet provides an opportunity for further satiric ridicule. His Excellency is "terrified of his new job" and is afraid of public demonstrations. This causes Chris to wonder "why the military armed to the teeth as they are can find unarmed civilians such a threat" (*Anthills* 12).

Most important, with the portrayal of Ikem Osodi, Achebe develops more fully the role of the writer, or as one critic noted, "Achebe assigns enlightened intellectuals a significant role in imagining alternatives to the nation-state" (Erritouni 50). Ikem, who hails from Abazon, suffering from drought and other ills, is critical of Sam's relationship with that part of the country. Ikem's "tragedy," as expressed by Simon Gikandi, derives from his "attempt to understand the African situation differently, to develop a logic for explaining a condition which appears illogical" (Gikandi 134).

Ikem's *Hymn to the Sun*, in which he expresses a national conscience, is a poetic prose statement that contains the title of the novel and offers another level of "logic." The hymn is an entreaty to "the Great Carrier of Sacrifice to the Almighty: Single Eye of God" to address the "hideous abomination," which has caused strife and disunity in Kangan, symbolized by the landscape and the destruction of the environment:

> The trees had become hydra-headed bronze statues so ancient that only blunt residual features remained on their faces, like anthills surviving to tell the new grass of the savannah about last year's brush fires. (28)

The tone of the hymn is of ominous doom in that it describes choking goats, cattle, and "[s]tray dogs in the market-place in a running battle with vultures" (*Anthills* 28). The hymn is also a nightmare of destruction, disintegration of the land, and the dissolution of traditional patterns. This element of the novel, the representation of the earth and traditional reliance on the planting cycle and spiritual rebirth, may suggest reclamation of non-Westernized structures, a sense that the communalism associated with the past may be a source for reform. Later in the novel, Ikem's speech before the Student Union at the University of Bassa, after he is suspended from the *National Gazette*, is one of the central statements concerning corruption within the military state but also an indictment of intellectuals and a clarification of "the new radicalism." Here the play of internal and external forces is blended with a somewhat ambivalent conclusion: "First and foremost, this radicalism must be clear-eyed enough to see beyond the present claptrap that will heap all our problems on the doorstep of capitalism and imperialism[.] . . . Please don't get me wrong. I do not deny that external factors are still at the root of many of our problems" (*Anthills* 146). Perhaps the logic Gikandi refers to is exemplified here when Ikem reminds his audience to distinguish between "remote and immediate causes" (*Anthills* 146). Interestingly, the speech, which echoes images in Ngũgĩ's *Matigari*, published the same year as *Anthills of the Savannah*, describes His Excellency's colleagues as "parasites" and uncritical students as "parroting" ideas of "'half-digested radical rhetoric'" (*Anthills* 146, 147, 148). Similarly, Emmanuel Obiechina called those state officials who submit to His Excellency's wishes "an array of puppets and chorus-boys who kowtow to him like so many marionettes" (Obiechina 18).

The other writer-intellectual in the novel, Chris, is part of the regime, and in earlier parts of the novel, he contests Ikem's positions despite the fact that at one time they had somewhat of a shared intellectual experience. Chris and Ikem had attended Lord Lugard College, the imaginary institution in Kangan named after Lord Lugard, the actual British proconsul responsible for elements of the British colonial system. As Minister for Information, Chris is torn between his admiration of Ikem's integrity and his own need to support the political expediency of the state. However, Chris can be interpreted as the intellectual who ultimately faces the truths about his nation after he is falsely accused of involvement in the "coup plot" to overthrow His Excellency and flees northward (171). Chris becomes a "wide-eyed newcomer to the ways of Kangan" (186), and his killing is in many ways metaphorically sacrificial.

Most important, Achebe uses Beatrice, B.B., Chris's mate and also a politically conscious intellectual, to emphasize the overall critique of the state. As Gordimer observed, "[I]t is Mr. Achebe's victory that she is also one of the most extraordinary, attractive and moving women characters in any contemporary novel" (Gordimer 1). In the closing, Beatrice signifies the progressive direction of Abazon arising from the death of Chris and the military coup that ousts the current regime. Beatrice's decision to name the child of Ikem and Elewa with a male name demonstrates her position of leadership. For Beatrice, the usual act of naming is "an ideological attempt by society to imprison girls by the citation of authorized time-honoured modes of (female) conduct" (Diala 194). The traditional ceremony of naming is modified when it becomes a collective decision initiated by Beatrice and ultimately accepted by the elder, the "old man": "We shall call this child AMAECHINA: *May-the-path-never-close*" (*Anthills* 206). Beatrice and her group, which had included Chris and Ikem, signify a future coalition, a new consciousness, which is connected to traditional culture but which goes beyond its rituals or especially gender restrictions. Although this intergenerational reconciliation contains the promise of a new "path," of the ending of the drought in Ikem's *Hymn*, it does not solve the political crisis in a state where the new leadership has arrived through yet another coup.

In *Anthills of the Savannah*, the coup is not necessarily attributed to global or Western intervention, as in *Jacob's Ladder*, which echoed Ghana's 1966 coup and the complicated subplots on both internal and external levels. Although Achebe acknowledges the possibility of external causes, especially in Chris's speech, which allows for "external factors," he focuses on what can be achieved by the will of the people, intellectuals, an open media, and a reform that includes women's voices, a point that Ngũgĩ emphasizes as well in *Wizard of the Crow*. The internal-external concept is an inextricable element of novels that challenge African dictatorial or military regimes, although certain critics may view the historical chain that links colonialism, neocolonialism, and globalization as no longer a productive causative relationship. However, if certain African novelists choose to revisit the independence era in order to re-vision it in fictional terms, they might, like Williams, find it unavoidable to unearth the excesses of the past with their attendant complexities, many of which have corollaries in successive eras.

Works Cited

Achebe, Chinua. *Anthills of the Savannah*. New York: Anchor, 1988. Print.

———. *A Man of the People*. London: Heinemann, 1966. Print.

———. "What Has Literature Got to Do with It?" *Hopes and Impediments: Selected Essays.* New York: Doubleday, 1989. 154–170. Print.

Armah, Ayi Kwei. *The Beautyful Ones Are Not Yet Born*. Boston: Houghton, 1968. Print.

Ayittey, George B. N. *Africa Betrayed*. New York: St Martin's, 1992. Print.
———. *Africa in Chaos*. New York: St. Martin's, 1998. Print.
———. *Africa Unchained: The Blueprint for Africa's Future*. New York: Palgrave, 2005. Print.
———. *Defeating Dictators: Fighting Tyranny in Africa and Around the World*. New York: Palgrave, 2011. Print.
Blum, William. *Killing Hope: U.S. Military and CIA Interventions Since World War II*. Monroe, ME: Common Courage Press, 2004. Print.
Brown, Michael Barratt. *Africa's Choices: After Thirty Years of the World Bank*. Boulder, CO: Westview, 1996. Print.
Collier, Paul, and Jan Willem Gunning. "Why Has Africa Grown Slowly?" *Journal of Economic Perspectives* 13.3 (1999): 3–22. Print.
Diala, Okeawolam Isidore. "Mythic Mediation and Feminism: Achebe's *Anthills of the Savannah*." *Ariel* 36.3/4 (2005): 185–202. Print.
Erritouni, Ali. "Contradictions and Alternatives in Chinua Achebe's *Anthills of the Savannah*." *Journal of Modern Literature* 29.2 (2006): 50–74. Print.
Ezenwa-Ohaeto. *Chinua Achebe: A Biography*. Bloomington: Indiana UP, 1997. Print.
Farah, Nuruddin. *Close Sesame*. London: Allison Busby, 1983. Print.
———. Rev. of *Anthills of the Savannah*, by Chinua Achebe. *West Africa* 21 Sept. 1987: 1828-1831. Print.
———. *Sardines*. London: Allison Busby, 1981. Print.
———. *Sweet and Sour Milk*. London: Allison Busby, 1979. Print.
Gebe, Boni Yao. "Ghana's Foreign Policy at Independence and Implications for the 1966 Coup D'état." *Journal of Pan African Studies* 2.3 (2008): 160–186. Print.
Gikandi, Simon. *Reading Chinua Achebe: Language and Ideology in Fiction*. Oxford, UK: James Currey, 1991. Print.
Glocke, Aimee. "The Path Toward Literary Liberation: The Role of the African Worldview in Conducting an African Centered Analysis of *Jacob's Ladder*." *Journal of Pan African Studies* 4.5 (2011): 196–217. Print.
Gordimer, Nadine. "A Tyranny of Clowns." Rev. of *Anthills of the Savannah*, by Chinua Achebe. *New York Times Book Review* 21 Feb. 1988: 1. *New York Times*. Web. 13 Jan. 2012.
Gross, John. "Books of the Times: *Anthills of the Savannah*." Rev. of *Anthills of the Savannah*, by Chinua Achebe. *New York Times* 16 Feb. 1988: C18. Print.
Jaffe, Andrew M. "A Black American in the New Africa." Rev. of *Jacob's Ladder*, by John A. Williams. *Los Angeles Times Book Review* 29 Nov 1987: 5. Print.
Kalb, John D. Rev. of *Jacob's Ladder*, by John A. Williams. *Melus* 16.4 (Winter 1989–1990): 129–131. Print.
Kirkpatrick, Jeane J. *Dictatorships and Double Standards: Rationalism and Reason in Politics*. New York: Simon and Schuster, 1982. Print.
Lerner, Max. "The Pattern of Dictatorship." *Dictatorship in the Modern World*. Ed. Guy Stanton Ford. Minneapolis: U of Minnesota P, 1935. 3–20. Print.
Ngugi wa Thiong'o. *Matigari*. 1987. London: Heinemann, 1989. Print.
———. *Wizard of the Crow*. New York: Pantheon, 2006. Print.
Nkrumah, Kwame. *Neo-Colonialism: The Last Stage of Imperialism*. New York: International Publishers, 1965. Print.
Obiechina, Emmanuel. "Parables of Power and Powerlessness: Exploration in Anglophone African Fiction Today." *Issue: A Journal of Opinion* 20.2 (Summer 1992): 17–25. Print.

Packer, George. Rev. of *Jacob's Ladder*, by John A. Williams. *New York Times* 15 Nov. 1987: 26. Print.

Pryce-Jones, David. Rev. of *Anthills of the Savannah*, by Chinua Achebe. *Times Literary Supplement* 9 Oct. 1987: 1106. Print.

Simpson, C. L. *The Memoirs of C.L. Simpson*. London: Diplomatic Press and Publishing Company, 1961. Print.

Soyinka, Wole. *Kongi's Harvest*. London: Oxford UP, 1967. Print.

———. *The Open Sore of a Continent: A Personal Narrative of the Nigerian Crisis*. New York: Oxford UP, 1997. Print.

Stockwell, John. *The Praetorian Guard: The U.S. Role in the New World Order*. Boston: South End Press, 1991. Print.

Thies, Cameron G. "The Political Economy of State Building in Sub-Saharan Africa." *The Journal of Politics* 69.3 (2007): 716–31. Print.

Waltz, Kenneth N. *Theory of International Politics*. Reading, MA: Addison-Wesley, 1979. Print.

Williams, John A. *Africa: Her History, Lands and People*. New York: Cooper Square Publishers, 1962. Print.

———. *!Click Song*. Boston: Houghton, 1982. Print.

———. *Clifford's Blues*. Minneapolis: Coffee House, 1999. Print.

———. *Jacob's Ladder*. New York: Thunder's Mouth, 1987. Print.

———. *The Man Who Cried I Am*. Boston: Little, Brown, 1967. Print.

The Dictator and His Objects: The Status of the Fetish in the African Dictator Novel

MAGALÍ ARMILLAS-TISEYRA

Fetish objects, invoked as the stuff of traditional culture, frequently appear in literary representations of dictators in African fiction. These objects are tied to the historical referents (actual African dictators) that the novels invoke, mock, and aim to subvert. The dictator in Ngũgĩ wa Thiong'o's *Wizard of the Crow* (2006), for example, carries what is referred to as a "traditional" staff and flywhisk and wears a suit decorated with animal skins that recalls Mobutu Sese Seko of Zaire, among others. The presence of these fetishes is part of the rich fabric of characterization, at once fictional and rooted in historical fact, of these novels. But characterization and critique by association are not the limit of the function the objects serve in these novels. As I will show, the presence of fetishes in African novels about dictators is more than an element of local color or a comic touch. Rather, fetish objects in these novels make visible the ways in which dictatorial power constructs and maintains its authority and are central to the analysis of authoritarian power that these novels put forward.

My reading of African novels about dictators borrows the term "dictator novel" from Latin American literature and criticism, where the genre has a long-standing tradition reaching back to the nineteenth century. The Latin American paradigm provides a useful conceptual and critical analog, a productive touchstone, in reading African dictator novels. As I will show, the Paraguayan novelist Augusto Roa Bastos's *I the Supreme* (1974) supplies a key to reading the dictator's fetish objects in African novels such as Ousmane Sembène's *The Last of the Empire*

(1981) and Ahmadou Kourouma's *Waiting for the Vote of the Wild Beasts* (1998) in particular; in both *I the Supreme* and *Waiting for the Vote of the Wild Beasts*, the dictator keeps a meteorite as a fetish and views it as the foundation of his power. Reading these texts and the various meanings given to the fetish objects together, I will unpack the function of the fetish in the dictator novel at large. In doing so, I will argue that the literary representation of the African dictator does not simply describe the nature of the dictator but also makes evident the ways in which the dictator is "made"—how he comes into existence and maintains his power. Fetishes are the nodes around which practices of meaning making are staged, demonstrating the ways in which the authoritarian state aims to control the construction of meaning. It is here, rather than in the parodic or farcical representation of the dictator, that the most cogent critique of authoritarianism takes shape.

Sembène's *The Last of the Empire*, which follows the unraveling of a dictator's rule and an eventual coup, begins with the disappearance of Léon Mignane, the Venerable One (*le Vénérable*).[1] The opening scene is a meeting of his ministers, who realize they have little claim to authority beyond their connection to the missing dictator. Afterward, Prime Minister Daouda remains alone, staring at the Venerable One's empty throne. The chair is an amalgam of traditional symbols, each drawn from a different culture. The symbolic excess here functions both as characterization and comic touch, recalling the very real excesses of the Venerable One's historical analogues.[2] Yet in spite of its comic potential, the dictator's throne also possesses a certain aura: Daouda has never sat in the chair, even when substituting for the dictator in his official function as prime minister. It inspires both awe and terror:

> He [Daouda] was fascinated, as if attracted by a supernatural power. Timidly he drew near. The hand-embroidered cushion of Kashmir silk charmed him. He held out his hand to touch the fabric. His heart beat twice as fast. A tide of warm blood flooded up his arm from his fingers. When his middle finger touched the cushion's seam, his blood flowed more quickly, piercingly chill. It seized his whole body. He withdrew his hand as if scorched, breathing heavily. He glanced fearfully at the walls, the folds of the curtains, the masks and statues. He was certain something was spying on him. He turned around quickly. No one! But the feeling remained. (17)

In the fascination and superstitious fear that it inspires, the dictator's throne functions as a fetish object. The term "fetish" is used in the sense inherited from anthropology and colonial ethnography: an inanimate object imbued with magical powers that stirs superstitious or irrational dread and yet also reverence. The pejorative connotations of this description are of a piece with the history of the concept of the fetish in anthropological discourses, particularly about Africa,

The Status of the Fetish in the African Dictator Novel

and this is part of the legacy with which authors who include fetish objects in their representation of African dictators engage.

The dictator's fetish objects are central to the narrative in Kourouma's *Waiting for the Vote of the Wild Beasts*. The story hinges on the disappearance of the dictator's two fetishes—a meteorite and a Koran—which he must regain in order to return to power. The novel describes the oral performance of the narrative of the rise and fall of Koyaga, the "president-dictator" (*président-dictateur*) of the fictional Republic of the Gulf (*la République du Golfe*).[3] Koyaga established his dictatorship during the Cold War only to see it unravel after the dissolution of the Soviet Union. His story is presented in the form of a *donsomana*, a genre of Malinke oral literature recited for members of the hunter clan; Koyaga himself is a master hunter and often referred to as a hunter of both beasts and men.[4] The *donsomana* is recited over the course of several days and is performed by a *sèrè*, the oral performer of the society of hunters. The *sèrè* is assisted by a *koroduwa*, a respondent who plays a role similar to that of the court jester: he is trenchant and occasionally insulting but allowed to be so. The *koroduwa*'s interjections provide an explicitly critical edge to the tone of the narration in the novel.

The occasion for the performance is, in fact, the disappearance of the dictator's fetishes. The *donsomana* is a purificatory narrative (*récit purificatoire*), and it is only once Koyaga's crimes have been narrated that the fetishes will reveal where they are hidden, making it possible for Koyaga to return to power. Although the performers initially seem to be in league with the dictator, the explanation of the purpose of the performance emphasizes the omission of substantive information about Koyaga's misdeeds as dictator throughout the narrative: little concrete information is given about his actual time in power, save for his visits to other dictators and the attempts on his life. Together with the critical edge of the *koroduwa*'s interjections, the absence of the promised narrative (Koyaga's crimes) raises questions about the performers' relation to the dictator. Their seeming complicity may in fact be a cover for their opposition and the narrative, therefore, an act of subversion. While the novel does not resolve these questions, the suggestion that the two narrators are not completely in the dictator's service opens a space for opposition to the dictator.

Similarly, the meaning of the novel's title is only suggested at the end of the performance; the *sèrè* remarks, "For you know, you are sure, that if by chance men refuse to vote for you, the animals (*les animaux*) will come out of the bush, seize ballots, and vote for you" (258). This claim is at once figurative and literal: it is impossible that, fetishes in hand, Koyaga will not return to power. In more literal terms, such an event is not outside the realm of possibility of the narrative world established in the novel, as animals have come out of the bush before. The ambivalence of the *sèrè*'s claim—that is, the budding of potential meanings and interpretations that attach to this statement—is of a piece with the ambivalent tone of the narration as a whole. It is also the impossible event that does not take place; the narrative, at the close of the novel, remains in suspension, the fetishes remain to be found, and Koyaga is still out of office. We are, in short, still waiting, and this links the *sèrè*'s closing remark to the title of the novel.

But the *sèrè*'s claim at the end of the novel both is and is not equivalent to the title, which refers to waiting for the vote of the wild beasts (*bêtes sauvages*).[5] In connection to Koyaga's role as a hunter, the word "beast" is more commonly used, and the two words are not semantically or contextually interchangeable. The *sèrè*'s claim does and does not refer to the title, just as the narration of the *donsomana* both is and is not in service of the dictator. This ambivalent structure recalls (although it is not identical to) that of the fetish, an object that is also a thing with supernatural powers: the Venerable One's throne is both a chair as well as the mark of the dictator's power. In turn, the ambivalence of meaning that the fetish reveals opens onto the political manipulation of language.

As in *The Last of the Empire*, the dictator is not the only one invested in the power of his fetish. Having survived yet another attempt on his life, Koyaga withdraws from the presidential palace but declares that he will return to office via democratic elections. Following Koyaga's disappearance, his fellow dictators launch their own searches for his missing fetishes, wishing to claim their power for themselves. Each dictator sends a team to Kogaya's village in search of the meteorite and the Koran: "[T]here were hundreds of secret agents searching and digging each tuft or parcel of ground" (257). The image is comical, but, like Daouda's superstitious reaction to the Venerable One's throne, the effect that Koyaga's special objects have on others is what confirms their status as fetishes. The value of the fetish object is constituted not by its intrinsic qualities but by the values imputed to that object by those who come into contact with it. This interpretation is central to the nature of the "fetish" whether within the realm of anthropology, psychoanalysis, or Marxist discourses of commodity fetishism. It is necessary, at this point in the argument, to ask how the fetish object achieves its meaningfulness and, further, how it comes to gain an aura of unassailability.

In *On the Postcolony*, Achille Mbembe describes the way in which the dictator (or, authoritarian ruler) establishes his *commandement* (authority) in the postcolonial African state. The term *commandement* originally appears in the context of Mbembe's discussion of colonial authority and is used to name a particular mode of colonial control. In the postcolony, the colonial *commandement* becomes what Mbembe calls "the authoritarian modality *par excellance*" (134, n8). The historical phenomenon of dictatorship is directly linked to the colonial experience, not merely as an after-effect but also as an expression of the neocolonial relations former colonial powers, as well as global powers more generally, attempted to institute after independence. Dictator novels take up this assertion in their representation of dictatorships: the presence of foreign actors or the effects of foreign influence are one of the tropes of the genre in both Latin America and Africa.

Mbembe's analysis of the way in which the dictator institutes his authority, in the chapter "The Aesthetics of Vulgarity," refers directly to the questions under discussion:

> In the postcolony the *commandement* seeks to institutionalize itself, to achieve legitimation and hegemony (*recherche hégémonique*), in the form of a *fetish*. The signs, vocabulary, and narratives that the *commandement* produces are meant not merely to be symbols; they are officially invested with a surplus of meaning that are not negotiable and that one is officially forbidden to depart from or challenge. To ensure that no such challenge takes place, the champions of state power invent entire constellations of ideas; they adopt a distinct set of cultural repertoires and powerfully evocative concepts; but they also resort, if necessary, to the systematic application of pain. The basic goal is not just to bring a specific political consciousness into being, but to make it effective. (103)

The form of the fetish names the excess or additional meanings attached to the signs (symbols, narratives) produced by the dictator and presented as the bases of his authority. Later in the same section, Mbembe also refers to the dictator's *commandement* as a cosmology. The excessive meaningfulness of these objects functions as an aura whose inaccessibility needs to be maintained by supplemental systems and practices, including violence.

In the context of his argument on vulgarity as an aesthetics of authoritarian power, Mbembe engages a critical tradition that reads vulgarity and vulgar representations of power as a subversive act, showing that this is not necessarily the case. In the postcolony, the mobilization of vulgarity functions not as a criticism but rather as part of the practice and aesthetics of power. It is one of the many repertoires to which the dictator makes recourse in maintaining the fetishistic aura of his *commandement*. For our purposes, Mbembe also shows that, while the fetish is seemingly unassailable, it needs to be maintained and protected by a larger symbolic and semantic system as well as, where necessary, recourse to violence. There is, then, a vulnerability to the fetish. This vulnerability originates in the surpluses of meaning attached to the object.

Although the fetishes in *The Last of the Empire* and *Waiting for the Vote of the Wild Beasts* have profound effects on those who come into contact with them, these novels also make clear that the meanings of these objects are not necessarily stable and often prove to be flexible. Even as fictional dictators invoke their fetishes, the objects carry additional meanings that complicate the dictators' relation to them. In order to unpack this, we should return to the origins of Koyaga's two fetishes: the meteorite, which he receives from his mother, Nadjuma, an animist priestess, and the Koran, which is a gift from the marabout (Muslim holy man) Bokano.

As Bokano presents Nadjuma with the fetishes for her son—the objects had previously chosen Bokano as their owner and now demand a transfer to the child Koyaga—he outlines a problematic tension: "Men of your son's race can never be just humane, while neither the aerolitic stone nor the Qur'an can tolerate iniquity and ferocity" (41). The meteorite and the Koran can be of little use to a dictator, for whom iniquity and ferocity are part of standard operating procedure. The fetish objects would seem to be rendered powerless by this founding condition. However, as the interest that other dictators show in finding the meteorite and the Koran suggests, the meaning attributed to the fetish object operates regardless of any proven effectiveness. The narrative itself never asserts, one way or the other, whether the fetishes are the reason for Koyaga's apparent invincibility. These objects are instead the expression of the dictator's authority: that is, of the dictator's ability to define the surplus of meaning attached to an object and to render it non-negotiable.

Kourouma uses the dictator's fetishes to demonstrate the contingency of meaning, made particularly evident as characters move between epistemological systems. There is critical potential in tracing these moves. For example, although Koyaga intends to find his fetishes in order to return to power, the real means by which he will regain his authority (*commandement*) is via democratic elections. The recourse to elections is a political move to appease Western governments that have made their support contingent on the democratization ("democratic" has replaced "anti-communist") of the Republic of the Gulf. Here democratic elections are rhetorically equated with the recuperation of the meteorite and the Koran. "Democratic elections" is rendered as much of a fetish as the meteorite or Koran: each is a symbolic imprimatur of the ruler's hold on power. The narrative points to fissures in the semantic foundations of the fetish object: it becomes clear as the *donsomana* unfolds that Koyaga himself often violates the original meaning of these objects. The force of the fetishes, such as it may be, comes not from the power imbued in them by the holy man but rather from the meanings imputed to them at various points in the novel.

In *Waiting for the Vote of the Wild Beasts*, the fetish is not a specifically "African" thing but rather the mark of overlapping or shifting economies of valuation. The fetish here stands not as an artifact of precolonial African traditional culture, as the dictator would have it, but rather as the signal of an economy of surplus meanings conditioned by the encounter between various and often competing interests. These interests, as so many dictator novels emphasize, are rooted in the competitions of global powers, which run counter to the interests of the emerging nation. While Mbembe offers a cogent explanation of the function of the fetish for the dictator, it is also necessary to consider the constitution of the fetish object as the mark, or consequence, of the encounter between different epistemological systems—these are the conditions of possibility for the fetish as we understand it.

As William Pietz explains in his exploration of the fetish in European Enlightenment discourse, the concept originates in the heterogeneous space of European contact with other cultures prior to and contemporaneous with the establishment of colonial relations; specifically, the fetish originates in "the cross-cultural spaces of the coast of West Africa during the sixteenth and seventeenth centuries" (5). In "The Problem of the Fetish," a series of essays on the topic, Pietz takes a historicist approach, beginning with the etymology of the term, which has its roots in the creolized Portuguese *fetisso* (*feitiço*), referring to witchcraft or magical practices. The term *feitiço* itself derives from the Latin *facticius*, meaning "manufactured." The fetish object is *made*, and these novels stage the making and unmaking of the fetish as part of the project of unraveling its aura of unassailability.

The fetish is what we could call, borrowing a term of Mary Louise Pratt, a phenomenon of the contact zone: it is constituted in the encounter between different cultural (epistemological) systems, often involving uneven relations of power, and, most importantly, it points to the simultaneous presence of diverse semantic or epistemological systems.[6] The excess of meaning ("superstition") attached to the fetish object is visible to the external observer who does not read the object within the same semantic code as it is presented. This is why the fetish marks the presence of multiple symbolic systems. It is also the reason for the fundamental vulnerability of the fetish. In this sense, the fetish signals the problem of contingency of value brought about by the existence of multiple and often conflicting systems, which are also the condition of its creation. We should recall here the Venerable One's throne in *The Last of the Empire*, which is composed of symbols drawn from throughout Africa. *Waiting for the Vote of the Wild Beasts*, with its play on cultural, religious, and political symbolic objects, uses the coexistence of multiple epistemological systems to both comic and critical effect. In turn, these objects point to the ways in which the dictator constructs and attempts to maintain his hold on power, and the exposure of the epistemological vulnerability of the fetish suggests the possible subversion of the dictator's authority.

The richest examples of rapid, and strategic, shifts between epistemological systems, which alternately make possible the fetish and threaten to undermine its power, come in the portion of the narrative dedicated to Koyaga's henchman, Macledio. In one episode, as he is escaping from a Bamileke royal court, Macledio takes with him the skulls of their ancestors to ensure his safe passage, knowing that the Bamileke king draws his authority from these skulls.[7] Macledio's transgression—which includes the desecration of the sanctuary where the skulls are kept—is only possible because he is an outsider to the epistemological system that renders these objects untouchable. To underline this point, the narrators inform us that a band of fierce warriors pursued Macledio, but none dared to attack for fear of harming the skulls.

However, once Macledio reaches the port, he negotiates with a group of Bamileke businessmen and exchanges the skulls for a briefcase filled with money. He explains:

> It was not so much the money (I have never tried to get rich). It was so I would not seem to be an idiot. I knew and admired the Bamileke for their cupidity and their business sense. The rich businessmen would have taken me for the most naïve person in the universe had I not traded the skulls of the ancestors for solid cash. (92–93)

Macledio does not accept the money because it is of value to him while the skulls are not: he accepts the exchange because the money he takes in return for the skulls is of great (if not greater) value to the Bamileke businessmen. In this scene, Macledio is not the only one who maneuvers multiple value systems at once. The Bamileke, too, can value the skulls and their money at once and strategically move between the logic of the two systems in order to achieve their goals. These various epistemological systems not only coexist but also interact, and the characters in the novel are able to shift between them as suits their immediate goals. Nothing, we are shown repeatedly, is truly fixed. This particular example also collapses the temporality of the narrative of the arrival of (implicitly European) modernity by pointing out the extent to which the sequentially ordered narratives of "barbarism-animism" and "civilization-modernity" are more often coterminous.[8] In turn, their simultaneous presence reveals the equivalence between the skull-fetish and the money-fetish of capitalist modernity.

Although we have to this point established that the dictator institutes and maintains his authority in the form of a fetish, made possible but also vulnerable by the co-existence of multiple and occasionally conflicting epistemological systems, some questions remain. First, what does the fetish object mean to the dictator? Second, in the context of the dictator novel, what interpretative possibilities do these objects offer? At this point, it is useful to turn to a Latin American dictator novel, Augusto Roa Bastos's *I the Supreme*, a fictionalized exploration of the final days of the nineteenth-century Paraguayan dictator, José Gaspar Rodríguez de Francia.[9] The novel is composed of "found" historical documents organized by a mysterious figure referred to as the "Compiler;"

the texts include Francia's dictations to his secretary as well as his personal log. Many of these texts are incomplete or overlapping and include marginal notes whose provenance is unclear. The narrative is filled with objects that function as fetishes, for Francia as well as for other characters; these include Francia's pen, a skull, a stone found in the intestines of a favorite cow, and a meteorite. For our purposes, I will discuss the object that offers an uncanny echo with Kourouma's *Waiting for the Vote of the Wild Beasts*: the meteorite. In the novel, Francia has the meteorite brought to the capital from the provinces, forces it into his house (the meteorite is said to resist), and keeps it chained to his desk chair.

As becomes clear over the course of the novel, the meteorite is the symbolic basis for Francia's conception of the Paraguayan Republic and his role as dictator. The capture of the meteor represents a victory over chance (*el azar*) and the guarantee of total control:

> I understood then that it is only by ripping this sort of thread of chance out of the weft of events that the impossible can be made possible. I suddenly realized that to-be-able-to-do [*poder hacer*] is to-be-able-to-enable [*hacer poder*]. At that instant a shooting star traced a luminous streak across the firmament[.] . . . I had read somewhere that falling stars, meteors, aeroliths, are the very picture of chance in the universe. The force of power lies then, I thought, in chasing down chance: *re-trapping* it[.] . . . Tracing down counter-chance. Removing from the chaos of the improbable the constellation possessed of probity. A State revolving on the axis of its sovereignty[.] . . . In the political universe, States confederate or explore. Exactly like the galaxies in the cosmic universe. (95–96)

Francia's authority as dictator is based on the submission of all aspects of national life to his ordering imperative. The state in this imaginary matrix functions as a universe, with the dictator as the gravitational force at its center. We should recall here Mbembe's language of the dictator's *commandement* functioning as a "constellation of ideas" as well as his comparison of it to a cosmology. The term "cosmology" is the most fitting description of the way in which Francia—and the dictator more generally—envisions the state, precisely because of the totality the term connotes.

As both the founding figure of the metaphorical economy through which the dictator understands the state and the mystical power from which he draws his strength—literally, in the form of the hyper-precise rifles he has made from the stone—Francia's meteorite is the cornerstone of his authoritarian power. But Francia's presentation of the meteorite draws scorn from the anonymous voice (*Unknown hand*) that keeps interrupting in the text: "Did you believe that you were thereby doing away with chance? [. . .] One aerolith does not make a sovereign" (99–100). This interruption removes the aura of the fetish-meteorite, its surplus of meaning, reducing it to a mere artifact. Francia replies, "You don't understand what I write. You don't understand that the law is symbolic. Twisted minds are unable to grasp this. They interpret the symbols literally. And so you make mistakes and fill my margins with your scoffing self-importance. At least read me correctly" (100). From the dictator's perspective, this is an instance of misreading as the meaning of the fetish object is not negotiable. The dictator's understanding of the metaphor ("I understood then") is contrasted to the unknown reader's lack thereof ("You don't understand"). The differentiation is between reading practices; more precisely, it is a distinction between symbolic systems, although the dictator will not acknowledge this.

As Mbembe makes clear, above, the non-negotiability of the fetish is part of the symbolic systems established to protect the dictator's power. In the above exchange, we are once again faced with the presence of a gap or break that reveals the contingency of the values attached to these objects. To make this contingency visible emphasizes the instability of historical knowledge, as these objects outlive their interpretations and take on new meanings. This epistemological uncertainty is the source of the panic that unravels in the dictator Francia over the course of the novel. *I the Supreme* uses such moments to demonstrate how the dictator might be misread, or, alternately, how it is possible to read against the dictator. In more general terms, if the fetish objects in these novels reveal the ways in which the dictator constructs his authority—concurrently, that his authority is in fact constructed—then they also function as starting points for the subversion of the dictator's semantic system.

While the Venerable One's throne in the scene from Sembène's *The Last of the Empire* referenced above initially inspires fear in the Prime Minister Daouda, his reaction is contextualized. Daouda knows the Venerable One practices "fetishist rites" for symbolically strategic reasons rather than for his own investment in their value: "One day the Venerable One, in an expansive mood, had whispered to him: 'Africa is irrational! Or else its rationality is such as to startle the modern world[.] . . . One has to make use of such practices . . . to protect oneself against enemies within'" (17). The Venerable One here offers us a more cynical version of the dictator's relation to the fetish object: it is explicitly strategic. For the dictator in the African novels under discussion, the adoption of any particular fetish object is a tactical decision. The point is not the dictator's feeling for the fetish object or rite but rather the feeling that the object inspires in others. Daouda's initial reaction confirms this; convinced that the Venerable One is alive and watching, Daouda refuses to assume the mantle of power. But the aura of the fetish object only holds for so long.

In *The Last of the Empire*, Daouda's perspective shifts as political chaos spreads. Deeply frustrated with the still-missing Venerable One and his political machinations, Daouda moves closer to taking power. This shift is dramatized in terms of his relation to the throne, which he now reads differently:

> The throne seemed bare. The carved details were no longer visible. He laid his hand on it. The smooth polished wood invited him to sit down. He listened to his heart... Not a cry, not a howl. He recited the *Fatiha-al-kitab* and other incantations. His Koranic training had returned to his memory. He sat down. From the Venerable One's raised seat, his veiled gaze (because of the glasses) swept the two sides of the table. There was nothing there, just emptiness. Now calm, he felt a new sensation flooding gently through his veins. To be so close to power and lose it? To be Number One. A man of caste, was he? Good... I'll play it close... He leaned back on the panther. (182)

The power of the throne has faded, and this makes it possible for Daouda to take the dictator's place. This occupation is, in turn, accompanied by the institution of other rites on which Daouda's authority (*commandement*) will be based. After Daouda has sat on the throne, two assistants enter; their reaction mirrors Daouda's former reverence for the Venerable One's throne.[10] For a moment, the narrative focus shifts to one of these men, and his reaction confirms Daouda's ascension to the position of dictator: "[He] had seen in this occupation of the throne, the Father's place, a sacred continuity. He left quickly. He was eager to show the new leader how active he was in his service" (183).

As we learn here, fetish objects can rather quickly be re-inscribed with new meanings and put to new uses. More to the point, having established that the dictator's relation to the fetish is instrumental, the novel makes it possible for Daouda to assume and re-inscribe the dictator's fetish, constituting it as the mark of his (Daouda's) own dictatorial authority. In *The Last of the Empire*, Daouda's rise is cut short by the military coup. While the larger argument of the novel is about the involvement of external (European) governments in the internal affairs of African countries, within that framework Sembène presents an argument about the fetishistic nature of the dictator's authority. In this context, the traditional symbols of the Venerable One's throne are little different from the democratic elections to which Koyaga hopes to take recourse. Key here is the fact that the same object can be re-inscribed and used to bolster the authority of another.

The example of Daouda's relation to the Venerable One's throne in *The Last of the Empire* centers on a shift in the reading practices of a single character: understanding the throne's power as metaphorical rather than literal is fundamental to this shift. What makes this shift possible, in turn, is the very nature of language as the primary symbolic system through which authority is constituted. The portion of *Waiting for the Vote of the Wild Beasts* that focuses on Macledio's peregrinations offers answers. As Kourouma has stated in interviews, Macledio's story is the key through which the novel should be read: "All of the elements [in the novel] participate in the meaning [*le sens*] Macledio allows [one] to understand Koyaga, just as Koyaga allows [one] to understand Macledio" (Chemla 27).[11] Although initially the shift to Macledio seems an interruption and a deviation from the purpose of the performance, within the novel, the portion of the narrative dedicated to Macledio is the thematic core of *Waiting for the Vote of the Wild Beasts*.

As a young boy in his village, Macledio is charged with killing and eating the soul of a close friend who has died. The body of the dead boy is reanimated by the local sorcerer and seems to implicate Macledio. At first, Macledio resists the accusation, but he cannot withstand the force of the narrative put forward by the sorcerer that conducts the ceremony:

> [T]he facts, details, specificities followed one after another and finally became evident. At first, as if in a kind of dream, Macledio began to doubt himself, his own awareness, his memory. With the insistence and perseverance of the sorcerer, all the accusation took shape and the dream took on substance. The vague reality became experience. So it was true—he was, in fact, a sorcerer, a consumer of souls. It was true, that was really him. (86–87)

Here Kourouma demonstrates the way in which language—fictive or literary language—can harden into apparent fact. Narrative imposes itself onto and molds reality through repetition, accumulation, and insistence. The accused gives way, incorporating the false narrative as experience. To return to Mbembe's language, Macledio here is made to accept the cultural repertoire that renders him a murderer and consequently an outcast.

Much later, after spending some time in France, Macledio returns to another country in Africa—the Republic of the Mountains—and goes to work for the dictator Nkutigi, known as the Man in White. In entering into the service of the dictator, Macledio shifts from the position of victim to aggressor: he becomes the champion of state power who produces the constellation of ideas that shore up the authority of the dictator's fetishes.[12] While working for the national radio of the Republic of the Mountains, Macledio specializes in inventing and denouncing plots against the dictator. He proves particularly adept at the task:

> Whatever he dreamed up out of whole cloth [*de toutes pièces*] became fact, the true phrases of a veritable plot, for the police, the judicial system, the party, and the international press[.] ... Subjected to instruments of torture, victims repeated Macledio's phrases, adorning them with many details, and finally made them sound accurate, logical, and irrefutable. (111–12)

The language of dreaming, of facts, and of truth recalls the prior scene from Macledio's childhood. Once again there is a combination of the imposition of language and the use of physical force in order to maintain a structure of authority. The similarities between the two scenes draw an explicit connection between

The Status of the Fetish in the African Dictator Novel

fetishistic rites and the mechanics of authoritarian power. However, by shifting the creation of the dictator's epistemological system—the making-fetish of his *commandement*—to the writer or secretary Macledio, Kourouma is able to more clearly demonstrate the ways in which authoritarian power functions: Macledio is part of the vast system necessary for upholding the dictator's power. In making visible the structure of that system, the novel shows that it is unstable and suggests that it can be shifted or subverted.

The implications of Macledio's move from the position of victim to aggressor do not escape the two performers, as the *koroduwa* (the jester) notes: "Truth and lie are never distant, one from the other, and rarely does truth win out. Macledio's lies became solid truths, even for their originator, who always ended up believing that he had discovered the threads of plots rather than having created them" (112). This observation offers the opportunity to consider what it means to read against the dictator. In the passage from *I the Supreme* cited above, the dictator Francia berated his unknown reader and critic for not understanding that the law is symbolic. Taking Macledio as a generator of the symbolic system that bolsters the dictator's *commandement*, Kourouma demonstrates how it is possible for someone—even the writer of the fictive narrative—to take the narrative (or symbolic system) as truth. Macledio here is simultaneously in the position of "dictator," as the generator of the symbolic system, and also in the position of the "public" or the "masses," for whom that system becomes fact. As a figure that straddles these two realms, Macledio demonstrates both the mechanics of the language of power and the power of language to bring a particular political consciousness into being. Recalling Francia's outburst against his critic above, Macledio fails to read the symbolic narrative literally—in this case, to remember that he himself has written it. To read the dictator's fetish literally is to remember that it has been composed, that it is maintained by an epistemological system to which there is always an outside. This is the danger of the fetish, as a phenomenon of the contact zone, and also its potential.

In the African dictator novel, the dynamics of the language of power become visible in the making and unmaking of fetish objects that the dynamics of the language of power become visible. The fetish in this analysis functions as vulgarity does in Mbembe's analysis of what he calls the "aesthetics of vulgarity." Just as the elaboration of the dictator's physical excesses cannot simply work as a critique when those excesses have been incorporated into the aesthetics of power, the mere presentation of the dictator's fetish objects (as "traditional" objects) does not effectively critique the dictator as "anti-modern" or "barbaric." Instead, the presence of the fetish object signals a larger dynamic of meaning-making of which it is an expression. The fetish figures the way in which the dictator institutes and maintains his authoritarian power.

As a phenomenon constituted in the overlap of multiple epistemological systems, the fetish also marks the vulnerability of authoritarian power. It is necessarily excessively meaningful (it has a surplus of meaning) and therefore open to multiple and mis-interpretations. It is the site where the dynamics of power become visible, and it is also the point from which it becomes possible to read against the dictator. This is not to say the presence of fetish objects in African dictator novels renders them instruction manuals for the dismantling of authoritarian regimes. But it is to argue that, in showing us how authoritarian power works, these novels do more than simply show the negative effects of dictatorship or the dictator as a monster. Rather, they make viscerally present the experience of the dictator's *commandement* by suggesting that there is something beyond its limits.

Notes

1. English quotations refer to Adrian Adams's translation, *The Last of the Empire: A Senegalese Novel* (1983).
2. "This throne was carved of *ekume* wood, with decorative motifs and legendary symbols belonging to the various peoples of the continent. Its mass rested upon four legs each bearing the dignified mask of a bearded Ibibio; the arms were reinforced by two ebony *tyiwarra*; on the back a couched [sic] leopard, fangs bared, lay ready to leap upon its prey" (17).
3. In an uncanny intertwining of literature and history, during the unrest that followed the November 2010 election in Côte d'Ivoire, the opposition leader Alassane Ouattara established his headquarters in the Hotel du Golf in Abidjan. Government newspapers began to refer to the opposition as the "Republic of the Golf" (*République du Golf*), echoing Koyaga's *République du Golfe*.
4. For a general introduction to oral literature in Africa, which effectively locates the *donsomana* in its broader context, see Johnson, Hale, and Belcher's *Oral Epics from Africa*. Jean Derive, in "Le *donsomaana*: quelques réflexions sur la spécificité d'un genre," discusses the extent to which the *donsomana* can and cannot be distinguished from other Malinke oral genres. Broadly speaking, the *donsomana* is a hunter's story performed within the community (caste) of hunters; importantly, the bard of the hunter clan is not properly speaking a *griot*—who is the member of an endogenous social caste. The Malinke word *donso* means hunter, and the *donsomana* is literally the story of the hunter. The narrator of the *donsomana* is the *sèrè* (differentiated from the performers of other types of narratives), and the content deals with hunting and wild animals.
5. Coates, in his translation, establishes a direct equivalence between the *sèrè*'s claim and the title, choosing to render *bêtes* in the title as "animals" (*animaux*). My rendering of the title in English aims to preserve a certain ambiguity about this moment in the novel.
6. Mary Louise Pratt uses the term "contact zone" to refer to the space of colonial encounters, "the space in which peoples geographically and historically separated come into contact with each other and establish ongoing relations, usually involving conditions of coercion, radical inequality, and intractable conflict" (8).
7. As Macledio explains, interrupting the narration of the *donsomana*: "The Bamileke are Bantu. Like every Bantu king, the Bamilkeke Fundoing receives his political, social, and mystical power

from the skulls of his ancestors, which the *gnwalaä* worshipped once every week with libations of wine and anointments of palm oil" (91).

8. The relation between fetish objects (presumed to be part of "barbaric Africa") and money as fetish object (part of capitalist modernity) is often raised in *Waiting for the Vote of the Wild Beasts*. A little later in Macledio's adventures the close identification of these two types of fetishism becomes the basis for one of the novel's many small jokes. Macledio is rescued by a Nigerien patrol from a Tuareg community where he was being held as a slave, after being robbed and left for dead in the desert. The soldiers return to him his "fetish" which they have found on their patrols: "What the soldiers had called a fetish—because it was covered with coagulated blood and feathers—was the sack, Macledio's purse with the gold. They had handled it with great precautions, without daring to open it, and had given it back with all its contents" (107–08). The bag of money—key fetish of capitalist modernity—is taken to be another type of fetish simply because it has been soiled. The joke turns on the problem of the contingency—and misperception—of value. Had the soldiers not thought the purse an animist fetish, they would have emptied it of its contents before returning it, if at all.

9. English quotations refer to Helen Lane's translation, *I the Supreme* (1986).

10. "Intimidated, the two new arrivals walked along the carpet, their eyes lowered" (182).

11. My translation; the original reads: "Tous les éléments participent au sens. Maclédio permet de comprendre Koyaga, comme Koyaga permet de comprendre Maclédio" (Chemla 27). Thank you to Katharina Piechocki for her help in rendering the difficult phrase "participent au sens."

12. "Nkutigi's faith in Islam and in socialism had not excluded his daily practice of traditional African customs (sorcery, sacrifices, charms). Macledio's principal task consisted in inventing the words, the lies, the cynicism, and the eloquence that would supply an element to rational justifications to acts that had none, since they came from the various prognostications of marabout-fetishists" (111).

Works Cited

Chemla, Yves. "*En attendant le vote des bêtes sauvages ou le donsomana*: Entretien avec Ahmadou Kourouma." *Notre librairie: Revue des littératures du Sud* 136 (1999): 26–29. Print.

Derive, Jean. "Le donsomaana: quelques réflexions sur la spécificité d'un genre." 2005. HAL-SHS (Hyper Article en Ligne—Science de L'Homme et de la Société), Open Archive. HAL-SHS, 2008. Web. 15 July 2011. <http://halshs.archives-ouvertes.fr/halshs-00344123/en/>.

Girard, Renaud. "Côte d'Ivoire: dans le camp retranché de Ouattara." *Le Figaro* 1 Jan. 2011. Web. 29 July 2011.

González Echevarría, Roberto. *The Voice of the Masters: Writing and Authority in Modern Latin American Literature*. Austin: U of Texas P, 1985. Print.

Johnson, John William, Thomas A. Hale, and Stephen Belcher. *Oral Epics from Africa: Vibrant Voices from a Vast Continent*. Bloomington: Indiana UP, 1997. Print.

Kourouma, Ahmadou. *En Attendant le vote des bêtes sauvages*. Paris: Éditions du Seuil, 1998. Print.

———. *Waiting for the Vote of the Wild Animals*. Trans. Carrol F. Coates. Charlottesville: UP of Virginia, 2001. Print.

———. *Waiting for the Wild Beasts to Vote*. Trans. Frank Wynne. London: Vintage, 2004. Print.

Mbembe, J. A. *On the Postcolony*. Berkeley: U of California P, 2001. Print.

Ngũgĩ wa Thiong'o. *Wizard of the Crow*. Trans. Ngũgĩ wa Thiong'o. New York: Pantheon, 2006. Print.

Nossiter, Adam. "Ivory Coast Leader's Rival Remains Under Blockade." *New York Times* 5 Jan. 2011. Web. 25 July 2011.

Pietz, William. "The Problem of the Fetish, I." *Res* 9 (1985): 5–17. Print.

Pratt, Mary Louise. *Imperial Eyes: Travel Writing and Transculturation*. 1992. 2nd ed. New York: Routledge, 2008. Print.

Roa Bastos, Augusto. *Yo el Supremo*. Buenos Aires: Editores S.A., 1974. Print.

———. *I the Supreme*. Trans. Helen Lane. New York: Knopf, 1986. Print.

Sembène, Ousmane. *Le Dernier de L'Empire*. Paris: Edition L'Harmattan, 1981. Print.

———. *The Last of the Empire: A Senegalese Novel*. Trans. Adrian Adams. London: Heinemann, 1983. Print.

Shaefer, Judith. "*En Attendant le Vote des Bêtes Sauvages*, by Ahmadou Kourouma: A Comparison of Two English Translations." *Translation Review* 67 (2004): 58–71. Print.

Fimbo ya Nyayo:
When the Kenyan Dictator Called the Tunes!

MAINA MŨTONYA

When Daniel arap Moi, at a relatively young age of fifty-four, took over as Kenya's second president in 1978, after the demise of the founding president Jomo Kenyatta at eighty-four, he immediately vowed to follow in the footsteps of the late president.[1] This pronouncement was significant in several ways; the young president sought to command similar respect that Kenyatta had and who, due to old age, deserved the title *Mzee*, a revered title for an elder, in Swahili. In this way, Moi was appropriating the idiom of age to justify his authoritarian stance by bestowing upon himself the paternal metaphor of a male, fatherly and old, which was the mask of political power in Kenya. As Ogola argues, this paternal imagery as used at the national level has always legitimized gerontocracy (582).

The oral tradition in Africa epitomises how age and its attendant variables are given prominence. The conceptualisation of the aged as the custodians of the culture responsible for imparting the ancestral knowledge to their juniors cannot be gainsaid. Likewise, in the political arena, especially in Africa, age is equated with wisdom, leadership skills, and foresight. In contrast, Western industrialised societies have given "more and more cultural centrality to youthfulness, symbolised by hard work, sports, playfulness and productivity" (Aguilar 289).

In this oral tradition, whose resonance in contemporary life persists hitherto through the arts, music, and literature, the valorization of old age over the folly of youth is always overemphasized.² The following proverbs best capture this fact:

Palipo wazee hapaharibiki neno (Swahili) [In the presence of elders, nothing goes wrong.]

Agba ko si ni ilu, ilu baje, bale ile ku, ile di ahoro' (Yoruba)³ [Without the elderly people, communities and villages will collapse.]

Mũthuri aikarĩire njũng'wa onaga haraihu gũkĩra kĩhĩĩ kĩrĩ mũtĩ igũrũ (Gĩkũyũ) [An elder seated on a stool sees far beyond what a boy on top a tree can see!]⁴

These proverbs are mostly invoked in asserting the authority of the elder, especially in terms of wisdom and leadership. In the political scenery, the contest between the young and old is played out in contemporary life in Africa.⁵ As Adeboye rightly argues, the idiom of age, despite several changes over the years, remains very relevant today in Africa both in structuring power relationships and also as a political weapon.

As discussed below, the politics of gerontocracy have had a huge bearing on the practice of politics in Africa. This is politics, however, that has had cultural antecedents in precolonial Africa. While addressing the question of the configuration of the dictator in Kenya through music, this chapter argues that Moi, like his predecessor, inherited and appropriated this idiom of age and its various manifestations to sustain and consolidate power during his reign. By inheriting the elderly status from Kenyatta in vowing to follow in his footsteps, Moi managed to ensure allegiance and compliance to his authority through various strategies. Moi's penchant for music as a propaganda tool led to a proliferation of songs that were a hallmark of his authoritarian rule.⁶ These songs were erroneously referred to as patriotic songs despite the fact that they served the sole purpose of praising Moi and his Nyayo philosophy. The dictatorial regime in its practice inadvertently led to an upsurge of underground networks of art dissemination and political opposition but was met by the full force of government repression. This in turn produced memorable works of theatre, music, and literature that to date serve as stark reminders of the Moi regime. Music, however, is the mainstay of this chapter, although reference is made to literary works born of this period. The attempted coup in 1982 and the Mwakenya period in the late 1980s are important epochs in the timeline of the Moi regime that fall within the scope of this chapter. All these issues clearly inform the relationship between music and politics during the dictatorial regime of Moi, towards the development of the objectives of this chapter.

Going back to the politics of gerontocracy, it is prudent to point out that the cultural metaphor that the elderly in Africa represent relegates the role of the youth in political leadership to the future, a future that never materializes. The youth are often regarded as the leaders of tomorrow, *viongozi wa kesho*, in an effort to sideline them from mainstream politics (Musila, 2010; Lukalo, 2006; Odhiambo, 2010; wa Mungai, 2010). As Abobo argues, "[R]espect for the elderly is so strong in Africa that it sometimes seems as though Africa is practicing *gerontolatry* –the worship of the elderly." This practice that is embedded in gerontocracy "cuts across the cultural, political and intellectual landscape wherein lies a particular trope of veneration of both age and masculinity" (Musila 18). The gerontocracy myth[7] becomes a pertinent issue while addressing political leadership on the continent.

Similarly, Odhiambo and wa Mungai highlight this close-knit relationship between old age and political authority. By extension, as this chapter argues, this has necessitated the reproduction of dictatorial regimes in Africa, as elderly leaders, who erroneously see themselves as custodians of their respective cultures, would hardly listen to counsel from other quarters. Odhiambo postulates that in Africa and the world over, "the reverence to old age gives automatic qualification to leadership and authority" (98).

Wa Mungai observes that the title *mzee*, that has been present in the Kenyan political scenario since the time of the founding President Jomo Kenyatta, has been redefined by gerontocracy in contemporary Kenya to go beyond "the salutary invocation of respect for those advanced in age and becomes a signifier of economic and political worth" (78). This is what Musila has aptly captured as the fetishization of old age (281) and complements Schatzberg's analyses of the paternal and familial metaphors that have characterized postcolonial African political leadership.

Schatzberg engages with political legitimacy in sub-Saharan Africa by studying the common cultural images of father, family, and food that are useful in deciphering the actions of leaders and the resultant acceptance by the citizenry. Of importance to this chapter is the paternal metaphor that manifests itself in clear ways when looking at the configuration of the dictatorial regime of Daniel arap Moi in Kenya. Schatzberg's study in Senegal, Côte d'Ivoire, Ghana Nigeria, Cameroon, Tanzania, the Democratic Republic of Congo, and Kenya presents duplicated efforts in the leaders' cultivation of "cults of personality that always presented themselves as loving, caring, solicitous national fathers" (10).

In efforts to stem an opposition tide from dissidents who were under the pay of foreign masters envious of Kenya's development record[8] during his twenty-four-year rule, Daniel arap Moi always saw himself as

> [t]he grand wise old man, the head of a great family. He knew what was good for everybody. He had the moral right to punish the delinquent children as a way to put them back on track for their own good. (Peter and Kopsieker 19)

To perpetuate this image of the father of the nation, Moi appropriated music as his powerful propaganda tool that became important in imparting his Nyayo philosophy that he assumed once he took over power following the death of Mzee Jomo Kenyatta in 1978.

Arap Moi, in vowing to follow in the footsteps of Jomo Kenyatta, ensured that just like his predecessor, he would not brook any dissidence or opposition from his competitors in politics. In this sense, he evolved his *Nyayo* philosophy of Love, Peace, and Unity, which, in essence, went contrary to these principles. *Nyayo* is Swahili for "footsteps." Not only did he attempt to replicate Jomo Kenyatta's leadership style, but he also expected everybody under him to follow duly and unquestionably his orders. See below his political speech in September 1984 while addressing the public at the Jomo Kenyatta International Airport on arrival from Ethiopia:

> I would like ministers, assistant ministers and others to *sing* like a parrot after me. During Mzee Kenyatta's time, I sang only Kenyatta until it came a time when people said 'he has nothing except singing Kenyatta.' I didn't have ideas of my own. Who was I to have my own ideas? I was in Kenyatta's shoes and therefore I had to sing whatever Kenyatta wanted (Applause). Do you think Kenyatta would have retained me had I sung a different song? So, you play my tune. Where I put a full stop, you also put a full stop. When time comes for you to be big, you play your tune and the masses will sing after you.[9]

Coincidentally, it was partly through music, amongst other political machinations, that arap Moi ensured that his leadership was respected by all and sundry in Kenya. While Kenyatta, too, encouraged the performance of traditional music at most state functions, Daniel arap Moi went a notch higher by encouraging formation of choirs as well as taking direct control over the music that was performed in events over which he presided.[10]

In 1982, the Permanent Presidential Music Commission[11] (PPMC) was formed under the patronage of the president himself. For a commission whose primary mandate was "to enhance research, development and education in the performance of music and dance in Kenya" (Okumu 162), it ended up with a responsibility of vetting all songs and dances that were to be performed in public presidential functions. As Mindoti and Agak observe, "[P]atriotic songs in particular, were vetted to ensure the inclusion of only those songs propagating the Nyayo philosophy of love, peace and unity" (159).

Because the government of Moi facilitated the performing groups in terms of financial logistics, transport, and honoraria, the number of choirs that produced "patriotic songs" but which, in essence, were indeed praise songs to the dictatorial regime of arap Moi and the ruling party, the Kenya African National Union

(KANU), proliferated.[12] Universities, parastatal bodies, high schools, churches, and mass choirs all competed to catch the eye of the president[13] with flattering lyrics about the person of the President of Kenya. Titles of the songs included *Fimbo ya Nyayo* (Kiswahili: "Moi's cane/staff"), *Tawala Kenya Tawala* (Kiswahili: "Reign over Kenya"), *Rais Moi Ndiye Nanga* (Kiswahili: "President Moi is the anchor"), *Moi Astahili Heshima* (Kiswahili: "Moi deserves respect"), and *Heko Baba Moi* (Kiswahili: "Congratulations Moi, our father").

Other songs touching on topical issues like soil erosion, family planning, agriculture, and health also featured prominently, but always reminding the listeners that only under the wise leadership of arap Moi would these programs succeed. A fitting example here would be Thomas Wesonga's song, *Wakulima Ongezeni Kilimo*:

> *Wakulima, ongezeni kilimo* [farmers, improve on your productivity]
>
> *Watoto wa Nyayo wawe na afya njema* [so that Nyayo's children will have great health].

Out of the sheer concern for "his children," president Moi started a food program that gave free milk to all primary school-going pupils once every week. In this act, Moi not only added the father role to his political cap but also a role that can best be seen as representative of the provider, the *mother* of the country. This school milk program, which gave free *maziwa ya Nyayo* ("Nyayo's milk") to pupils, was a service that was sometimes tied to the recitation of the loyalty pledge, (which is discussed below) at least in some schools. In this way, Moi and, by extension, the ruling party KANU were *Baba na Mama* ("father and mother") to Kenyans during his reign and from whom he expected nothing less than putative loyalty.

The milk packets carried clear instructions that support our hypothesis that far from being a measure to counter malnutrition among Kenyan school-going children, the program existed purely for the political expediency of the dictatorship:

> *Maziwa yanatolewa bure na serikali kwa watoto wote wa shule za msingi nchini Kenya kufuatana na uamuzi wa busara wa rais Daniel arap Moi aliye pia Amiri Jeshi Mkuu*
>
> This milk has been provided for free by the government to all primary school pupils under the wise counsel of President Moi who is also the Commander-in-Chief of the Armed Forces.

Therefore, consuming the milk implied unconditional support of the government and of the president of the nation, even to children whose sense of political consciousness was still largely undeveloped. The image of the president was not only visible in inanimate objects like packets of milk, or currency, but the president himself was literally involved in every activity that concerned the lives of Kenyans. He was the chancellor of all public universities, and was present at all graduation ceremonies, as the number one teacher, in "full academic regalia, dignified and solemn"; the commander in chief of the armed forces; the provider and number one soccer supporter, as Schatzberg (145) captures the paternal figure that most African presidents cut, in a way, to legitimate their authority.

Apart from parastatal bodies forming choirs that used to entertain Moi, one of the mandatory routines especially in public functions was the national anthem, as is protocol, but followed by what was referred to as the Loyalty Pledge.[14] This pledge in most schools even existed in a musical form, which school-going children were forced to recite every Friday morning:

> I pledge my loyalty to the President and Nation of Kenya. My readiness and duty to defend the flag of our Republic. My life, strength and service in the task of nation building. In the living spirit embodied in our national motto "Harambee,"[15] and perpetuated in the *Nyayo philosophy* of Peace, Love and Unity. (Widner 1)

Such was the pervasiveness of the symbols of political power that arap Moi wielded, power that assumed the physical, social, and the mental spaces of the Kenyan. Apart from the ever-present portrait of the president in every government office, as well as business premises, most educational institutions, hospitals, projects, and parastatals scrambled for the tiniest connection to Moi's larger-than-life profile. Aluanga observes that "to have the Moi name appended to one's educational institution was a mark of prestige and quality. But in other circles, it also served as a mark of allegiance, leaving no doubt to where one's loyalties lay" (2). There were the Nyayo Tea Zones, Nyayo Stadium, Nyayo House, Nyayo Bus, Nyayo monuments, Nyayo Wards, Nyayo Car, and institutions like Moi University and Moi High School Kabarak, among others. Most of these names have served as reminders of the dark past that characterized the Moi regime.

In an effort to entrench his iron-fisted rule, one may argue that the music was useful in retaining arap Moi in power, amongst many other factors that are beyond the scope of this chapter. However, it is clear that when Daniel arap Moi took power in 1978, one of his primary strategies was to emphasize and gain the most benefit possible from the praise side of the praise-poet tradition. In 1979, Moi instigated the formation of his premiere propaganda ensemble, the Muungano Choir, a mass choir whose membership represented the diversity of Kenyan society. The president's enthusiasm for, and support of, this kind of music stimulated many state corporations to form their own choirs—all of which sang the praises of the KANU party and President Moi.

The first three years of the Moi era saw the recording of a large body of pro-Moi and KANU praise songs that came to form a new genre termed "patriotic songs." Performed both by choirs and by commercial popular musicians, these songs enjoyed extensive airplay on the Kenya Broadcasting Corporation radio and TV (then the only broadcasting station, which was under strict government control) over the following two decades. Some of the most famous patriotic songs recorded by commercial bands included *Rais Moi* (Kiswahili: "President Moi") by the Kenya-based Congolese band Mangelepa; *Hongera Moi* (Kiswahili: "Congratulations Moi") by Them Mushrooms, a popular music group, now renamed Uyoga Band; Joseph Kamaru's *Safari ya Japan* (Kiswahili: "Trip to Japan") and *Chunga Marima* (Gĩkũyũ: "Watch Your Steps").

Chunga Marima dwelt on the politics of the day. The then attorney general, Charles Njonjo, was accused by fellow politicians of being behind the attempted coup of 1982 and was branded a "traitor." Kamaru joined this lobby with a song castigating Njonjo and supporting the government:

Huko nĩ cietherwo itatĩ ikwa itanathira
Ciarema ciĩkĩrwo maaĩ
Mwendia bũrũri
Nĩ ahĩtwo, nĩ ahĩtwo narua atanaturũkia

Let us get traps for the moles before they finish our yams
Or better still, pour water in their holes
Sellouts in our country should be hunted down
Before they disappear.

It is important to note here that musician Kamaru had an on-and-off relationship with both regimes of Kenyatta and arap Moi. He was on record for defending the leadership of Jomo Kenyatta against allegations of complicity in the assassination of Tom Mboya in 1969, but was quick to change tunes when populist Member of Parliament, J. M. Kariuki was killed in 1975. He composed a song in Kariuki's memory, whose scathing lyrics heavily castigated the same government he had praised a few years back. As Hofmeyr is wont to argue, "[T]he careers of popular musicians will often traverse almost absurdly different positions as performers, chameleon-like, improvise around and explore and indeed dramatize the chaotic plurality of the postcolony" (131). After Kenyatta's death, notes Mutonya, "the same Joseph Kamaru, whose 1975 song had been banned released another song, *Musa wa Andũ Airũ* (The Black People's Moses), that drew an analogy between the Biblical Moses and Kenyatta" (34).

In the Moi era, the same vacillating nature of praising and criticizing was clearly evident in Kamaru's compositions, but in ways that explain the complex relationship between the rulers and ruled in postcolonial Kenya. Thus, despite all President Moi's efforts to retain control over the political power of music, unmitigated praise of his government by musicians was not to last. In 1982,

Kenya faced the first attempted *military coup d'état*, which lasted only a few hours. Hundreds lost their lives, and much property was destroyed. This precipitated a deluge of songs. One of these, *Kenya ya Ngai* (Gĩkũyũ: "Kenya Belongs to God") by Joseph Kamarũ, starts thus:

> Nĩ Kenya ĩrĩa yakwa ndahũragĩrwo
> Kana nĩ ĩrĩa itũ mwahunyĩrĩra
> Yainainio ta thaara ta ĩtarĩ mwene
> Kuma ũmũthĩ Kenya ngũmĩne Ngai
> Is it the Kenya I suffered for?
> Or is it our Kenya you play around with?
> Which had been shaken like it belongs to no one?
> From now onwards I deliver it to God.

The song goes on to castigate politicians who get into power just to enrich themselves:

> Ngũigua ta ingĩrĩra ndaririkana
> Tũgũikĩirie mĩtĩ ũgatũtetere
> Na rĩu nĩ Kenya woha mũgoto
> Ngũria, ũkũmĩendia kũ Kenya ya Ngai?
> I feel like crying when I remember
> We voted you into power to represent our interests
> And now you intend to sell Kenya
> Where shall you sell this Kenya of God?

The song then challenges the politicians by asking them whether they have no mercy for the children, the women, and the aged who suffer as a result of power-hungry leaders. The song concludes by warning politicians that if they were in Nairobi during the time of "Power" (the attempted coup), then they would know that power is God-given.

The coup heralded a period of intense political repression of those who criticized the state. In music this was manifested most obviously in heavy censorship. *Kenya ya Ngai*, for instance, was never given airplay by the Kenya Broadcasting Corporation (KBC), the only broadcasting station at the time, because, as Mucoki asserts, "the policy makers felt that these songs and others with similar lyrics were undermining their positions" (18).

The relationship between politics and music is best captured by this attempted *coup d'état* fronted by members of the armed forces. One of the key institutions that the forces managed to capture was the government broadcaster, KBC. The duty announcer, Leonard Mambo Mbotela, was forced to announce that the government had been overthrown. Then, in between the messages, the insurgents forced Mbotela to repeatedly play the soothing tunes of Tabu Ley's song *Maze*, a love song.[16] But when the coup was crushed by forces loyal to the government of arap Moi, the *lingala* music of Tabu Ley was immediately substituted by Kenyan musician Joseph Kamaru's song *Safari ya Japan* (Kiswahili: "Trip to Japan"), which included the refrain *Moi songa na mbele tujenge Kenya yetu* (Kiswahili: "March forward, Moi; let's build our Kenya").[17]

And march forward Moi did. The attempted overthrow marked a turning point in Moi's regime, and it could be rightly argued that the dictator in him was born around this time and was to be felt in every facet of the lives of Kenyans.[18] For starters, Moi banned music that was not in either English or Kiswahili on the state broadcaster. To Moi, this was done in the spirit of promoting local music. But as Peter and Kopsieker rightly note, in reality, "this action sought to create the needed space for 'patriotic songs' which were many and all of them geared towards playing certain ideological objectives" (22).

It was only after Tabu Ley corrupted lyrics of his song *Nakei Nairobi* (Lingala: "I am heading to Nairobi") with Mbilia Bel to include a few lines in Swahili to praise *Baba Moi* that the ban on *lingala* music was lifted in 1986:

Twende Nairobi [Let's go to Nairobi]
Tukamuone baba Moi [To see Moi, our father]
Twende Nairobi [Let's go to Nairobi]
Tukamwimbie baba Moi [to sing for our father Moi].

In Kenya, the 1982 constitutional amendment had made Kenya a one-party state, and the government of Daniel arap Moi intensified its crackdown on individuals who were not toeing the official line. In the 1990s, Moi also became increasingly suspicious of even close political allies. In this environment of mistrust, Moi dealt ruthlessly with real or imagined enemies: fellow politicians, academics, lawyers, church leaders, musicians, farmers, university students, etc. This background created a situation in the country in which "the government was afraid of its citizens and the citizens were afraid of their government. There was a mutual fear of the ruler and the ruled; a condition that was dubbed '*paramoia*'" (Kariuki 70), a pun on the president's name. While the 1980s in Kenya were characterized by silence and fear, as well as the zenith of the dictatorial regime of Moi, the 1990s witnessed heightened political electricity in the clamor for multi-party democracy, a dream that was actualized in 1991 but which did not come with a change of regime.

Years later, in a newspaper interview after Moi's departure, Muungano Choir Director Boniface Mgangha asserted that his choir was unique in that it had to represent the aspirations of the country at the time. He says that Muungano's objective was to sing patriotic songs as part of the broader role to enhance sociopolitical development. He cites *Kenya Kipenzi Changu* (Kiswahili: "Kenya, My Love") by his choir as the most remarkable recording in its genre. The formation of government-sponsored choirs is a classic example of what Stokes describes as "the intensive involvement of music as a tool in the hand of new states to propagate the dominant modes of classification" (10).

Writing on politics and popular culture largely in Europe and America, John Street argues that "artistic creativity depends upon the freedom of expression to which state interference is antithetical" (77). In many postcolonial states, however, there are many instances of state censorship of popular culture. Typically, this indicates the existence of an authoritarian regime. During apartheid, for instance, the South African government banned countless books, plays, songs, and films, and, as Street notes about a different context, "the Nazis took particular exception to 'swing youth,' a group of young bourgeoisie, who chose to dance to the 'decadent Jewish' and 'degenerate' prohibited music of Benny Goodman, Louis Armstrong, amongst other giants of the age of jazz" (86). The interference of the state in the form of censorship constitutes negative political power: "the power to prevent" (Street 88). Power, Street argues, can also be used to facilitate what the audience listens to, where, through broadcasting policies: the audience is made to differentiate actively rather than to be entertained passively. In this way, state decisions influence popular culture, and the ambiguities and complexities between popular culture and politics are highlighted. The ambiguity is more pronounced by the thought that "the quality of cultural life is important to the quality of political life. This parallels a general argument about the relationship between democracy and the system of broadcasting" (97).

Despite censorship and other authoritarian measures taken in attempt to silence his opposition, President Moi ultimately lost the battle and was forced to accept multi-party politics. Music was central in achieving this end. Commenting on the changing and volatile political tide that swept Kenya in the early 1990s, Haugerud notes that music and theatre became important avenues through which criticisms of the ruling regime "coalesced, influencing individual consciousness" as the opposition grew bigger and became more public by late 1991 and early 1992 (28).

In Kenya, a different version of patriotism emerged with time, far more beyond the flag and the national anthem. Conflict arises when leaders are perceived as not acting in the best interests of the people. In this case, patriotic supporters of the leaders may be perceived as traitors of the people and vice versa. Patriotism here demanded the courage of one's conviction and the willingness to speak the truth as one saw it for the good of the country. When the disillusionment narrative became widely recognized, as was the case in Kenya during the early 1990s, musicians who performed "patriotic songs" suddenly found themselves being critiqued as traitors of the people. The standard of their art was also more openly critiqued:

> The divide between sycophancy and art disappeared, as was the case in communist regimes. In the new genre, the "correct" political content was all that mattered. Genuinely patriotic compositions such as *Kenya Nchi Yetu* [Kiswahili: "Kenya Our Country"] were apparently too aloof. The president had to be praised or "disgruntled elements" criticized for a song to be patriotic. Praising the motherland wasn't enough. Its leader deserved a special mention. (Wambua 13)

This was patriotism as sanctioned by the regime. Although some patriotic songs recorded by commercial artists were deemed as good compositions, in many cases the content of the lyrics took precedence over musical quality. A good majority were rush recordings whose sole purpose was to pitch for attention from those in power in the hope of gaining support and getting some reward from the head of state or others in high office. Similarly, while some commentators suggest that, on an artistic level, the formation of in-house choirs by state corporations was a positive factor for music development nationally, others assert that such choirs were open to widespread abuse by opportunists who used them to pitch for political favors and by choir members who saw them as a means to make easy money and advance personal agendas.

Another focus of scathing criticism directed at these choirs is that they altered gospel songs in order to introduce lyrics in praise of the president. The music set new, explicitly political texts to a variety of pre-existing religious compositions for the purposes of praising the governing establishment. The debasing of the Christian liturgy became an issue with the St. Stephen's Choir's tribute to the late Mzee Jomo Kenyatta when it altered lyrics in popular church hymns in order to pass them off as tribute songs to the late president. Most of these songs were eventually dropped from Christian worship because it was felt that they had been debased since they had acquired loaded political meanings and praised mortal human beings instead of God. The practice of adapting Christian songs continued into the Moi era, although the resulting repertoire did not enjoy widespread exposure.

However, this transformation of hymns for political purposes has a pre-independence history. As early as the 1920s, as well as during the Mau Mau struggle for independence, Christian hymns[19] were corrupted by the Gĩkũyũ to suit the struggle. Ogot notes, "[W]hen meetings were apparently swaying in religious fervour to the strains of 'Abide With Me' or 'Onward Christian Soldiers' the congregation was in reality being exhorted to fight for their independence or regain their stolen land" (276).

When Kenyatta took over from the colonialists, the use of the same praise songs and Christian hymns altered to serve secular and political purposes continued unabated. This is one of the instances in which shifts in the political landscape either threatened the existence or subsequently reworked the significance of particular musical practices. The protest songs of the 1950s were adapted as praise songs in the postcolonial regime.

At the height of one-party dictatorship in Kenya, choirs that performed praise songs to the ruling party KANU and the then president Daniel Moi were endemic features in the life of ordinary Kenyans. Such songs were played out loud after every news bulletins on the state-owned Kenya Broadcasting Corporation on a daily basis. The trend has continued even after multi-party democracy, where state corporations and academic institutions all form part of national day celebrations every year. Their songs serve as a tool for pledging loyalty and praise to ruling regimes.

At the onset of colonialism, the missionary arrived. The missionaries and the proselytisers introduced Christian hymns with simple choruses. The choruses were widely adapted by the early mission stations and were used to teach basic tenets. The seeds of colonial penetration of East Africa "were planted initially in the Christian missions and schools. Music was used from the beginning in the indoctrination and the teaching of Western ideology. Songs and hymns therefore were important tools in the processes of subjugation to new moral values and systems" (Barz 57). However, to draw similarities between the role of songs as a means of the indoctrinating Western ideology by mission schools, as stated above, and the praise songs in postcolonial Kenya would seem to oversimplify a complex issue. But for the purposes of this chapter, this should suffice. The underlying fact here is that music, and, in my case, choral music, during arap Moi's regime was a useful ingredient in the diffusion of his ideology.

In a newspaper interview in 2002, shortly before Moi's fall from power, musician Kamaru, who featured in many public functions officiated over by President Moi, denied that musicians were being used by the government. He said that, in his case and in the case of many other artists who performed such songs, the objective was purely commercial because there was a market for songs praising Moi and KANU: "I had good sales with *Chunga Marima* because it had commercial appeal and I believe others saw it from commercial perspective." Kamaru adds that he received no reward from State House for his praise songs, but does admit that President Moi was generous to musicians singing at his functions and gave generous cash hand-outs. When the political tables turned, President Moi refused to believe that the deluge of anti-KANU songs released during the run up to the 1992 general election was a response to a market desire for the expression of such political sentiments. He distanced himself from musicians, asserting that they were in the payroll of opposition parties.

One of the praise songs that exalted Daniel Moi as the father of the nation contained suggestive lyrics:

Fimbo ya Nyayo

> *Moi Moi rais wa Kenya* [Moi, Moi, president of Kenya]
> *Tunakutakia maisha mema* [we wish you good life]
> *Maisha mema ya amani na umoja* [good life full of peace and unity]
> *Ukabila hatutaki Kenya yetu* [we don't want tribalism in our country, Kenya]
> *Sisi wanakenya wote tumeungana* [all Kenyans are united]
> *Kwa mwito wako wa amani na umoja* [behind your philosophy of peace, love and unity]

The mention of tribalism in the song highlights one of the major challenges in fostering national unity in post-independence Kenya. Upon assuming power, Moi had promised reforms in all sectors. However, rather than provide reforms, "his anti-corruption drive was in fact a tool against the Kikuyu elite who had accumulated power and wealth during the Kenyatta era" (Kariuki 74). This strategy was, however, resented because it was reminiscent of Kenyatta's antics between 1963 till his death in 1978 when most "non-Kikuyus were marginalized in the country's political economy" (Kariuki 77). To consolidate his power in later years, Moi engineered a remake of Kenyatta's "multi-ethnic elite alliance in a way that seriously diminished the economic and political power of the Kikuyu faction" (Berman, Eyo and Kymlicka 10). Adar and Munyae note:

> To bolster his grip on power, Moi embarked on the gradual Kalenjinization of the public and private sectors from the 1980s. Moi is a Tugen, one of the smaller Kalenjin ethnic groups. He began to "de-Kikuyunize" the civil service and state-owned enterprises previously dominated by the Kikuyu ethnic group during Kenyatta's regime. (5)

This sentiment is shared by Hempstone, the former U.S. ambassador to Kenya:

> [Moi] enlisted and promoted his tribesmen in disproportionate numbers in the army and civil service. Promotion in both depended, not on competence but on unquestioning loyalty and subservience to the accidental Big Man, from whom all power, privilege and wealth derive. (39)[20]

Politicised tribalism in Kenya has continued egregiously under different regimes since independence. This aspect is partly a colonial legacy, whereby colonialists categorised their subjects in relation to their ethnic backgrounds to prevent some form of unity. Post-independence governments have, however, perfected the art in an attempt to hold on to power. As Odhiambo shows, ethnicity in Kenya permeates the lives of ordinary Kenyans who "talk and think about it as the regular experience of their everyday lives, in its many enabling capacities, its incapacitating impediments on the hopes of individuals and the blocking of opportunities for whole communities" (171–2). As Schatzberg rightly argues,

"[E]thnicities may arise in opposition to the state specifically when a group feels excluded from the benefits the state has to offer and thus relatively disadvantaged" (*Dialectics* 22). This perspective is helpful in illuminating the patron-client relationships that define Kenyan politics.

Musicians, like authors, engage in the construction of symbolic economies and in transforming real economic relationships into symbolic ones. They help to generate explanations of (mis)fortune that will touch the experiences of their listeners. Through such lyrics, listeners can rationalise their own poverty. In his song *No ngainūkia Itaha* (Gĩkũyũ: "I will surely take home my share"), musician Joseph Kariuki details the travails of living in Nairobi in the 1990s, coupled with social challenges. But most of the problems have a basis in the economic downturn, occasioned by poor management and bad leadership, in the song and in the reality of the 1990s. After all, as Kariuki contends in his song:

> *Ona wīna ndingirii, ūtarī na mbeca no tūhū* [your academic achievements are useless if they can't get you a job]
> *Baba nī ahurunjīte thīna būrūri wothe* [For father has spread poverty countrywide]

The "father" in the song alludes not only to the head of state but also to his government for the rise of poverty in the country, for the mismanagement of resources and high unemployment cases, which led many to the streets as hawkers. The 2002 Human Rights Watch Report noted that about half of Kenya's workers made their living in the informal economy as street hawkers, roadside vendors at stalls (kiosks), and as bus touts, maids, garbage scavengers, prostitutes, or casual labourers: "The government has few official policies dealing with the informal sector and workers on the margins of society are vulnerable to arbitrary and harsh treatment by the authorities" (20). Musician Queen Jane's lament of the plight of the hawkers, in another song, *Hawkers*, is symbolic of the many struggles that a great proportion of Kenyans were going through. Such lyrics as those above offer critique of officialdom for the everyday problems of the non-elite and elite listeners alike.

When arap Moi took over from Kenyatta, he vowed to follow in his (Nyayo) footsteps. Kenyatta as the first president was "the universally accepted 'father of the nation'" (Kariuki 75), and Moi in line with following the footsteps inherited the title as well, as *Baba wa taifa* ("Father of the nation"). This is what the musician alludes to in the song. Bayart's position on postcolonial leadership in African states is that "the link between holding positions of power within the State apparatus and the acquisition of wealth is clearly related to the political hierarchy" (87). Thus, in its attempts to acquire and accumulate wealth, the general populace is left wallowing in poverty in this predator-prey relationship.

What more apt way to capture this than in the musician's own words, "father has spread poverty countrywide"? The father figure is supposed to be the benevolent provider for and custodian of the domestic space. It is ironic here that instead of being the provider, the "father" is the source of poverty.

Some of the music also makes explicit mention of the symbols of power that the dictatorial regime of arap Moi will best be remembered for. Arthur Kemoli's song heaps praise on Moi's cane/sceptre, which just like his predecessor's flywhisk, or Kaunda's white handkerchief, signified power for he who wielded it. During Moi's reign, especially in the late 1980s, it was forbidden for Kenyans to carry any item that was longer than thirty inches, which would be considered as a weapon. But Moi's cane was in clear contravention to this rule for it was beyond the length as provided by the law. It was around the same time that the then fashionable camouflage clothes were banned, as they "imitated" the power of the army, in which he was the Commander-in-Chief![21]

The song *Fimbo ya Nyayo* (1981), as mentioned above by Arthur Kemoli, goes as follows:

Fimbo ya Nyayo [Moi's staff]
Yatuongoza kwenda wapi? [where is it leading us to]
Fimbo ya Nyayo [Moi's staff]
Yatuongoza kwenda mbele [is taking us forward]

Like a cattle owner controls his herd with the whip, Moi's *fimbo* was meant to ensure unquestioned loyalty and adherence to the Nyayo Philosophy of Peace, Love, and Unity, which actually went against the very same principles it propounded. The *fimbo* cynically portrayed the "pastoralist president," not because he hailed from the Tugen pastoralist community, but because he was "constantly on the move" engaging in "development" activities, such that Nyayo came to mean "development in motion" (Nyairo 4). These were just populist schemes in an attempt to make himself stand out as the only protector of national interests and to legitimise his leadership: "Moi went round the Republic fund-raising for schools, building gabions against soil erosion and waging war on what was called *pombe haramu* (illicit traditional brew)" (Peter and Kopsieker 18).

In his song, *Nīguo Kūrī* (Gīkūyū: "This is How Things Are"), John Demathew alludes to the *fimbo* as well. The song is a call for the unity of the Kikuyu people who suffered immensely under the dictatorship of Moi:

Nīkīo ita ritū, rīinainagio nī kahīī kamwe na karūthanju!
[This is the reason our army is always shaken by a small boy wielding a stick!]

He warns that if the community doesn't pull together, they will forever be herded like cows. But the stick symbol can also be seen to refer here to the walking cane that Kenyatta used to support his aging body but also served as a rod to punish errant leaders and artists.[22]

In the run-up to the democratisation process that culminated in the repeal of Section 2A that ushered in multi-party politics, Kenyans had outgrown the dictatorship that had reached its peak in the late '80s. The growing political and social displeasure manifested itself in several art forms that emerged. An example of the prison/dungeon literature below is a clear illustration of the proliferation of the arts during the time of political upheaval in the history of Kenya.

A growing body of prison literature has captured the memories of the torture chambers of the infamous Nyayo House, where real or perceived "enemies of the state" were incarcerated, especially during the Mwakenya[23] crackdown in the '80s way into the '90s. The Mwakenya period in the 1980s carved an epochal niche in Kenya's postcolonial history. Political incarceration and the attendant assassinations and the torture of the so-called dissidents that marked this period gave rise to a new sub-genre of literature. The mid-1980s witnessed the most intense siege on political dissenters by the Moi regime, which consequently spawned a proliferation of literature with a thematic consistency that has been referred to as the literature of the dungeon. The period was the apogee of one-party dictatorship in Kenya under arap Moi. During this time, the government of arap Moi was involved in arbitrary arrests and detentions without trials of those who were seen to go against the grain. With Moi having appropriated the paternal figure, this repression would have appeared as punitive exercises against errant kids in the family, to paraphrase Peter and Kopsieker (19).

In this brief period, a corpus of literature was born. Most of the books were written in the early 1990s soon after the institution of political reforms. What are loosely referred to as "Kamiti stories"[24] during the Mwakenya arrests include a number of literary productions. The works of Wahome Mutahi were among the first books to detail the horrors of Kenyan prisons in the period under study. They include *Jail Bugs* (1992) and *Three Days on the Cross* (1991). In addition to *Kenya: A Prison Notebook* mentioned earlier, historian Maina wa Kinyatti wrote *A Season of Blood: Poems from Kenyan Prisons* (1995). Benjamin Garth Bundeh's ordeal at Kamiti Maximum Security Prison is recounted in *JailBirds of Kamiti* (1991). Karuga Wandai's *Mayor in Prison* (1993), Kimani Kiggia's *Prison is Not a Holiday Camp* (1994), and Wanyiri Kihoro's *Never Say Die: The Chronicle of a Political Prisoner* (1998) are other examples of works narrating the horrid prison experiences. *We Lived to Tell: The Nyayo House Story* (2003) details a collection of prison experiences by a number of political prisoners. In recent times, Njuguna Mutonya's *Crackdown* (2010) is the latest addition to this growing body of literature that best paints the portrait of torture under the dictatorship of Daniel arap Moi.

While most of these authors compiled their memoirs after going through imprisonment under the repressive regime, and not necessarily for their actions as writers, it is also imperative to highlight here that during his reign, Daniel arap Moi had an uneasy relationship with writers and literature in general. Writers like Ngũgĩ wa Thiongo, Micere Mũgo, Ngũgĩ wa Mĩriĩ, and Abdilatif Abdalla are some of the writers in Kenya that suffered in the hands of the state purposely because of their writings.

Ngũgĩ wa Thiong'o was a victim of both the Kenyatta and Moi repressive regimes, because of his writings. His book *Petals of Blood* (1977) particularly was a penetrating critique of independent Kenya. The novel may have upset members of Kenyatta government, but as Thomas argues, "[I]t appears to have been Ngũgĩ's role in community activism and self-help in the village of Kamĩrĩĩthũ that led directly to his detention" (285). Public performances of Ngugi's play *Ngaahika Ndeenda* ("I Will Marry When I Want") were banned, and Ngũgĩ sent to detention without trial for one year, experiences captured in his *Detained: A Writer's Prison Diary* (1981).

In a state where the political power holders did not share the same intellectual horizons with the citizens, and in this case the writers, the Moi regime relied more on violence than ideas to govern and control the masses. Violence visited upon the writers through imprisonment is an extension of the violence of both the mind and ideas by the dictatorial state. As Adebayo contends, "African rulers have usually responded with panic to the lethal immediacy of the popular arts and their devastating political consequences." He gives the example of Okot p'Bitek, who was thrown out of Uganda precisely because of his attempts to use popular poetry for social commentary (358). Ngũgĩ's open-air peasant theatre at Kamĩrĩĩthũ, as seen above, was part of the popular arts, with which the Kenyatta government was uncomfortable.

Mbembe, in an attempt to understand the postcolony in Africa argues that, when a body is thought to be disfiguring the public place, or is considered to be a threat to public order, the state steps in to have the body neutered. The government for two main reasons carefully orchestrates the process of imprisonment, especially on political grounds. First, it is devoted to removing the victims from the society, and secondly to shifting them to a confined place where the state may carry out its operations on them with the knowledge that they are no more its visible opponents in the eyes of the public (1).[25]

As wa Mungai rightly argues, the incarceration of the writer, or the artist, was the Moi regime's way of stopping them from interfering with the state's control of public discourse (46). In tandem with Mbembe, the "official narrative" of the repressive state is meant to produce fables and stupefy its subjects, as in Moi's appropriation of music (16). Literature provided an alternative way of subverting this narrative, by offering not only criticisms to the regime but by also willing new realities.[26]

During the reign of arap Moi, apart from banning books, by local writers, like Ngũgĩ wa Thiong'o's *Matigari*, his government also silenced magazines and periodicals such as *Beyond*, *Financial Review*, *Sauti ya Mwananchi*, and *Inooro*, as well as the staging of plays like *Animal Farm* by George Orwell, *An Enemy of the People* by Henrik Ibsen, and *Fate of a Cockroach* by Tewfik al Hakim from Egypt.

These bans have a historical antecedent in that during the struggle for independence in Kenya, the colonial government, especially in 1952, when the State of Emergency was declared, saw many writers, editors, and publishers prosecuted for publishing what the then government regarded as seditious articles in the vernacular press and political pamphlets.[27]

The ban of the staging of Ngũgĩ's plays *Ngaahika Ndeenda* and *Maitũ Njugĩra* particularly defined new coordinates in the relationship between the dictator Moi and authors of creative works of literary and theatrical productions. Mbugua and Gĩchingiri credit Ngũgĩ's Kamĩrĩĩthũ experience for bringing to the realisation that people's theatre was a useful tool in the direct social mobilisation of the masses, and in effect producing narratives that countered those of the regime of arap Moi. It is this fact that led to the eventual ban and the subsequent criminalisation of theatre by the Moi government.

This situation above clearly depicts one fact: that Moi was very uncomfortable with musicians, journalists, scholars, the clergy, and Kenyans at large. Moi harbored serious suspicion of the intellectual society, probably buoyed by the fact that he did not have a sound academic foundation as contrasted to his predecessor, Jomo Kenyatta. Kariuki traces this paranoia from Moi's lack of "Kenyatta's charisma, self-confidence and political credentials" that led him to iron-fisted rule that aptly entered him in the annals of history of the African dictators (76). As if to compensate for his skimpy education, Moi, on several occasions, declared himself a "professor of politics" (Rasmussen 444). However, he had a reputation of outwitting his political opponents through cunning strategies (Rasmussen 444).

Barber notes that in times of rapid social change, the art forms "with their exceptional mobility (whether through technology such as the radio, record and cassette tape, or through physical transportation from place to place by travelling performing groups) will play a crucial role in formulating new ways of looking at things" (4). In this light, music and theatre then became crucial avenues through which criticisms of the ruling regime coalesced. As Haugerud argues, "the music heavily used social and religious symbols, as well as drawing from the popular anticolonial songs from the 1920s and the Christian hymns of the

1950s whose lyrics were altered to praise Kenyan political leaders who opposed colonial rule" (28).

This music carried themes that continually expressed the dissatisfaction of Kenyans towards the ruling regime. Musicians protested against the official corruption, rapid increases in the cost of living, and the government efforts to silence political opposition. There were scathing political lyrics that were evident in the music. These expressive forms, like music and theatre, Haugerud argues, "create, as well as enact political understanding and consciousness" (28). The government was uncomfortable with these expressive forms and made attempts to ban the music. However, the artists and their audiences alike found creative channels for expressing versions of current history that differed from official scripts.

One of the channels they appropriated was to play the music in public transport vans, known as *matatu*; they would also play music in bars and in shops. The informal sector vendors and street hawkers were also instrumental in the sale and distribution of this music. But while not overtly political, the themes carried in most of these songs were themselves a pointer to the disillusionment of the Kenyans.

The musicians, in voicing their concerns about a united Kenya and highlighting the tribulations of the ordinary person, had sensed that there was "no room for exchange of political views: any communication [was] in essence a dialogue of the deaf" (Kariuki 70). Rather than engage with the politician, the artist opted for just naming and shaming the injustices. Cultural performances are important tools especially for the marginalized. In Conquergood's words:

> Through cultural performances, many people both construct and participate in "public" life. Particularly for the poor and marginalized people denied access to middle class "public" forums, cultural performance becomes the venue for public discussion of vital issues central to their communities as well as an arena for gaining visibility. (189)

Though not explicitly mentioning the disillusionment, unlike most artists, musicians found subtle ways of raising the concerns about the hurly-burly of everyday politics in Kenya. Messages of corruption, tribal cleansing, and dysfunctional democracy amongst other concerns filtered through most lyrics of the songs. In agreement with Christopher Waterman (8) and John Chernoff (154), the argument made here is that African popular music has been broadly conditioned by competition within colonial and postcolonial economies. As Barber puts it, it is "under conditions of pervasive political and economic change that music continues to play a crucial role as a medium of symbolic transaction and a means of forging and defending communities" (4).

CONCLUSIONS

Kenyan music has not only been pandering to the interests of the regime. Studies by Ndĩgĩrĩgĩ (1994), Gecau (1995), Nyairo and Ogude (2005), Mutonya (2004 & 2006), Njogu and Maupeu (2007), amongst many others, have highlighted the importance of music in the social and political change in Kenya, especially during the regime of arap Moi. In fact, it was the same power of song in power politics that assisted in a huge way towards the exit of the repressive KANU regime in 2002. A coalition of opposition parties under the umbrella NARC (National Rainbow Coalition) was buoyed up by the electric performances of a rap duo Gidi Gidi Maji Maji's hit *Unbwogable* (Sheng: "Invincible"), which increasingly became an anthem during campaign rallies. The popular Christian homily *Yote yawezekana kwa imani* (Kiswahili: "All is possible in God's faith"), was subverted to *yote yawezekana bila Moi* ("all is possible without Moi"), a rallying call that popularised the dislike for the ruling party and its preferred candidate for presidency, Uhuru Kenyatta, whom Moi had hand-picked as his successor. In its widest sense, "project Uhuru denoted President Moi's strategy of whipping up generational sentiments and giving a new youthful shade to Kenya's body politic by elevating the 'uhuru generation' to the higher echelons of his party and government to upstage challengers both within his party and among the opposition" (Kagwanja, 57). For once, the self-proclaimed "professor of politics" had erred in his calculations as youthful Uhuru lost to seasoned politician Mwai Kibaki, but, again, this served to reinforce the gerontocracy myth of the youth as "leaders of tomorrow."

Kenyan musicians have not, however, always retained the moral high ground in the eyes of the people. Indeed, many have been accused of propping up despotic regimes by performing patriotic praise songs for them.[28] Accused of sycophancy for the sake of personal aggrandizement, or to increase their individual access to power and money, such musicians reply that their motives were economic, not political, and that they only perform what many people wish to hear. This argument brings to the fore the fundamental conflicts that emerge around the complex transactions that occur at the intersections between money and power. Musicians have constantly needed to negotiate the conflicts and congruencies between the political power effected through voicing the interests of rulers or those of the nation's subjects. They also have to weigh the economic benefits of doing so, gained either from handouts from politicians or through accessing the mass market populated by the ordinary citizens. Whatever their actions, however, they seem ultimately to be judged according to the moral expectations of a traditional praise poet: that they should use their privileged access to a platform appropriately—that is, to raise their voices for the common good.

Notes

1. This note refers to the essays main title *Fimbo ya Nyayo* (1981) (Kiswahili: "Moi's Cane/Staff"), by Arthur Kemoli, which is derived from the title of a praise song during the reign of Kenya's second president, Daniel arap Moi, whose symbol of authority was the cane. Upon assuming presidency in 1978, he evolved the Nyayo philosophy of Peace, Love, and Unity, vowing to follow in the footsteps (*nyayo*) of his predecessor, Jomo Kenyatta.
2. Aguilar further contends that in Western societies, like the United States, the old are seen as a problem because they are not producers but consumers of the economic and public resources. This is in stark contrast to the expectations of traditions in many communities in Africa.
3. See Olubanke and Adeboye, who look at Yoruba cultural practices in rethinking political and social dynamics in contemporary Nigeria.
4. Odinga (145), in his memoirs, had described Moi as a "giraffe with a long neck that saw from afar," an interesting compliment from a politician who was much older than him, in view of the proverb above. This proverb of the Kikuyu in Kenya is similar to one from the Nembe of the Niger Delta: *What an old man sees seated / A youth does not see standing.*
5. Youthful Uhuru Kenyatta, a forty-two-year-old (Kenya African National Union) KANU presidential aspirant, lost in the third general elections in Kenya held under multi-party democracy to septuagenarian Mwai Kibaki, fronted by the opposition coalition National Rainbow Coalition (NARC), who won in a landslide majority.
6. Jomo Kenyatta, the first leader of independent Kenya also presided over a regime that suppressed political opposition, detentions without trial, strangulation of the intellectuals, as well political assassinations. According to Muigai, it is President Kenyatta who "entrenched ethnicity as the dominant basis of political mobilization" (251). In vowing to follow in his predecessor's footsteps, Daniel arap Moi, who forms the backbone of this chapter, ensured that such tendencies continued unabated, as a way of maintaining political power and control.
7. Abobo grapples with what he refers to as the fallacies of the gerontocracy myth; that the older one is, the wiser he becomes, or that the judgement of the elderly is always right. Abobo contends that this myth should be revised in Africa, especially in relation to political leadership.
8. When under local pressure, Moi always whipped up national emotions by claiming that those against his leadership (anti-Nyayoists) had been mercenaries of unnamed foreign powers, who were bent on disturbing the prevailing tranquility perpetuated in the Nyayo philosophy of Peace, Love, and Unity.
9. See "End of an Era," 13. As Sicherman (137) notes, Ngugi wa Thiong'o mocked this advice by creating a Professor of Parrotology in his novel, *Matigari*.
10. The difference between Kenyatta's and Moi's taste in music is also visible in the latter's preference for the dancers to use well-designed attires, as opposed to them using "old skins and torn clothes as costumes" (Mindoti 179). The use of skins, it was argued, went against president Moi's wildlife conservation policy. Hence, his insistence on uniforms for the choirs "stopped the killing of wild animals to obtain skin" (Mindoti, ibid.).
11. In the Kibaki government (2002-2013), the PPMC was a department within the Ministry of State for National Heritage and Culture, with a similar vision and mission to the one envisaged during arap Moi's regime. However, it was not under direct patronage from the office of the president, as it was prior to Moi's exit from power.
12. In 1963, immediately after independence from the British, the founding president centralized power and introduced a *de-facto* one-party state that was to be under KANU. When Moi took over, many of the key functions of the government were shifted to the powerful Office of the

President. In 1982, under Moi, through a constitutional amendment that was debated for only twenty minutes, KANU was enshrined in the constitution, effectively turning Kenya into a one-party state *de jure*. See Kariuki; Brown; and Jeffrey.

13. In Lukalo's analysis of political patronage during the regime of Moi, "catching the eye" of the president also involved "fraternizing with the ruling elite, and was seen to symbolize power" (20).
14. The Loyalty Pledge existed before Moi's ascendancy to the presidency. As Widner rightly comments, the Kenyatta government rarely used to enforce the loyalty pledge because the "provincial administration, not the party, was Kenyatta's chosen vehicle for securing compliance with government policies and stances" (1). Moi continued to use it but added the last part to reflect his philosophy.
15. *Harambee* is the official motto of Kenya, which literally means "self-help development," or "let us pull together." When Kenyatta took power in 1963, this spirit already existed in an un-institutionalized form. It was in 1965, in the Sessional Paper No. 10 on African Socialism that this spirit "assumed a new and more important role than it had previously occupied" (Widner 62). During Kenyatta's reign, he would end his political speeches with a chant of *Harambee* with the audience responding with a cheer. In Moi's reign, the cheer from the audience changed to *Nyayo*, in response to the *Harambee* chant. For more on the transition from *Harambee* to *Nyayo*, see Widner.
16. This song ended up capturing the social imaginary in Kenya in the sense that the word *Maze* entered into Kenyan slang language, *sheng*, a word that is used for emphasis. This is one instance in which songs tend to create new insights for the audience. For a long time, Tabu Ley's love song was seen as a protest song to the regime of Moi by Kenyans. I am grateful to Kakozi Kashindi and Denis Owaga for their insights into the translations and interpretations of the *lingala* music.
17. Oduor Ong'wen
18. As Peter and Kopsieker contend, the 1982 coup and the flurry of song recordings that followed marked "the emergence of the construction of the big man through songs" (22).
19. Pugliese notes,

    Biblical analogies were often used to convey messages. For instance, Kenyatta was referred to as 'the shepherd of black people' . . . and as God's instrument for the salvation of the Gĩkũyũ since He was given the rod of leadership from God like Moses in Egypt. Songs in praise of Gĩkũyũ colonial chiefs were fairly common in the 1930s. In the 1940s, new songs were composed to pay tribute to the Gĩkũyũ politicians who were fighting against the colonial government. (24)

20. Widner's statistics underline this fact:

    Under Moi, Kalenjin gained control of the governor-ship of the Central Bank, the Ministry for Cooperative Development, the Ministry of Local Government, and the post of commissioner of cooperatives. The chairs of the Kenya Commercial Bank and Kenya National Insurance were both Kalenjin. Moi's community also gained the directorships of Kenya Posts and Telecommunications, the Agricultural Finance Corporation, the Agricultural Development Corporation, Kenya Industrial Estates, the National Cereals and Produce Board, the Kenya Grain Growers' Cooperative Union, Nyayo Tea Zone, Nyayo Bus Company, and the Kenya Broadcasting Corporation. The government decided to de-register the Kenya Coffee Growers' Union, the representative of smallholder coffee interests, which were predominantly Kikuyu, and sidelined the other body whose officers are elected by coffee growers, the Kenya Planters' Cooperative Union. (180)

21. Schatzberg sees these symbols as faces of power, which the heads of states in middle Africa are reluctant to share (*Political Legitimacy* 60).
22. Musician D.K. Kamau produced a song about the 1975 brutal murder of politician J. M. Kariuki. Some of the lyrics pointed to the popular belief that the murder was state-engineered: "It is rumoured that the musician was summoned to Gatundu [Kenyatta's home] and thoroughly caned by the President, Jomo Kenyatta, which was the late President's preferred punishment for dissent even among his fellow politicians." See www.enchanted-landscapes.com.
23. *Mwakenya* is an acronym for *Muungano wa Wazalendo wa Kuikomboa Kenya*, literally translated as "The Progressive Movement to Liberate Kenya." According to Maina wa Kinyatti in his memoirs, *Kenya: A Prison Notebook* (169), it was an underground revolutionary movement started in the 1970s. Originally it was referred to as the "December Twelfth Movement" before it changed to *Mwakenya*. The movement was indigenous and transcended class and ethnicity, despite Moi's claims that it was foreign-controlled (Kariuki 77). A crackdown on the movement by the government led to the arrest of mainly university lecturers, students and their leaders, and later of other professionals. In the 1990s, a number of ex-prisoners wrote novels and autobiographies detailing the torture in government cells. For more on the literature of this period, see Mutonya, *Laughing Cry*.
24. According to Kabaji, Kamiti Maximum Prison in Kenya has come to symbolize suffering, anguish, and horror. The experiences in this prison have given birth to the most memorable fiction that epitomizes the excesses of the Moi dictatorship.
25. Gikandi (380) argues that in the postcolonial situation, the nation is not the manifestation of a common interest but a repressor of desires.
26. According to Oliver Lovesey (32), the imprisonment of African writers is the incarceration of the creative national spirit seeking to define and celebrate national freedom. He continues that this imprisonment of the writer in Africa must been as a search for the efforts to retrieve the power to write the national narrative from the state.
27. See Pugliese. However, Gikandi (379) contends that trying to understand the postcolonial situation as simply an extension of the colonial experience comes with its own complexities and contradictions. In this chapter, however, I am attempting to draw parallels with the excessive use of state authority (by both colonial and post-independence Kenyan governments) to stigmatize narratives that contest those of the state.
28. In recent times, a group of choir masters and musicians who were at the forefront of producing praise songs for Moi and his government have consolidated their efforts in a book entitled *Music in Kenya: Development, Management, Composition and Performance: A Tribute to Daniel T arap Moi*. The book contains essays that discuss the contributions of arap Moi to the development of the praise music tradition in Kenya during his reign. For the most part, the book is a documentation of sampled music scores of largely praise songs to Moi accompanied by an 80-song CD.

Works Cited

Abobo, Williams. "Revising the Gerontocratic Myths in African Political Leadership." *GhanaWeb*. GhanaWeb, 11 Feb. 2010. Web. [Accessed 3rd February 2012]

Adar, G. Korwa and Isaac Munyae. "Human Rights Abuse in Kenya Under Daniel Arap Moi, 1978–2001." *Africa Studies Quarterly* 5 .1 (2001): 1-17. Print

Adeboye, Olufunke. "The Changing Conception of Elderhood in Ibadan, 1830–2000." *Nordic Journal of African Studies* 16.2 (2007): 261-278. Print.

Aguilar, Mario, ed. *Rethinking Age in Africa: Colonial, Post-Colonial and Contemporary Interpretations of Cultural Representations*. Trenton: Africa World Press, 2007. Print.

Allen, Lara. "Music and Politics in Africa." *Social Dynamics* 30.2 (2004): 1–19. Print.

Aluanga, Lillian. "Moi: Seven Years after Retirement." *The Standard* 9 Oct. 2010: 16-17. Print.

Barz, Gregory. *Performing Religion: Negotiating Past and Present in Kwaya Music of Tanzania*. New York: Rodopi Publishers, 2003. Print.

Bayart, Jean-Francois. *The State in Africa: Politics of the Belly*. London: Longman, 1993. Print.

Berman, Bruce, Dickson Eyoh and Will Kymlicka. *Ethnicity and Democracy in Africa*. Oxford: James Currey, 2004. Print.

Brown, Stephen. "Authoritarian Leaders and Multiparty Elections in Africa: How Foreign Donors Help to Keep Kenya's Daniel arap Moi in Power." *Third World Quarterly* 22.5 (2001): 725-39. Print.

Chernoff, John Miller. *African Rhythm and African Sensibility: Aesthetics and Social Action in African Musical Idioms*. Chicago: Chicago UP, 1979. Print.

Conquergood, Dwight. "Rethinking Ethnography: Towards a Critical Cultural Politics." *Communication Monographs* 58.2 (1991): 179–194. Print.

"End of an Era." *Sunday Nation*. 24 Dec. 2002: 1-24. Print.

Gikandi, Simon. "The Politics and Poetics of National Formation: Recent African Writing." *From Commonwealth to Postcolonial*. Ed. Anna Rutherford. Sydney: Dangaroo Press, 1992: 377-389. Print.

Haugerud, Angelique. *The Culture of Politics in Modern Kenya*. Cambridge: Cambridge UP, 1995. Print.

Hempstone, Smith. *The Rogue Ambassador: An African Memoir*. Sewanee: U of the South P, 1997. Print.

Human Rights Watch. *Kenya's Unfinished Democracy: A Human Rights Agenda for the New Government*. 14.10A, December 2002. Print.

Kabaji, Egara. "The Kamiti Stories and the Bad Toilet Paper Joke." *Sunday Standard* 23 July 2000: 23-24. Print.

Kagwanja, Peter. "Power to Uhuru? Youth Identity and Generational Politics in Kenya's 2002 Elections." *African Affairs* 105.418 (2005): 51–75. Print.

Kariuki, James. "'Paramoia': Anatomy of a Dictatorship in Kenya." *Journal of Contemporary African Studies* 14.1 (1996): 69–86. Print.

Kariuki, John. "Flashback to Praise Songs Era." *The Sunday Nation* 3 Nov. 2002: 19 Print.

Lovesey, Oliver. "Chained Letters: African Prison Diaries and 'National Allegory'" *Research in African Literatures* 6.4 (1995): 31–45. Print.

Lukalo, F. Kavulani. *Extended Handshake or Wrestling Match? Youth and Urban Culture Celebrating Politics in Kenya*. Discussion Paper 32. Uppsala: Nordika Afrikainstitutet, 2006. Print.

Mbembe, Achille. "Provisional Notes on the Postcolony." *Africa: Journal of the International African Institute* 62.1(1992): 3–37. Print.

Mbogo, Fred. "Daniel arap Moi Used the Power of Choral Music to Rule Kenya." *ArtMatters.Info*. ArtMatters.Info, 19 Nov. 2008. Web. [Accessed December 10th 2011].

Mindoti, Kaskon W and Hellen Agak. "Political Influence on Music Performance between 1963-2002." *Bulletin of the Council for Research in Music Education* 161/162 (2004): 155–164. Print.

Morton, Andrew. *Moi: The Making of an African Statesman*. London: Michael O'Mara Books, 1998. Print.

Mucoki, Mburu. *A Study of Themes in Kenya's Popular-Political Music in the Last 15 Years*. Research Report. Nairobi: School of Journalism, U of Nairobi, 1992. Print.

Muigai, Githu. "Jomo Kenyatta and the Rise of the Ethno-Nationalist State in Kenya." *Ethnicity and Democracy in Africa*. Eds. Bruce Berman, Dickson Eyoh and Will Kymlicka. Oxford: James Currey, 2004. 200-217. Print.

Musila, Grace. "Redykyulass Generation's Intellectual Interventions in Kenyan Public Life." *Young* 18.3 (2010): 279-299. Print.

Mutonya, Maina. "Joseph Kamaru: Contending Narrations of Kenya's Politics through Music." *Cultural Production and Social Change in Kenya: Building Bridges*. Eds. Kimani Njogu and G. Oluoch-Olunya. Nairobi: Twaweza Communications, 2007: 27-45. Print.

———. *The Laughing Cry: (Mwa)Kenya Prison Literature of Wahome Mutahi*. MA Thesis. U of Witwatersrand, 2001. Print.

———. "Praise and Protest: Music and Contesting Patriotisms in Postcolonial Kenya." *Social Dynamics* 30.2 (2004): 20-35. Print.

Ndĩgĩrĩgĩ, Gichingiri. "Kenyan Theatre after Kamĩrĩĩthũ." *The Drama Review* 43.2 (1999): 72-93. Print.

Nyairo, Joyce. *The Grammar of the State: Kenya's Three Regimes and a Lexicon of Oppression*. Unpublished manuscript. Print.

Odhiambo, E.S. Atieno. "Hegemonic Enterprises and Instrumentalities of Survival: Ethnicity and Democracy in Kenya." *African Studies* 61.2 (2002): 223-249. Print.

Odhiambo, Tom. "Gerontocracy and Generational Competition in Kenya Today: An Observation." *(Re)membering Kenya: Identity, Culture and Freedom*. Vol. 1. Nairobi: Twaweza Communications, 2010. 96-107. Print.

Odinga, Oginga. *Not Yet Uhuru*. New York: Hill & Wang, 1967. Print.

Oduor, Ong'wen. "Where Were You On August 1 1982." *Standard Digital News*. Standard Digital, n.d. Web. [Accessed December 10th 2011].

Office of the Vice President, Ministry of State for National Heritage and Culture. <http://marsgroupkenya.org/pdfs/2011/01/Ministry_PDFS/Ministry_of_National_Heritage/NATIONAL_MUSEUMS_KENYA/Publications/The_national_records_management_policy.pdf>. [Accessed September 25th 2013].

Ogola, George. "The Idiom of Age in a Popular Kenyan Newspaper Serial." *Africa: Journal of the International African Institute* 76.4 (2006): 569-589. Print.

Ogot, Bethwell A. "Politics, Culture and Music in Central Kenya, a Study of Mau Mau Hymns." *Kenya Historical Review: Special Issue on Some Perspectives on the Mau Mau Movement* 5.2 (1977): 275-286. Print.

Olubanke, Akintunde. "Rethinking HIV/AIDS Prevention: Exploring Some Yoruba Cultural Practices." *Kinaadman: An Interdisciplinary Research Journal* 19.2 (2008): 1-13. Print.

Peter, Chris Maina and Kopsieker Fritz. *Political Succession in East Africa: In Search for a Limited Leadership*. Nairobi: Kituo Cha Katiba and Friedrich Ebert Stiftung, Kenya Office, 2006. Print.

Pugliese, Cristiana. "Complementary or Contending Nationhoods? Kikuyu Political Pamphlets and Songs: 1945-1952." *Mau Mau and Nationhood: Arms, Authority & Narration*. Eds. E. S. Atieno Odhiambo and John Lonsdale. Oxford: James Currey, 2003. 97-120. Print.

Rasmussen, Jacob. "Outwitting the Professor of Politics? Mungiki Narratives of Political Deception and their Role in Kenyan Politics." *Journal of Eastern African Studies* 4.3 (2010): 435-449. Print.

Schatzberg, Michael. *The Dialectics of Oppression in Zaire*. Bloomington and Indianapolis: Indiana UP, 1998. Print.

———. *Political Legitimacy in Middle Africa: Father, Family, Food*. Bloomington: UP, 2001. Print.

Sicherman, Carol. "Revolutionizing the Literature Curriculum at the University of East Africa and the Soul of the Nation." *Research in African Literatures* 29.3 (1998): 129–148. Print.

Southall, Roger and Henning Melber, eds. *Legacies of Power: Leadership Change and Former Presidents in African Politics*. Uppsala and Pretoria: The Nordic African Institute and Human Sciences Research Council Press, 2006. Print.

Steeves, Jeffrey. "Presidential succession in Kenya: The Transition from Moi to Kibaki." *Commonwealth & Comparative Politics* 44: 2 (2006): 211–233. Print.

Street, John. *Politics and Popular Culture*. Cambridge: Polity Press, 1997. Print.

Stokes, Martin. *Ethnicity, Identity and Music: The Musical Construction of Place*. Oxford: Berg, 1994. Print.

Thomas, Roger. "Exile, Dictatorship and the Creative Writer in Africa: A Selective Annotated Bibliography." *Third World Quarterly* 9:1 (1987): 271–296. Print.

Wa Kinyatti, Maina. *Kenya: A Prison Notebook*. London: Vita Books, 1996. Print.

Wambua, Sammy. "Songsters Outdid themselves in their Rush to Praise the President's Regime." *Sunday Nation* 24 Dec. 2002: 13. Print.

Wa-Mũngai, Mbũgua. "Iconic Representations of Identities in Kenyan Cultures." *(Re)membering Kenya: Identity, Culture and Freedom*. Vol. 1. Nairobi: Twaweza Communications, 2010. 72–95. Print.

Wa-Mũngai, Mbugua. "The Big Man's Turn to Dance in Kenyan Bar-rooms: Wahome Mutahi's Parody of Power."*Leeds University Centre for African Studies Bulletin* 65 (2003): 37–48. Print.

Wanyama, Mellitus, Rose Ongati, Frederick Ngala and Caleb Okumu. *Music in Kenya: Development, Management, Composition and Performance: A Tribute to Daniel T. Arap Moi*. Kabarak: Kabarak University, 2010. Print.

Waterman, Christopher Allan. *Jùjú: A Social and Ethnography of an African Popular Music*. Chicago: U of Chicago P, 1990. Print.

Widner, Jennifer A. *The Rise of a Party-State in Kenya: From "Harambee!" to "Nyayo!"* Berkeley: U of California P, 1992. Print.

Williams, Adebayo. "Literature in the Time of Tyranny: African Writers and the Crisis of Governance, Politics and Letters: Some Paradigmatic Observations." *Third World Quarterly* 17.2 (1996): 349–362. Print.

Diagnosing Dictatorship: Illness, Medicine, and the Critique of Sovereignty in *Wizard of the Crow*

ROBERT L. COLSON

Ngũgĩ wa Thiong'o's *Wizard of the Crow* opens with five short chapters wherein the reader learns that the Ruler of Aburĩria is ill and that there are several popular diagnoses being discussed around the country. Although it will be many hundreds of pages before the Ruler actually succumbs to a mysterious illness, the novel's opening diagnostic rumors serve as a set of prolepses that foreground in the reader's mind the Ruler's medical condition, long before that condition becomes a reality in the text. The suspended question of the Ruler's ill body is a fundamental undercurrent of the novel's critique of his brutal authoritarian regime. It creates an ironic counterpoint to the Ruler's own bodily imaginary, which he not only lays out to his sycophantic ministers, but also presents to the country as his political philosophy.

Early in the novel the Ruler challenges Minister Sikiokuu with a set of questions: "Why do you go on and on about *my* enemies and those of the Country? Is there a distinction between me and the Country?" (136). Only a little later, Minister Sikiokuu needs to be reminded yet again as the Ruler fiercely interjects: "There is a difference between me and the Country?" (161). The Ruler's aggressive self-fashioning as the country should not be understood in terms of metonymy or synecdoche. He is not arguing that he relates, as a representative part, to the country as a whole. Rather there are three ways—semantic, rhetorical, and religious—to understand the Ruler's imagined embodiment of the country.

On a semantic level the Ruler's relationship to the country is figured in terms of substitution and synonym, typified late in the novel when the Ruler orders Minister Machokali to "[s]ubstitute the word *Ruler* for *the country*, as I am the country" as he reads from a document (513). This semantic substitution is significant because the dictator, in an etymological sense, "is the person who gives orders and he who creates his own world" ("es el personaje que da órdenes y el que crea un mundo propio"; García 30). He is, symbolically and literally, the one who speaks and whose words serve a performative function, shaping reality to his capricious desires and ends. Ngũgĩ's novel makes this explicit when it recounts the hidden history of the Ruler's rise to power. When he assumes power, after the "mysterious death of the First Ruler," he authorizes the execution of prisoners and experiences a terrible epiphany about the power of his words: "When he saw that his signature on paper or a word from his mouth could bring about the immediate cessation of a life, he there and then truly believed in his omnipotence. He was now sovereign" (Ngũgĩ 233). The Ruler's power over life demonstrates his sovereignty if we think, along with Michel Foucault, that "sovereign power's effect on life is exercised only when the sovereign can kill" (*Society* 240). Because of his verbal sovereignty, the Ruler is capable of enforcing his embodiment of or equivalence to the country.

The Ruler's embodied equivalence with the country extends beyond the semantic to the rhetorical register as well. The Ruler imagines himself to embody Aburĩria, in a sort of reverse personification or antiprosopopoeia.[1] The notion of adequately and fully representing a national space calls to mind the ultimate and absurd extension of cartography described by Jorge Luis Borges in "On Exactitude in Science." Here the Cartographers Guilds, seeking to fully capture and represent the empire, "struck a Map of the Empire whose size was that of the Empire, and which coincided point for point with it" (325). Although the Ruler certainly doesn't imagine that his physical body contains the country of Aburĩria, this figure of the ultimate map suggests the level of coextension and correspondence between nation and body imagined by the Ruler. In contrast, one might think of the famous illustration, by Abraham Bosse, from Hobbes's *Leviathan* of the sovereign's body where the body is composed of many small figures, culminating in the head, the sovereign. The Ruler's image of sovereignty is of a single body, his own, that represents the totality of the nation, not the Hobbesian Commonwealth that is comprised of the members of the body politic who have given their consent and invested power in the sovereign (*Leviathan* "Chapter XXVIII"). This contrast is further emphasized in the novel when the Ruler's *Political Theory* is published and distributed. A central tenet of this political theory is that "what was important in any given country was . . . the character of the person who personified the head, heart, arms, and legs of the state" (703).

The Ruler's personification of Aburĩria almost represents the apotheosis of his notion of sovereignty. The body itself becomes a signifier for the Ruler's dictates. As Achille Mbembe notes, "The body of the despot, his frowns and smiles, decrees and commands, the public notices and communiqués . . . these are the primary signifiers, it is these that have force" (108). However, there is one further level invoked in this comparison between body and nation, the divine.

Near the end of the novel, after the terrifying explosions that seem to bring an end to the Ruler's illness and appear to signal a *coup d'etat*, the Ruler makes a long overdue appearance before Parliament to attempt to re-solidify his power. The Ruler's prolonged absence from public view, as a result of his real and rumored illness, coupled with the signs of a *coup*, had seriously shaken public confidence in him. As part of the announcement, the Ruler says, "Every Aburĩrian child knows that I am the Country and the Country is Me, which means that *this* Excellency, *this* Country, and *this* Nation are like the mystery of Three in One and One in Three creating the Perfect One" (698). The Ruler's invocation here of the metaphor of the Christian trinity to describe his inextricable connection to Aburĩria, along with his other divine pretensions such as the Marching to Heaven project which would see him as God's own neighbor, will most likely seem far more surprising to Ngũgĩ's readers in the English translation. For Ngũgĩ's Gĩkũyũ readership, the Ruler's aspirations for the divine are always already figured in his name. The "Ruler" is a title, not a name. In fact, we never learn his name. The Gĩkũyũ word that is translated as "Ruler" is *Mwathani*, which most closely translates as "Lord" (as used in the Bible). Ngũgĩ's choice here seems deliberate. He could have used the Gĩkũyũ word for leader, *mũtongoria*, but this would neither have implied the Ruler's claim to unquestionable political authority, nor would it have fully reflected his pretensions to divine authority. These pretensions of divinity mark an absurd manifestation of what has often been the case with historical dictators. Jackson and Rosberg note:

> Like monarchs of old, they stand above their subjects. In all save a very few states not only do they enjoy unrivaled power, privilege, wealth, and honor—that is, overt public rewards—but also in some cases a kind of political divinity. In many an African country the ruler is portrayed as embodying the idea, dignity, and even the sacredness of the state—a concept most evident in countries with long-surviving rulers who have governed for a decade or more or who have ruled continuously since independence. In those countries the idea of the state and the person of the ruler are intertwined to a degree that is difficult to imagine in institutionalized systems. (22–3)

Although Jackson and Rosberg astutely describe the way a ruler can come to embody his country, they neglect to explain adequately the means by which this embodiment comes into being. This "political divinity," Jackson and Rosberg seem to claim, is conferred by the people on the ruler, in some sort of passive accretion of the sacred to the political. However, in the case of Ngũgĩ's dictator at least, the sovereign's imaginary embodiment of country is actually created by the authoritarian ruler and foisted on the people. Ngũgĩ's Ruler has conferred on himself a political divinity and, in a period of turmoil, draws on this idea in an attempt to reassert his power.

The question of the sovereign's body, in the context of a kind of political divinity, has been the concern of political theology for many years. In *Homo Sacer: Sovereign Power and Bare Life*, Giorgio Agamben returns to the work of Ernst Kantorowicz on the king's two bodies. Kantorowicz's work represents the definitive examination of sovereignty in the context of medieval Christianity. The idea of the king's two bodies refers to the notion that while the monarch's physical body may die, the monarch's "political body" lives on. This is aptly summarized in the expression: "The King is dead. Long live the King." This phenomenon represents "the continuity of the state's *corpus morale et politicum* (moral and political body), without which no stable political organization could be conceived" (Agamben 57). To Kantorowicz's medieval Christian context, Agamben introduces the Romans' treatment of the sovereign's two bodies in order to better illustrate how this doubleness reveals "what is sovereignty's clearest feature, its perpetual nature" (58). By supplementing the Christian practices from Kantorowicz with the Roman practices, Agamben concludes that:

> the king's political body cannot simply represent . . . the continuity of sovereign power. The king's body must also and above all represent the very excess of the emperor's sacred life, which is . . . passed on to the designated successor. However, once this is acknowledged, the metaphor of the political body appears no longer as the symbol of the perpetuity of *dignitas*, but rather as the cipher of the absolute and inhuman character of sovereignty. The formulas *le mort saisit le vif* and *le roi ne meurt jamais* must be understood in a much more literal way than is usually thought: at the moment of the sovereigns [sic] death, it is the sacred life grounding sovereign authority that invests the person of the sovereigns [sic] successor. (61–2)

The question of succession is centrally important for both Kantorowicz and Agamben. The "inhuman character of sovereignty" underpins the king's embodiment of sovereign power, but is also transferable to his successor in the form of the king's undying political body. The political situation of the Ruler in *Wizard of the Crow* demonstrates the inhuman perpetuity of sovereignty.

The Ruler in Ngũgĩ's novel is not at all interested in the question of succession. There is no concern over producing a viable heir, and only token interest is paid, near the end of the novel, to any kind of democratic transition. The Ruler is ultimately concerned with the opposite—he seeks, at the very end of the novel, to "freeze or abolish the future of [his] country" (Ngũgĩ 750). Ironically, these last efforts to forestall the march of time are what lead to his death and the end of his rule. In sharp contrast to the Ruler's efforts to permanently foreclose his end, the progression of his rule leads to its logical conclusion, his death. As Jackson and Rosberg observe, "There is a vicious circle of tyranny: the more a Tyrant persists in his rule, the more violence he must do; tyranny cannot come to an end except by the only justice inherent in it, which is the overthrow of the Tyrant and his regime—if necessary, by the killing of the Tyrant" (239). As Tajirika takes power, he moves to supplant the Ruler, to kill off his memory, not just succeed him. He brings to an end the Baby D program and begins construction of a "modern coliseum on the site once earmarked for Marching to Heaven" (754). The perpetual, inhuman nature of sovereignty is here expressed in the erasure of one's predecessor. The public announcement of the Ruler's death emphasizes that "this was not a coup d'etat. It was premeditated SID [self-induced disappearance]" (753). The Ruler doesn't die so much as he disappears from Aburĩria and from history, and the cover story has him disappearing himself. This pattern of erasure is merely a repetition of what the Ruler himself had done. After assuming control of the country after the "mysterious death of the First Ruler," his rule extends for so long that, in the popular conception, "even [the Ruler] could not remember when his reign began. His rule had no beginning and no end[,] . . . his rule had survived all the generations" (233, 5). The people speak as if they are convinced that "Aburĩria had never had and could never have another ruler, because had not this man's reign begun before the world began and would end only after the world ended?" (6). However, hidden from the arms of the state's hegemony in the popular memory, there remains a sense of the actual historical narrative. Nevertheless, this sentiment of the Ruler's eternal rule reinforces the idea of "political divinity" put forth by Jackson and Rosberg. But the Ruler's disappearance from official history after his death demonstrates the divorce between the Ruler's physical and political bodies, in direct opposition to his semantic and rhetorical efforts at eliding the difference between the two.

In conjunction with the expression of the "absolute and inhuman character of sovereignty" that challenges and unseats the Ruler's hegemony, the Ruler's own physical body plays an even more apparent role in unsettling his power. The novel's focus on the Ruler's material body, his illness, and the attempts to diagnose and treat that illness all serve to further undermine and eradicate the linkage between his body and the sovereign state. In addition, the Ruler's illness and the attempts to diagnose and treat him also subjugate the sovereign to some of the same aspects of biopower that his authoritarian regime wields against the general population. In his lecture of March 17, 1976, collected in *Society Must Be*

Defended, Michel Foucault briefly draws on an historical example of a dictator stricken with a debilitating illness as an illustration of the pervasive force that political biopower has on everyone, even on those who wield that biopower to maintain their own political power.[2] Foucault invokes the contemporary, to him, example of Franco and his death. He makes an important observation about Franco's situation that illuminates the Ruler's situation in *Wizard of the Crow*, even though the Ruler's illness was not directly fatal. Foucault remarks that

> the man who died had, as you know, exercised the sovereign right of life and death with great savagery, was the bloodiest of all the dictators, wielded an absolute right of life and death for forty years, and at the moment when he himself was dying, he entered this sort of new field of power over life which consists not only of managing life, but in keeping individuals alive after they are dead" (248).

Foucault marks, in this passage, the powerful transition that physical illness signals for a sovereign who has ruled savagely and violently. The man who has exercised power over life and death has now lost control of his own body and is now subjected to some of the very same disciplinary and biopolitical mechanisms that he has used to control the population he rules.[3] Foucault grants to medicine, in this context, a "new field of power over life" that supersedes, in this special instance, the sovereign's own power. This ultimately humanizes the dictator because his body is susceptible to the same maladies as anyone else's, albeit he probably has the option of much better medical treatment than his average subject. Where the Ruler's invocation of equivalence between the nation and his political divinity draws him into the realm of what Agamben calls the "inhuman character of sovereignty," the Ruler's illness and his loss of control over his own material body signal his absolute humanization and subjection to the frailties of mortality. It would seem that the Ruler is, as it were, pulled in two directions at once by these two inexorable forces in the novel.

Ngũgĩ's depiction of the physically ill Ruler in *Wizard of the Crow*, however, moves the Ruler in a single direction, towards humanity and mortality. Where the inhumanity of sovereignty divorces the Ruler from his most grandiose claims and aspirations to eternal rule and divine powers, the Ruler's medical condition pulls him down into the masses of humanity and makes him a subject, just like any other political subject. He is, in a manner of speaking, removed from a state of exception and brought back to earth. The humanization of the figure of the dictator is not an uncommon trope in dictator novels. Speaking of Latin American dictator novels, Jorge Sherman observes that "[the] recourse to parody . . . includes a strong literary element of play or burlesque fundamentally designed . . . for two objectives: i) the demystification of the figure of the dictator; and ii) the humanization of the character in spite of his brutality" ("[el] recurso de la parodia;

incluye con fuerza un elemento literario de carácter lúdico o burlesco destinado fundamentalmente ... a dos objetivos: i) demistificar la figura del dictador; y ii) humanizar al personaje a pesar de su brutalidad"; Scherman 41). The demystifying and humanizing forces in Ngũgĩ's narrative make the Ruler a man and nothing more. Although he might be, like Franco, "the bloodiest of all dictators," he is, in the end, just a man who can and will die. So while the power he wields is terrifying and his actions are brutal, he is nothing more than a man. Much like the iconic scene in the film *The Wizard of Oz*, the dictator novel pulls back the curtain on the tyrant and exposes that behind the curtain and all the pyrotechnics and scary voices, there is just a man using a microphone and some machines.

It is fitting that the focus returns to the Ruler as a human who possesses a body because this reduces him to his most vulnerable political and physical state. Because all of his power depends on his ability to control and manipulate others, he must be in control at all times. A loss of control could prove deadly. This is why "personal rule is marked by inherent uncertainty. At the best of times, when a ruler appears most firmly in control, there is nevertheless a possibility for fate or fortune to change things or, indeed, for the ruler himself unwittingly or incautiously to cause disruption[.] ... The ultimate uncertainty in a system of personal rule lies in the key point of vulnerability: the ruler" (Jackson/Rosberg 26). As the "key point of vulnerability" in the system he rules, the Ruler lives in a state that lies somewhere between hyper-vigilance and fear and paranoia. However, all the while that he works to protect himself from the scheming of his ministers and resistance movements in the country, one of the greatest threats to his power is his own body, which betrays him for a time. Although the novel opens with the five rumors that serve as popular diagnoses of the Ruler's illness, there is not even a mention of this illness again until the beginning of Section I at the opening of *Book Three: Female Daemons*. Here the narrator alludes to the paper and diary entries of one Professor Furyk of Harvard "about the Ruler's strange illness" (Ngũgĩ 273). However, there is no immediate elaboration on this "strange illness" at that time either. At the end of Section II of the third book, we learn from an email from one rival minister to another that "[t]he Ruler was not feeling well," but nothing more (421). Finally, after so much anticipation and delay, we get firsthand accounts of the Ruler's condition at the beginning of *Book Four: Male Daemons*.

To begin the presentation of the facts, the narrator first draws on the work and diary of Dr. Din Furyk, a "distinguished Harvard professor," in order to "supplement [the narrator's] other sources" (469). That this initial presentation of the Ruler's illness and his symptoms is mediated through the lens of a distinguished medical professional sets the tone for all the further descriptions of the Ruler's illness and symptoms. The illness first manifests itself during his trip to America. Concern builds as "the Ruler's body had started puffing up like a balloon, his whole body becoming more and more inflated, without losing the proportion of parts" (469). When he appeared "on the verge of bursting," his personal physician, Dr. Kaboca, called in a specialist, Dr. Clarkwell, who called in his mentor, Professor Furyk (470). When authoritarian regime and official medicine coincide, the "cure (and before that still the diagnosis) [is] no longer a private but a public function, the doctor's responsibility [is] no longer exercised in relation to those who [are] sick, but rather to the state, the sole (and also secret) depository for archiving the conditions of the patient" (Esposito 139). In a way, the narrator's inclusion of the official and unofficial records of Dr. Furyk enacts this tendency of the state, but the narrator is not state-sponsored, so there is an element of resistance in presenting these revelations. The fourth chapter of *Book Four: Section I* presents the Professor's notes on his initial examination:

> The patient was seated on the floor, his back to the wall. I felt his forehead, took his temperature, listened to his heartbeat. All was normal, though he seemed to be panting a bit from fatigue. But his eyes, those eyes, I have never encountered a look like that in an adult. They looked scared and helpless, like the eyes of a child stricken with fear at the unexpected and the unknown. (471)

A variety of things happen in this short passage. The image of the panting, fatigued Ruler with his back to the wall is a blow that undercuts him. He is weakened and in a position of weakness. This image of the Ruler's eyes, however, is really striking. Furyk sees in the Ruler's eyes the fear and helplessness of a child. At once this is a humanizing image that provokes a sympathetic and compassionate reaction as the reader faces human suffering and a critical image that reduces the Ruler to a scared little boy, stripping away all his pretensions to political divinity and power. If the eyes are the windows of the soul, as the cliché goes, then the Ruler is just a scared little boy. To see him brought so low is striking indeed.

But the first and most significant thing that happens as Furyk examines him, even before he describes the Ruler's physical condition, is that the Ruler is classified as a "patient." This fixes him in a particular discourse, in a particular power relationship, and to classify him as a patient poses a very real challenge to his sovereign power (Foucault, *Discipline* 190). Although Foucault discusses the power-knowledge of medicine and its disciplinary and biopolitical effects on bodies in several texts, he most thoroughly dissects the doctor-patient relationship in *The Birth of the Clinic*, long before he began talking of "medicine [as] a biopolitical strategy" (qtd. in Esposito 27). For the physician to "know the pathological fact, the doctor must abstract the patient" (Foucault, *Birth* 8). As he or she does this, "the doctor's gaze is directed initially not towards that concrete body, that visible whole ... that faces him—the patient—but towards intervals in nature, lacunae . . . [that] like negatives" serve as signs of the disease (Foucault, *Birth* 8). In medical practice, then, the doctor really doesn't see the person, or even their concrete body; the doctor sees past the patient, who is an abstraction more than a person, and sees what is missing or out of harmony. One must "subtract the individual" in order to discover the malady (*Birth* 14). The Ruler becomes just a list of conditions that match some or all of his symptoms. The man who stresses again and again his equivalency with Aburĩria is here reduced to a list of possible conditions that could be the cause of his uncontrollable inflation. The Ruler as patient becomes a set of blood samples to determine if the ailment is "hyperthyroidism, nephritic syndrome, polycystic kidney disease, or some form of Cushing's syndrome brought about by cortisal hormones in the blood, or any disorders associated with obesity known to science" (Ngũgĩ 471). The symptoms occupy a "uniquely privileged position" because they "allow the invariable form of the disease . . . to *show through*" (Foucault, *Birth* 90; emphasis in the original).

For the Ruler to become Dr. Furyk's patient and to submit to the examination, the Ruler enters this framework whereby the patient almost ceases to exist as an individual, which is about as powerless a state as one can imagine in a power relationship. The patient/individual is not completely obliterated, however. The patient is fundamentally necessary for the process. The doctor and patient are "bound together, the doctor by an ever-more attentive, more insistent, more penetrating gaze, the patient by all the silent, irreplaceable qualities that, in him, betray—that is reveal and conceal—the clearly ordered forms of the disease" (*Birth* 15–6). Yet the patient is silent and is betrayed by the disease which plagues him, placing him in a state of extreme powerlessness, a state that certainly would explain the look of a scared child that the doctor sees in the Ruler's eyes. The fear he feels is not just a result of the troubling illness that affects his body but also a sign of power that he has lost in the eyes of those around him. Some portion of this power is swept up by the doctor's gaze "in which the sovereignty of the gaze gradually establishes itself—the eye that knows and decides, the eye that governs" (*Birth* 89). These last two phrases could have been easily applied to the Ruler to describe him as dictator. His is the voice that knows and decides, the voice that governs. But now he has lost his voice, and, more troubling yet, he has been betrayed by his body, a sort of biological *coup*, and is now subject to the sovereign gaze of those who would try to heal him, including Dr. Furyk and the Wizard of the Crow. The Ruler no longer exercises supreme sovereignty; he is now subjected to this "eye that governs," and this will ultimately prove to be his undoing. The effects of this gaze linger whenever the illness is mentioned/described. The Ruler is now always already a patient in need of diagnosis and treatment; he is a subject who can be and must be abstracted and subtracted in order to arrive at the essence of truth.

The Ruler's illness, his "self-induced expansion," as Dr. Furyk calls it, has a profound effect on those who come into contact with him in an official, political capacity (Ngũgĩ 472). The obvious manifestation of his body's betrayal collapses the normal power distance between the sovereign and the governed. Normally "the body of the king ... is at the opposite extreme of this new physics of power represented by panopticism; the domain of panopticism is, on the contrary, that whole lower region, that region of irregular bodies" (*Discipline* 208). But when the medical gaze is brought to bear on the Ruler, his body is no longer contrary to the irregular bodies; his body becomes visible as a most irregular body. Early in *Discipline and Punish*, Foucault makes his own mention of Kantorowicz's analysis of the king's two bodies, and invokes an image from the "opposite pole[,] ... the body of the condemned man" (29). This condemned man becomes the public repository for the exercise of "monarchical 'super-power'" which demonstrates the sovereign's power (Foucault, *Discipline* 80). The Ruler's illness, by effacing the difference between sovereign and irregular bodies, displaces him from a position where he can wield his "super-power" and leaves him vulnerable to the exercise of power; it condemns him to precisely the position of any subject or citizen living in a dictatorship of this kind where anyone and everyone is subject to the whims of the dictator and the regime. This displacement effect takes hold almost immediately after Dr. Furyk's encounter with the patient. When the Wizard of the Crow is brought to New York to treat the Ruler's other condition, his speechlessness, he is confronted with the juxtaposition of his expectations of the Ruler's appearance and the reality he encounters:

> The Wizard of the Crow had never met the Ruler face-to-face, and his image of him—tall, big-bodied but not fat—had been formed from watching television and reading newspapers. The Ruler cared about his appearance[.] ... He had expected a difference, especially in one now so afflicted, but never this that appeared before his eyes. He was struck by a stench such as he often detected in the streets of Eldares, except that now it seemed to be oozing out of the Ruler's body. The Ruler's eyes were full of fear. (Ngũgĩ 489)

The imposing image the media created in one of the citizens of Aburĩria is debased by his actual presence. To describe him in terms of "stench" and "ooze" lowers the Ruler into the register of the strong and unpleasant smells of the streets and is an image that will be important in the final stages of the illness. And the Wizard of the Crow also makes note of the fear-filled eyes. These descriptions of him would be unthinkable if he were healthy. The fear would be in the eyes of the citizen, not the Ruler. Because of this effect the ministers make extra efforts to conceal the Ruler from the public eye after he returns to Aburĩria. This decision has its own destabilizing effect and assures the public that "something had to be wrong; The Ruler always appeared on live television whenever he returned from abroad" (517). The lack of media appearances even leads to speculations about his death. Nevertheless, those who have been close to him still come into contact with him. Their reactions are telling. Minister Sukiokuu is "taken aback by the new size and shape of the Ruler, [but] he did not show it by look or gesture" (519). Kaniũrũ calls him "the expanded Ruler," and foreign envoys call on him to express their concern about his "health and condition" (656, 581). Tajirika's encounter is the most striking: "Tajirika saw before his very eyes a human monstrosity emerge. Tajirika was about to bolt but . . . recognizing a semblance of the Almighty Ruler in the figure" he reconsidered and "took courage and sat still" (523). To go from being a feared dictator to a human monstrosity in the eyes of one of his political cronies shows the deep humiliation brought on by the Ruler's illness. He becomes a curiosity. His ministers even concoct a last ditch effort to display his ballooning body in an extensively painted room designed to turn him "into a righteous deity looking down from the sky in judgment," but they do this in an attempt to turn "a thing of shame and weakness into one of power and glory" (667). Their attempts to reverse the trajectory of debasement and humiliation started by his illness are unsuccessful, just as all attempts to treat his self-induced expansion have been.

To this scene of a ballooning demi-god in a painted sky Dr. Furyk returns to examine the patient again who, after "suffer[ing] another bout of bodily expansion . . . was now floating in the air" (654). At this point the doctors are the Ruler's "only beacons of hope . . . [to] stop his body from conspiring against him." After a new examination the doctors find "nothing amiss" except that his expansion "had increased tenfold" and a new symptom had appeared, "the lightness of the body" (673). This examination serves as the prelude to the climactic moment of the novel—the public assembly convened to celebrate the Ruler's birthday and the "Day of National Renewal" (677). At this assembly the Wizard of the Crow, before the crowd and the nation, present via television, reveals his role in the rumors of the Ruler's pregnancy that have flourished in his lengthy absence from the public eye. The Ruler and his physicians watch these proceedings in the faux-celestial state house. As the assembly turns from an enactment of sovereign hegemony into a site of public resistance and a call for democracy, the patient begins to experience a distressing new symptom, pain. This new symptom seems to be a direct response to the events at the televised assembly. Dr. Furyk observes that the onset of the pain is sudden and is manifested by "a sharp, anguished cry, his airborne body writhing in pain" (680). The pain is intermittent and interrupts the Ruler's attempts to monitor the proceedings at the assembly or intervene by calling his minister Big Ben Mambo (682). This latest symptom is at once both the most humanizing and the most potent subtraction of the individual. Elaine

Scarry notes that "the success of the physician's work will often depend on the acuity with which he or she can hear the fragmentary language of pain, coax it into clarity, and interpret it," yet many people's experiences lead to the "opposite conclusion, the conclusion that physicians do not trust (hence, hear) the human voice, that they in effect perceive the voice of the patient as an 'unreliable narrator' of bodily events, a voice which must be bypassed as quickly as possible" (6). This opposite pole represents an aspect of the subtraction of the individual that I have previously discussed. This is not, however, simply an effect of the medical gaze and the doctor-patient power relationship. Pain adds a new wrinkle to the Ruler's situation and poses its own challenge to him and his sovereign power. The Ruler's pain both heightens the sense of his weakness and serves as a commentary on the events playing out at the assembly for the whole country to see. Scarry makes three observations about pain that shed light on how the Ruler's pain affects him and the perception of him. First, "[t]he feeling of pain entails the feeling of being acted upon" (16). This first aspect of the body in pain reinforces the passivity of being a patient. Pain's second effect is "that [it] destroys a person's self and world, a destruction experienced spatially as either the contraction of the universe down to the immediate vicinity of the body or as the body swelling to fill the entire universe" (35). The coincidence here of the image of a swelling body is ironic, but of greater significance is the sense of isolation expressed. And third, "[p]ain is a pure physical experience of negation, an immediate sensory rendering of 'against,' of something being against one, and of something one must be against" (52). This final aspect of the experience of intense pain best explains the origins and significance of this latest symptom. The Ruler experiences fits of intense and sudden pain as he watches the public gathering that he planned to re-solidify his power and eliminate his enemies. However, his efforts backfire, and he watches horrified as the Wizard of the Crow and Nyawĩra and the Movement for the Voice of the People take control of the assembly.

In the face of this political catastrophe, the Ruler's body swells to "tak[e] up the whole chamber" (689). Then something unexpected happens: "[T]hunder split the sky... then another crack of thunder, followed by six more, each louder than the previous one" (690). People in the square and people in the state house panic, assuming that a "coup was taking place at the State House... pointing to the sky and saying, It is doomsday." After the seven cracks of thunder, "mushroom clouds" appear near the state house. The next day there is a "vile stench ... from the dark mist of the day before, issuing from the State House[;] ... the whole country seemed enveloped in a sickening pollution" (692). The next several chapters of the novel are devoted to the popular and official explanations for the thunder and pollution. This is the moment in the novel when the Ruler visits Parliament, now healed from his illness, "tall and thin" (695). He gives a speech

Diagnosing Dictatorship

blaming the explosions and deaths on the Movement for the Voice of the People and sets forth his plan for Baby Democracy wherein he "would be the nominal head of all political parties" (699). Only after all this misinformation do we get the real story. In the eighth chapter of Section II of *Book Five: Rebel Daemons*, almost at the very end of the novel, we get the Ruler's account, which will be confirmed later by the official biographer's account. He recalls his symptoms, the ballooning and the pain, and confesses that "he felt as if his being was on the verge of bursting through the orifices of his body. When he later emerged from unconsciousness, he found himself mired in the darkness of his filth, still slowly escaping through the roof, blasted by the force of his corruption" (706). This "day of autoexplosion" is confirmed for him in the account of his official biographer who "faithfully read how blasts of thunder like stealthy missiles had fired from each of his seven orifices and then exploded in turns" (707, 709). The biographer's account, of course, makes him dangerous because it contradicts the official version that has the Ruler battling terrorist bombs, so the Ruler has him and his record eliminated. This final symptom, or perhaps the cure, of autoexplosions from his bodily orifices is the ultimate sign of the sovereign's incontinence and was present even at the beginning of the illness (as reported by the Wizard of the Crow at his first encounter). This grotesque and satirical image of the Ruler, covered in his own filth after blasting thunder from his orifices, recalls Mbembe's chapter "The Aesthetics of Vulgarity" in *On the Postcolony*. Here he draws on the Bakhtinian notion of the grotesque and obscene and C. Toulabor's work to discuss the way people play with images of "orifices, odors, and genital organs" to critique despotic authority (106). In this framework of popular political derision, the "body in question is first a body that eats and drinks, and second a body that is open" (107). These bodily representations of the Ruler are not merely "outbursts of ribaldry and derision" but are "taking the official world seriously, at face value or the value, at least, it gives itself" (Mbembe 107). The depiction of the filth-covered Ruler is certainly a symbolic signification of his corruption, but it also is the magical realistic depiction of a very ill man, reducing him from the quasi-divine status to the absolutely and basely human through its deployment of hyperbolic flatulence and human waste.

This final image of the Ruler's body, before the disappearance of his illness, represents the ultimate blow in eradicating not only his control of the country but also his symbolic embodiment of Aburīria. After all, it is Tajirika, the one who saw the sick Ruler as "a human monstrosity," who arranges to assassinate the Ruler and seize control of the country shortly after the Ruler's apparent return to physical health (523). There was another possible cause for the Ruler's condition, one not discussed at any length here. That possibility lay in the popular rumor, inadvertently started by the Wizard of the Crow, that figured the Ruler's illness as a kind of pregnancy. Because the pregnancy represented a symbolic condition, rather than the "real" condition presented by the Ruler's self-induced expansion, I chose to focus entirely on the Ruler's condition as illness. However, the Ruler's rumored pregnancy is another important challenge to his authority and is made possible because of the Ruler's strange illness. Pheng Cheah, speaking of the novels before *Wizard of the Crow*, notes that "Ngũgĩ's novels evoke the teleological time of the nation's birth and imminent resurrection through recurring images of pregnancy" (365). Much like other instances in Ngũgĩ's work, "the scene of nativity" in *Wizard of the Crow* "is haunted by the shadow of death" (366). That the pregnancy rumor, which is a popular rumor expressing hope for the future, is tied to the Ruler's illness is a fitting embodiment of just what Cheah observes in Ngũgĩ's other fiction. This rumor unsettles the Ruler because it challenges his macho image by figuring him as a woman and potential mother, but it gives hope and promises of the future. Sadly, Tajirika's "new era of imperial democracy" preempts the potential for a popular movement to bring real change to the people of Aburĩria (754). But Tajirika himself suffered an illness in the novel, so perhaps there is some small hope in the frailty of a ruler's human body.

Notes

1. The Ruler's pretensions to embody the nation might also be considered within the lengthy tradition of the organismic metaphor for the political body. In *Spectral Nationality*, Pheng Cheah presents an excellent analysis of this tradition and then turns to postcolonial nations and texts, including a lengthy meditation on Ngũgĩ's work. Although published before *Wizard of the Crow*, Cheah anticipates some of the concerns of Ngũgĩ's most recent novel.
2. Although "biopower" and "biopolitics" are often used interchangeably, I tend to agree with Roberto Esposito about "the lexical bifurcation between the terms, used indifferently sometimes, of 'biopolitics' and 'biopower.' By the first is meant a politics in the name of life and by the second a life subjected to the command of politics" (15).
3. Esposito provides an interesting genealogy of "biopolitics" before and after Foucault. Of particular interest to my work here is Esposito's discussion of Morley Roberts' work in the 1930's on the "connection, not only analogical, but real, between politics and biology, and particularly medicine" (18).

Works Cited

Agamben, Giorgio. *Homo Sacer: Sovereign Power and Bare Life*. Stanford, CA: Stanford UP, 1998. Print.
Borges, Jorge Luis. "On Exactitude in Science." *Collected Fictions*. Trans. Andrew Hurley. New York: Penguin, 1998. Print.
Cheah, Pheng. *Spectral Nationality: Passages of Freedom from Kant to Postcolonial Literatures of Liberation*. New York: Columbia UP, 2003. Print.
Esposito, Roberto. *Bíos: Biopolitics and Philosophy*. Minneapolis: U of Minnesota P, 2008. Print.

Foucault, Michel. *The Birth of the Clinic: An Archaeology of Medical Perception*. New York: Vintage Books, 1994. Print.

———. *Discipline & Punish: The Birth of the Prison*. New York: Vintage Books, 1995. Print.

Foucault, Michel, et al. *Society Must Be Defended: Lectures at the Collège De France, 1975–76*. New York: Picador, 2003. Print.

García, Juan Carlos. *El Dictador en la literatura hispanoamericana*. [*The Dictator in Latin American Literature*]. Santiago: Mosquito Editores, 2000. Print.

Hobbes, Thomas and Ian Shapiro. *Leviathan, Or, the Matter, Forme, & Power of a Common-Wealth Ecclesiasticall and Civill*. New Haven: Yale UP, 2010. Print.

Jackson, Robert H. and Carl G. Rosberg. *Personal Rule in Black Africa: Prince, Autocrat, Prophet, Tyrant*. Berkeley: U of California P, 1982. Print.

Mbembe, Achille. *On the Postcolony*. Berkeley: U of California P, 2001. Print.

Ngũgĩ wa Thiong'o. Wizard of the Crow. Trans. Ngũgĩ wa Thiong'o. New York: Anchor Books, 2006. Print.

Scarry, Elaine. *The Body in Pain: The Making and Unmaking of the World*. New York: Oxford UP, 1985. Print.

Scherman, Jorge. *La parodia del poder: Carpentier y García Márquez: desafiando el mito sobre el dictador latinoamericano*. [*The Parody of Power: Carpentier and García Márquez: Challenging the Myth of the Latin American Dictator*]. Santiago: Editorial Cuarto Propio, 2003. Print.

Performing Resistance in Ngũgĩ's *Wizard of the Crow*

GĨCHINGIRI NDĨGĨRĨGĨ

In an interesting essay titled "Why I Write," Nuruddin Farah says that "Somalia was a badly written play[:] ... Siyad Barre was its author[;] ... he was also the play's main actor, its centre and theme; as an actor-producer, he played all the available roles" (1597). Though written in the 1980s, Farah's description of Barre matches the portrait of the protean fictional dictator in Ngũgĩ wa Thiong'o's *Wizard of the Crow* (2006), who dominates the fictional Aburĩria's stage and is a composite of several postcolonial dictators, including Barre. Elevated to divinity, coterminous with the state/country, its history, and seemingly controlling time and all space in Aburĩria, the Ruler and his henchmen seek the ultimate prize: the construction of a tower high enough that, as the natural occupant of its topmost floors, the Ruler will be right next to God in the skies and can periodically drop in for a morning chat. In any case, with the tower complete, the Ruler would be the first person God saw when He woke up in the morning. All this would be fancy stuff for a clown show, but convinced about the genius of its modern Tower of Babel, the ruling elite attempts to mobilize the citizenry to participate in an elaborate staging of consensus that would help to convince the Global Bank to fund the tower, and thus enable the impoverished country to match its superwonder with the superpowers of the world.

Two of the most climactic events in the novel happen in relation to the planned tower—its unveiling on the Ruler's birthday and his mooning on the day of its dedication— and the two events lead to a growing disaffection with the state's grab at modernity without a corresponding extension of rights to its citizenry. This disaffection achieves its most articulate expression at a climactic ceremony during which the state hopes to receive Nyawĩra, the instigator of otherwise apolitical subjects according to state propaganda. Central to all these events is the element of performance, with the state performing its majesty, its asymmetrical power, in a grand simulacrum that simultaneously constructs the people as citizens participating in a consensus-building process and as spectators with nothing to contribute. The Ruler is center-stage in all this as a transcendental apex below which everybody else prostrates. But the play, like Barre's, is badly written, and its other principal players—such as they are—all appear to be reading from different scripts that ultimately undermine each other. The competition between Machokali and Sikiokuu, the two rival cabinet members, over who is the better sycophant—and therefore qualified to occupy stage center with the Ruler or in his place—gives hints that they are playing from their own scripts. At the end of the novel, the state's invitation to Kamĩtĩ to take center-stage in the nationally televised drama is bound to produce unpredictable results. As a character who has not been a participant in any of the state's rehearsals, his interpretation of his role is clearly at odds with the state's intentions.

The idiom of performance is preponderant throughout *Wizard*. During the first state ceremony to celebrate the Ruler's birthday, Machokali "dramatically" unfolds a huge cloth that has an artist's impression of Heavenscape, the tower that was being planned to immortalize the Ruler (15). He plays up the sense of suspense so well that when Kaniũrũ, the artist who drew the impression, seeks to share in the limelight, he is quickly shoved to the side and the people's attention is "riveted on the bigger drama on the platform" (16). Thinking that he has mesmerized his audience with the grandeur of the project, Machokali then pauses "dramatically to allow for an ovation" that never comes (17). After the Ruler is shamed by the women who scatter plastic snakes halfway through his diatribe, he stages a "performance, carried live on all the airwaves, [that] was visually compelling" (24). When he later rides a donkey to a local church in a parody of Jesus's entry into Jerusalem, we are told that the particular church was chosen because it stood on a hill "and this would make a dramatic scenic background for television pictures" (26). His seemingly impulsive gestures are "choreographed by his image builders. . . . The long camera shots showing the Ruler at the foot of the hill and the church on the hill made him look as if he was leading a pilgrimage to the City of God" (27). Followed by his entourage that "allowed the principal actor a foot or so," we are told that "the performance was almost flawless" (27). On the day of the dedication of the site, the performances are supposed to culminate in "a grand finale with all the singers and dancers

Performing Resistance in Ngũgĩ's *Wizard of the Crow*

joined together." The Ruler is set to "mingle with the dancing women and even attempt a step or two himself" in a show meant to convey the impression that he is "truly a man of the people" (249). The performance does not go flawlessly, and the implications of this failure will be addressed shortly. However, it is noteworthy that the Ruler has nightmares about the mooning by the women, remembering it as "the treacherous drama . . . at Eldares" for days on end (235). In the elaborately scripted ceremony staged towards the end of the novel, the Ruler thinks that he controls the event during which the whereabouts of the subversive heroine, Nyawĩra, were to be revealed. Rendered from the Ruler's character perspective, the references to "dramatization," "performance" (670), "the entire drama," "the entire script, the actors their allotted lines only" (672), and the comparison of the Ruler to "a director helplessly watching his actors straying from the script" (682); his orders to "stop straying from the script" (683); and his futile attempt to take his "teledirecting role back" (689), all point to the Ruler's performance of a role and/or directing a show. The Ruler is upstaged at his own performance and later overthrown and "disappeared" from the national stage.

Given the frequency with which we encounter the idea of performance in the novel—including the idea of identity as performance—the novel therefore invites a reading through a performance lens. This chapter reads the dramaturgy of the state ceremonials in *Wizard* and presents the Ruler as a bungling scriptwriter/actor/director. Since the state deploys ceremonialism as a means of staging its majesty, the analysis pays attention to the people's staging of their resistance by seizing on the inherently dialogic nature of performance. Guided by the understanding in performance studies that an audience is actively involved in the construction of the meaning of a performance, the analysis shows how as co-participants, the people appropriate and deform state ceremonies.

The chapter proceeds in four stages. First, it develops a theoretical framework that connects performance, spectacle, and state ceremonialism with the reproduction of the social hierarchies of the imagined community. Since most of that performance and ceremonialism happens around or in connection with the Ruler, the second section of the chapter pays attention to the Ruler as the apex of precedence and to the bluff that he stages as part of the public transcript. My analysis presents the Ruler as a colonial creation, historicizing colonial and postcolonial despotism. Building off Achille Mbembe's description of the postcolony "as a dramatic stage on which are played out the wider problems of subjection and its corollary, discipline" (102–103), the third section analyzes the Ruler's absence in Book Three for signs of the people's internalization of surveillance and discipline. Particular attention is paid to Kamĩtĩ who, as the dreaded Wizard of the Crow, becomes an alternative center of power in the Aburĩrian popular imagination. This name evokes Kamĩtĩ Prison, the notorious maximum security jail in Kenya, and analysis of this central character presents him as a synecdoche that concretizes the internalization of the imprisoning logic of the state and the recognition that one has to make a political choice. Finally, since the state performs its majesty by masculinizing the public sphere and constraining women and powerless men to the private space, Nyawĩra's re-genderization of "woman" as an actor in the public space concludes the discussion.

PERFORMANCE, SPECTACLE, AND CEREMONIALISM

Reflecting on the focus on performance in current scholarship, Julia Walker observes that privileging the metaphor of performance "with its emphasis upon actors acting upon the world" addresses the problematic role of individual agency and "allows for the possibility of resisting the otherwise deterministic structures of social and political relations" (149). Walker ponders the idea of gender performativity in ways that are appropriate to a reading of the Aburĩrian people's parodic performance of the codes that interpellate them as docile, apolitical, and "women." The focus on gender performativity is also central to Diana Taylor's *Disappearing Acts*, a fascinating study of the role of women in Argentina's crisis years (1970s) that has interesting parallels with the repression of political dissent and women's roles in democratizing the public sphere in Ngũgĩ's *Wizard*. Taylor's informative study foregrounds the constructedness of state spectacles that "function as the locus and mechanism of communal identity, the 'imaginings' that constitute social systems. They reflect and (re)produce the spatial configurations of the imagined community, establish both the parameters and organizational structures" (73). This perspective will be useful in reading the spatial configuration of the state ceremonials that stage the imagined Aburĩrian community in *Wizard*. It will be found that spectacle reinforces domination by simultaneously dramatizing the majesty of elites and the powerlessness of the non-elites. Reading the positioning of bodies in state ceremonials in *Wizard* yields clues about the power relations in the fictional Aburĩrian society. Further, Taylor argues correctly that in making communal imaginings visible, "spectacles are the glue that holds communities together in kinship. . . . The metaphor of the glue underlines the non-organic nature of the scenarios, the "man"-made-ness of the construction. By making obvious that the whole was once otherwise, the constructedness offers the hope that the pieces might one day be imagined otherwise" (76). This chapter ponders how the space of the state's ceremonial performance is subverted by non-state actors who stage their imagined, alternative Aburĩrian society.

In a cogent article entitled "Prestige as the Public Discourse of Domination," James C. Scott observes that in a situation where elites are anxious to dramatize their prestige, some events are planned "essentially as discursive affirmations of a particular pattern of domination" (147). Explaining how hierarchical relations are routinized, Scott states that "[e]lites naturally have the greatest political investment in such affirmations, since each of them signals a pyramid of precedence of which each forms the apex." Noting that elites "would like every performance to follow their scenario and to go off without a hitch," Scott probes the struggles surrounding the performance: "[T]o the degree the performance demonstrates the claim of the dominant, it encourages a certain resistance from those at the bottom whose *inferiority*—whose lack of status—is thereby being reciprocally demonstrated" (148). Scott's benign observation that "[o]ccasionally when they venture on-stage subordinates may spoil, interrupt, or ridicule the performance in an attempt to turn it into a disconfirmation of power relations" (148) is relevant in the analysis of *Wizard*, where the disruption becomes an imperative rather than an "occasional" accident. The despotic ruler in the novel cares little for legitimacy itself, and a lot more for the appearance of legitimacy. He seems to think that he can coerce both prestige and charisma. In his study of Mobutu's Zaire, Schatzberg concludes that that state—like most despotic African states—had not planted deep roots and Mobutu and his clique deployed the metaphor of the nation as family and Mobutu as father "to build on the complex, culturally based moral matrix of legitimate governance," using symbols and images "that help to maintain political quiescence" (141). This model is particularly applicable to the Ruler in *Wizard*. An analysis of the character and his power benefits tremendously from the preceding discussion of spectacle and the state's monologic performance, ceremonialism, and paternal imagery.

RULER'S BADLY WRITTEN SCRIPT/ACTING/DIRECTING

It is important to historicize both the African "Big Man" and the Ruler himself before turning attention fully to the Ruler and his performance of power. In his cogent discussion of the emergence of centralized despotism in postcolonial Africa, Mahmood Mamdani recognizes that the African despot did not spring up fully-grown as a product of a postcolonial African political pathology: there was nothing particularly democratic about colonialism. Mamdani notes that in the acephalous societies, the colonizers imposed chiefs "shorn of the rule-based restraint." He shows that this restraint on precolonial authority "flowed from two separate though related tendencies: one from peers, the other from people." Without these, "the full-blown village-based despot" emerged (43). Further, he says, "[f]rom African tradition, colonial powers salvaged a widespread and time-honored practice, one of a decentralized exercise of power, but freed that power of restraint, of peers or people. Thus they laid the basis for a decentralized despotism" at the local level, serving a centralized and equally despotic state (48). In centralized states the traditional rulers were shunted aside to make way for colonial governors who had enormous powers without corresponding accountability to the governed. The colonial state thus created the foundation for the centralized despotism of the postcolonial era. Mamdani notes that "the hallmark of the modern state was civil law through which it governed citizens in civil society. The justification of power was in the language of rights, for citizen rights guaranteed by civil law were at the same time said to constitute a limit on civil power" (48). In the colonies, the colonized had few civil rights and even less ability to limit colonial power. Whereas Schatzberg shows that the paternalism of the African Big Man was a corruption of traditional African cultural modes, Mamdani posits that even the most liberal and sincerely motivated colonizer "displayed a deep-seated paternalism" in the formulation and implementation of colonial policy (85). As the good boys of the colonial administration, the new African rulers of the 1960s would carry this authoritarian paternalism into the postcolonial phase. Such is the situation in *Wizard*: having inherited authoritarian power from the colonial state, the Ruler resists democratization. Any challenge to his authority is characterized as the reactions of children who need a spanking to get them back in line, or as women straying from their natural "service to power," which, in the patriarchal logic of the state elite, belongs to the male (235).

As a leader, the Ruler is a man of fairly modest abilities. The story of his unremarkable ascent up the ladder in the colonial military is told in some detail early in the novel. Though his "reputation for making minister plot against minister, region against region, and community fight against community was now a matter of legend[,] . . . in his long ascendance to ultimate authority, the Ruler had himself been the nonpareil master of humility and self-abnegation," "a champion of an unquestioning humility before power" (*Wizard* 231). We are told that "[h]e was first widely known during the colonial times for seeming meek and mild-mannered. . . . Whether in school, the government bureaucracy, or the army, his servile bearing facilitated his climb up the ladder of success" (231). Having bowed to others, he cannot understand why others will not bow down to him when his turn in power comes: "[T]he more he humbled himself to his superiors, the more he expected the same from his underlings to assuage a deep-seated self-doubt. This need for assurance often resulted in acts of implacable brutality against the weak" (233). Having ordered the execution of all condemned prisoners awaiting clemency at the time of his ascension to power, he is amazed that his signature on a paper or a word from his mouth "could bring about the immediate cessation of a life." After exercising this power over life and death, "he there and then truly believed in his omnipotence. He was now sovereign" (233). And, thus, his conception of sovereignty is not founded on the individual rights of his people and popular sovereignty. Rather, he is the sovereign that unifies the state, and his powers become absolute. His crowning achievement would reportedly come when he "mowed down a million Aburīrian Communists" at the behest of the West, whose media celebrated him as "AN AFRICAN STATESMAN OF WORLD STATURE" and whose presidents, queens, and kings welcomed him into their countries on his "numerous state visits" (234). Having broken the opposition into fragments and grown "adept at stifling all other nascent opposition through the carrot and the stick" and keeping a pacific military happy with patronage goods, the Ruler would become "our man" to the military leadership, the same honorific with which the former colonizers had fondly referred to him. With time, the disconnect between the Ruler and the ruled would be ironically given voice in his frequent reminders to the nation "that the only votes that mattered were those cast for him by the armed forces" (234) and his other boast that he and the country were one and the same, that his might is the might and light of the nation (25). To him, his sovereignty went hand in hand with the exercise of unquestionable power.

Accepting that maintaining domination will always be problematic and resistance inevitable, James C. Scott finds that "[a] substantial portion of the public transcript of the dominant thus consists in crafting a stage presence that appears masterful and self-confident[:] . . . there is a certain amount of bluff and pretense in almost any display of power" (152) that seeks to naturalize the domination and that hides "whatever might detract from their grandeur and authority" (154–5). In *Wizard*, the desire to conjure up, to coerce prestige—which is supposed to be conferred by others—speaks to a hollowness haunting the ruling elite's claim to actual power and thus the desire to keep hidden any behavior that would threaten the official story. As Scott observes, "Those whose claim to authority is based on the superior performance of a verifiable skill have less reason for elaborate, staged presentations, either of their power or of the reciprocal deference of subordinates" because the difference between "the public and hidden transcripts is not so great nor, for that reason, is its exposure to public view so dangerous" (156–7). The Ruler has no verifiable skill, and thus he needs to craft a public transcript that gives the illusion that he is masterful and self-confident, and that absolute power is his to exercise, particularly over women.

As the least privileged members of the society, the women of Aburīria overcome their marginalization and erasure in society by deconstructing the seemingly "immutable truths" of the paternalistic Big-Man and the euphemisms that are used to mask his setbacks. Likewise, the dominated out-perform/upstage the Big-Man on the political landscape. On the Ruler's birthday, the women subvert the state ceremonialism performatively. Spatially designed as an affirmation of the hierarchies in the society, state guests are positioned on the covered raised platform "relative to the seat of might" (13), depending on their relative seniority or usefulness to the regime or the Ruler. Unlike the public that sits in the hot sun, the dignitaries have shade and cold water (13). The only woman on the covered platform reserved for state guests is Yunice Immaculate Mgenzi, who is "conspicuous by her silence" (*Wizard* 13). Indeed, no woman speaks in the official program. The women who upstage the Ruler on his birthday are forced to sit in the hot sun, reflecting their perceived marginality to the occasion. But they end up making the loudest statement by releasing the snakes that create the pandemonium, thus bringing the celebration to a premature end before the Ruler can impart his paternalistic wisdom to his "beloved children" (21). Even that image of the benevolent father has already been destabilized in the people's minds by the time the event gets underway: most of them came expecting to be given food, which they do not get. In addition, the fantastic idea that the Ruler was going to stage a miracle—like Jesus multiplying the five loaves to feed the multitudes—is called into question. The absence of food or any drink for the public signals the disconnect between the state and the people (12). Though they invert the power between the Ruler and the ruled on this occasion, the women are only toying with the Ruler's power. Having tested its absolute reach, they organize a much more spectacular inversion when they moon the Ruler.

On the day they moon the Ruler, the women move in choreographed but natural rhythm, and their performance incorporates the spectators as participants. Unlike the privileged performance space occupied by the state—the raised, shaded platform—the women's performance space recreates a communal social sphere that is not discontinuous. They bridge the gulf between the stage [state] and the seemingly redundant public that the state assumes to be nothing more than an applause machine. But the women's performance is dialogic: it involves call and response and some elaborate synchrony. Their lines merging with the people, they recreate the imagined community that is the nation, and their refrain is that Marching to Heaven is a pile of shit which is ascribed to the Ruler's anus. In addition, Marching to Heaven is described as a modern ogre with two mouths, and the people analogically become the persecuted wife of the blacksmith who was being exploited by the ogre in the traditional Gĩkũyũ folktale that Nyawĩra tells later. But whereas the wife's comfort in the tale was that the husband would come back, the women and the oppressed become their own liberators.

Predictably, the Ruler cannot understand "what drove the women to do what they had done" (235), a euphemism that masks his mooning by the women from his consciousness. If they had come to him for money, "he would gladly have given them thousands of Burĩs [Aburĩria's virtually useless currency]. If they had come to him to beg for a piece of land, he would have heard [but not acted upon?] their entreaty. If they had ... he would have given them ... but they had asked for no favors. Why then their need to shame the nation?" (235). Couched as favors that are his to give, and not as rights, these requests would only reinforce his dominance. As Scott allows, elites will tolerate two forms of dissent: "those couched in terms which affirm the subordination itself" by affirming loyalty, devotion, and subordination and by recognizing the ruler's prestige. The second form is that couched in subtle, veiled, and muted forms, not direct challenges in public. This "does not constitute a direct challenge to the symbolism of power and, hence, does not require a public refutation or attack" (164). The Ruler has enough sycophants doing the first, but it is illustrative that the Old Man who calls the Ruler everything from "cheap arsehole" to "reckless/directionless child" is not thrown into jail because he appears to have had a bad case of what we can only read as Freudian slips (*Wizard* 18). It is not a direct challenge to the Ruler, but, ultimately, the references to the Ruler's orifices defetishize him and bring him down to the level of the common man. But the direct challenges that the women stage go beyond the realm of regulated dissonance and call into question the majesty and the very masculinity of the Ruler. Both the mooning and the old man's "misuse" of language devalue/detract from the majesty of both the Ruler and his phallocentric regime. They are acts that emasculate the Ruler at the apex of his own performance, reducing him from the omnipotence of his masculinity to a level marked by the orifices associated with lowly bodily functions—the evacuation of wastes, the posterior as opposed to the front/the lead.

The mooning is first reported to us in posterior narration as a traumatic event that has made the Ruler "unsure as to what to do or where or with whom to start the vengeance like that which he had shown Rachael. Unable to act, his torturous thoughts always returned to the treacherous drama at Eldares in which the women shamed the nation before the eyes of foreign dignitaries and, worse still, in front of the Global Bank missionaries" (235). Seeing himself as Lord of all Aburīrian women, the Ruler's inability to channel his vengeance like an Old Testament God is remarkable. But even more remarkable are the euphemisms used to mask the Ruler's mooning. Seen from his perspective, the treacherous women shamed the nation, but we later learn that they shamed his person when the event is presented from Nyawīra's simultaneous perspective. All along, the Ruler has emphasized that he and the country are one and the same. But it is illustrative that this time he refers to the country as nation, an affect-laden term that assumes that sovereignty resides in the people. Even seen from the perspective of the elites, the disconnected sequencing between event and its telling is significant: in a cabinet meeting, Machokali reports that he had already told the Global Bank agents the same thing that the Ruler will later try to say when the event is presented in simultaneous narration, "that what they *saw* was a sacred Aburīrian dance performed only before honored guests" (242). But told from Nyawīra's perspective, the Ruler tried to assure the dignitaries that "what they had seen and heard or thought they had seen and heard was *black humor* from an ancient Aburirīan ritual" (252). In Machokali's version, there is no obfuscation (as in Ruler's) that the audience "thought they had seen": the seeing is actually foregrounded in italics. It is ironic that in the Ruler's scale of values, black humor is apparently a positive thing. Read through Tajirika's logic that "truth is in the eyes of the interpreter" (110), the slips between the two versions are illustrative of the state's attempt to control the construction of meaning and its reception. Euphemism helps to hide the egg on the Ruler's face. For a person who dotes on public adulation, the Ruler secludes himself in State House and then escapes to the US.

Scott delineates the three functions of the public transcript: one to "*magnify* the visible awe, prestige, or terror in which elites are held" (157), while, second, the other side "serves cosmetically to beautify power, to highlight its beneficent side, and to obscure nasty truths"—what Scott, borrowing from Bourdieu's *Outline of a Theory of Practice*, calls "euphemization[,] . . . [the] infallible sign that one has stumbled on a delicate subject" (157). Both state occasions when the Ruler was upstaged were meant to magnify the majesty of the Ruler. Having failed to do that, state propaganda resorts to euphemization. Scott states that the third function of public transcripts "[is] to create the appearance of unanimity among the ruling groups and the appearance of consent among subordinates" (161), but the competition between Machokali and Sikiokuu during the two major state ceremonies signals the absence of consent among the Ruler's subordinates.

The Ruler's visit to the US would help him to kill three birds with one stone. First, it would help him to temporarily escape the feeling of impotence that overwhelms him when the women moon him. As the narrator reports, "[T]he chance to go to New York to be wined and dined while lobbying for support for Marching to Heaven was medicine for the Ruler's wounded soul" (243). In addition, it would hopefully give him an opportunity to address the UN General Assembly and, thus, a global audience on the superwonder. Finally, it would also be an opportunity to demonstrate that he has important friends by hopefully bringing back bagfuls of dollars. The spectacle of a triumphal re-entry is already being planned even before the delegation finds out whether the Global Bank (GB) will fund the tower, with Sikiokuu being ordered to prepare the greatest airport reception ever to receive the Ruler (353). As it happens, he has to be sneaked back into the country (517).

The Ruler's hubristic attempt at performance of power on the world stage is informed by a deep-seated anxiety about his power. Unfortunately, the West calls his bluff by reminding him how insignificant he is on the world stage. The changes in the Ruler's power can be read as a symptom of the radical shift in North/South relations after the end of the Cold War. Where buffers were needed before—hence the usefulness of the Barres, Mobutus, and Mois as bulwarks against "Communist influences in Africa"—these were no longer necessary in the early 1990s. The end of the Cold War was very quickly followed by a new civil rights discourse, in which the same dictators—so-called "friends of the West" in the Cold War—were quickly urged by the West to democratize their own political spaces. When the recalcitrant ones resisted change, Western governments had few qualms sponsoring civil society groups pushing for change. The Ruler could previously count on the support of the West and cannot understand the new global order that requires him to be accountable.

To the question of why the Mobutu state lasted so long, Schatzberg notes that "the political, economic, and military support the regime enjoys from its allies in the West . . . [such as] IMF, World Bank, and other creditors indicates to its population that the regime has friends abroad" (140–41). In similar fashion, the Ruler hopes to add "glamour and dignity to the business" of firming up loans for Marching to Heaven (MtH) from GB by making state visits to England, Germany, France, and Scandinavia, but official invitations to these countries do not materialize. Mistaking the earlier adulation by the West as genuine recognition of his worth in global affairs, and not being a particularly keen student of global politics, the Ruler laments that "earlier state visits, despite the Cold War, had taken no time to arrange—why not now when the war was over?" (255). The choice of the preposition "despite" is telling, an indication that the Ruler never quite realizes that he was merely a bit player in the global drama of the Cold War. The West mesmerized him by staging state receptions for him that were just empty rituals, and the Ruler could not see through them. Now hoping to impress the Global Bank, Machokali tries in vain to arrange a meeting "between the Ruler and the American president to take place before the one with the chiefs of the Global Bank. Even an hour or two with the president of the United States would send a positive message to the bank" (256), and, of course, to his own people. The Ruler instructs Machokali to fit in "as many state visits as you can. I don't want these Global Bank people to think that I am making the trip for the sole purpose of negotiating with them," thus confirming the element of bluff (244). As it happens, Machokali is only able to arrange for the Ruler to attend a face-saving Prayer Breakfast presided over by the US president in which the Ruler does not get any personal audience with the US president (484). In addition, the GB refuses to fund the tower, citing its dubious economic value and the unrest and instability in Aburīria. After GB minions (not the head) deliver the message to the Ruler, he becomes struck by the Self-Induced-Expansion (SIE), and his handlers are forced to cancel any further public events, including the address to the UN (509).

Forced to make a hasty and messy exit from the US, the Ruler's already bad situation is made worse by the discovery of a cryptic note that analogically relates the brewing problems in Aburīria to a pregnancy (510). Since the Ruler holds that he is the country, he therefore takes umbrage at the assumed link between his illness and pregnancy, and thus his feminization. Thinking that he is being called a woman because his power is waning in the West, the Ruler ponders ways of showing "them that I am still the man I was" (518). The performance of power therefore becomes enmeshed with the performance of masculinity with the Ruler conjuring ever-desperate measures that would enable him to look the Global Bank directors in the eye "and tell them to shove it" (549). His hopes for "[a] *national massacre. To be televised. Live*" (579) are complicated by the new push for civil liberties to accompany the free flow of goods and services now being advocated by the West. Ever conscious of the need for a public transcript that reinforces his power, the Ruler thinks of sending his goons to provoke the citizens gathered in a people's assembly in Eldares to march on State House, but he rethinks the idea because the "images would not play well on television screens around the world" (640). Pushed by Western governments and his own people to democratize the political space and step down, the Ruler decides that "enough is enough; he must find a way to remind these Westerners that in Aburīria he was still the man, regardless of the loans for Marching to Heaven, and there was nothing these arrogant bastards could do about his slaughter of his own people" (643). He stages a desperate performance of masculinity, deploying the military to break up the People's Assembly. We are told that "[t]he sight of armored cars on television, their long guns poised to murder, relentlessly moving down the streets of Eldares made him feel manlier. The media swarming around the columns excited him. Let them see blood . . ." (643). Instead of mowing down his people as the Ruler hoped, the army joins the people's revolt in the full glare of television cameras, forcing the Ruler to wonder: "But who choreographed it?" (643). Characteristically, the Ruler thinks in the idiom of performance. It would be useful to read a final scene in which the Ruler's script comes unstuck.

Seeking to have Nyawīra flushed out of her hiding place by the Wizard of the Crow—whose intimate relationship with Nyawīra the Ruler does not know, in spite of the vaunted omnipresence of his surveillance apparatus—the Ruler stages what he hopes will be a dramatization of his control over time and space in the country. Having sent different agents into the People's Assembly, the Ruler tightly controls the "entire drama" from his haven in State House, and he thinks that he alone knows "the entire script, the actors their allotted lines only" (672). But the people rewrite the script in a way that in the end reduces the Ruler to "a director helplessly watching his actors straying from the script" (682). His order to one of his agents to "stop straying from the script" is only partially successful (683). That script features the Ruler as the principal actor or puppeteer who, if he could, would want to play all the available parts in the national spectacle. He is the actor, while the people are supposed to be passive repositories of his paternalistic wisdom. But at the end of the event, the Ruler tries in vain to take his "teledirecting role back" (689). The hermeneutic puzzles posed by this scene merit a closer reading.

Each of the actors to whom the Ruler allots lines reads his individual role differently from the Ruler's intentions. Each of them sees himself as the principal actor riding his role to greater glory with or in spite of the Ruler. Kaniūrū thinks that he has license to "dispatch the sorcerer to hell" (675) because his script is silent on what to do with the Wizard after he has flushed out Nyawīra; but Sikiokuu has specifically been tasked to snatch the Wizard and take him back to State House where the Ruler would be waiting. Kaniūru is motivated by revenge against Kamītī for having attracted the affection of Nyawīra, his former wife (684). Sikiokuu is motivated by the need to execute his task well and thus get back into the good graces of the Ruler, a position he lost when his own aspiration to power was discovered. The Ruler needs the Wizard back in State House so that he can divest him of his occult powers and then dispatch him to his death, leaving the Ruler as sorcerer supreme, as we later learn (707). The Ruler sees his contest with the Wizard as "a battle of wills" that he has to win (705), marking the climax of a dramatic conflict. None of these actors had contemplated the possibility that Kamītī might have his own script or the ability to improvise. He uses the occasion to stage his own resistance by rallying the People's Assembly into answering back to the Ruler as a collective voice.

Writing of Mobutu's Zaire, Schatzberg presents the different organs of the state as a complex entity, "a complicated congeries of only imperfectly controlled organizations and institutions [administrative, coercive, ideological] each motivated by different imperatives" (69). As he argues, the state cannot possibly act monolithically, or even speak with a single voice: "Interstitial crevices exist between the state's various administrative and coercive organs[.] . . . Since these organizationally distinct components of power grow and decline at different rates, and possess differing values and visions of the shape of society and polity . . . [, they are like] . . . a series of imperfectly meshed gears. Conflict and pockets of resistance internal to the state result . . ." (114). Looking at the Ruler's Aburīria, one is persuaded to think of the different actors reading from different scripts as these imperfectly meshed gears. In addition to the instability created by the competing state agents, external pressure from the West does not help the Ruler. He is forced to make some contextual modifications to his performance as a Big-Man. Before Western powers, he displays the self-abnegation that he expects his inferiors to show to him, but the allure of his power motivates his own subordinates to replace him as head of state. To this end, the competitions between Machokali and Sikiokuu on the one hand, and that between Tajirika and Kaniūrū as well as the one between Kaniūrū and Sikiokuu, on the other, only weaken the Ruler before his intended audiences. Scott says of competition among elites:

> If the dominant are at odds with one another in any substantial way, they are, to that degree, weakened, and subordinates may be able to exploit the divisions and renegotiate the terms of subordination. An effective façade of cohesion thus augments the apparent power of elites, thereby presumably affecting the calculations which subordinates might make about the risks of non-compliance or defiance. (162)

The people of Aburīria are able to penetrate the façade of cohesion among the elite and to progressively enlarge their own space of civil liberties. While the Ruler thinks in terms of script, roles, drama, television, and dance, and he sees himself as the principal actor and director who constructs the meaning of the performance, this is called into question consistently throughout the novel. The people become actors in the drama of their lives: they stage a reconfigured imagined nation that is a horizontal comradeship.

If bluff and a crafted stage presence that appears masterful and self-confident defines the public transcript of elites, as Scott indicates (152), the Ruler's bluff is repeatedly called in the novel: by Rachael, by the women, by the Global Bank, by the West, and, ultimately, by all Aburīrians. Despite his love for spectacle, he seems to mismanage the staging of his stage presence at every turn. As was already indicated, Scott observes that elites would prefer that their performances go off without a hitch so as to naturalize the domination and hide "whatever might detract from their grandeur and authority" (154–5). If the public transcript of elites is meant to display its awe and to euphemize power so that people take domination as natural, the Ruler mismanages his script and the public spectacle. Rather than controlling the script as the principal actor in a drama about himself and assigning others to bit roles, it would appear that it is the Ruler who is trapped in reactive roles. The script is anything but masterful and self-confident.

The Ruler seeks to occupy the whole space of power relations in Aburīria, but as the foregoing discussion has shown, the Ruler's omnipresent apparatus of surveillance cannot really secure his repressive power. And one can reach that tentative conclusion from reading the Ruler's badly written script and his own poor execution of his stage presence. The perspective is reinforced by looking briefly at Kamītī and Nyawīra, the other major players in the novel.

HEGEMONY, SURVEILLANCE, AND SUBJECTION

Foucault suggests that once the panoptic modality of power has successfully conditioned the incarcerated to surveil themselves, then the agent monitoring the surveillance apparatus need not be visible (201). In *Wizard*, the idea that the

Performing Resistance in Ngũgĩ's *Wizard of the Crow*

Ruler controls people's actions even in his absence is inculcated into the minds of the people. But soon after the Ruler's departure for the US, Sikiokuu effectively takes over the running of the country. Thinking about Sikiokuu's gestures that usurp some of his powers, Tajirika reflects: "[T]he Waswahili say *paka akienda, panya hutawala* [when the cat leaves, rats will play]. Might he not be devoured by the rat that now ruled in the absence of the cat? But then he quickly dismissed those fears. There was nothing Sikiokuu could do to the chairman of Marching to Heaven, for that would be interfering with a special envoy of the Ruler" (299). It is remarkable that Tajirika thinks of the Ruler's dominance through predatory animal imagery. But contrary to Foucault's analysis, Tajirika specifically thinks of the rat behaving out of character in the absence of the cat. Sikiokuu is daring enough to go against an appointee of the Ruler, and he stages his own performance of power modeled on the Ruler's, complete with a majestic seat and costume (398, 413). And thus, even as he executes the Ruler's wishes, Sikiokuu is advancing his own. Such a scenario is supposed to be inconceivable in Aburĩria because the Ruler is supposed to occupy all the available political space and to be able to control both time and space in the whole country. By the end of the novel, this will be revealed as idle bluff. But it is noteworthy that the Ruler is absent from Aburĩria for the whole of Book Three, or a total of 193 pages. It would seem to follow that everything in the country should either grind to a halt or go strictly according to his wishes even in his absence. While it might be a productive endeavor to analyze the power play pitting Tajirika, Sikiokuu, and Kaniũrũ against each other in the Ruler's absence, they compete as part of the dominant elite seeking to extend their own power. It is therefore much more productive to analyze the character of Kamĩtĩ for indications of the people's subversion of the repressive state apparatus.

Mbembe describes the postcolony "as a dramatic stage on which are played out the wider problems of subjection and its corollary, discipline" (*Postcolony* 102–103). Aburĩria is a fairly dramatic stage, but the Ruler's absence in Book Three reveals that the people have only partly internalized state surveillance. The subjection is called into question through the character of Kamĩtĩ, and the reach of the disciplinary apparatus of state power is increasingly called into question. Mbembe's discussion of the limitations of Gramscian hegemony becomes useful in developing an understanding of the shared authoritarian episteme in Aburĩria. To criticism that his original reading of the postcolony was unnecessarily pessimistic and his controversial assertion that both state and people were involved in processes of mutual zombification, Mbembe poses the question: Why do "dominated and oppressed groups accept not only their position in the social hierarchy, but also an understanding of the world defined by elites as 'common sense'"? (128) As he says, this notion of "hegemony" led Gramsci to conclude that "by accepting the dominant understanding of how the world works, subaltern classes are collaborators in their own oppression" ("Prosaics" 128). But Mbembe flags the deficiency of the Gramscian approach as a possible explanation of the postcolony because there the elites improvise around rules. They "seek to establish the legitimacy of their power and privilege but, at the same time, they can do without legitimacy," and the "coercion and the quest for legitimacy, rather than being opposed, go hand in hand" ("Prosaics" 128). Mbembe posited that "the dominated simultaneously accept and reject their position in the social hierarchy, and also collaborate in their own oppression and also fight against it" ("Prosaics" 128). Kamĩtĩ's characterization helps to test this notion.

Tajirika is temporarily imprisoned by Sikiokuu in Book Three, and he encounters Kamĩtĩ in the same prison. To Tajirika's desire for release from prison, Kamĩtĩ poses the important question: which prison? He posits that there is the prison of the mind and the other of the body (379). Given his investment in the fetishism that surrounds the Ruler, it is illustrative that even before his body was imprisoned, Tajirika's mind had already been imprisoned by the Ruler. On the contrary, Kamĩtĩ's body may be temporarily imprisoned, but he refuses to let the state imprison his mind. An analysis of the process that brings Kamĩtĩ to this moment of recognition would be appropriate.

Kamĩtĩ's name is polysemous. On the one hand, it is a family name that connects him to the *mĩtĩ* clan, which has a heritage of herbalists and fortune tellers (294). But, on the other, as an apolitical citizen at the beginning of the novel, Kamĩtĩ is effectively complicit in his own oppression. That would seem to be the suggestiveness that Ngũgĩ was aiming for by naming the character Kamĩtĩ. The name recalls the maximum-security prison in Kenya where a lot of the freedom fighters in the independence struggle were imprisoned. It is also the prison where Ngũgĩ himself was detained without trial for most of the year 1978, and he writes about how the jail was supposed to break the inmate (*Detained* 100–170). Most of the other political dissidents who became political prisoners between the late 1960s and early 1990s were also locked up here. While Kamĩtĩ naturally takes to herbology, it takes Nyawĩra's conscientization to get him to see that he, like a lot of people in Aburĩria, is living in a mental prison. As a synecdoche of the oppressed country, Kamĩtĩ would therefore be the ideal character to study for signs of the disciplinary machinery of state power and prison as the site of regulation and subjection à la Foucault.

Prodded by Nyawĩra to take a side in the theater of politics—either on the side of those who fight for justice and civil liberties or the side of those who refuse to fight and, therefore, perpetuate oppression by default—Kamĩtĩ at first thinks that society should leave him alone in his idealistic belief in "humanity, divine, indivisible. We all need to look deeply in our hearts and the humanity in us will be revealed in all its glory. Then greed and the drive to humiliate others will come to a halt" (87). Seeing no possible role for him to play in a corrupt society and seeking to remain uncontaminated, Kamĩtĩ temporarily withdraws to live as a hermit in the wilderness outside the city. He even tries to convince Nyawĩra to abandon human community and its problems and join him there. But in showing him how everybody is imbricated in politics, Nyawĩra concretizes her social activism for Kamĩtĩ by comparing Marching to Heaven to the folkloric ogre that snatched food and water from the mouth of the expectant mother whose husband had gone to the smithy (She tells this story earlier to Gachĩgua and Gachirũ) (209). Like the expectant mother, the people can subvert the ogre even as they send for help, or they, like Kamĩtĩ, can resign themselves to their fate. Eventually, Nyawĩra is able to convince Kamĩtĩ to use his God-given powers of divination to heal the wounded souls of the people. Like most things in Aburĩria, his role involves performance, the enactment of a role, and Kamĩtĩ is the first to recognize this (207). But it also involves the play with authority that Mbembe recognized so well: resisting it by seeming to do its dictates.

Kamĩtĩ plays his role as the Wizard of the Crow so well that, with time, his mythologized image supersedes that of the Ruler and he effectively becomes the alternative center of power—though beneficent—in Aburĩria. Since the Ruler cannot countenance an alternative source of power in Aburĩria, he orders the Wizard's arrest with two intentions. If the Wizard is genuine, he is supposed to be as corruptible as everybody else in Aburĩria, and for a price, he can be made to reveal the whereabouts of Nyawĩra, whom the Ruler acknowledges as the greatest threat to his power. Having done that, the Ruler would then divest the Wizard of his occult power so that he can become the supreme sorcerer. In a series of encounters mediated through the idiom of performance, the Wizard outwits the Ruler and his surveillance apparatus.

When he is first arrested under orders by the Ruler, Kamĩtĩ performs a role as a speech-impaired person and only repeats the word "if" (602). His performance signifies on the actual ailment afflicting both Tajirika and the Ruler, whom he had treated for the condition earlier. While those who came to him for a cure for the ailment were blocked by a frustrated wish, Kamĩtĩ's is simply a performance, and Kamĩtĩ is conscious of the performance role he enacts (624).

The Ruler prides himself in his ability to coerce people to do his will. He summons all sorcerers to the state house to cure the Wizard's speech defect, but only the so-called Limping Witch lives up to the challenge. She turns out to be Nyawĩra in disguise. Nyawĩra essentially outperforms the Ruler. Playing her role to the hilt—complete with a convincing limp, a face made up to look repulsive, an eye that oozes, twitching lips, and a walking stick—Nyawĩra improvises around AG's slip that the man was the Wizard. AG reveals this information to the Limping

Witch in a bid to get due credit for discovering the drunken Kamĩtĩ in a bar earlier (628–9). It is a classic example of the conflicts that confront state agents depending on different circumstances. Though seeking to advance the interests of the state in giving the Limping Witch as much information as she might need to heal the Wizard, AG is also being protective of the Wizard, to whose occult powers he thinks he owes his rise in the state apparatus, having been the earliest client of the Wizard. It is also ironic that only AG would know that the Wizard works through both a male and a female persona, though at this point he does not know that he is interacting with the two personas, both of them acting a role.

The Limping Witch's diagnosis is a classic instance of double-talk couched in the mystery of witch talk. In a country in which the Ruler assumes that he controls all meaning and its performance, Kamĩtĩ and Nyawĩra are able to communicate with each other in a code that reveals their true identities to each other but which the security apparatus grouped around them cannot crack. Performance scholars observe that bodies on stage do not have a prediscursive transparency, that they require context for the interpretation of the hermeneutic puzzles they send (Conway 89), and that "[u]nlike verbal signification, vocal signification can create, augment and/or reverse the presumed meaning of words by using pronunciation, tone coloration, and inflectional variation to speak to an emotional as well as conceptual register of 'meaning'" (Walker 160). Kamĩtĩ and Nyawĩra's bodies communicate using multiple codes, but the state assumes that the two bodies will send just one decodable sign. The Limping Witch is able to outwit the state apparatus by showing that she can get Kamĩtĩ to talk. A better scriptwriter who anticipates complications and plans entrances and exits better, Nyawĩra tempts the state by telling its agents that if Kamĩtĩ is to be fully cured, he would have to be delivered to her shrine at the state's leisure (628). Greed motivates the Ruler's orders that he be taken to her shrine immediately. Despite all the care that the police escort takes with the two, an accident conveniently happens, and the two are able to escape.

Having fumbled by allowing Nyawĩra to stage her walk-on performance as the Limping Witch that results in the state's loss of the prized prisoner, the Wizard of the Crow, the state fumbles yet again upon re-capturing the Wizard. The state requires him to reveal Nyawĩra's whereabouts during the massive People's Assembly, which, as we saw earlier, the Ruler thinks that he is tele-directing. But it is revealing that in agreeing to address the assembly, Kamĩtĩ makes the decision that it is better to die in public view than to be "disappeared" like Machokali and others (668). In addition, he seizes his public stage appearance to give voice to the history of anticolonial resistance, the betrayed hopes in the postcolonial order, and the justice of their present struggle (681). In speaking truth to power, Kamĩtĩ knows that he was "almost certainly performing his own death" (687), but he is motivated by his earlier rescue through Nyawĩra's daring performance as the Limping Witch. Surrounded by the might of the state, Kamĩtĩ rallies the people to performatively re-voice themselves as Nyawĩras—the soul of the exploited and oppressed workers and citizens in the country. His performance is a far cry from the indecisive idealist who wanted to be left alone to discover himself in the wilderness earlier in the novel. Despite the pervasiveness of the instruments of surveillance, it would appear that Kamĩtĩ, the character named after the prison that haunted Kenyans principally for the colonial era detentions of the 1950s to the postcolonial ones of the 1960s and 1990s, refuses to let the panoptic modality of power naturalize itself in his own mind and in the minds of the average Aburĩrians that he motivates to rebellion. The postcolony may be a dramatic stage, and it may be filled with the disciplinary apparatus of state power as Mbembe says, but through Kamĩtĩ and Nyawĩra, *Wizard* challenges Mbembe's assertion that subjection is the natural corollary of discipline. Nyawĩra now merits some individual attention.

STAGING THE RE-GENDERED NATION

Asked to give his first report on the Movement for the Voice of the People, the movement Nyawĩra heads, Sikiokuu tells the Ruler, "These renegades are cowards meeting under the cover of darkness. They dare not come into the light because they are not men at all. They are women, cowards" (238). And thus, the dissent over governance, rights, and state vs. popular sovereignty is reduced to a conflict that is only conceivable between men. The structural equivalence syntactically established between women and cowards points to the patriarchal cast of the state elites' mindset. Towards the end of the novel, having been mistakenly informed that Nyawĩra is dead, the Ruler hopes to "trumpet her fate as an example to presumptuous women who dare assume male prerogatives" (705). But, ironically, the Ruler soon falls into a depression because he has no more worthy adversaries (707), a tacit admission that Nyawĩra was a worthy one. Even more tellingly, having put Rachael effectively in a prison to signify his might as Ruler and as a man, his visit to her prison ends with the Ruler's running from a mysterious ball of fire that puts paid to his dream of stamping his authority on the body of Rachael (708). Because the state delegitimizes opposition by women by deploying paternal imagery that constructs the political space of the nation as masculine, a study of Nyawĩra's re-gendering of the nation is therefore appropriate. Central to this analysis is Nyawĩra's transformation of the passive viewer role apportioned by the state into that of the spect-actor, and her mobilization of the people to do the same: to become spectators who act on their reality.

In her fascinating study of the role of women in Argentina's crisis years, Diana Taylor pinpoints the re-gendering of the population by the state, "a reorganization of the social and political 'body' into active (male) and passive (feminine/effeminate) positions that had more to do with the us/them divide than with biological sex differences." As she shows, "[t]his recasting dramatically expanded the numbers of people who now fell into the feminine category: female-sexed members of the population, regardless of their active or passive roles, were biologically female; male-sexed individuals who had been rendered passive either directly by torture or indirectly by the culture of fear were also part of the effeminate mass..." (156). Taylor's finding that "the self-referentiality of the monologic gender system in which the defining subject is male and the 'female' is merely the projection of the male fear or desire" (156) is helpful in reading the character of Nyawīra in *Wizard*.

Like the Madres in Taylor's study, the women of Aburīria "rearticulate and position the 'feminine' in a masculinist structure and language predicated on its erasure" (208). The country is equated to a family, and the father's authority is presented as unquestionable. As a sign that power is superstructural—that is, existing on the basis of other power relations, kinship, family, sex, gender, etc.—the state has recourse to the father image to contain Nyawīra, casting her as an errant child who needs to come home, or else she would be disowned by her biological father (291). In the paternalistic logic of the state, ideological opposition to the despotic state's excesses is a result of parental failure to inculcate respect for authority, thus the call to the father (Wangahū) to assert greater paternal authority. *Wizard* shows that the same paternal metaphors can be destabilized in ways that empower the people.

The "parenting" performed by the state is supported by other logics based on patriarchy. In his first appeal to Nyawīra's father to summon his daughter back home and thus arrest her anti-government activities, Kaniūrū appeals both to the father and the man in him simultaneously. Assuming that Wangahū would have control over his daughter as a father, he casts Nyawīra's mother's opposition to the public appeal for her return as an example of female irrationality (291). The family is used to repress the individual with the state targeting familial bonds to break down the opposition. In the same way that Kaniūrū appeals to Wangahu's parental responsibility, Tajirika will be persuaded by Sikiokuu to see his wife as an evil pretender who ruins his relationship with the Ruler.

Given the patriarchal cast of the ruling elite, Nyawīra is therefore refreshing in her defiant self-representation. A trained performance artist, Nyawīra masquerades as male as situations demand, and she deprivileges marriage and childbearing. She recognizes gender as performative, depending on the repetition of socially sanctioned codes that produce the bodies interpellated as docile, daughterly, apolitical, and maternal. She refuses to reproduce herself according to the socially sanctioned codes that would disempower her. Seeing gender, like identity, as a performance, she changes the codes of that performance by adapting to male and female roles situationally. In a society where social activism is constructed as male, she performs as both male and female and fudges the essential differences between the two. Nyawīra inverts the paternalism (and sexism) the Ruler exerts on the postcolonial state by moving beyond familial/kinship structures of Big-Man/Small-Man/woman based on reciprocal gifts that re-energize the paternal hold to the language of rights to citizenship, free expression, and free choice unfettered by patriarchal discourse.

The women's inversion of the power relations in the novel and their departure from the state's scripted performances merit further analysis. Physically upstaging the Big-Man is agentive, but it is equally important to reflect on the way the people upstage the image of the Big-Man in their minds, for in so doing, they are able to destabilize the master codes subjecting them. The women are responsible for subversively re-organizing three state events that end up upstaging the Ruler. In addition, Tajirika—who is taken into the Ruler's confidence specifically because the latter thinks that Tajirika is effeminate—overthrows the Ruler in the end. And thus, women and supposedly emasculated men—Kamītī included—overthrow a masculinist state elite.

Scott notes that "[f]orms of domination that rely on elaborate codes of public ceremony do generally prevent surprises in the short run by monopolizing public discourse. They are, however, like radios that can send signals but cannot receive them. As a result, if they are surprised, the surprise is likely to be a large one" (152). Such is the Ruler's surprise, then, first when women—of all people—disrupt his birthday celebrations; then moon him on the day of dedication for the site where the tower immortalizing him is to be built; and mobilize men to adopt Nyawīra's name on the occasion of her public "outing"; and, finally, when he is overthrown by Tajirika. A major feature of the patriarchal logic in *Wizard* is connected with the notion of hypermasculinity that the Ruler, Tajirika, and Sikiokuu all enact and the feminization of the population. Insulated in his simulacral world, the Ruler cannot reconcile himself to the idea that women (in "masculine" military formations, no less) are able to achieve agency by disrupting the socially sanctioned codes, refusing to reproduce themselves as the interpellated docile, apolitical, dutiful, maternal, irrational, and house-bound objects of his paternalistic and sexist generosity.

Led by Nyawīra, the women disrupt the Ruler's birthday; they toy with his power during the dedication of the site for Marching to Heaven; and then they moon the Ruler. After the mooning, the women become as adept as the state in staging their spectacles, which culminate in the final staging of the nation during which everybody answers to Nyawīra's name. Like the Madres in Taylor's *Disappearing Acts*, the women move "the site of their enactment from the private sphere ... to the public" square where they take stage center (194). Thinking that he controls the final event, the Ruler requires that Nyawīra should give up in public watched by the entire territorial audience on TV and apologize for leading astray people who otherwise adore the Ruler. Like the monarch in Foucault's *Discipline and Punish*, the Ruler seeks to overmaster the body of the criminal and thus reactivate his power. This "discursive affirmation from below," to contextualize Scott to *Wizard*, would be "all the more valuable since it contributes to the impression that the prestige of the symbolic order is willingly accepted by its least advantaged members" (166). As Scott illustrates, "[T]he flow of symbolic taxes [is] vital to the moral economy of domination. To be sure, dominant elites would prefer a willing affirmation of their norms, but if this is not available they will extract, whenever they can, at least the simulacrum of a sincere obedience" (166). It is this simulacrum that the people of Aburīria reject in the end. Given center-stage to affirm "the moral economy of domination," Nyawīra and Kamītī upstage the script-reading Ruler in their own unscripted, spontaneous spectacle that flows from the people and involves them in seizing back the public sphere. By all—including the men—answering to Nyawīra's name, they act out the difference between Nyawīra as an individual, female identity and the collective. It becomes a political identity. Problematically, but due to the value system operative in Aburīria, the efficacy lies in the fact that multitudes adopt a woman's name as a subversive act of collective political performance. They re-gender the feminine as the identity of the imagined nation as the previously hypermasculine Ruler is himself feminized.

In the end, the women defetishize the divinities in the political space and refocus the people's efforts into a search for the inner divinity within them. They also dethrone maestro performers reading from bad scripts. Because the Ruler and his henchmen seek to occupy all the available political space in Aburīria, upstaging them starts out as a rehearsal of the imagined community. Since state power is disseminated through the medium of performance, the people seize the performance space and stage their own imagined nation. At first their performance parodies the social codes that disempower them. In the end, the people move from mere acting of a role to being free subjects unfettered by gender codes.

Works Cited

Conway, Brian and Lyn Spillman. "Texts, Bodies, and the Memory of Bloody Sunday." *Symbolic Interaction* 30.1 (2007): 79–103. Print.
Farah, Nuruddin. "Why I Write." *Third World Quarterly* 10.4 (1988): 1591-1599. Print.
Foucault, Michel. *Discipline and Punish*. Trans. Alan Sheridan. New York: Vintage, 1979. Print.
Mamdani, Mahmood. *Citizen and Subject: Contemporary Africa and the Legacy of Late Colonialism*. Princeton, N.J.: Princeton UP, 1996. Print.

Mbembe, Achille. *On the Postcolony*. Berkeley: U of California P, 2001. Print.

———. "Prosaics of Servitude and Authoritarian Civilities." *Public Culture* 5.1 (1992): 123–145. Print.

Ngũgĩ wa Thiong'o. *Detained: A Writer's Prison Diary*. Nairobi: Heinemann, 1981. Print.

———. *Wizard of the Crow*. New York: Pantheon, 2006. Print.

Schatzberg, Michael G. *The Dialectics of Oppression in Zaire*. Bloomington: Indiana UP, 1988. Print.

Scott, James C. "Prestige as the Public Discourse of Domination." *Cultural Critique* 12 (1989): 145–166. Print.

Taylor, Diana. *Disappearing Acts: Spectacles of Gender and Nationalism in Argentina's "Dirty War."* Durham: Duke UP, 1997. Print.

Walker, Julia. "Why Performance? Why Now? Textuality and the Rearticulation of Human Presence." *Yale Journal of Criticism* 16.1 (2003): 149–175. Print.

Fraternal Oppression and the "Aesthetics of Vulgarity" in Alain Mabanckou's *Broken Glass*

AWA SARR

Despotism was at the heart of colonization. Imbued with their superiority complex, their advanced technology and their dreams of empires, Europeans conquered and subdued different regions of the world, including Africa, whose writers used literature to denounce the exploitation of the continent. Almost always anticolonial, the literature produced in francophone Africa during the colonial period castigated colonialism and called for the liberation of the continent. The works of Mongo Béti (*Ville cruelle/Cruel City, Le Pauvre Christ de Bomba/The Poor Christ of Bomba*) and Ousmane Sembène (*Les Bouts de bois de Dieu/God's Bits of Wood, Oh pays mon beau people!/Oh Country, My Beautiful People!*) are good examples of the literature of the time. Fifty years after many African countries gained their independence, however, we have to agree with Albert Memmi that "if decolonization was a triple hope: economic, political, and cultural," Africans have not been successful in any of them (86). Indeed, decolonization has turned out to be a big disillusionment; the change hoped for did not happen. African leaders, often in collusion with the former colonial powers, ruthlessly and shamelessly subjugate their countrymen in the same way the Europeans did. In other words, in postcolonial Africa, an indigenous minority exploits an indigenous majority.

It is therefore not surprising that while the first generation of writers favored realism often associated with nationalism to denounce colonial occupation, the new generation is opting for surreal and burlesque modes of representation to portray postcolonial Africa stifled by its own people.[1] Indeed, as authors born after the colonial period, the new generation of African writers did not experience the "colonial night," and, as a result, they blame the failures of the continent on Africans more than anybody else. Alain Mabanckou is one of the most prolific writers of the new generation of Francophone writers. Born in 1966 in Congo-Brazaville, he won the Renaudot prize in 2006[2] for his novel *Mémoirs de porc épic*. In this contribution, I will analyze how he mixes the grotesque, satire, and scatological writing in *Broken Glass* to represent the postcolonial African state in its most repulsive aspects—despotism and cynicism—and how he characterizes the disintegration of individuals that results from such maladministration. I will also analyze how the mixing of the genres itself reflects the disorder being described as well as it expresses the writer's freedom.

I borrow the expression "aesthetic of vulgarity" in the title of this discussion from Achille Mbembe who reexamines the concept of carnival from Bakhtin by applying it to the ways some African states are run in the postcolonial era. Mbembe argues in *On the Postcolony* that the lower classes are not the only practitioners of the carnivalesque. Vulgarity is the very principle by which the all-powerful postcolonial state machinery functions. As will be apparent, *Broken Glass* offers a literary translation of Mbembe's theory.

THE GROTESQUENESS OF THE DOMINANTS

Broken Glass is the narrative of the eponymous character of the novel. He is charged by the owner of Credit Gone West, Stubborn Snail, to tell its story. The novel opens with these lines:

> [L]et's say the boss of the bar Credit Gone West gave me this notebook to fill, he's convinced that I—Broken Glass—can turn out a book [. . .] when he gave me this notebook he said from the start it was only for him, no one else would read it, and when I asked why he was so set on this notebook, he said he didn't want Credit Gone West just to vanish one day, and added that people in this country have no sense of the importance of memory. (1)

Memory undoubtedly occupies a privileged place in the novel; the obvious and abundant intertextual references inside the text sufficiently demonstrate this. Pierre-Yves Gallard writes:

> [B]efore designating the name of the eponymous character of Manbanckou's novel, Broken Glass is the title of a song by Lutumba Simaro, a Congolese poet and singer [. . .]. The book that Broken Glass writes is therefore immediately in a filial relationship with previous texts and if it is the memory of Credit Gone West Customers'

lived experiences, it is also the memory of books read, films seen and songs heard by the author and his characters.³

However, what is remembered can at first appear trivial and disconcerting, mainly when one considers the importance given to the particular and allegedly only appropriate way memory is supposed to be seriously kept. Indeed, Stubborn Snail adheres to the idea of the primacy of the written word over the spoken word. Broken Glass writes: "The boss of Credit Gone West doesn't like ready-made phrases like '*in Africa, when an old person dies, a library burns,*' every time he hears that worn-out cliché he gets mad, he'll say '*depends which old person, don't talk crap, I only trust what's written down*' (1).

The opening of the bar was from the beginning an ordeal. The "church people," "the Week-end-and-Bank-Holiday-Cuckolds," "the guardians of traditional moral values," among others, opposed Stubborn Snail's project. In fact, the various groups abhorring the idea of having a bar in their neighborhood and their different arguments are listed in the first pages of the novel. These arguments overlap with each other, forming a mass of exaggerated and ridiculous complaints. Given that opening a bar is, *a priori*, a very ordinary and simple procedure, the magnitude of this particular list is likely to amuse many readers. This trivial matter will, however, become a national issue known as the "Credit Gone West Affair" that is discussed in cabinet meetings, until the day the minister for agriculture, commerce, and small and large businesses, Albert Zou Loukia, decides to solve the problem once and for all by addressing the whole country. The speech the minister delivered to this end is henceforth regarded "as one of the finest political speeches ever made," mainly because he repeated several times the phrase "I accuse": "I accuse, I wish to distance myself from our current moribund social climate, I refuse to condone this witch hunt by my presence in the government [. . .] I accuse the cowardly and retrograde machinations [. . .] I accuse the uncivil nature of these barbarous acts [. . .] I accuse the indecency and insubordination which have become common currency in this country" (6), and so on. The reader is thus introduced to ridicule at the very beginning of the novel. It is obvious that the controversy around the "Credit Gone West Affair" is a caricature of the "Dreyfus Affair," and the juxtaposition of the two affairs enhances the grotesqueness of the "Credit Gone West Affair." If the minister's speech, which is cynicism in the rough, is also one of the finest speeches of all time, one can imagine the scandal of the other speeches that history has not retained. Furthermore, the minister's very long title reminds us of the very common overlapping of functions in many African governments. It could also be that Mabanckou is highlighting the unlikely associations governments engage in. One wonders whether it is appropriate to gather agriculture, commerce, and small and large businesses in one ministry. The comedy continues when the president, Adrien Lokouta Eleki Mingi, becomes jealous of his minister's pet phrase and orders his staff to find him one "that would be remembered by posterity" as Zou Loukia's "I accuse" (8). After endless ruminations and sleepless nights, the president's cabinet will find the competitive slogan. The following Sunday precisely at lunch time, the president appears on national television to present his finding. As prelude he will condemn Europeans who still exercise their domination over African countries, attack those he refers to as "the lackeys of imperialism and colonization," congratulate Stubborn Snail for his admirable initiative, and, finally, "arms stretched wide as though clasping a sequoia," he unleashes his sentence: "I have understood you" (16). Henceforth, the phrase is as famous as the minister's. For a joke, Broken Glass explains, "we common folk often say that 'the minister accuses; the president understands'" (16). This story is representative of the high level of buffoonery and cynicism that some African leaders can reach. They reduce the art of governing to the art of finding a magical slogan. If we refer to Mbembe's analysis in *On the Postcolony*, the exaggeration that Mabanckou uses to make his characters fabulous is the same technique that real governments in Africa turn to in order to invent fables they think will keep them in power. The *work* of power (le travail du pouvoir), he explains,

> also involves a process of "enchantment" to produce "fables." But there can be no "fable" without its own particular array of clichés and verbal conventions notable for their extravagance and self-regard, intended to dress silliness in the mantle of nobility and majesty. In short, there is no "fable" in the post-colony without the apparatus to captivate the mind's eye (l'imaginaire) with a Gulliverian vision of the *commandement's* deeds, in which the tiny becomes huge and the familiar strange, accompanied by the emptiness of gestures; here, excess and distortion are the style. (117)

The gesticulation, the defamiliarization process, and the silliness Mbembe talks about are all present in Adrien Lokouta's slogan-delivery performance. Besides, Mbembe writes that "the erection of the ordinary into an event" is politics in Africa (*De la postcolonie* 166). This particular politics frames the first part of *Broken Glass*. Indeed, after the fabulous performances of the minister and the president, Mabanckou serves the reader another grotesque spectacle: a piss competition. Such a contest is most futile and gross, and he devotes nearly ten pages to its description. However, the status of the contestants gives this episode its whole political meaning.

The competition is between Casimir and Robinette. Like Broken Glass, "the queen of piss" is a veteran of Credit Gone West but even more fond of the bottle than Broken Glass:

Fraternal Oppression and the "Aesthetics of Vulgarity" in *Broken Glass*

> Robinette drinks and drinks, and never gets drunk, and when she drinks like that she goes to piss behind the bar instead of in the bathroom like everyone else, and when she pisses behind the bar she can urinate nonstop for ten minutes, it just flows and flows as though someone had turned on a public fountain, and it's not a trick, it's incredible, but true, men have even tried to compete with her at endurance pissing, but have been forced to say farewell to arms, defeated, crushed, wiped out, mocked, rolled in the dust, in cornstarch. (56–57)

Casimir is a dandy who has never been in the bar before. Robinette challenges him, and he demands to sleep with her if he wins. At the beginning of the competition, we learn that Robinette is well-endowed whereas Casmir has an "indivisible element" (61) at the sight of which the regulars of the bar burst out laughing, convinced in advance that Robinette will win. However, the newcomer will prove to be the most talented and enduring. Five minutes into the contest, Broken Glass writes:

> the flow of his urine increased several notches, and we all stretched our eyes and stared, because the braggart was now pissing with much more conviction, and we could see that his original indivisible element was twice, three times its original size, and we rubbed our eyes in disbelief, as his pouches swelled up and hung there now like two old gourds filled to the brim with palm wine, and there was jubilation in his pissing. (63)

For a moment, Robinette was the star of the show; then Casimir "turned a decisive corner, a miracle deserving of papal beatification," as Broken Glass reports:

> we all dashed over to get a closer look, you should never miss a miracle [. . .] so we all went hurtling over to Casimir High-Life to get a look at his historic miracle, we were all knocked aside, something unbelievable was happening right before our eyes, you had to be there to believe it, we saw how Casimir High-Life had sketched in the dust with his urine a perfect outline of the map of France, his unremarkable output was now falling in the very heart of the city of Paris. (64)

Dazzled by the "miracle," the audience nicknames the magician Casimir the Geographer. Exhilarated, Casimir promises to exhaust Robinette in bed, and they "applauded more and more as he added the various regions of France to his map" (64). A witness overwhelmed by Casimir's talent wonders about the "thing" on the side: "'that's Corsica, idiot,' replied the artist, without interrupting his flow, and [they] all gave a round of applause for Corsica, and for some the word Corsica was a new discovery, and people started mumbling, and arguing" (64). The show ends when Robinette surrenders and the winner claims his prize. In a theatrical way, then, Casimir dazzled and entertained his audience. Instead of being a random moment of grotesqueness in the novel, the piss competition is as politically charged as the "Credit Gone West Affair" which directly evokes the buffoonery of power in Africa. The same way Adrien Lokouta Eleki Mingi is a caricature of an African president (the length of the name, though shorter, reminds us of Mobutu Sese Seko Nkuku Ngbendu wa Za Banga), Casimir can be read as representing a certain African ruling class. He is described as a charming person dressed "like a man of substance, in his black jacket, white shirt, red tie, and polished shoes" (58). His straightened hair "fastened behind at the neck [...] in a country where frizzy hair is the greatest of curses [. . . and] brought him just a little bit closer to the white man" (58). This description (relaxed hair, black jacket, white shirt, white man) undeniably evokes Frantz Fanon's *Black Skin, White Masks* and makes Casimir the embodiment of alienation. In addition, his alien status in the Credit Gone West, his arrogance towards the regulars of the bar presented in terms of class difference ("what did he take us for, beggars, bumpkins, in short, a band of workers of the world who wouldn't unite" [58]), his name which denotes royalty and thus power, his claim of living "the high life," and his demand to sleep with Robinette, all these suggest we read Casimir as a representative of the ruling class. As Mbembe wrote, in colonial times *Commandement* "was simultaneously a tone, an accoutrement, and an attitude. Power was reduced to the right to demand, to force, to ban, to compel, to authorize, to punish, to reward, to be obeyed—in short, to enjoin and to direct" (32). This is also true for the postcolonial era. We have a long list of post-independence African dictators, and Casimir behaves exactly like a monarch who has the right to punish his challenger and appropriate her body.

During the competition, we also witness the bewilderment of common people by the representative of power. Small at first, and described as an "insignificant object," Casimir's "feeble little member" (61) will take on extraordinary dimensions. As Mbembe convincingly demonstrates in his book, the art of turning tiny things exceptionally huge or non-events into events is politics in many African states. In addition, Casimir's drawing of France with his urine and his pissing right in the heart of Paris—or, in the witnesses' terms, his miracle—is but another fable among the many vulgar fables leaders like president Adrien Lokouta Eleki Mingi spend their time creating to entertain and divert people's attention from real problems. Mbembe writes:

> [T]he production of vulgarity [...] needs to be understood as a deliberately cynical operation. It is political in the sense intended by S. Wilentz when he argues that every polity is governed by "master fictions" little by little accepted into the domain of the indisputable. The postcolonial polity can only produce "fables" and stupefy its "subjects," bringing on delirium when the discourse of power penetrates its targets and drives them into the realms of fantasy and hallucination. (118)

Fraternal Oppression and the "Aesthetics of Vulgarity" in *Broken Glass*

Held in contempt at first, Casimir will earn the admiration of all after his spectacular win over Robinette. If for Bakhtin the dominated use the obscene to undermine official power, in the African postcolony, the state and its representatives use it as a way to exercise or cling to power. Effective because it is a distraction, it easily turns the dominated into accomplices in their own subjugation. Indeed, when state vulgarity dazzles and drives common people "in the realms of fantasy and hallucination" (Mbembe 118), it also hinders or tames revolt. That is why contrary to Bakhtin, Achille Mbembe sees nothing in the performance of vulgarity in the postcolonial era that can be equated with resistance. He writes, "[A]t any given moment in the postcolonial historical trajectory, the authoritarian mode can no longer be interpreted strictly in terms of surveillance, or the politics of coercion. The practices of ordinary citizens cannot always be read in terms of 'opposition to the state,' 'deconstructing power,' and 'disengagement'" (128). He instead speaks of a certain "conviviality" between the state and ordinary people that impedes resistance. However, by using the slogans of the president and the minister as jokes, it is obvious in *Broken Glass* that the public sees through the game of their rulers and makes fun of them. It is consciously, and not accidentally as Mbembe argues, that the popular laughter clashes with the vision of the state and the world that the dominants seek to impose. Nevertheless, the effectiveness of this form of resistance seems to be very limited. Even when they are cognizant of their leaders' game, the dominated appear resigned and fatalistic in Mabanckou's novel.

EXCESSES OF POWER AND THE DISINTEGRATION OF THE PEOPLE

After the story of the "Credit Gone West Affair," *Broken Glass* narrates the life story of the Pampers guy. One day, this bar patron returns from one of his excursions among prostitutes and finds the lock of his house changed. He calls the police, but soon his wife is accusing him of pedophilia against his own daughter. Shocked, the policemen and women handcuff him, take him to a police station, and then straight to Makala, "the place all the criminals in [. . .] town dreaded" (32). After a sojourn of two and a half years at Makala and being subjected daily to the torture of "the middle way" (33), sodomy, the Pampers guy confides his desolation to Broken Glass, "they destroyed me, I can show you my backside, you could make a fist and put it up me, no problem, that's the truth, I never even got a trial, in this shit-hole of a country" (34). When the man gets up to leave, Broken Glass has this comment: "[T]hen I got a close-up of his backside, bulging with four layers of Pampers, a damp backside, buzzing with flies, and he saw fit to tell me 'don't worry about the flies, it's always like that, Broken Glass, flies are my best buddies these days, I don't even bother brushing, they always find me again, wherever I go, I get the feeling it's always the same flies following me'" (34). Even if the accusation of pedophilia was true, the man was entitled to a fair trial. However, as soon as he is accused, the policemen and women start to bully him physically and verbally before expressly announcing he would not benefit from a trial: "I didn't deserve the honor of a legal trial, besides which they're a complicated business" (32). Obviously, the police were being dramatic, overzealous, and out of control. Justice is not or should not be about honor; similarly, a trial need not be complicated. The police's behavior therefore exhibits the excesses of power also evident in Mouyaké's story. Mouyake is a charlatan who swindles his customers. Caught, he is lucky to get a trial. However, he will try to defraud the judge, claiming he has mystical power to enlighten him and make his convictions impeccable. This audacity enrages the judge, who decides to ignore the jury and directly sentence him: "I'll deal with it personally, because I am the Law" (78–79). Here also power is presented as excessive and burlesque. So, through these examples, a window on the excesses undermining many African countries is offered. A consequence of such a lack of control is destruction, symbolized in the novel by the overflow of liquids: beer, piss, shit associated with the country[4] and which drips from the behind of the Pampers guy. The latter has not only lost the control of his body at Makala but also the control of his destiny. He is powerless before the flies that stigmatize him as social waste, and he must beg for food to survive. Described at the beginning of the story as "a man," Broken Glass refers to him towards the end as a "wreck with a leaking butt" (80). The liquefaction process he went through is a metonymy of the liquefaction of the country under the wrath of tyrannical leaders. Broken Glass predicts that the Pampers guy will one day "flip the lid" and kill someone: "I don't know how anyone can kill, he says, life is essential, that's what my mother always told me, and even if she's dead now, I'll always stick to that rule of the thumb" (34), a pronouncement full of tragic irony since Broken Glass's mother drowned in a river and he will end his life by diving in the same waters.

Broken Glass wants the reader to know why he has fallen "so low without a parachute" (99). At sixty-four, he considers himself a "fossil" of Credit Gone West. His wife thinks he started drinking after the death of his mother, which he denies. On the contrary, he contends he stopped drinking during the mourning period out of respect for his mother. He took the "full swing," as he puts it, the day he was fired as a teacher. Alcoholism is, however, the official rationale of his dismissal. But again, Broken Glass refutes the argument; alcoholism was not the reason but, rather, the "pretext" for his firing (124). He was a good teacher but a bit non-conformist: he called his country "still by the name that was hers at the time of royalty" (143), which won him sanctions, but, he insists, "[T]his country's shit, we inherited these borders when the whites carved up their colonial cake in Berlin, so this country doesn't even exist, it's just a reserve where the cattle die of famine" (113). After losing his job, Broken Glass takes up residence in Credit Gone West and lets his life crumble, his wife eventually leaving him. Alone and disillusioned, he thinks about putting an end to his life. A testimony to his mental state is the day he relieves himself underneath a tree in broad daylight. A young resident asks him to pick up his excrement, to which he replies, "There is nothing sickening about picking up your own shit, it's other people's shit that's revolting," (86) so he plunges his hands in the pile, causing the young man to vomit in disgust.

As with the Pampers guy, Mabanckou uses excrement to represent the disintegration of individuals. The association of feces, a symbol of the abject, with some of his characters suggests that they have undergone a transformation in the heart of which is the tyranny of the arbitrary. Degeneracy cannot indeed be greater for a father than being forced to wear diapers at all times like an infant. Similarly, it is only in a deregulated world that a sixty-four-year-old man is admonished by a youngster, particular in Africa wherein the elderly are regarded as the incarnation of wisdom. Thus, characters such as Broken Glass and the Pampers guy reflect the disorder of a society wherein power is always cynically exercised in excess. Trapped between the anarchy and the tyranny of such a system, the weak, lacking the tenacity of a Stubborn Snail, break up or liquefy without any hope of rehabilitation. Broken Glass once discussed the importance of plural nouns with a student: "[L]ife is a banal business of singulars and plurals, locked in daily combat, loving, hating, condemned to live together" (114). In this ongoing struggle between the singular and the plural, his name evokes the crack and tear of the defeated. If the name of Stubborn Snail reflects the persistence of the character, Broken Glass's indicates fragility. When his family took him to consult the charlatan that was supposed to cure his alcoholism, he rebelled in vain. Exasperated he asked, "[W]ho ever heard of mending a Broken Glass" (105)? He only hopes to recover his sanity when he joins his mother in the afterlife:

> [I]n a short time I will at last be alone, face to face with my mother, in less than two hours now, and we we'll talk for a long while, and on the stroke of midnight I will plunge into the depths of these narrow waters, I'll just need to get past the bridge, then I'll be off on my adventures, I'll be happy, because I'll be reunited with my mother, and the next day, there will be no Broken Glass at Credit Gone West, and for the first time, a broken glass will have been repaired by the good God. (163)

While waiting to join his mother, Broken Glass and the Pampers guy live the lonely life of the marginalized whose only companions are associated with the excremental.

"Excremental writing," as Joshua Esty calls it,[5] has tempted writers from diverse backgrounds. In Francophone Africa, Sony Labou Tansi is a pioneer. He used it to show the greed of the ruling class: the overconsumption that is their privilege manifests itself primarily by the amount of waste they eject. Talking about the defecation of presidents is also an opportunity for their subjects to laugh at them and see them for what they are, human beings, thus negating the almost divine image that many African heads of state have of themselves.[6] Joshua Esty has, however, argued that one main element of excremental writing that has not been reflected upon is that it carries "a secret load of self-involvement":

> [E]xcrement's primary symbolic value—as both psychoanalytic and anthropological theory would suggest—is that it marks the fuzzy boundary between inside and outside, between the self and the not-self. Psychoanalysis codified (but did not invent) this reading: 'shit, the first extension of the self, is also the first instancing of the other' [. . .]. It makes sense in this light that shit figures complicate moral and political binaries by diffusing guilt and shame. (34)

My analysis of *Broken Glass* reaffirms this idea. Guilt is indeed a widespread feeling in this novel: victims also have their share of responsibility in their tragedy. The Pampers guy and Broken Glass, the two characters primarily associated with feces, are also the most involved in their own degradation. The Pampers guy left his wife to be with prostitutes. He refutes having touched his daughter, but the "young girls" he meets in the cinema Rex could be his daughters. Similarly, his wife's participation in a sect that has all the appearance of a scam has contributed to the collapse of their home. So, behind the destruction of the Pampers guy are personal, familial, and institutional shortcomings. Similarly, if Broken Glass was not drinking, alcohol could not have been used as an excuse for his dismissal. The arbitrariness of the system allows administrators to get rid of whomever they want to and when they want to, but in his case, alcoholism has greatly facilitated their task. According to Esty, "[W]hat the new currency of scatology in postcolonial cultures suggests is that excremental satire is also an index of national or collective self-implication in folly or excess" (34–35). In other words, if Broken Glass and the Pampers guy were a little more responsible, holding off their libido or penchant for alcohol, maybe their fates would have been different. Esty underlines the fact that there is the possibility in excremental writing that the victims are blamed for their misfortunes, but the reality is that "at the level both of national politics and of individual ethics, excremental writing tends toward complex models of systemic guilt, rather than toward the sharp absolutions and resolutions that attend moral or political binaries" (35). So there is a link between excremental writing and anti-nationalism. The heroes of the revolution or the struggle for decolonization are no more. There is now an exploitation of Africans by Africans and the general rush towards enjoyment.

Even though the situation in the postcolony is appallingly described in *Broken Glass*, Mabanckou does not fall into what he denounces elsewhere and considers a trap: sentimentalism.[7] Indeed, Broken Glass and the other characters are grotesquely funny. He uses satire and scatological language for a comic effect. This in turn tempers the brutality of the topics addressed and helps the writer to avoid being pathetic. However, scatology is also used for its shock value. As Dieter and Jacqueline Rollfinke write, "In order to call attention to the world's vices and follies, satirists must have the courage to offend and shock their public; one of the very few means by which most contemporary audiences can still be shocked is the use of scatological elements" (54). Of course, some might find the ribald content distasteful or disrespectful. The vulgarization of the language is also part of a general project in which the author claims his independence to write whatever and however he wants. The mixing of the genres can equally be understood in this general framework of the writer's assertion of his freedom.

Victor Hugo wrote in the preface of *Nouvelles Odes* that "[r]ules are to literature what laws are to morality: they cannot anticipate everything, [. . .] the arbitrary distinction of genres quickly crumbles before reason and taste."[8] In other words, rules are binding and not always efficient, and writers ought to not follow them. One could contest such a statement, but it is clear in *Broken Glass* that the rules of no one "pure" genre are being followed. The novel reflects a realistic image of the postcolony but this realism is achieved only because the juxtaposition of satire, the carnivalesque, and scatology renders a fantastic image of the postcolony. At another level, the writer consciously violates some rules in the name of freedom. One of the most commented aspects of *Broken Glass* is how Mabanckou ignores punctuation rules; the text is written as one giant, never-ending sentence full of commas and with no stop. Furthermore, Broken Glass explains at the very beginning of the novel that even if he enjoys writing in the notebook handed him by Stubborn Snail, he will refrain from showing his excitement because if he does, the bar owner would start pushing him to write at all times. Whereas he writes: "I want to be free to write when I want, when I can, there's nothing worse than forced labor, I'm not his ghost, I'm writing this for myself as well (2)." The moment Broken Glass accepts the mission to write, he appropriates the project; he writes for himself and proceeds according to his will. Later, he gives a "theory" of what he considers as good writing, the depiction of "real life," and how such a project should be carried out. If he were to write something worth writing, he claims,

> I'd write down words as they came to me, I'd begin awkwardly and I'd finish as awkwardly as I'd begun, and to hell with pure reason, and method, and phonetics,

and prose, and in this shit-poor language of mine things would seem clear in my head but come out wrong [. . .] and what I really want people to say when they read is 'what's this jumble, this mess, this muddle, this mishmash of barbarities [. . .] and my mischievous answer would be "this jumble of words is life." (129–130)

Broken Glass's writing technique based on the rejection of any "method" translates very well the socio-political disorder, the cacophony he describes. A carnivalesque ruling class presiding over the destinies of a carnivalesque society is transcribed in a carnivalesque manner; in other words, there is coincidence between what is said and how it is said.

The classical writing style of early Francophone writers such as Camara Laye, Mongo Beti, Cheikh Hamidou Kane, or Ferdinand Oyono was deemed "paradoxical." The choice by these authors to follow the rules of the language of the master was at odds with their writing project intended as a critique of colonialism and an unveiling of Africa's unique situation. Therefore, they were sometimes criticized for their "classicism," or conformism that did not reflect the idea of breaking off and rebellion that promulgated their literature. Since independence, however, the way Francophone African authors write has changed dramatically. In an almost obsessive way, each writer seeks to create a language freed from any constraints or rules of "good usage." It has been said that Ahmadou Kourouma "Malinkélizes" the French language, Sony Labou Tansi "tropicalizes" it, and so on. Now we can add that Mabanckou "jumblelizes" it. If we are to believe the analysis of Albert Memmi, there is nothing original in these writers' manipulation of language since it is each and every writer's role as an artist to rework and transform the language in which they write. Feeling vaguely guilty, he writes: "[T]he decolonized writer will engage in some grimaces and contortions to apologize for the use of the former colonizer's language, he will claim for example that he has hijacked, raped, destroyed the language of the colonizers, and other nonsense as if other writers were not doing the same!" (146). However, from the perspective of African authors, their manipulation of the language is the expression of their freedom. By writing as they "want" and not as they "should," they make the French language their own, and it ceases to be a borrowed or imposed language. In *Lettre à Jimmy*, his essay on James Baldwin, Mabanckou devotes considerable space reiterating the African-American fight for freedom, in its literary and political dimensions, and describing his own determination to write freely by establishing his distance with a certain African literature he does not like. It is not surprising, then, that this theme of the freedom of the writer is an integral part of *Broken Glass*.

As promised in the second page of the novel, the author does not spare anybody in his text. The bizarre competitions between the president and his minister and between Casimir and Robinette, as well as the arrogance of the judges and policemen, show how the State and its agents erect the grotesque and the obscene as techniques of power management while the questioning of the rights of individuals are set as administrative principle. The novel reflects the general mismanagement of the postcolonial state, the deception and "zombification" of the populations that excessive powers and resignation are always pushing a little further into degradation. Textually, the mixing of genres and the vulgarization of the language express the socio-political disorder and malaise rampant in the postcolony as well as showing the writer's wish to be in control of his writing.

Notes

1. See Appiah.
2. One of the highest distinctions in French and Francophone literature.
3. Pierre-Yves Gallard: "Mémoir et intertextualité dans Verre Cassé, d'Alain Mabanckou." *Malfini*. Ens de Lyon, n.d. Web. July 2012. http://malfini.ens-lyon.fr/document.php?id=140>. Translation mine.
4. Many characters refer to the country as "a shit-hole of a country."
5. See Esty.
6. See Mongo-Mboussa.
7. Alain Mabanckou, *Lettre à Jimmy* (Paris: Fayard, 2007), 76.
8. Cited by Tim Farrant in "Balzac et le mélange des genres," *L'année Balzacienne* 1 (2000): 109–118. Translation mine.

Works Cited

Appiah, Kwame Anthony. *In My Father's House: Africa in the Philosophy of Culture.* New York/Oxford: Oxford UP, 1992. Print.
Béti, Mongo (Eza Boto). *Le Pauvre Christ de Bomba.* Paris: Laffont, 1956. Print.
———. *Ville cruelle.* Paris: Présence Africaine, 1954. Print.
Esty, Joshua D. "Excremental Postcolonialism." *Contemporary Literature* 40.1 (1999): 22–59. Print.
Mabanckou, Alain. *Broken Glass.* Trans. Helen Stevenson. New York: Soft Skull Press, 2010. Print.
Mbembe, Achille. *On the Postcolony.* Berkeley: U of California P, 2001. Print.
———. *De la postcolonie: essai sur l'imagination politique dans l'Afrique contemporaine.* 2e éd. Paris: Karthala, 2000. Print.
Memmi, Albert. *Portrait du décolonisé.* Paris: Gallimard, 2004. Print.
Mongo-Mboussa, Boniface. "Sony Labou Tansi et l'écriture du corps: la subversion par le bas." *Africulture.* N.p., June 1999. Web. July 2011.
Sembène, Ousmane. *Les Bouts de bois de Dieu.* Paris: Le Livre Contemporain, 1960. Print.
———. *Ô Pays- mon beau peuple!* Paris: Le Livre Contemporain, 1957. Print.

"A Nation of One's Own": Fictional Indictment of Cannibalistic African States

NG'ANG'A MŨCHIRI

This chapter brings together two different kinds of texts: fictional and legal, showing that reading one kind illuminates our understanding of the other. The discussion begins by engaging with the ubiquity of the nation-state as a political community as well as highlighting its near-universal and cannibalistic traits. This background then enables an analysis of *Johnny Chien Méchant* by Emmanuel Dongala and *La Vie et Demie* (*Life and a Half*) by Sony Labou Tansi to explore the cannibal-like nature of contemporary regimes in the Congo region. Both authors expose the trauma and dystopia visible in present-day Congo to demonstrate the human "sacrifices" states are willing to make in order to maintain a hold on political power. In both novels, contrary to popular belief, an invocation of democratic ideals does not guarantee social justice. While national constitutions are typically presented as foundational texts that set the tone for equitable and sustainable civic engagement, Dongala and Tansi show this is not always true. The chapter ends by re-visiting the premier human rights documents on the African continent and outlining the idealism encompassed therein. Of particular interest is Dongala's cynicism of human rights discourse, and how it mirrors Tansi's ridicule of national constitutions. Overall, the analysis problematizes human rights praxis in postwar and/or authoritarian societies as a possible strategy for grassroots movements seeking to deploy and achieve democratic ideals.

I

Ivan Vitanyi argues that the "nation" is a concept without a "universal and global definition," rather we can only discuss it on a case-by-case basis (19). The myriad social arrangements that have been identified as nations challenge our ability to classify. However, the presence of death seems to accompany nation-states in their expressions of nationalism: Pheng Cheah characterizes nationalism as the "exemplary figure for death," even as patriotic subjects attempt to build a nation that outlasts "mortality and death" ("Spectral Nationality" 226). In its unique role as the purveyor of military might, the nation has indeed become associated with death, especially at moments when states seek to prolong or preserve their own lives. Despite the nation's etymological association with "natality" and birth, pointing towards moments of fruitful origin, the contemporary nation-state does have an unchallenged monopoly on death ("Spectral Nationality" 227). When the deaths in question are those of outsiders, the nation can simply be termed murderous; however, when it kills its own citizens, the nation becomes associated with cannibalistic behavior.

Johnny Chien Méchant by Emmanuel Dongala and *La Vie et Demie* by Sony Labou Tansi, in unique ways, demonstrate violations of people's right to life, property, and political participation. This behavior is cannibalistic since it allows the state—in its various manifestations—to oppress and subjugate its own people as mechanisms for survival. This oppressive nature of postcolonial African states provides a continuum of violence that can be traced back to European colonial enterprises on the continent, highly complicating anticolonial efforts of the Fifties and Sixties (Cheah, "Rationality of Life" 9). In such spaces as described by Dongala and Tansi, "opposition" to the state is not only "uneasy" but also fraught with danger (Cheah, "Violent Light" 173). Dipesh Chakrabarty identifies the almost universal permeability of the nation-state and goes on to discuss the importance of the "imagination" in constructions of nationalism (41). As a result, when structural adjustment programs by international financial institutions reduce a regime's capacity to make economic decisions, the cultural sphere becomes a target for states seeking to prop up and display their might (Paley 481). Ethnic nationalism, which can sometimes be "militant" and "aggressive," may emerge in such instances (Vitanyi 23). This combination leads to authoritarian regimes, which, as can be seen from subsequent analysis of Dongala's and Tansi's work, depend upon brute force for their longevity. However, as Achille Mbembe argues, IMF and World Bank interest in local affairs not only curtails a state's financial sovereignty, it might also lead to its actual "disintegration" (73). Mobutu Sese Seko's Zaire is a classic example; after nearly three decades of dominance, once starved of foreign funds to offer political clientele the state quickly crumbled in the face of Laurent Kabila's advance.

Sony Labou Tansi's novella is the tale of a fictional African state, Katamalanasie. The long line of dictators, self-styled as Providential Guides, are the antagonists to Tansi's main characters—Martial and his progeny Chaidana.[1] We follow Martial as he resists the oppression of the Guides, and because Martial dies at the very beginning of the plot, the text takes a turn for the mythical. While Martial takes part in Katalamanasie's events as a living-dead, his daughter, Chaidana, and his grandchildren continue the fight against political hegemony. Although the Providential Guides are much invested in procreation to ensure a continuation of their political dynasties, it is very clear from the beginning of the text that citizens' right to life has been usurped by the ruling regime. The Guide's violence upon Martial's body using a "table knife," "revolver," "machine gun," and a "long, gold-sparkling saber" is meant to bring death (Tansi 5–7). That Martial is immune to the Guide's murderous acts, infuriatingly remaining suspended in mid-air while "his dangling guts were bled white," wholly perplexes the Providential Guide (Tansi 6). The rest of Martial's family suffers the same fate; they are murdered by the Guide using his table knife, and even worse, are forced to eat the cadavers of their family members (Tansi 11). Only Chaidana, Martial's daughter, survives this horror—small wonder that she will later in the text seek revenge on the Guide and the ministers in his government.

Unfortunately, the regime's homicidal streak does not end there. The execution of political dissidents in Katamalanasie causes street protests; Colonel Obaltana de Kienzo, the Guide's assistant, "gave the order to open fire on a crowd of nearly thirty thousand men" seeking the cessation of extra-judicial killings (Tansi 33). Visibly, life in Katamalanasie is a precious commodity cheapened by the regime's actions. The sanctity endowed human life is lost to this oppressive regime. Cannibalism as a metaphor of political life is clearly visible in the Guide's actions: he consumes the bodies of his subjects not only to nourish his body, but also to instill fear and further elongate his reign. That such events happened in the former Congo Free State is worth noting. This Belgian colonial project was known for mutilating its indigenous communities in an effort to maximize profits; the additional funds, of course, were deployed to further entrench European hegemony and colonial rule.

Emmanuel Dongala's *Johnny Chien Méchant* shows that Tansi's Katamalanasie is not an exception. Set in an unnamed African country in the throes of civil war, Dongala's novel evokes memories of recent events in the two states that go by the name Congo, Sierra Leone, Liberia, and Ivory Coast. The book's title arises from the name of the antagonist, Johnny, also known as Mad Dog—a child soldier who is both traumatized and vicious. By the end of the plot, he has killed many innocent civilians, and it is almost with a sigh of relief that the reader witnesses Mad Dog's death at the hands of the protagonist, a young woman named Laokole. It is at Laokole's home that we first learn of the cost of the civil war in terms of human life. Laokole's brother, Fofo, exhibits signs of Post-Traumatic Stress Disorder after he is informed that armed rebel soldiers might be headed to their house. Fofo, "panic in his eyes . . . began to cry, his whole body trembling. He was terrified . . . dreading a repeat of the day when members of the first militias . . . had killed Papa right in front of him" (Dongala 4). The death of the children's father is only one in a long line of murders that are carried out by weapon-toting youths. Mad Dog and his militia group attack a radio station; in addition to raping a female TV presenter, Mad Dog's companion burns three male broadcasters alive: "Gator turned his flamethrower on the panicked men—transformed them into human torches shrieking with pain and writhing on the ground. It was pretty funny. They squealed like pigs" (Dongala 20).

Cannibalistic regimes turn normal modes of social life upside down. In Dongala's and Tansi's texts, parents' quotidian ability to protect their children from harm has been challenged. Furthermore, in Dongala's novel we see Mad Dog reacting with humor at human suffering, rather than with empathy and compassion. This is quite similar to Tansi's portrayal of a dictator who responds to human weakness as displayed by his subjects with more cruelty. Death in both novels is closely associated with state hegemony, as well as competition for political power. Moreover, the connection between political supremacy, physical force, and material acquisition is clearly demonstrated. Dongala's text is a register of items that Mad Dog and his fellow militia loot and steal. From 4x4 vehicles, to food, alcohol, stereo systems, a live pig, and books, the rebel soldiers enjoy material acquisition far and beyond their wildest dreams. They become intoxicated by the "power" that "lies at the muzzle of a gun" and repeatedly deploy it for their personal gain (Dongala 24). Similarly, Tansi narrates the great wealth that Providential Guides have accumulated at the expense of their subjects: palaces, trips abroad, luxury goods, weaponry and security training for their armed forces. Across the two texts we can read a high disregard not only for individual rights to possess wealth but also for society's right to its national resources. Both are wholly desecrated either as armed rebels plunder private homes or as the Guides portion out national wealth to foreign countries in exchange for personal gain.

If the two novels depict similar chaotic social moments, the corresponding political setups could not be more dissimilar. A closer look at the fictional texts reveals a stark difference in the *kind* of political power described. While Dongala exhibits a much-contested state ascendancy and only fleetingly mentions the top executive in charge, Tansi's work displays an omni-present dictatorial personality. These two extremes can be instructive as we attempt to further comprehend nation-states that are malignant for their citizens' well-being. In the first case, Tansi writes about the Presidential Guides whose presence is felt throughout the text. The most important spectacle of the dictator's powers surrounds his copulation with fifty young maidens. In what becomes an annual national event, the country's TV network broadcasts the Guide in one of his palatial rooms "readied with fifty blue comforters, fifty blue sheets, fifty napkins, fifty nightgowns, fifty pairs of flip-flops, fifty washcloths, fifty masseurs, and fifty tablets. Fifty virgins were ushered in . . . undressed and laid on numbered beds" (Tansi 102). Not surprisingly, sometime later the young women give birth to fifty male children, all potential heirs of their father's power (Tansi 103). The very public nature of the moment of conception privileges a reproductive stance that is otherwise missing in the regime's denigration of human life. Once more, we can read the Guide's acts of procreation as a logical result of his sacrificial actions on his subjects' bodies. The Katamalanasie regime takes great pains to self-generate precisely so it can maintain its carnivorous and cannibalistic devouring of its citizens, literally and figuratively. In stark contrast, Dongala offers us a window into a society whose government is largely ineffective. The *de facto* power has been usurped by murderous gangs who assert their newfound dominance by meting out death and destruction. Despite the obvious differences, both of these regions can be classified as nation-states, clearly exemplifying the challenges discussed earlier in categorizing political communities as nation, state, or nation-state.

II

If the nation-state has become ubiquitous, so too has its invocation of democracy; paradoxically, this might occur in an effort to entrench authoritarianism. Julia Paley invites us to closely examine the competitive and "strategic deployment of the term democracy" and what this implies for "power" relations within the nation space (475). It turns out that in social relations characterized by inequitable power sharing, what "democracy" means is "hotly contested" among various groups: political parties, civil society, military regimes, among others (Paley 476). Democratic ideals are enshrined in national constitutions, which serve as the blueprint for building societies oriented towards justice. The primacy of constitutional documents and their multiple implications for democracy cannot be overstated, and hence Tansi's ridicule of national constitutions is a profound critique that attacks the very base upon which Katamalanasie society is built, exposing the decay therein. *La Vie et Demie* explores ways in which constitutional documents, rather than increasing government transparency, actually make regimes more obscure to people's scrutiny. In this way, Tansi satirizes our belief in national legal structures as potential mechanisms for achieving social justice. Jean-Heart-of-Father, one in a long line of Guides, devoted political energy to refurbishing his country's laws. Through a national referendum he added

> two articles to the constitution. Article One: Power belongs to the Guide, the Guide belongs to the people. The second article was written in a language that nobody could ever understand. It was said to be the language of madmen. Article Two: *Gronaniniate mese botouete taou-taou, moro metani bamanasar karani meta yelo yelo-manikatana.* (Tansi 89)

This incident parodies people's democratic involvement in their own government. First, while the presence of a referendum points towards the citizenry's ability to choose, the fact that "one hundred percent of the ballots cast were in favor of the constitutional referendum" shows that in reality the people have no choice (Tansi 89). Either they all voted "yes" in fear of repercussions, or the announced results were falsified to portray fictional unity. In stark contrast to Article 6 in the Congo-Brazzaville constitution which decrees that "every citizen shall have the right to take part in the direction of the public affairs," it appears that all eligible voters have been turned into automatons that make political decisions as advised by the Guide.

Second, the incomprehensibility of Article Two serves to show that the electorate has very minimal means of keeping their government accountable. The people struggle to understand the article, interpreting the phrase "*yelo yelo-manikatana* [to mean] 'sovereign for life'" or debating that the complete article actually means "hell" (Tansi 89–90). Nevertheless, they cannot make head or tail of it. It is quite ironic that constitutional documents, meant to clearly articulate how a society's government will be run, actually leave the people more confused. Also ironic is the fact that tools of democratic governance—such as elections and referendums—have been co-opted by a totalitarian regime to reduce people's involvement in civil life. The national constitution, rather than being an empowering text that increases people's agency has been transformed into background noise to provide companionship as life flows by. Later in Tansi's novella, we encounter a moment of political dissent that is resolved when one Katamalanasie province breaks away from the rest of the country. Typical of most coup d'etats, Jean-Cold-Blooded deploys radio communication to inform the people of Darmellia about their newfound sovereignty:

> A radio relay station ... proclaimed independence for the state of Darmellia after the death of Jean-Heart-of-Stone. The constitution, the formation of the provisional government, and the reinstatement of colors other than Jean-Heart-of-Stone's national blue were all announced over the radio. Jean Cold-Blooded's constitution decreed that there would be three political parties. (Tansi 109–110)

The good news of possible future peace now that the region has seceded from Katamalanasie is dampened by the fact that most people might not even believe Jean-Cold-Blooded's announcement. Because of the Guide's continued use of the radio to spread rumors and propaganda, "people had lost the habit of believing. They listened to the radio for the noise it made" (Tansi 34). Thus, the advent of a new political age and the crucial document that outlines the hopes of the new administration are relegated to the inconsequential part of everyday life. The constitution, it turns out, is an insignificant manuscript whose presence is largely disregarded by the very people whose lives it affects. This insignificance is also demonstrated by the provincial secession, which flies in the face of constitutional documents that strictly command regional integrity.

The population's shrouded animosity towards this vital political script is not unfounded. When Jean-Heart-of-Father first added the two extra articles to the constitution, he also decreed that it be "written above every doorway in the country" (Tansi 89). Presumably, he hoped to ensure that citizens were familiar with the changes to the laws of the land so they could more fully participate in civic life. Thus, "it was ordered that every article of the People's Constitution be painted in every room, in the kitchen, everywhere" (Tansi 90). Unfortunately, the length to which the Guide goes in enforcing this law wholly detracts from the functionality of the constitution. If the constitution is a text that enshrines individual and collective rights to economic, social and political life, its saturation in society brings about the opposite effect. Jean-Heart-of-Father commanded that "those who took longer than the nine-day time limit decreed" by him to paint the constitution on their walls were to be punished (Tansi 90). They "watched elements from the Special Forces lay waste to their huts with rifle butts or blow them up with dynamite" (Tansi 90). Because of a document that protects individual rights to property, families lost their homes, or worse, their lives. The fanaticism of the regime, it turns out, only further impoverishes the very society it is supposedly serving and protecting.

III

The writers' critique of constitutional documents demonstrates the inadequacy of the national space to nurture and support democratic ideals. Unfortunately, as both authors show, the transnational public sphere is not a viable alternative. On the African continent, as elsewhere, human rights discourse is deliberately couched in language that would appear exemplary across national borders. The inherently transnational nature of human rights activism is depicted by the premier global text: The Universal Declaration of Human Rights. On a continental level the Organization of African Unity, at its 1981 gathering held in Kenya, adopted what has subsequently been termed the Banjul Charter. Although the legislation only came into force in 1986, work had begun seven years earlier at the meeting convened in Monrovia, Liberia. The Banjul Charter, or the African Charter on Human and People's Rights, was a revision of the OAU's anticolonial mandate. It sought to make the organization meaningful for an increasing number of postcolonial African nations (OAU 2). Although coming several decades after European and American Human Rights documents, the Banjul Charter was still a trailblazer in its day for several reasons. One, unlike its American and European counterparts, it had no derogation clause; states could not abrogate their commitments to the Banjul Charter even during states of emergency or moments of civil war (Manby 176). Two, the Banjul document placed equal importance on basic rights, as well as on socio-economic wellbeing and the right to political self-determination; neither of these categories of rights was considered to be more important than the other (Baldwin & Morel 273). Nevertheless, it had some serious shortcomings. It overlooked the primacy of women's rights in healthy societies with the internal capacity for growth. To correct this omission, the Protocol to the African Charter on Human and People's Rights on the Rights of Women in Africa was adopted by the African Union in July 2003. The Women's Protocol championed the rights of imprisoned mothers, elderly women, and those living with disabilities. Its insistence on women's access to inheriting parents' and husbands' property, women's right to sustainable development, healthy environments, and the elimination of harmful practices gave it the capacity to be a revolutionary document for women's well-being on the continent (AU Articles 5, 7, 13, 18).

If the preceding legal documents indicate an African utopia, the reality could not be more different. Emmanuel Dongala's text shows that African Human Rights discourse has been compromised and rendered largely ineffective. First, human rights rhetoric has been co-opted by violent militia groups. Mad Dog, previously known as Matiti Mabe, is a self-proclaimed intellectual. As a result, he asserts his understanding of contemporary politics better than his compatriots in General Giap's ragtag army, the Mata Mata. Mad Dog's first foray into violence is enabled by the appearance of a dubious "intellectual doctor" who proceeds to sow discord between urban communities that had previously been coexisting in relative peace. That the language of democracy and representative government spewed out by the rebel recruiter is false and empty can be seen by Mad Dog's recollection of how he and a group of other young people were invited to join "the Movement For the Democratic Liberation of the People, the MFDLP, and [fight] against the partisans of the Movement For the Total Liberation of the People, the MFTLP;" when Mad Dog took up arms in the struggle between "MFDLP versus MFTLP, it was six of one and half a dozen of the other" (Dongala 83–4). Dongala's play with language challenges the reader to catch the difference between the two armed groups. Their similarity, it turns out, lies not only in their ill-prepared political manifestos, but also in their ability to coerce civilians into contributing towards the war effort. Laokole, Dongala's female protagonist, describes how "all of the warring factions claimed to be fighting in the name of the people, so it was up to the people to pay the expenses of both those who were winning and those who were losing" (Dongala 14). People's right to political self-determination and participation in their desired form of government is nullified when militia groups forcefully assert their prerogative to politically represent civilians without the people's mandate. This is in direct violation of Articles 13 and 20 of the Banjul Charter. As it turns out, rebel factions explicitly cite human rights as their raison d'etre, further exemplifying Dongala's cynicism of such language. Mad Dog explains to the reader the difference between the real intent for the rebels' desire to fight versus the fictional reason given to win support for their cause. He says, "[L]ooting . . . was the main reason we were fighting. To line our pockets . . . to have all the women we wanted . . . to be the rulers of the world" (Dongala 64). However, rebel soldiers have been warned by their superiors not to confess to outsiders the benefits they enjoy as a result of their position. The rebels' military leaders, as well as President Dabanga, had commanded them, instead, to say that they "were fighting for freedom and democracy" since that way they could "win the sympathy of the outside world" (Dongala 64). This becomes another moment when the meaning of the word democracy is disputed by several factions, each seeking to maximize its self-interest.

Secondly, Dongala's fiction demonstrates that African human rights discourse has been superseded by animal rights. He portrays two scenarios where people's rights are either violated or simply ignored in preference to animal welfare. Such events problematize the assumed universality of human worth and dignity. Laokole's family spends the first half of Dongala's novel running away from armed groups. When the family finally finds safe haven at the United Nations High Commission for Refugees, their shelter is only temporary. Mad Dog and his gang threaten the UNHCR workers, and in response Western governments send in an armed search-and-rescue team to extract all foreign nationals. The successful operation comes at a high cost; Laokole's childhood friend, Melanie, is run over by one of the armed vehicles involved in the commando operation. Melanie's body is run over twice after her death as soldiers rush to retrieve a foreign national's pet. The dog, Dongala shows, is worth more than any refugee's life, even Melanie's. But it is not only domesticated companions that Dongala privileges over humans; wild beasts, too, rank higher than African refugees, despite what the Banjul Charter might say to the contrary. Towards the end of the novel, we follow Laokole deep into the jungle as she escapes armed men who have attacked a small village in which she was living. Laokole comes across a clearing in the forest and soon discovers a group of veterinary doctors who have come to airlift gorillas out of the war zone. The protagonist's hope that if the foreigners "could save animals, they could also save" her is soon proved utterly wrong (Dongala 281). Despite much pleading, Laokole's cries for help are met with apathy and a determined refusal by the doctors to do anything that might jeopardize their mission. "We're not authorized to take passengers," the animal saviors tell her, and with that they leave her to her own devices (Dongala 283). The foreigners' indifference to the young woman, alone in a jungle and at the mercy of pursuing soldiers, is in sharp contrast to their carefully orchestrated gorilla protection scheme. Dongala subverts the reader's expectation that as much care and consideration is given to human life as to animals, if not more. Parallel to contemporary political events, he overturns an African human rights dialogue that seeks to uphold the sanctity of human dignity.

In light of cannibalistic nation-states, and untenable transnational spheres, where else could citizens seek a life simultaneously free of suffering and based on social justice? Pheng Cheah proposes that culture can be a key instrument in the achievement of self-determination due to its potential for "causality" ("Rationality of Life" 17). Cultural production is deliberately opposed to "nature" or what could be read as "given conditions," and in this opposition lies culture's capacity for transformation ("Rationality of Life" 18). Organizations interested in reversing dismal human rights trends and manifesting ideal social experiences would benefit from anchoring their activism and political agitation in local cultures and vernacular forms of expression. Dongala and Tansi offer us examples of communities finding within themselves the strength to confront injustice and stand up to hegemonic oppression. Towards the end of Dongala's novel, a Swedish journalist speaks with a rape victim. The female survivor not only confronts social stigma and shame by confidently stating her name, she also indicts the ruling regime with the words, "[A] responsible government can't expect to get away . . . and let such terrible crimes go unpunished" (Dongala 303). Her testimony draws other women to listen to her story of survival, empowering them to speak and share their own trauma with each other and with viewers around the globe. These women not only push back against communal taboos on speaking about sexual violence, but they also envision themselves justified to take their governments to task for recent conflict. While human rights charters gather dust in government cabinets, these women have made the first step towards deploying the Banjul Charter for increased well-being. The oral nature of the women's stories invokes earlier modes of African cultural production—folktales, riddles, and myths—exemplifying the autochthonous character of this mobilizing force. At the same time, the mass media serves as a connection to a transnational public sphere, which could play a supporting role in such transformational efforts. The centrality of local arts in campaigning for social justice is also underscored by Tansi's novella. One Christmas Eve Chaidana Martial gathers "three million" men and women and together they paint her father's defiant phrase, "I do not want to die this death" (Tansi 28). These words, a political rallying call, not only enrage the ruling Guide for their defiance, but also offer agency to those who oppose repressive regimes. Just like the women in Dongala's text, these youths form a community that puts into practice the ideals of self-determination laid down in the Banjul Charter. Unlike Dongala, however, Tansi views the international space as sinister. Tansi's text does not attempt to connect the indigenous with the foreign; in *La Vie et Demie* the transnational space is at best filled with ominous foreboding and at worst plays a supporting role to Katamalanasie's dictators.

I find the practice of social justice endeavors, while deliberately anchored in local cultural production, to hold much potential for future work in African democracy. From such praxis, it is not much farther to the experiences of the Endorois and Ogoni peoples. Both communities have taken their respective state governments to the African Commission on Human and People's Rights (ACHPR) for perceived infringements. The Endorois community pursued the Kenyan state for compensation for their land, which was confiscated and turned into a national game reserve. The Ogoni community, on the other hand, went before the commission to pursue a clean and healthy environment, free from pollution by oil drilling corporations. They also sought part of the proceeds gathered from the extraction of natural resources on their land. It is a big step for small communities to charge their own sovereign states at an international legal space. However, it is even more inspiring that both cases were won by the complainants. Both experiences give us real-life corollaries to Dongala's and Tansi's fictional communities that rally together to achieve the aspirations of the Banjul Charter. Furthermore, both examples serve as key indicators of the primacy of local knowledge and the necessity for social movements to incorporate such indigenous expertise into the idealistic rhetoric of the Banjul Charter, the Women's Protocol, and other unique constitutional documents.

Nevertheless, it is imperative not to romanticize the Endorois and Ogoni incidents as novel exemplars of resistance against despotic regimes. Deeper analysis soon displays the inherent inadequacy of human rights frameworks in initiating change. Firstly, rulings by the ACHPR may not always be recognized by authoritarian governments. Dictatorial states develop, in the first place, by ignoring the kind of international pressure embodied in this continental human rights body. Coupled with the ACHPR's lack of an enforcing agency, it quickly becomes clear that implementation of court rulings relies upon the exact kind of goodwill and political maturity that is lacking in dictatorships. Secondly, pursuing international legal assistance against one's government has the potential for increased persecution; hence, not many communities are willing, or even have the ability, to initiate such action. Ken Tsaro Wiwa's demise at the hands of the Sani Abacha regime is one of the few much-popularized instances when activists have been targeted. Other numerous, but equally violent, repressions continue—recorded by indigenous human rights organizations yet unbeknownst to the world. Finally, even when such judicial decisions are acceptable to state parties, they do not translate into immediate changes in the living conditions of the affected communities. Administrative policies simply may not react fast enough for such instantaneous transformations to take place.

Notes

1. Achille Mbembe's *On the Postcolony* mentions the fact that Cameroon's Ahmadou Ahidjo (president 1958–1982) was once titled "Providential Guide" by sycophants.

Works Cited

Baldwin, Clive & Cynthia Morel. "Group Rights." *The African Charter on Human & People's Rights: the System in Practice, 1986-2006*. Eds. Malcolm Evans & Rachel Murray. Cambridge: Cambridge UP, 2008. 244–288. Print.

Chakrabarty, Dipesh. *Provincializing Europe: Postcolonial Thought and Historical Difference*. Princeton: Princeton UP, 2000. Print.

Cheah, Pheng. "The Rationality of Life: On the Organismic Metaphor of the State." *Radical Philosophy* 112 (2002): 9–24. Print.

———. "Spectral Nationality: The Living on [sur-vie] of the Postcolonial Nation in Neocolonial Globalization." *Boundary* 2.6.3 (1999): 225–252. Print.

———. *Spectral Nationality: Passages of Freedom from Kant to Postcolonial Literatures of Liberation*. New York: Columbia UP, 2003. Print.

———. "Violent Light: The Idea of Publicness in Modern Philosophy & in Global Neocolonialism." *Social Text* 43 (1995): 163–190. Print.

Cooper, Frederick. "Possibility & Constraint: African Independence in Historical Perspective." *Journal of African History* 49 (2008): 167–196. Print.

Denitch, Bogdan. "National Identity, Politics & Democracy." *Social Science Information* 35.3 (1996): 459–483. Print.

Dongala, Emmanuel. *Johnny Mad Dog*. Trans. Marie L. Ascher. New York: Farrar, Straus & Giroux, 2005. Print.

Manby, Bronwen. "Civil & Political Rights in the African Charter on Human & People's Rights: Articles 1- 7." *The African Charter on Human & People's Rights: the System in Practice, 1986-2006*. Eds. Malcolm Evans & Rachel Murray. Cambridge: Cambridge UP, 2008. 171–212. Print.

Mbembe, Achille. *On the Postcolony*. Berkeley: U Of California P, 2001. Print.

Paley, Julia. "Toward an Anthropology of Democracy." *Annual Review of Anthropology* 31 (2002): 469–496. Print.

Salam, Reihan. "The Confounding State: Public Ignorance & the Politics of Identity." *Critical Review* 14.2,3 (2000): 299–324. Print.

Tansi, Sony L. *Life and a Half*. Trans. Alison Dundy. Bloomington: Indiana UP, 2011. Print.

Vitanyi, Ivan. "Does a Homogeneous Conception of Nation Exist? A Typology of National Identities." *Beyond Nationalism? Sovereignty & Citizenship*. Eds. Fred Dallmayr & Jose M. Rosales. Boulder: Lexington Books, 2001. 15–28. Print.

CONTRIBUTORS

MAGALÍ ARMILLAS-TISEYRA is Assistant Professor of World Literature in the English Department at the University of Mississippi, where she specializes in African and Latin American, postcolonial, and world literatures. Her research focuses on the literature of dictatorship in transnational contexts, and she is currently completing a book manuscript on novels about dictators in Latin American as well as Anglophone and Francophone African literatures. Her writing has appeared in the *Latin American Literary Review* and *Comparative Studies of South Asia, Africa, and the Middle East*; she is also the guest editor for a special issue of the journal *The Global South* on "The Aesthetics of Dislocation" (7.2).

ROBERT L. COLSON is Assistant Professor of interdisciplinary humanities at Brigham Young University where he teaches courses on African fiction and film, postcolonial studies, and European modernist art and literature. His research focuses on modernist and postcolonial fiction. Previous work on *Wizard of the Crow* has been published in *Research in African Literatures*. He is currently working on a book project about nationalism and narrative form in the work of Virginia Woolf, James Joyce, Salman Rushdie, and Ngũgĩ wa Thiong'o.

GĪTAHI GĪTĪTĪ is Professor of English, Film and Media Studies, Africana Studies, and Comparative Literature at the University of Rhode Island. His scholarly and creative work has appeared in *The Johns Hopkins Guide to Literary Theory and Criticism, Atlantic Literary Review, Paintbrush, Current Writing, Left Curve, Race in the College Classroom: Pedagogy and Politics, The Companion to African Literatures, ATQ: Nineteenth Century American Literature and Culture, Ngũgĩ wa Thiong'o: Texts and Contexts, Metamorphoses 2, Routledge Encyclopedia of African Literature, Barrow Street, Mũtiiri*, etc. His research and teaching interests encompass Africa and the African diaspora, Latin America, postcolonial studies, and world literature. He is a critic, poet, and translator.

NADA HALLOWAY is Assistant Professor of English at Manhattanville College. Her research and teaching interests include twentieth-century and contemporary Anglophone literature, Victorian literature, literary and cultural history, theory and feminist studies.

OLIVER LOVESEY is Associate Professor of English at the University of British Columbia, Okanagan, Canada. He is the author of monographs on Ngũgĩ wa

Thiong'o and also on George Eliot, and most recently the editor of *Victorian Social Activists' Novels* (2011) and *Approaches to Teaching the Works of Ngũgĩ wa Thiong'o* (2012).

JOSEPH MCLAREN is Professor of English at Hofstra University in New York. A specialist in African, Caribbean, and African American literatures, his publications include numerous articles on literary and cultural subjects. He is the author of *Langston Hughes: Folk Dramatist in the Protest Tradition, 1921-1943* (1997). In addition, he co-edited *Pan-Africanism Updated* (1999) and *African Visions* (2000) and edited two volumes of the *Collected Works of Langston Hughes*: *The Big Sea* (2002) and *I Wonder As I Wander* (2002). He is coauthor with legendary jazz saxophonist-composer Jimmy Heath of Heath's autobiography, *I Walked with Giants* (2010).

NG'ANG'A WA MUCHIRI is a PhD candidate at the University of Miami. His dissertation project is concerned with the question of natural/national resources in Eastern Africa, especially land rights. Using literary, legal, and visual texts, as well as personal narratives, he investigates the conversation between nation-states and their subjects on "who" gets to assert their rights to land ownership, and "why." He has presented at the following conferences: African Theatre Association (2010), African Studies Association (2012), African Literature Association (2013), and the Africa Conference convened by UT-Austin's Dr. Toyin Falola (2013). He is the recipient of a travel award from the Association for the Study of Literature and the Environment (ASLE), a departmental research award for archival visits to Nairobi and Dar es Salaam, as well as the African Literature Association's Best Graduate Student Paper award (2012).

MAINA WA MŨTONYA has taught African Studies (Literature, Philosophy and Swahili) in México. His research interests include a study of the politics of remembering, violence and its representation in the popular cultural terrain of Kenya. Mutonya is currently involved in a research on Afro-Mexican identities in México. His recent publications include, a book which explores the politics of everyday life in the popular music of the Gĩkũyũ people in Kenya, a path-breaking addition to the field of African popular culture and literature and articles; "La Negociación de Identidades Urbanas en el Mũgithi y la Ejecución de One-Man Guitar en Kenia" (2012) and "The Beat Goes On: Performing Postcolonial Disillusionment in Postcolonial Kenya" (2011). He is a member of the African Literature Association, the African Studies Association and the International Society for African Philosophy and Studies.

GĨCHINGIRI NDĨGĨRĨGĨ is Associate Professor of English and Africana Studies at the University of Tennessee, Knoxville. His work has appeared in *Approaches* to *Teaching the Works of Ngũgĩ wa Thiong'o, Canadian Review of Comparative Literature, Journal of the African Literature Association, Indian Journal of Ecocriticism, Mũtiiri* and *The Drama Review*.

AWA COUMBA SARR is an Assistant Professor of Francophone Studies and Africana Studies at the University of Tennessee, Knoxville. Her research is focused mainly on Francophone African literature, including colonial and postcolonial intellectual theories and movements, the publishing industry, and women's writings. She has articles published or forthcoming on Calixthe Beyala and Khadidjatou Hane, Aminata Sow Fall, Alain Mabanckou, as well as on plagiarism and literary politics, and « littérature-monde ». She is currently working on a book project on the new generation of Francophone African writers.

INDEX

abject, 215
Achebe, Chinua, xi–xiii, xv, 102, 111
African Americans, 114, 115
African Charter on Human and People's Rights on the Rights of Women in Africa, 228
African Commission on Human and People's Rights, 231
African leaders, 113, 114, 116
African novelists, 111
Agamben, Giorgio, 170, 172
agency, 186
Amin, Idi, 30, 69, 85–109
Anthills of the Savannah, 61, 112, 116
Arab Spring, 85–86
Armah, Ayi Kwei, 111
Astles, Robert 95, 105n14
Atlantic Slave Trade, 115
attempted coup, 142, 147–49, 162n18
authoritarianism, 13
autonomy, 8, 26
The Autumn of the Patriarch (Márquez), 69

Baba, 154; *wa taifa*, 154; Moi, 145, 149; *na Mama*, 145
Babel (Tower of), 183
Banda, Hastings, 30
Banjul Charter, 228–31
Barre, General Siyad, 2, 3
Benjamin, Walter, 100
Big Brother (*1984*), 16
Big-Man, xviii, 187, 189, 195, 203; and Small-Boy Syndrome, xxi, 2
biopolitics, 174, 180n2
biopower, 171, 180n2
Biya, Paul, 69
bloodwealth, 22
bluff, 189, 192, 193, 197
body, 169, 179; symbology of, 74; *See also* embodiment
Bokassa, Jean-Bédel, 30, 36–37, 69, 85, 97, 98, 104n1
buffoonery, 210, 212
burlesque, 208, 214
Butler, Judith, xv

cannibalism, 86, 92, 94, 101, 222–23
caricature, 209, 212
carnivalesque, 208, 217, 218
Central Intelligence Agency (CIA), 32, 114, 115
ceremonialism, xvii, xxvii; of state, 185
Chakrabarty, Dipesh, 222
chieftains (colonial), 25
Christian: gospel songs, 151; homily, 160; hymns, 151–52, 158; liturgy, 151; missions, 152; schools, 152; worship, 151
City of God, 184
civil law, xx
civil society, 188–89
Cold War, 127, 192, 193
colonialism, 112, 121, 152
commitment, 47–63
Congo-Brazzaville Constitution, 226
coup d'etat, 169, 178
Coupland, Douglas, 104n6
cynicism, 208, 209, 210

debt, xvii, xviii
defetishization, 20, 191
Demathew, John, 155
democracy, 111, 225
despotism, 208; centralized, xix, 3–4; decentralized, xix; and incomplete modernization, 21, 185, 187
destabilization, 112, 115
dictator, 141, 149, 212; configuration of, 142; definitions of, 29; lifestyles, 86, 104n6; novels about, 47–48, 61, 66, 125; in popular culture, 86, 100, 104n6; regime, 142; regimes in Africa, 143; regime of Moi in Kenya, 143–144, 149; stereotypes, 92–93
dictatorship, 111, 145, 152; and colonialism, xix, 50–51, 55; and megalomania, 80; and paranoia, 70, 81; rhetoric of, xxix
Diderot, Denis, 57–58
disappearance (mode of eliminating political opponents), xiii, 185
disillusionment (theme), 66
domination, 186
Dongala, Emmanuel, 223
doppelganger, 91

INDEX

elites, 187, 204
embodiment, 167–68; See also body
Emechetta, Buchi, 102
ethnic nationalism, 222
euphemization (Bourdieu), 192
excremental writing, 216

fables, 210, 212
Fairhall, John, 104n5
Fanon, Frantz, 31, 56, 91
Farah, Nuruddin, 31, 36, 43, 117, 118, 183
fascism, 86, 88, 105n16
father, 154–55; paternal metaphor of the, 141; cultural image of the, 143; of the nation, 144, 152, 154; Moi as, 145, 149; and mother, 145
fetish: definition, 126–27, 130–131, 137–138; objects, 73, 126–27, 130–32, 133, 134–35, 139; See also Mbembe, Achille
Fimbo ya nyayo, 141, 145, 155, 161n1
Foden, Giles, 86, 87, 90–93, 101, 104n3, 105n14
Foucault, Michel, xiii, 168, 172, 174–75; discipline, xxvii, 5, 185, 194, 196; subjection, xxvii, 196, 198, 204; See also medicine
Franco, Francisco, 172

Gadaffi, Colonel Muammar, 89
gender: performance of, 203; self-referential, 202
genres: mixing, 208, 217, 219
gerontocracy, 141, 143; politics of, 142; myth of, 143, 160, 161n7
gerontolatry, 143
Ghana, 112, 114, 121
Gikandi, Simon, xii, 119, 120
Gĩkũyũ/Kikuyu, 151, 162n19, 169; ethnic group, 153, 155, 162n20; elite, 153; *kikuyunize*, 153; non- 153; proverb, 142, 161n4
Gordimer, Nadine, 117, 121
governance, xvii, 73
Greene, Graham, 88
grotesque, 208, 210, 215, 219
grotesqueness, 209, 211

Hamlet, 91
Harambee, 146, 162n15
Heart of Darkness, 91–92, 93
hegemony (Gramsci), 196, 197
Hitler, Adolf, 87, 90, 106n18
Holocaust, 90
Hypermasculinity, 19, 74

idiom of age, 141–142
illness, 167, 172, 174–75, 179, See also medicine, pain, patient
imagined community, 185, 186, 190, 204
imperialism, 112, 120
internal-external theory, 111, 113
Isegawa, Moses, 87, 93–100, 101, 105n10–11, 105n15, 106n17–18, 107n21
I the Supreme (Roa Bastos), 125, 132–34, 137
Ivan Vitanyi, 222

Jerusalem, 184
justice 21, 23

Kamaru, Joseph (musician), 147–49, 152
Kamĩtĩ Maximum Security Prison; 156, 163n24,185, 198; Kamiti: stories, 156;
Karlström, Mikael, xv-xvii
Kemoli, Arthur (composer), 155, 161n1
Kenya African National Union (KANU), 145–46, 152, 161n12; anti-KANU songs, 152; regime, 162; presidential candidate, 161n5
Kenyatta, Jomo, 69, 141–44, 147, 151, 153–54, 156–57, 161n1, 161n6, 161n10, 162n14, 162n15, 162n19, 163n22
Kenyatta, Uhuru, 160, 161n5
Kony, Joseph, 85, 104n2
Kourouma, Ahmadou: interview with, 135–36; *Waiting for the Vote of the Wilds Beasts*, 61, 125–40
Kyemba, Henry, 86
Kyomuhendo, Goretti, 87, 90, 100–104, 105n11, 106n20, 107n21

Labou Tansi, Sony, *Life and a Half*, 49, 61
legitimacy (political), 8, 187
Leviathan, 168
lex talionis, 21, 25
Liberia, 113, 114
literature: during the Moi regime, 142, 157; of the dungeon, 156, 163n23; and oral tradition, 141; as subversion to official narratives, 158
Lopès, Henri: *African Geopolitics*, 60–61; interview with, 56, 61; "My Novels, My Characters, and Myself," 56, 60; *The Laughing Cry*, 47–65
loyalty, 22; pledge, 145, 146, 162n14
Lumumba, Patrice, 103

INDEX

Mabanckou, 208, 209, 215, 217; *Broken Glass*, 208, 213, 217
Mamdani, Mahmood, xix, 106n17, 187
Mangue, Teodoro Nguema Obiang, 104n1
Mariam, Alemayehu, 66
Mau Mau, 86, 92, 98–99, 104n3, 151
Mbasogo, Theodoro Obiang Nguema, 104n1
Mbembe, Achille, 208, 210, 212, 213; aesthetics of vulgarity, xv, xxviii, 129, 208; *Commandement*, xv, xxviii, 67, 70, 128–29, 133, 137; fetish, 75, 79, 129, 134; necropolitics 77; *On the Postcolony*, 48, 66–67, 128–29; tension (convivial), 3, 12; zombification, xv, 185, 197, 198, 199, 204
medicine, 173–75; *See also* illness, patient
metafiction, 90
Mobutu Sese Seko, 69, 74, 98, 103; honorifics, 75
modernity, xx
modernization: challenges of, 79
Moi, Daniel Arap: 141–45; as *father* of the nation, 144, 154; as Kenyatta's successor, 144; use of choirs for patriotic songs, 144, 146, 151,163n28; and KANU, 144; songs about, 145, 147, 152–53; pervasive presence, 146, 155, 161n1; control over music and musicians, 148–49, 161n10; 1982 attempted coup and one-party rule, 149, 161n12; and multiparty politics, 50; and tribalism, 152, 62n20; and Mwakenya, 156, 163n23; relationship with writers, 156–58, 163n24; end of an era, 160
mooning, 183, 190, 203
multiparty democracy, 149, 152, 156, 161n5
music as propaganda, 142, 144, 146
Mutahi, Wahome, 156
Mwakenya, 142, 156, 163n23
Mzee, 141, 143–44, 151

Napoleon, 85
nation state, 222
Nazareth, Peter, 87, 88–91, 92, 93, 105n8, 105n11
neocolonial mimicry, 97
neocolonialism, vii, 112, 128–129, 130
Nguema, Francisco Macias, 30, 104n1
Nkrumah, Kwame, 29–30, 37–38, 41, 44n1, 112, 113, 114, 115, 116; Preventive Detention Act of 1958, 41–43, 44n5
Nyayo, 144, 154–55, 161n1, 161n8, 162n15; bus 146, 162n20; car, 146; house, 146, 156; *maziwa ya*, 145; monument, 146; philosophy, 142, 144, 146, 155, 161n8; stadium, 146; tea zones, 146, 162n20; wards, 146; *watoto wa*, 145
Nyerere, Julius, 87

Obama, Barak, 104n2
Obote, Milton, 30, 85, 89, 106n16
Ogre (story of), 190, 199
Okigbo, Christopher, 88
one-party state, 149, 161n12; dictatorship, 152, 156
Operation Entebbe, 86, 91
oral literature: *donsomana* (Malinke), 127, 137, 138
oral tradition in Africa, 141
Organization of African Unity (OAU), 86, 227
"Osagyefo," 40–41; *See also* Nkrumah, Kwame
Ousmane Sembène: *The Last of the Empire*, 61, 125–27, 128, 134–35

pain, 177–78
Paley, Julia, 225
paternalism, xvii, xix, 188; father-of-the nation types, 68
patient, 174–75, 178, *See also* illness, medicine, pain
patriotic songs, 142, 144, 146–47, 149–51, 162
patriotism, 150, 51
p'Bitek, Okot, 107n23
performance, 184, 186, 194, 200, 204; dialogic 190, 200; of masculinity 194; monologic, 187
performativity, 186, 202
Pheng Cheah, 222, 230
political divinity, 169–71; *See also* sovereignty
politics, 210, 212, 213
polyphony: in *The Laughing Cry*, 81
popular arts, 157
popular music, 147, 151
postcolonial, 86, 89, 90, 93, 97, 98
Posner, Daniel, 9
power, 210, 212, 213, 214, 215; as agency, xxix; asymmetrical, 184, 213, 219; as limitation xxix; panoptic modality of xxiii, 2, 5, 196, 201; superstructural, 2, 24, 202
Pratt, Mary Louise: contact zone, 131, 138
prestige, 186
proverbs (African), 142, 161n4, 160
public memory, 20
pyramid, 187

239

INDEX

rape: political, 17
realism, 207, 217
reciprocity: circuits of, xvi, xvii
re-gendering; 201
resistance, 187,189; sites of, xv
ridicule, 209
ruling class, 212, 216, 218
rumor, 12, 167, 178–80

Sani Abacha, 232
satire 216, 217
Scarry, Elaine, 177–78; *See also* pain
scatological writing, 208
scatology, 217
Schatzberg, Michael, xii–xiii, 73, 74, 80, 187, 193
Scott, James, 187, 189, 191, 192, 203, 204
Selassie, Haile, 97
Sese, Seko, Mobutu, 36
Simons, Anna, 26
simulacrum, 184, 203, 204
social identity, 8; ethnic, 8; strategic, 8; clan, 15
Sony Labou Tansi, 223
sovereignty, 72, 77, 168, 170–72, 176, 188, 191, 201; popular, xiii; *See also* political divinity
Soyinka, Wole, 31, 35–38, 42–43, 111, 117; "Future Plans," 37; *Kongi's Harvest*, 38–39, 42; *Opera Woyonsi*, 35, 69; *A Play of Giants*, 35–37;
spectacle, 78, 80, 185, 186, 196, 204
state: carceral, 4, 6; as social glue, 26; solvency, 26
subjection, xxvii, 185, 196, 197, 198, 201

surveillance, 1, 5, 72, 185, 194, 196
Tansi, Sony Labou, 67, 104n7
Taylor, Diana, 186, 201
teledirecting, 185
Thomas, Dominic 67
tradition, invented or false, 88, 93, 96–97
traditional: brew, 155; music, 144; praise poet, 160
truth (knowledge), 10
tyrannical leaders, 214

Uhuru: generation, 160; project, 160
United Nations High Commission for Refugees, 229
Universal Declaration of Human Rights, 227

vulgarity, 208, 213

Walker, Julia, 186, 200
wa Thiong'o, Ngũgĩ, 56, 87, 93, 111, 118, 120, 121, 157–58, 161n9; *Devil on the Cross*, 48, 55; "The Language of African Fiction" (*Decolonizing the Mind*), 48–49, 55, 61; writing about dictators, 48–49, 55, 58; *Wizard of the Crow*, 61, 125
Wiwa, Ken Tsaro, 232
writer's freedom, 208

Yewah, Emmanuel, xiii
youth: in 2002 elections in Kenya, 160; in African proverbs, 161n4; folly of, 142; in industrialized societies, 141; as leaders of tomorrow, 143; in political leadership, 142